Longman Guide to

BIBLE

QUOTATIONS

Longman Guide to

BIBLE

QUOTATIONS

Kenneth McLeish
Valerie McLeish

Longman

Longman Group UK Limited,
Longman House, Burnt Mill, Harlow,
Essex CM20 2JE, England
and Associated Companies throughout the world.

First published 1986

British Library Cataloguing in Publication Data

[Bible. *English. Selections* 1986]. Longman
  guide to Bible quotations.
  I. McLeish, Kenneth   II. McLeish, Valerie
  220.5'2   BS391.2
  ISBN 0-582-55573-6

Set in 10/11 Linotron 202 Ehrhardt
by Computerset (MFK) Ltd., Ely, Cambridgeshire, England
Printed in Great Britain
by Mackays Ltd., Chatham, Kent

Contents

Abbreviated titles for books of the Bible

OLD TESTAMENT

Gen	I Kgs	Eccles	Obad
Exod	II Kgs	S of S	Jonah
Lev	I Chr	Isa	Mic
Num	II Chr	Jer	Nahum
Deut	Ezra	Lam	Hab
Josh	Neh	Ezek	Zeph
Judg	Esther	Dan	Hag
Ruth	Job	Hos	Zech
I Sam	Ps	Joel	Mal
II Sam	Prov	Amos	

APOCRYPHA

I Esd	Wisd	Bel & Dr
II Esd	Ecclus	Pr of Man
Tobit	Baruch	I Macc
Judith	S of III Ch	II Macc
Rest of Esth	Sus	

NEW TESTAMENT

Matt	II Cor	I Tim	II Pet
Mark	Gal	II Tim	I John
Luke	Eph	Titus	II John
John	Phil	Philem	III John
Acts	Col	Heb	Jude
Rom	I Thess	Jas	Rev
I Cor	II Thess	I Pet	

Preface

THE WRITING AND ASSEMBLING of the books of the Bible took at least a thousand years, from the days of King David to the time of the early Christian Church. The 'canon' of the Old and New Testaments was settled in the second and third centuries AD, and the Bible as a whole was given wide currency in the fourth century AD, when Constantine the Great declared the Roman Empire Christian and when St Jerome made his Latin translation of the Bible, the Vulgate. From that time on, at least in the Western world, no book has ever equalled the Bible for availability: for 1,700 years it has been the first and most essential item on every literate person's bookshelf, a pillar not only of religion but of literature and culture.

The Bible contains three sections, the Old Testament of 39 books, the Apocrypha of 14 (often excluded from printed Bibles) and the New Testament of 27. The 'books' range widely in length (from one page to several dozen) and in content. The books of the Old Testament, written originally in Hebrew, are a collection of religious teachings, historical accounts, wise sayings, prophecies, poems and stories made by the Jewish people over a thousand years and enshrining their relationship with God. The Apocrypha, written in Greek, is a collection of additions to or adaptations of these teachings, made between the third century BC and the second century AD and widely used in the early Christian Church. The New Testament contains accounts of Christ's life and teaching, a series of pastoral 'letters' meant to establish the doctrines and practices of early Christianity, and the account of a vision of the Day of Judgment, an attempt to harmonize the teachings of the Old Testament with those of Christianity, to show Christ as the Messiah and Redeemer foretold from earliest times. The Bible has been current in three 'versions' above all: in the original languages, in St Jerome's Latin translation, and in the various vernacular translations of more modern times, such as Martin Luther's German version or the Elizabethan English of the Authorized Version.

The concern of this present book is less with doctrinal matters than with the 'literature' and 'culture' mentioned in the first paragraph above. We were aware from the start that the Bible is far more than words, that it or parts of it are fundamental to the beliefs of orthodox Jews, Muslims and Christians of every kind and creed. But we decided to avoid religious controversy as far as possible, and to concentrate on the context of each quotation and on the first layer of meaning in the words: that is, on what the actual English of the Authorized Version meant. Inevitably, our own religious background – we were both brought up as Protestant Christians – colours what we say, but we have tried to keep our own views, and indeed any specific religious views, as muted as possible. In the same way, we chose the Authorized Version not for doctrinal reasons but because it seemed the most culturally resonant of all the Bible translations, because its words and phrases haunt our language, our literature and our whole intellectual experience. Much of its language is as comprehensible as it is magnificent; where words have changed their meanings since Elizabethan times, we have given brief explanations.

The quotations are identified according to their verse-numbers in the Authorized Version. Cross-references use the abbreviated book titles listed on page iv, together with the quotation number as set out in the left-hand column in this book. In the index, many quotations, and certainly the most familiar, are identified by two or even three keywords: 'clothed, and in his right mind', for example, is indexed under both 'clothed' and 'mind'.

We should like to thank Donald Fraser for reading and commenting on the text and Janet Musson for typing practically every word.

Kenneth McLeish and Valerie McLeish

OLD TESTAMENT

Genesis

1   **In the beginning God created the heaven and the earth. And the earth was without form, and void; and darkness was upon the face of the deep. And the spirit of God moved upon the face of the waters.**
(1:1–2)
Genesis contains two accounts of creation, and this is the start of the first. From the primeval void is created heaven and earth and everything in them, ending in the human race itself. Various dates have been calculated for the actual moment of creation itself: the most specific, 9 am Tuesday, 23 October 4004 BC, was proposed by Archbishop Ussher of Armagh in AD 1654.

2   **God said, Let there be light: and there was light.**
(1:3)
This is God's second act on the first day of creation: the division of light from dark. Until it was completed, the days of creation themselves could not be numbered.

3   **And God saw that it was good.**
(1:10)
This phrase rounds off the account of each day of creation: God looks at his work, sees that there is no evil in it, and is content.

4   **God said, Let us make man in our image, after our likeness: and let them have dominion over the fish of the sea, and over the fowl of the air, and over the cattle, and over all the earth, and over every creeping thing that creepeth upon the earth.**
(1:26)
On all previous days of creation, God merely acted, bringing things into being by commanding their existence. By contrast, before the final act he announces his purpose and makes it clear that he envisages the human race as superior to all other created things, and as having a relationship with him which none of them shares.

5   **Male and female created he them.**
     (1:27)
     This is the general account of the creation of humanity; it is
     expanded in Gen 8 and Gen 12 into specific accounts of the making
     of Adam and of Eve.

6   **Be fruitful, and multiply, and replenish the earth.**
     (1:28)
     After blessing the founding parents of the human race, God gives
     them the impulse to fertility – an order which has provoked later
     scholars to trace the descent from Adam and Eve of every one of the
     present-day inhabitants of the earth (recently estimated at
     4,159,000,000 people).

7   **On the seventh day God ended his work which he had made;**
     and he rested on the seventh day from all his work which he
     had made. And God blessed the seventh day, and sanctified
     it: because that in it he had rested from all his work which
     God created and made.
     (2:2–3)
     This is less a statement that God needed rest or enjoyed a day off,
     like any human artisan, than a priestly interpolation into the
     creation account, giving a precedent to respect for the Sabbath.

8   **The Lord God formed man of the dust of the ground, and**
     breathed into his nostrils the breath of life; and man became
     a living soul.
     (2:7)
     Many religions share these traditions, of the making of the human
     race from dust, and of the gift of the breath of life; only Genesis
     goes on to credit humanity with 'a living soul'. The Hebrew word
     for 'man', that is 'humankind', is *Adam*.

9   **The Lord God planted a garden eastward in Eden; and there**
     he put the man whom he had formed. And out of the ground
     made the Lord God to grow every tree that is pleasant to the
     sight, and good for food; the tree of life also in the midst of
     the garden, and the tree of knowledge of good and evil.
     (2:8–9)
     The Hebrew word *Eden* means literally 'delight', and the earthly
     Paradise which God made for the human race was thought to lie
     'eastward' of the Mediterranean, that is in Mesopotamia, at the
     northern end of the Persian Gulf.

10   **But of the tree of the knowledge of good and evil, thou shalt**
     not eat of it: for in the day that thou eatest thereof thou shalt
     surely die.
     (2:17)

God allows Adam and Eve to enjoy every fruit in the Garden of Eden except one. The theological thinking behind this prohibition is shared by many other early religions: morality, 'knowledge of good and evil', is not a concern of the human race, but a matter for the deity. By acquiring knowledge, human beings fall from their state of primal innocence, the unblemished perfection of the inhabitants of Paradise.

11 **Out of the ground the Lord God formed every beast of the field, and every fowl of the air; and brought them unto Adam to see what he would call them: and whatsoever Adam called every living creature, that was the name thereof.** (2:19)

Adam asserts human authority over all other created beings by naming them.

12 **The Lord God caused a deep sleep to fall upon Adam, and he slept: and he took one of his ribs, and closed up the flesh instead thereof; And the rib, which the Lord God had taken from man, made he a woman.** (2:21–2)

This is a more specific account of the creation of Eve, just as Gen 8 was of Adam. The phrase 'Adam's rib' became proverbial, and has often been scornfully used of women from the time of the Authorized Version onwards.

13 **This is now bone of my bones, and flesh of my flesh: she shall be called Woman, because she was taken out of Man.** (2:23–4)

Just as human beings stand in a unique relationship with God, so this passage announces a unique relationship between men and women, sanctified by God. The English 'man/woman' wordplay has no parallel in Hebrew; in the Middle Ages it led to the chauvinistic view that 'woman' should really be spelt 'woe-man', because Eve brought woe to man.

14 **Now the serpent was more subtil than any beast of the field which the Lord God had made.** (3:1)

Snakes were widely worshipped in the Mediterranean, and the abhorrence generally expressed for them in the Old Testament has probably more to do with their prominence in non-Judaic religions than with any natural dangers: few Mediterranean snakes are venomous. This is the first Biblical reference to the 'serpent', and it is presented, from the start, as a major force for evil on the earth.

15   **God doth know that in the day ye eat thereof, then your eyes shall be opened, and ye shall be as gods, knowing good and evil.**
(3:5)
The serpent uses bribery and innuendo – stating that knowledge will make human beings like God, and that God knows this and wants to prevent it – to persuade Eve to eat the fruit of the tree of knowledge, and so bring about humanity's fall from grace.

16   **The eyes of them both were opened, and they knew that they were naked; and they sewed fig leaves together, and made themselves aprons.**
(3:7)
Knowledge of sexuality here stands for all moral knowledge; also, knowledge of guilt gives Adam and Eve the first conscience-pangs ever felt by the human race. The translation 'aprons' in the Authorized Version is one of several, the most notorious of which was 'breeches' in the Geneva Bible of 1560. It should be said that fig-leaves are not the dainty affairs shown on most paintings or sculptures of this scene: they are large (up to 12 inches (30 cms) long) and more like palm-fronds than the leaves of more northerly trees.

17   **The man said, The woman whom thou gavest to be with me, she gave me of the tree, and I did eat. And the Lord God said unto the woman, What is this that thou hast done? And the woman said, The serpent beguiled me, and I did eat.**
(3:12–13)
Faced with their guilt, Adam and Eve behave like children caught out in naughtiness: vestiges of paradisal innocence still cling to them.

18   **In the sweat of thy face shalt thou eat bread, till thou return unto the ground; for out of it wast thou taken: for dust thou art, and unto dust shalt thou return.**
(3:19)
Adam's punishment for eating the fruit of the tree of knowledge of good and evil is that the paradisal fecundity of the earth is no longer guaranteed: for simple day-to-day survival, he has to work.

19   **Adam called his wife's name Eve; because she was the mother of all living.**
(3:20)
Eve's punishments for eating the fruit of the tree of knowledge are to suffer the pains of childbirth and to be subordinate in all things to her husband. This subordination is symbolized by Adam's naming her, just as he earlier named all other created things. The word

'Eve' probably originally meant something between 'life' and 'fertility': procreation personified.

20 **Abel was a keeper of sheep, but Cain was a tiller of the ground.**
   (4:2)
   Of Adam's and Eve's first two children, the elder, Cain, shares his father's punishment, the need to work the earth, and the younger, Abel, extends his father's dominion over other created beings by being the first human to herd and tame them.

21 **The Lord said unto Cain, Where is Abel thy brother? And he said, I know not: Am I my brother's keeper?**
   (4:9)
   Jealous that his brother Abel found favour in God's eyes while he did not, Cain has killed Abel, and now responds to God's questioning with a display of mingled surliness and guilt which has become proverbial.

22 **The voice of thy brother's blood crieth unto me from the ground.**
   (4:10)
   Despite circumstantial evidence, God still offers Cain the chance to confess his guilt.

23 **A fugitive and a vagabond shalt thou be in the earth.**
   (4:12)
   The punishment received by Cain for murdering Abel is that the ground, poisoned by Abel's blood, will no longer respond to Cain's tilling: he has lost both his livelihood and his reason for existence.

24 **And the Lord set a mark upon Cain, lest any finding him should kill him.**
   (4:15)
   The 'mark of Cain' became identified in the Middle Ages as the port-wine birthmark which appeared on some people's faces: in earlier times this led to such people being persecuted as criminals.

25 **Cain went out from the presence of the Lord, and dwelt in the land of Nod, on the east of Eden.**
   (4:16)
   No one has finally identified the 'land of Nod', but if the Garden of Eden was sited somewhere in the 'fertile crescent' north of the Persian Gulf, the area east of there is dominated by high, trackless mountains (the Zagros Mountains in Iran) and by stony desert.

26   **All the days of Methuselah were nine hundred sixty and nine years: and he died.**
(5:27)
The Old Testament patriarchs all lived to ripe old ages – two and three hundred years were commonplace – but none lived longer than Methuselah. Even more remarkable than his longevity (which led to the saying 'as old as Methuselah'), is the fact that he 'begat sons and daughters' throughout his long and vigorous life.

27   **There were giants in the earth in those days.**
(6:4)
Though this phrase has become proverbial as an expression of the belief that people in former times – any former times – were nobler and mightier than we are now, its meaning here is literal. The descendants of the giants, together with the children of ordinary mortals, are the 'wicked and evil generation' which leads God to propose sending a flood to cleanse the world.

28   **I will cause it to rain upon the earth forty days and forty nights; and every living substance that I have made will I destroy from off the face of the earth.**
(7:4)
God tells Noah of the coming flood, whose purpose is to cleanse the earth of human violence and of what he calls the 'corruption of all flesh'.

29   **Noah did according unto all that the Lord commanded him.**
(7:5)
This refers to the building of an ark, a kind of houseboat of gopher wood (probably cypress) caulked with pitch. The verse also emphasizes Noah's total obedience to God, the factor which marks him out from everyone else on earth.

30   **There went in two and two unto Noah into the ark, the male and the female, as God had commanded Noah.**
(7:9)
Despite washing human violence and corruption from the world, God proposes the continuation of life by making Noah fill his ark with one male and one female of every species that live on earth.

31   **In the six hundredth year of Noah's life, in the second month, the seventeenth day of the month, the same day were all the fountains of the great deep broken up, and the windows of heaven were opened. And the rain was upon the earth forty days and forty nights.**
(7:11–12)

Archbishop Ussher (see Gen 1) worked out that Noah was born 1056 years after the day of creation, and therefore that the flood occurred in 2348 BC. Remarkably, this date coincides with the approximate time of devastating floods described in other ancient traditions, for example Sumerian, Aegean and Egyptian. The expression 'forty days and forty nights' was a standard Hebrew phrase for 'a long time'.

32   **Every beast after his kind, and all the cattle after their kind, and every creeping thing that creepeth upon the earth after his kind, and every fowl after his kind, every bird of every sort.**
(7:14)
This is the tally of all the creatures in Noah's ark.

33   **The ark rested in the seventh month, on the seventeenth day of the month, upon the mountains of Ararat.**
(8:4)
Mount Ararat in Turkey is over 17,000 feet (5,000 m) high, and this flood account led to centuries of folk legends of flotsam, pieces of wood and animal remains lying scattered on its inaccessible upper slopes long after the water finally subsided.

34   **The dove came in to him in the evening; and, lo, in her mouth was an olive leaf plucked off: so Noah knew that the waters were abated from off the earth.**
(8:11)
After forty days perched on Ararat, Noah sent out a raven and a dove to look for dry land. The raven never returned. The dove first came back without success, but returned from a second flight with an olive leaf in its beak, showing that the floodwater had subsided enough to uncover trees. Ever since this story, a dove carrying an olive leaf (or branch) has been a symbol of peace – of the end of violence on earth.

35   **Bring forth with thee every living thing that is with thee, of all flesh, both of fowl, and of cattle, and of every creeping thing that creepeth upon the earth; that they may breed abundantly in the earth, and be fruitful, and multiply upon the earth.**
(8:17)
After the dove returns with the olive leaf, Noah waits another seven days till the ground is dry, then opens the ark and hears these instructions from God. The flood and its aftermath have cleansed the earth of evil, and it is ready to be replenished.

36   The Lord smelled a sweet savour; and the Lord said in his
heart, I will not again curse the ground any more for man's
sake; for the imagination of man's heart is evil from his youth;
neither will I again smite any more every thing living, as I
have done. While the earth remaineth, seedtime and harvest,
and cold and heat, and summer and winter, and day and night
shall not cease.
(8:21–2)
After Noah disembarks and makes sacrifice, God gives this promise
for the future, and follows it up by giving Noah and his sons the
same dominion over all the earth's creatures as he once gave to
Adam.

37   I do set my bow in the cloud, and it shall be for a token of a
covenant between me and the earth.
(9:13)
The rainbow is a sign of God's blessing on the earth and on the rule
of the human race over every other living thing.

38   Even as Nimrod the mighty hunter before the Lord.
(10:9)
Nimrod, one of Noah's great-grandsons, was the first named
hunter in human history. The frequent use of 'Nimrod' to mean
'hunter' in later literature derives from this verse.

39   So the Lord scattered them abroad from thence upon the face
of all the earth: and they left off to build the city. Therefore is
the name of it called Babel; because the Lord did there
confound the language of all the earth.
(11:8–9)
In the fifth generation, Noah's descendants settled in the 'land of
Shinar' (the plain of Babylon between the rivers Tigris and
Euphrates), and began building a tower to symbolize their unity.
Fearful that if they succeeded there would be no limit to the
arrogance of the human race, God frustrates their plans by giving
each branch of Noah's descendants – the offspring respectively of
Shem, Ham and Japheth – a different language, so that failure of
communication leads to the tower being abandoned. 'Babel' is
probably an ancient name for Babylon, and the 'tower' was actually
a *ziggurat*, a tiered temple (as if built from piled rectangles of ever-
decreasing size) sacred to its gods. Ever since this story, 'Babel' has
been a synonym for confusion and nonunderstanding. The word
'babble' is sometimes associated with it.

40   The angel of the Lord said unto her, Behold, thou art with
child, and shalt bear a son, and shalt call his name Ishmael;
because the Lord hath heard thy affliction. And he will be a

wild man; his hand will be against every man, and every man's hand against him; and he shall dwell in the presence of all his brethren.
(16:11–12)

Sarai (Sarah), the wife of Abram (Abraham), felt that she was past childbearing age, and encouraged Abram to sleep with her maid Hagar and beget a son. But when Hagar became pregnant Sarai turned against her, and Hagar fled into the desert and hid beside a spring. Here God's angel finds her and speaks these none-too-comforting words before sending her back to Abram and Sarai. The name Ishmael, as the passage suggests, means 'may God hear'; his nature and destiny are also clearly sketched. Later, he became the ancestor of the Ishmaelites – the people of north-western Arabia and southern Sinai.

41 **Now Abraham and Sarah were old and well stricken in age; and it ceased to be with Sarah after the manner of women.**
(18:11)

God sent messengers to tell Abraham and Sarah that they would have a son, and Sarah laughed to hear it: this passage gives her reason, that she is too old to conceive.

42 **The Lord rained upon Sodom and upon Gomorrah brimstone and fire from the Lord out of heaven; And he overthrew those cities, and all the plain, and all the inhabitants of the cities, and that which grew upon the ground.**
(19:24–5)

No one has ever clearly spelt out what sins the inhabitants of the cities of the plain – Sodom, Gomorrah, Admah, Zeboiim and Zoar – indulged in, and over the years every wickedness from blasphemy to sexual perversion has been attributed to them. Whatever their guilt, God decides to blot them out, allowing only Abraham's nephew Lot, his wife and his two young daughters to escape.

43 **But his wife looked back from behind him, and she became a pillar of salt.**
(19:26)

Despite the terror of the fire and brimstone raining all round her, Lot's wife cannot restrain her curiosity about the fate of Sodom and Gomorrah, and turns back to look. The result is one of the pumice-stone-like stalagmites which can still be seen at the southern end of the Dead Sea, where the cities of the plain reputedly once stood.

44 **Take now thy son, thine only son Isaac, whom thou lovest, and get thee into the land of Moriah and offer him there for a**

burnt offering upon one of the mountains which I will tell
thee of.
(22:2)
God sends these orders to test Abraham's obedience, before
offering him a covenant. Isaac is the child miraculously born to
Abraham and Sarah in their extreme old age.

45   **Abraham said, My son, God will provide himself a lamb for a
burnt offering.**
(22:8)
Abraham's answer to Isaac's question shows either the remarkable
literal-mindedness of the truly devout, or a grim irony rare in the
books of the Old Testament until Job. All later uses of the phrase
have taken it literally, as an expression of absolute trust in God's
providence.

46   **Abraham lifted up his eyes, and looked, and behold behind
him a ram caught in a thicket by his horns: and Abraham
went and took the ram, and offered him up for a burnt
offering in the stead of his son.**
(22:13)
Abraham's faith in God's providence is justified.

47   **In blessing I will bless thee, and in multiplying I will multiply
thy seed as the stars of the heaven, and as the sand which is
upon the sea shore; and thy seed shall possess the gate of his
enemies; And in thy seed shall all the nations of the earth be
blessed; because thou hast obeyed my voice.**
(22:17–18)
After Abraham's ram-sacrifice, God's angel speaks these words,
outlining the new covenant between God and the human race.

48   **I am a stranger and a sojourner with you: give me a
possession of a buryingplace with you.**
(23:4)
After the death of his beloved wife Sarah at the age of 127, Abraham
begs the people for land to bury her.

49   **Esau was a cunning hunter, a man of the field; and Jacob was
a plain man, dwelling in tents.**
(25:27)
Esau, the elder brother, was the heir of Isaac, Abraham's son. But
Jacob, the younger brother, was not so 'plain' a man as he let it
appear: he was biding his time.

50   **And he sold his birthright unto Jacob.**
(25:33)
Faint with hunger, Esau begs food of his brother Jacob, and is
persuaded to buy it by giving up his birthright, the right of the eldest
son to inherit his father's position and wealth. All that now remains
is for Jacob to receive the blessing of Isaac their father in Esau's
place.

51   **Behold, Esau my brother is a hairy man, and I am a smooth
man.**
(27:11)
Jacob has been told that whichever of the brothers takes their blind
father Isaac his evening meal will receive his blessing. He decides to
impersonate his brother Esau, and overcomes the problem
mentioned in this verse by wrapping his arms in goatskins.

52   **The voice is Jacob's voice, but the hands are the hands of
Esau.**
(27:22)
Despite the qualms expressed here, Isaac is taken in by the
goatskins wrapped round Jacob's arms, and blesses him in Esau's
place.

53   **And he said, Thy brother came with subtilty, and hath taken
away thy blessing.**
(27:35)
Esau has railed against Isaac for his mistake, but there is no remedy:
as Isaac says, there was only one blessing, and Jacob has stolen it.

54   **He dreamed, and behold a ladder set up on the earth, and the
top of it reached to heaven: and behold the angels of God
ascending and descending on it.**
(28:12)
Jacob hears that Esau plots to kill him after their father Isaac's
death, and escapes into the desert. He sleeps in the countryside
north of Beersheba, and sees this vision, after which God promises
him the land he sleeps on, and all the land he can see, as a home for
his descendants. The phrase 'Jacob's ladder' came to be used for a
rope ladder with wooden rungs, much used on ships, and for a
Victorian children's toy – a ladder whose rungs folded down on
each other, one after another, so that it seemed as if the top rung
was tumbling towards the bottom.

55   **Jacob awaked out of his sleep, and he said, Surely the Lord is
in this place; and I knew it not. And he was afraid, and said,
How dreadful is this place! this is none other but the house of
God, and this is the gate of heaven.**
(28:16–17)

On waking up from his dream, Jacob is filled with holy awe; he
sacrifices and names the place Bethel, 'the house of God'.

56   **Jacob served seven years for Rachel; and they seemed unto
him but a few days, for the love he had to her.**
(29:20)
At his journey's end, Jacob has fallen in love with Rachel, the
daughter of his uncle Laban, and has agreed to work for him in
exchange for Rachel's hand in marriage.

57   **Therefore was the name of it called Galeed; And Mizpah; for
he said, The Lord watch between me and thee, when we are
absent one from another.**
(31:48–9)
Having asked Laban's agreement to let him take some of Laban's
flocks and leave for home, Jacob by a trick takes all the best animals;
when Laban pursues him, Jacob makes peace only by skilful
bargaining. They set up a boundary-cairn between their kingdoms,
and each vows never to pass it, adding the solemn invocation above.
The word *Galeed* means 'heap of witness', and the word *Mizpah*
means 'watch-tower'. In a more recent, and more genial, use of
these verses, the word 'Mizpah' is often engraved on lovers'
keepsake rings.

58   **Jacob was left alone; and there wrestled a man with him until
the breaking of the day. And when he saw that he prevailed
not against him, he touched the hollow of his thigh; and the
hollow of Jacob's thigh was out of joint, as he wrestled with
him. And he said, Let me go, for the day breaketh. And he
said, I will not let thee go, except thou bless me. And he said
unto him, What is thy name? And he said, Jacob. And he said,
Thy name shall be called no more Jacob, but Israel: for as a
prince hast thou power with God and with men, and hast
prevailed.**
(32:24–7)
Returning home, Jacob is still unsure of his reception from Esau,
whose blessing he long ago usurped. Accordingly, he sends him vast
flocks and herds, after which God sends an angel to wrestle with
him and bless him: a parallel experience to the dream of the ladder
between earth and heaven. On the evidence of this passage, it was
once thought that 'Israel' meant 'He who strives with God'; but
scholars now prefer the rendering 'May God prevail'.

59   **Now Israel loved Joseph more than all his children, because
he was the son of his old age: and he made him a coat of many
colours.**
(37:3)

'Israel' is the name given to Jacob after he wrestles with the angel. The point about Joseph's many-coloured coat is that it is a garment not for work but for leisure, the sign of a ruler and not of a workman. Joseph's brothers take it as proof that their father intends to pass them over and give their rightful inheritance to Joseph, much as Israel once stole his own elder brother Esau's blessing.

60 **Behold, we were binding sheaves in the field, and, lo, my sheaf arose, and also stood upright; and, behold, your sheaves stood round about, and made obeisance to my sheaf. (37:7)**
Joseph rashly tells his elder brothers of his dream that he will one day rule them.

61 **Onan knew that the seed should not be his; and it came to pass, when he went in unto his brother's wife, that he spilled it on the ground, lest that he should give seed to his brother. (38:9)**
Judah, the brother who persuaded Joseph's other brothers not to kill him but to sell him into slavery, had two sons, and when the elder offended God and was killed for it, Judah ordered the younger, Onan, to sleep with his brother's wife and beget a son. Sooner than do that, Onan 'spilled his seed on the ground'. Speculations about what this means have ranged from *coitus interruptus* to masturbation (for which 'onanism' was once a common alternative word).

62 **She caught him by his garment, saying, Lie with me: and he left his garment in her hand, and fled. (39:12)**
In Egypt, Joseph wins favour with his master Potiphar, captain of the guard – and also, to his horror, with Potiphar's wife.

63 **Pharaoh said unto Joseph, In my dream, behold, I stood upon the bank of the river: And, behold, there came up out of the river seven kine, fatfleshed and well favoured; and they fed in a meadow: And, behold, seven other kine came up after them, poor and very ill favoured and leanfleshed, such as I never saw in all the land of Egypt for badness: And the lean and the ill favoured kine did eat up the first seven fat kine: And when they had eaten them up, it could not be known that they had eaten them; but they were still ill favoured, as at the beginning. So I awoke. And I saw in my dream, and, behold, seven ears came up in one stalk, full and good: And, behold, seven ears, withered, thin, and blasted with the east wind, sprung up after them: And the thin ears devoured the seven**

good ears: and I told this unto the magicians; but there was
none that could declare it to me.
(41:17–24)
Joseph's reputation as an honest man, and as an interpreter of
dreams, reaches Pharaoh, who asks him the meaning of this dream.
Joseph's interpretation is that glut will be followed by famine, and
that food should be stored in the fat years ready for the lean.

64   He said, My son shall not go down with you; for his brother is
dead, and he is left alone: if mischief befall him by the way in
the which ye go, then shall ye bring down my gray hairs with
sorrow to the grave.
(42:38)
Joseph, promoted to control all the food supplies in Egypt, is
petitioned by his wicked brothers – who do not recognize him – for
corn for their people back at home. Joseph refuses, unless they
prove their honesty by bringing him their youngest brother,
Benjamin, the apple of their father's eye. Jacob refuses, in the words
quoted above, remembering how his previously best-beloved son,
Joseph, was taken from him.

65   And ye shall eat the fat of the land.
(45:18)
When Joseph hears of Jacob's grief at the thought of parting with
Benjamin, he relents and promises his brothers the food they ask.

Exodus

1   The children of Israel were fruitful, and increased
abundantly, and multiplied, and waxed exceeding mighty;
and the land was filled with them.
(1:7)
The Israelites driven to Egypt by famine consisted of Jacob's
seventy sons, their wives, children and grandchildren: an enormous
resident alien tribe.

2   Now there arose up a new king over Egypt, which knew not
Joseph.
(1:8)
The previous Pharaoh had trusted Joseph because of his skill at
interpreting dreams. Times are about to change.

3   The Egyptians made the children of Israel to serve with
rigour: And they made their lives bitter with hard bondage, in
mortar, and in brick.
(1:13–14)

The building work the Israelites were forced to do – alien labour for a nomadic, shepherd people – chiefly involved making bricks of mud and chopped straw, baking them in the sun, and then binding them with 'mortar' (probably a mixture of mud and lime).

4   **Pharaoh charged all his people, saying, Every son that is born ye shall cast into the river, and every daughter ye shall save alive.**
(1:22)
Pharaoh, alarmed at the population explosion among the Israelites, has ordered the Jewish midwives to kill every male child at birth, and the midwives have disobeyed on the transparent excuse that the children are born, every time, before they can get to them. Setting the babies to float on the river – a standard way of disposing of unwanted children in the ancient world, entrusting them to the gods and so absolving yourself of the guilt of murder – is Pharaoh's second plan.

5   **She took for him an ark of bulrushes, and daubed it with slime and with pitch, and put the child therein; and she laid it in the flags by the river's brink.**
(2:3)
'She' is a Levite, one of the Jewish sojourners in Egypt. An 'ark', whether Noah's, big enough for two each of every being in creation, or this one, big enough for just one baby, was a basket-shaped box with a domed lid. 'Flags' are reeds.

6   **She called his name Moses: and she said, Because I drew him out of the water.**
(2:10)
Pharaoh's daughter has rescued the baby in the ark, and given it by chance to the child's own mother to nurse. The Biblical explanation of the name 'Moses' is that it came from the Hebrew *Mashah*, 'to draw out'; it may equally well be the Egyptian name Mōsē, connected with the word *mesu*, 'child' and often featuring as part of longer Egyptian names, for example Thuthmose.

7   **And he said, Who made thee a prince and a judge over us?**
(2:14)
Moses, who has grown up as an Egyptian prince, tries to stop a quarrel between two Israelites, and is rejected as a foreigner.

8   **Moses was content to dwell with the man: and he gave Moses Zipporah his daughter. And she bare him a son, and he called his name Gershom; for he said, I have been a stranger in a strange land.**
(2:21–2)

Old Testament names are frequently explained in this way: see, for example, Ishmael (Gen 40), Moses (Exod 5). Gershom means simply 'stranger'.

9   **The angel of the Lord appeared unto him in a flame of fire out of the midst of a bush: and he looked, and, behold, the bush burned with fire, and the bush was not consumed.**
(3:2)
Moses flees from Pharaoh's vengeance to Midian, a desert place near the Gulf of Akabah, and works as a shepherd. God sends the angel in the burning bush to tell him of his mission to take the Israelites out of Egypt.

10   **Draw not nigh hither: put off thy shoes from off thy feet, for the place whereon thou standest is holy ground.**
(3:5)
God speaks in his own voice from the burning bush.

11   **I am come down to deliver them out of the hand of the Egyptians, and to bring them up out of that land unto a good land and a large, unto a land flowing with milk and honey.**
(3:8)
God promises to deliver the Israelites from Egypt: the 'land flowing with milk and honey' is Canaan, to the north. The phrase 'land of milk and honey' has become proverbial for a place of fertility and prosperity.

12   **God said unto Moses, I AM THAT I AM: and he said, Thus shalt thou say unto the children of Israel, I AM hath sent me unto you. And God said moreover unto Moses, Thus shalt thou say unto the children of Israel, The Lord God of your fathers, the God of Abraham, the God of Isaac, and the God of Jacob, hath sent me unto you: this is my name for ever, and this is my memorial unto all generations.**
(3:14–15)
God reveals his name to Moses. The word translated as I AM THAT I AM is *JHWH*, 'the one who was, is and always will be'. God's name is so sacred that it was forbidden to speak it; in Jewish ritual, the word *Adonai* (sovereign) was always read in its place, and I AM THAT I AM is more of an acceptable substitute than a translation. 'Jehovah' is a mixture of the two words, vowels from *Adonai* run together with consonants from *JHWH*.

13   **Moses answered and said, But, behold, they will not believe me, nor hearken unto my voice: for they will say, The Lord hath not appeared unto thee. And the Lord said unto him,**

What is that in thine hand? And he said, A rod. And he said,
Cast it on the ground. And he cast it on the ground, and it
became a serpent; and Moses fled from before it. And the
Lord said unto Moses, Put forth thine hand, and take it by the
tail. And he put forth his hand, and caught it, and it became a
rod in his hand.
(4:1–4)
God persuades Moses by a sign that Moses' vision is genuine.

14   The Lord said furthermore unto him, Put now thine hand
into thy bosom. And he put his hand into his bosom: and
when he took it out, behold, his hand was leprous as snow.
And he said, Put thine hand into thy bosom again. And he put
his hand into his bosom again; and plucked it out of his
bosom, and, behold, it was turned again as his other flesh.
(4:6–7)
God shows Moses a second sign. The disease and its cure
symbolize Moses' spiritual impurity (when he disobeys God) and
purity (when he obeys).

15   Moses said unto the Lord, O my Lord, I am not eloquent,
neither heretofore, nor since thou hast spoken unto thy
servant: but I am slow of speech, and of a slow tongue.
(4:10)
Although he is convinced that he has genuinely spoken with God,
Moses is still reluctant to undertake the task of asking Pharaoh to
release the Israelites.

16   The Lord said unto him, Who hath made man's mouth? or
who maketh the dumb, or deaf, or the seeing, or the blind?
(4:11)
God answers Moses' doubts, promising to give him eloquence to
persuade Pharaoh to release the Israelites.

17   I know not the Lord, neither will I let Israel go.
(5:2)
From the start, Pharaoh (who speaks these words) is depicted as a
scornful, hard-faced man – character-traits which God increases in
him to bring about his own destruction.

18   Go therefore now, and work; for there shall no straw be given
you, yet shall ye deliver the tale of bricks.
(5:18)
Pharaoh's response to the request for Israelite freedom is to make
their tasks even harder – trying to make mud bricks bake in the sun
without an admixture of chopped straw was a very laborious task.
The phrase 'making bricks without straw' has become proverbial for

achieving something immensely difficult with very little help. 'Tale'
here means 'tally' or 'full total'.

19   **I will harden Pharaoh's heart, and multiply my signs and my
     wonders in the land of Egypt.**
     (7:3)
     God declares that he intends to encourage Pharaoh not to let the
     Israelites go, and explains why.

20   **But Aaron's rod swallowed up their rods.**
     (7:12)
     The attempt to soften Pharaoh's heart begins with a contest
     between Aaron and the royal magicians. Aaron wins.

21   **All the waters that were in the river were turned to blood.
     And the fish that was in the river died; and the river stank,
     and the Egyptians could not drink of the water of the river;
     and there was blood throughout all the land of Egypt.**
     (7:20–1)
     This is the first of the ten plagues of Egypt, sent to soften Pharaoh's
     heart.

22   **Aaron stretched out his hand over the waters of Egypt; and
     the frogs came up, and covered the land of Egypt.**
     (8:6)
     This is the second plague. The point about frogs may be that their
     presence implies that the land was too wet to plough; they also
     polluted the water supply.

23   **The Lord said unto Moses, Say unto Aaron, Stretch out thy
     rod, and smite the dust of the land, that it may become lice
     throughout all the land of Egypt.**
     (8:16)
     God ordains the third plague. Apart from the irritation they caused
     and the disease they brought, lice were considered by the devout to
     be creatures of corruption and of death, which was the Devil's
     realm.

24   **Then the magicians said unto Pharaoh, This is the finger of
     God:**
     (8:19)
     The magicians are convinced that the Israelites' God is greater than
     Egyptian magic, but Pharaoh is not.

25   **Thus saith the Lord, Let my people go, that they may serve
     me. Else, if thou wilt not let my people go, behold, I will send
     swarms of flies upon thee, and upon thy servants, and upon**

thy people, and into thy houses: and the houses of the
Egyptians shall be full of swarms of flies, and also the ground
whereon they are.
(8:20–1)
Moses warns Pharaoh, in God's words, what the fourth plague will
be.

26 All the cattle of Egypt died: but of the cattle of the children of
Israel died not one .
(9:6)
This is the fifth plague, and it is coupled with a clear indication that
God favours the Israelites.

27 The Lord said unto Moses and unto Aaron, Take to you
handfuls of ashes of the furnace, and let Moses sprinkle it
toward the heaven in the sight of Pharaoh. And it shall
become small dust in all the land of Egypt, and shall be a boil
breaking forth with blains upon man, and upon beast,
throughout all the land of Egypt.
(9:8–9)
God ordains the sixth plague. 'Blains' are ulcers. The word survives
in the modern 'chilblains'.

28 Moses stretched forth his rod toward heaven: and the Lord
sent thunder and hail, and the fire ran along upon the ground;
and the Lord rained hail upon the land of Egypt.
(9:23)
This is the seventh plague, the first turning upside-down of the
order of nature which portended disaster. Frogs, lice, chilblains and
the others could be explained as natural disasters; this could not.

29 Moses and Aaron came in unto Pharaoh, and said unto him,
Thus saith the Lord God of the Hebrews, How long wilt thou
refuse to humble thyself before me? let my people go, that
they may serve me.
(10:3)
By the seventh plague, God's order to Pharaoh, 'Let my people go',
has become dauntingly insistent. 'Let my people go' has since
become a rallying cry from champions of the oppressed.

30 They covered the face of the whole earth, so that the land was
darkened; and they did eat every herb of the land, and all the
fruit of the trees which the hail had left.
(10:15)
The eighth plague is locusts.

31   And he said, I have sinned against the Lord your God, and
      against you. Now therefore forgive, I pray thee, my sin only
      this once, and intreat the Lord your God, that he may take
      away from me this death only.
      (10:16–17)
      Pharaoh gives way at last – only to change his mind again almost
      immediately.

32   The Lord said unto Moses, Stretch out thine hand toward
      heaven, that there may be darkness over the land of Egypt,
      even darkness which may be felt.
      (10:21)
      The ninth plague is more a supernatural warning than an affliction.

33   Thus saith the Lord: About midnight will I go out into the
      midst of Egypt: And all the firstborn in the land of Egypt shall
      die, from the firstborn of Pharaoh that sitteth upon his
      throne, even unto the firstborn of the maidservant that is
      behind the mill; and all the firstborn of beasts.
      (11:4–5)
      Moses warns Pharaoh of the tenth plague. Pharaoh refused to listen
      and the prophecy was exactly carried out.

34   Speak ye unto all the congregation of Israel, saying, In the
      tenth day of this month they shall take to them every man a
      lamb, according to the house of their fathers, a lamb for an
      house.
      (12:3)
      God tells Moses and Aaron to order the preparation of passover
      lambs in every Israelite house in Egypt. The idea of the lamb which
      by its blood saves true believers from destruction, gained added
      force in Christian times, thanks particularly to the teaching of John
      the Evangelist (see John 6).

35   Your lamb shall be without blemish, a male of the first year.
      (12:5)
      God instructs Moses to tell his people to choose the passover lamb,
      whose blood, smeared on the Israelites' door-lintels, will warn
      God's angels to pass over their children in the slaughter of the
      firstborn.

36   They shall eat the flesh in that night, roast with fire, and
      unleavened bread; and with bitter herbs they shall eat it. Eat
      not of it raw, nor sodden at all with water, but roast with fire;
      his head with his legs, and with the purtenance thereof. And
      ye shall let nothing of it remain until the morning; and that
      which remaineth of it until the morning ye shall burn with

fire. And thus shall ye eat it; with your loins girded, your
shoes on your feet, and your staff in your hand; and ye shall
eat it in haste: it is the Lord's passover.
(12:8–11)
God's instructions continue for the passover feast.

37   Pharaoh rose up in the night, he, and all his servants, and all
     the Egyptians; and there was a great cry in Egypt; for there
     was not a house where there was not one dead.
     (12:30)
     The tenth plague has struck: God has killed the firstborn of every
     household in Egypt, human and beast alike.

38   The people took their dough before it was leavened, their
     kneadingtroughs being bound up in their clothes upon their
     shoulders.
     (12:34)
     The Israelites prepare for a hasty departure, knowing that Pharaoh
     will not let them get far without pursuit. Haste, not doctrine, is the
     reason for the bread being unleavened: there is no time to knead it.

39   The Lord went before them by day in a pillar of a cloud, to
     lead them the way; and by night in a pillar of fire, to give them
     light.
     (13:21)
     God leads the Israelites out of Egypt.

40   They said unto Moses, Because there were no graves in
     Egypt, hast thou taken us away to die in the wilderness?
     (14:11)
     The Israelites have seen Pharaoh's hosts on the horizon, and panic.

41   The children of Israel walked upon dry land in the midst of
     the sea; and the waters were a wall unto them on their right
     hand, and on their left.
     (14:29)
     Moses parts the Red Sea, and the Israelites cross over to safety.

42   The Lord is my strength and song, and he is become my
     salvation: he is my God, and I will prepare him an habitation;
     my father's God, and I will exalt him. The Lord is a man of
     war: the Lord is his name.
     (15:2–3)
     This is part of the triumph-song Moses and the Israelites sang after
     the engulfing of the Egyptians in the Red Sea: a forerunner of
     several of the more exultant Psalms (see Ps 169 and 238).

43   **Who is like unto thee, O Lord, among the gods? who is like
      thee, glorious in holiness, fearful in praises, doing wonders?**
      (15:11)
      This verse from Moses' triumph-song after the Israelites are
      delivered from Egypt is often detached and set to music.

44   **The Lord shall reign for ever and ever.**
      (15:18)
      This verse from Moses' triumph-song after the Israelites are
      delivered from Egypt often appears separately in musical settings:
      one of the most famous is its adaptation in Handel's *Messiah*.

45   **Would to God we had died by the hand of the Lord in the land
      of Egypt, when we sat by the flesh pots.**
      (16:3)
      Lost and hungry in the wilderness (perhaps the area now known as
      the Negev Desert), the Israelites grumble against their leaders.
      'Flesh pots' is literal; in Egypt the Israelites ate stewed meat, but
      there is none in the desert.

46   **When the dew that lay was gone up, behold, upon the face of
      the wilderness there lay a small round thing, as small as the
      hoar frost on the ground. And when the children of Israel saw
      it, they said one to another, It is manna: for they wist not what
      it was. And Moses said unto them, This is the bread which the
      Lord hath given you to eat.**
      (16:14–15)
      Textual scholars suggest that what the Israelites actually said was
      'Man hu?' 'What is it?', and that the word *manna* means 'the
      Whatsit'. Whatever it was (guesses range from honeydew to fungus,
      and modern travellers in the area have found and eaten a variety of
      substances which fit the Biblical description) Exodus says that God
      provided it miraculously to feed the Israelites, that it was their staple
      diet for forty years, and that long before they reached Canaan they
      were sick of it.

47   **God spake all these words, saying, I am the Lord thy God,
      which have brought thee out of the land of Egypt, out of the
      house of bondage. Thou shalt have no other gods before me.
      Thou shalt not make unto thee any graven image, or any
      likeness of any thing that is in heaven above, or that is in the
      earth beneath, or that is in the water under the earth: Thou
      shalt not bow down thyself to them, nor serve them: for I the
      Lord thy God am a jealous God, visiting the iniquity of the
      fathers upon the children unto the third and fourth
      generation of them that hate me; And shewing mercy unto
      thousands of them that love me, and keep my**

commandments. Thou shalt not take the name of the Lord thy God in vain; for the Lord will not hold him guiltless that taketh his name in vain. Remember the sabbath day, to keep it holy. Six days shalt thou labour, and do all thy work: But the seventh day is the sabbath of the Lord thy God: in it thou shalt not do any work, thou, nor thy son, nor thy daughter, thy manservant, nor thy maidservant, nor thy cattle, nor thy stranger that is within thy gates: For in six days the Lord made heaven and earth, the sea, and all that in them is, and rested the seventh day: wherefore the Lord blessed the sabbath day, and hallowed it. Honour thy father and thy mother: that thy days may be long upon the land which the Lord thy God giveth thee. Thou shalt not kill. Thou shalt not commit adultery. Thou shalt not steal. Thou shalt not bear false witness against thy neighbour. Thou shalt not covet thy neighbour's house, thou shalt not covet thy neighbour's wife, nor his manservant, nor his maidservant, nor his ox, nor his ass, nor any thing that is thy neighbour's.
(20:1–17)

This is Moses' account, to the people, of the Ten Commandments, given to him on Mount Sinai by God himself. The formula is that of an ancient legal 'covenant' or treaty, the person named at the beginning first stating what he or she undertakes, and then outlining the obligations laid on the other parties to the covenant.

48   If any mischief follow, then thou shalt give life for life, Eye for eye, tooth for tooth, hand for hand, foot for foot, Burning for burning, wound for wound, stripe for stripe.
(21:23–5)

God continues his law-giving to Moses. The 'eye for an eye, tooth for a tooth' section of this law, often quoted as an example of Old Testament morality at its most implacable, is nowadays more widely remembered than the specific occasion (making a pregnant woman miscarry) for which it is here the prescribed judicial punishment.

49   They saw the God of Israel: and there was under his feet as it were a paved work of a sapphire stone, and as it were the body of heaven in his clearness.
(24:10)

God reveals himself to Moses, Aaron and others of the elders, seventy-four people altogether.

50   The glory of the Lord abode upon mount Sinai, and the cloud covered it six days: and the seventh day he called unto Moses out of the midst of the cloud. And the sight of the glory of the Lord was like devouring fire on the top of the mount in the eyes of the children of Israel. And Moses went into the midst

of the cloud, and gat him up into the mount: and Moses was
in the mount forty days and forty nights.
(24:16–18)
Moses leaves his people in Aaron's charge and climbs Mount Sinai
to hear more of God's instructions for the Israelites.

51   The people gathered themselves together unto Aaron, and
said unto him, Up, make us gods, which shall go before us; for
as for this Moses, the man that brought us up out of the land
of Egypt, we wot not what is become of him. And Aaron said
unto them, Break off the golden earrings, which are in the
ears of your wives, of your sons, and of your daughters, and
bring them unto me. And all the people brake off the golden
earrings which were in their ears, and brought them unto
Aaron. And he received them at their hand, and fashioned it
with a graving tool, after he had made it a molten calf: and
they said, These be thy gods, O Israel, which brought thee up
out of the land of Egypt.
(32:1–4)
Not knowing if Moses will ever come down again from Mount
Sinai, the people turn to Aaron, and he, despite the vision of God
he has seen with his own eyes on the mountainside, and the first of
the Ten Commandments newly sent down to guide them,
encourages them in their idolatry. The gold was Egyptian, given to
the Israelites by their lords and masters just before the Exodus, to
try to stop God killing the firstborn of every house in Egypt.

52   When Joshua heard the noise of the people as they shouted,
he said unto Moses, There is a noise of war in the camp. And
he said, It is not the voice of them that shout for mastery,
neither is it the voice of them that cry for being overcome: but
the noise of them that sing do I hear.
(32:17–18)
High on Mount Sinai, Moses and his assistant, Joshua, hear the
sound of the Israelites' orgiastic revelry from the desert below.

53   Moses' anger waxed hot, and he cast the tables out of his
hands, and brake them beneath the mount.
(32:19)
Moses reacts furiously to the sight of the Israelites dancing naked
round the Golden Calf. In most later depictions of the scene, the
'tables' he is shown breaking are the stone slivers on which the Ten
Commandments are incised; in Exodus, the Israelites have long
possessed the Ten Commandments, and these 'tables', closely
written on both sides, contain a vast body of other 'testimony',
instructions chiefly on making and consecrating the tabernacle.

54   I will not go up in the midst of thee; for thou art a stiffnecked
      people: lest I consume thee in the way.
      (33:3)
      Although God agrees to keep his promise to deliver the Israelites
      from the wilderness, he punishes them for idolatry by withholding
      his presence from them.

55   For there shall no man see me, and live.
      (33:20)
      Moses has begged God to let himself be seen once more in all his
      glory, but God will not reveal himself.

56   It shall come to pass, while my glory passeth by, that I will put
      thee in a clift of the rock, and will cover thee with my hand
      while I pass by: And I will take away mine hand, and thou
      shalt see my back parts: but my face shall not be seen.
      (33:22-3)
      Even Moses, who has 'found grace' in God's sight and who is
      known to God by name, is granted only this limited vision of his
      glory; even the following morning, when he climbs Mount Sinai to
      replace the broken 'tables' and talk once more with God, he keeps
      his head bowed in worship – as worshippers have done ever since.

57   He lighted the lamps before the Lord; as the Lord
      commanded.
      (40:25)
      In atonement for their idolatry, the Israelites have built the
      tabernacle, or shrine, according to the instructions given to Moses
      on Mount Sinai, and when it is finished Moses dedicates it.

58   Then a cloud covered the tent of the congregation, and the
      glory of the Lord filled the tabernacle.
      (40:34)
      God responds to the Israelites' exact obedience to his commands.

59   The cloud of the Lord was upon the tabernacle by day, and
      fire was on it by night, in the sight of all the house of Israel,
      throughout all their journeys.
      (40:38)
      God's presence in the tabernacle, a demonstration of his unbroken
      covenant with his chosen people, continues to sustain the Israelites
      in their long wandering towards the Promised Land.

Leviticus

1   **The Lord called unto Moses, and spake unto him out of the tabernacle of the congregation.**
(1:1)
God's law-giving, through Moses, continues. Leviticus is a series of instructions about every aspect of life, from worship to marriage-customs, from how to prepare food to how to treat disease. The book is called Leviticus, 'the Levite', because its teaching was entrusted by Moses to Aaron and his descendants, the priestly offspring of Levi the son of Jacob.

2   **Of a sweet savour unto the Lord.**
(1:13)
Originally referring to the smell of sacrifice – the part of the offering God took pleasure in (since he had no need of the meat, no need to be fed on human food). This phrase has come to describe any human action or thought which pleases God metaphorically.

3   **It shall be a perpetual statute for your generations throughout all your dwellings, that ye eat neither fat nor blood.**
(3:17)
Whatever its effect on later dietary laws, this prohibition originally applied to sacrificial offerings. The fat was to be burned on the altar, to please God with its aroma, and the blood was to be poured away.

4   **Whatsoever parteth the hoof, and is clovenfooted, and cheweth the cud, among the beasts, that shall ye eat.**
(11:3)
This law begins a long section on which creatures may and may not be eaten, laws on 'cleanness' and 'uncleanness' which have influenced the Jewish diet ever since.

5   **The leper in whom the plague is, his clothes shall be rent, and his head bare, and he shall put a covering upon his upper lip, and shall cry, Unclean, unclean.**
(13:45)
The cry 'Unclean, unclean' warns everyone to keep away from the leper, and he lives as an outcast until his disease is no longer infectious. This custom has led to the word 'leper' becoming almost a synonym for 'outcast' even in countries where leprosy is unknown.

6   **The goat, on which the lot fell to be the scapegoat, shall be presented alive before the Lord, to make an atonement with him, and to let him go for a scapegoat into the wilderness.**
(16:10)

Originally a scapegoat was a real goat, heaped verbally with the accumulated guilt of the people, and then allowed to escape (hence the name) into the desert, to carry the guilt far from human habitation. The word 'scapegoat' is now used more generally for any person or thing, guilty or innocent, given the blame.

7 **They shall no more offer their sacrifices unto devils, after whom they have gone a whoring.**
(17:7)
Leviticus lays down precise instructions about sacrifice. It is to be carried out only by appointed priests and in the proper place. 'Whoring after strange gods' is the more commonly used form of the phrase nowadays, and refers to any practices, religious or otherwise, zestfully carried out however outlandish they may seem to other members of the community.

8 **Whatsoever man there be of the children of Israel, or of the strangers that sojourn among you, which hunteth and catcheth any beast or fowl that may be eaten; he shall even pour out the blood thereof; and cover it with dust. For it is the life of all flesh; the blood of it is for the life thereof: therefore I said unto the children of Israel, Ye shall eat the blood of no manner of flesh: for the life of all flesh is the blood thereof: whosoever eateth it shall be cut off.**
(17:13–14)
These verses are the origin of kosher butchery (in which the blood is drained from the meat after slaughter), and they are also its explanation. The idea is that blood carries the life-force itself, and therefore that if any of it remains in a carcass, the animal is not truly dead.

9 **I am the Lord your God.**
(18:2)
Originally imitating the opening words of a covenant or legal document, this phrase is used more ritualistically throughout Leviticus. God precedes each new set of laws with it, stating his orders and reaffirming his own role in the covenant with mortals.

10 **Thou shalt not lie with mankind, as with womankind: it is abomination.**
(18:22)
This outlawing of homosexual acts is one of a long series of sexual prohibitions, designed originally to keep the Israelites free from the perversions of the Egyptians (who practised incest) and of the Canaanites (who practised bisexuality).

11   Thou shalt not avenge, nor bear any grudge against the
children of thy people, but thou shalt love thy neighbour as
thyself.
(19:18)
This verse, one of the most humane injunctions in what is otherwise
a grim catalogue of prohibitions and taboos, was quoted by Jesus in
answer to the man who asked which commandments he should
keep to guarantee eternal life (see Matt 127).

12   I am the Lord your God, which brought you out of the land of
Egypt. Therefore shall ye observe all my statutes, and all my
judgments, and do them: I am the Lord.
(19:36–7)
Just as ancient covenants had a formal opening (see Gen 47), so they
had a formal close. These words indicate the end of one complete
section of the law, in this particular case on general social
behaviour.

13   They shall not make baldness upon their head, neither shall
they shave off the corner of their beard, nor make any
cuttings in their flesh.
(21:5)
These instructions (originally to priests) have been rigorously
followed ever since by the most orthodox of Jews.

Numbers

1   Take ye the sum of all the congregation of the children of
Israel, after their families, by the house of their fathers, with
the number of their names, every male by their polls.
(1:2)
This verse accounts for the name of the whole book. It refers to a
'numbering' or census of all adult males (save those of the priestly,
Levite group) for military service. The book is, however, chiefly an
account of the thirty-eight years spent by the Israelites
discontentedly wandering in the desert before they reached the
Promised Land.

2   Behold, I have taken the Levites from among the children of
Israel instead of all the firstborn that openeth the matrix
among the children of Israel: therefore the Levites shall be
mine: Because all the firstborn are mine.
(3:12–13)

God makes a covenant with the Israelites, letting the Levites (priests) stand for the firstborn spared during the passover in Egypt, and taking them for his service. 'Matrix' is an Elizabethan word for womb: 'openeth the matrix' therefore simply means 'is born'.

3 **The Lord bless thee, and keep thee: The Lord make his face shine upon thee, and be gracious unto thee: The Lord lift up his countenance upon thee, and give thee peace.**
(6:24–6)
God gave this blessing for the Levites to say over the children of Israel; it has been used by priests and pastors of all denominations since.

4 **So it was alway: the cloud covered it by day, and the appearance of fire by night.**
(9:16)
God's presence in the tabernacle, and his continued guidance of his chosen people, were demonstrated by these signs. When the cloud was there the Israelites camped round the tabernacle; when it lifted they moved on until it appeared again.

5 **Rise up, Lord, and let thine enemies be scattered; and let them that hate thee flee before thee.**
(19:35)
Every day that God's cloud was lifted from the tabernacle and the Israelites pressed further into hostile territory, Moses prayed this prayer. It has been commonly used since by commanders of many religious denominations on the brink of battle.

6 **Who shall give us flesh to eat? We remember the fish, which we did eat in Egypt freely; the cucumbers, and the melons, and the leeks, and the onions, and the garlick: But now our soul is dried away: there is nothing at all, beside this manna, before our eyes.**
(11:4–6)
The Israelites complain about the bland taste of the endless manna, which is 'as the taste of fresh oil', and remember the sharper-flavoured foods of Egypt.

7 **Moses said, The people, among whom I am, are six hundred thousand footmen; and thou hast said, I will give them flesh, that they may eat a whole month. Shall the flocks and the herds be slain for them, to suffice them? or shall all the fish of the sea be gathered together for them, to suffice them?**
(11:21–2)

God has told Moses that he will respond to the Israelites' grumbles
about the lack of fresh meat. Despite Moses' consternation, he
treats God not with deference but with the affectionate sarcasm of
friend to friend.

8   There went forth a wind from the Lord, and brought quails
     from the sea, and let them fall by the camp, as it were a day's
     journey on this side, and as it were a day's journey on the
     other side, round about the camp, and as it were two cubits
     high upon the face of the earth. And the people stood up all
     that day, and all that night, and all the next day, and they
     gathered the quails.
     (11:31–2)
     God provides meat for the Israelites, ringing their camp with quails
     two cubits deep (that is, twice the distance from elbow to fingertips)
     in a band as wide as it would take a day to cross.

9   We saw the giants, the sons of Anak, which come of the
     giants: and we were in our own sight as grasshoppers, and so
     were in their sight.
     (13:33)
     Twelve scouts spy out the land ahead of the Israelites, and bring
     back this dispiriting, if circumstantial, report of giants.

10   The Lord said unto Moses, How long will this people provoke
     me? and how long will it be ere they believe me, for all the
     signs which I have shewed among them?
     (14:11)
     God is angry with the Israelites, who distrust the signs of favour he
     sends them and refuse to enter giant territory.

11   How long shall I bear with this evil congregation?
     (14:27)
     God's anger against the Israelites continues.

12   As for you, your carcases, they shall fall in this wilderness.
     And your children shall wander in the wilderness forty years,
     and bear your whoredoms, until your carcases be wasted in
     the wilderness.
     (14:32–3)
     God states how he will punish the Israelites for doubting him. Of
     the people who left Egypt for the Promised Land, all but two
     (Joshua and Caleb) will die before getting there; it is their
     descendants who will inherit it.

13 **Behold, the rod of Aaron for the house of Levi was budded, and brought forth buds, and bloomed blossoms, and yielded almonds.**
(17:8)

God demonstrates his approval of Aaron and his house by making his rod of office blossom. The phrase 'Aaron's rod', apart from being an English country name for such plants as golden rod, came to be used for the forked hazel-twig or willow-twig used in the divining of water or metal-ore.

14 **Moses lifted up his hand, and with his rod he smote the rock twice: and the water came out abundantly, and the congregation drank, and their beasts also.**
(20:11)

Through Moses, God works another miracle to provide for his people, despite their grumbles. By striking the rock, Moses goes beyond God's instruction merely to speak to it.

15 **They turned and went up by the way of Bashan: and Og the king of Bashan went out against them.**
(21:33)

The Israelites are battling their way through hostile territory to the Promised Land. Og, King of Bashan, is a giant; but his name has been used since to stand for any unreasoning, hostile, barbarian ruler.

16 **The Lord opened the mouth of the ass, and she said unto Balaam, What have I done unto thee, that thou hast smitten me these three times?**
(22:28)

Balaam the prophet of Pethor has originally favoured the Israelites, but is persuaded against them by terror of his king, Balek. God sends an angel to change his mind, and three times Balaam's ass refuses to pass the angel in a vineyard, to Balaam's fury. He beats the ass, and the ass turns and gently remonstrates. Somewhat unfairly, the name Balaam ever since has meant a babbling, foolish prophet, and 'Balaam's ass' has meant the gibberish-words (groups of the required number of letters) printers once used to fill up empty spaces at the ends of lines, a practice still occasionally seen in newspapers.

17 **How shall I curse, whom God hath not cursed? or how shall I defy, whom the Lord hath not defied?**
(23:8)

Convinced by the miracle of the speaking ass, Balaam refuses to curse the Israelites, as his master King Balek commands.

18   **What hast thou done unto me? I took thee to curse mine
      enemies, and, behold, thou hast blessed them altogether.**
      (23:11)
      Balek is furious with Balaam, who has refused to curse the Israelites
      as Balek ordered him.

19   **He hath not beheld iniquity in Jacob, neither hath he seen
      perverseness in Israel: the Lord his God is with him, and the
      shout of a king is among them.**
      (23:21)
      Balaam resolutely defends himself. The phrase 'the shout of a king'
      became proverbial for royal power.

20   **How goodly are thy tents, O Jacob, and thy tabernacles, O
      Israel!**
      (24:5)
      Balaam begins a hymn of praise to God, and in particular for the
      security he has given to the Israelites.

21   **I shall see him, but not now: I shall behold him, but not nigh:
      there shall come a Star out of Jacob, and a Sceptre shall rise
      out of Israel, and shall smite the corners of Moab, and destroy
      all the children of Sheth.**
      (24:17)
      Filled with God's spirit, Balaam prophesies. Whatever their specific
      references at the time they were written (for example to such now-
      forgotten enemies as the Moabites or the children of Sheth), his
      words have been taken since as a foretelling of the coming of the
      Messiah.

22   **Be sure your sin will find you out.**
      (32:23)
      The Israelites turn once more against God, and Moses gives them
      yet another warning.

Deuteronomy

1   **Only Og king of Bashan remained of the remnant of giants;
      behold, his bedstead was a bedstead of iron; is it not in
      Rabbath of the children of Ammon? nine cubits was the
      length thereof, and four cubits the breadth of it, after the
      cubit of a man.**
      (3:11)

From the size of King Og's bed – a cubit is about 18 inches (45 cms) – something of his giant size can be deduced.

2   **Take heed unto yourselves, lest ye forget the covenant of the Lord your God, which he made with you, and make you a graven image, or the likeness of any thing, which the Lord thy God hath forbidden thee. For the Lord thy God is a consuming fire, even a jealous God.**
(4:23–4)
Aware that his death is imminent, Moses warns the Israelites to keep God's commandments, and particularly to avoid idolatry. The last-quoted sentence became proverbial even in Biblical times.

3   **The Lord shall scatter you among the nations, and ye shall be left few in number among the heathen.**
(4:27)
Moses prophesies what will happen to the Israelites if they disobey God.

4   **The Lord thy God is a merciful God; he will not forsake thee, neither destroy thee, nor forget the covenant of thy fathers which he sware unto them.**
(4:31)
Moses reminds the Israelites of God's mercy, and of his special relationship with his Chosen People.

5   **Hear, O Israel: The Lord our God is one Lord: And thou shalt love the Lord thy God with all thine heart, and with all thy soul, and with all thy might.**
(6:4–5)
Moses begins his exposition of the Ten Commandments. The verses have been used ever since as one of the central prayers of the Jewish faith, and in many other traditions.

6   **Ye shall not go after other gods, of the gods of the people which are round about you; For the Lord thy God is a jealous God among you.**
(6:14–15)
Moses reminds the Israelites to keep the First Commandment.

7   **Ye shall not tempt the Lord your God, as ye tempted him in Massah.**
(6:16)
Moses is preaching spiritual obedience, not distrust of God. The 'tempting', or trial of God in Massah, was the occasion when the Israelites demanded water, and God sent it by ordering Moses to strike his staff on a rock.

8   **Man doth not live by bread only, but by every word that
        proceedeth out of the mouth of the Lord doth man live.**
        (8:3)
        Moses is reminding the Israelites that God kept his word to them
        and provided for their needs by sending manna, which they had
        never seen before. The phrase has since been used to remind
        people of the need for spirituality, that the soul needs food as well as
        the body; Jesus quotes the words, with this implication, to confound
        the Devil tempting him in the wilderness (see Matt 12).

9   **The Lord thy God bringeth thee into a good land, a land of
        brooks of water, of fountains and depths that spring out of
        valleys and hills; A land of wheat, and barley, and vines, and
        fig trees, and pomegranates; a land of oil olive, and honey; A
        land wherein thou shalt eat bread without scarceness, thou
        shalt not lack any thing in it; a land whose stones are iron, and
        out of whose hills thou mayest dig brass.**
        (8:7–9)
        Moses' description of the Promised Land is a fine verbal flourish,
        developing the phrase 'flowing with milk and honey'.

10   **Therefore shall ye lay up these my words in your heart and in
        your soul, and bind them for a sign upon your hand, that they
        may be as frontlets between your eyes.**
        (11:18)
        These words have been interpreted both metaphorically (God's
        word, and obedience to it, are a kind of armour for the righteous)
        and literally (Bible texts were rolled up and bound with thongs
        around the hands and forehead).

11   **If there arise among you a prophet, or a dreamer of dreams,
        and giveth thee a sign or a wonder, And the sign or the
        wonder come to pass, whereof he spake unto thee, saying, Let
        us go after other gods, which thou hast not known, and let us
        serve them; Thou shalt not hearken unto the words of that
        prophet, or that dreamer of dreams.**
        (13:1–3)
        Moses cautions his people against the false prophets of other
        religions. The phrase 'dreamer of dreams' has ever since had
        connotations of false learning, and has been linked with the Greek
        tradition that the Gate of Dreams leads from the Underworld to
        confusion: in the Middle Ages, for example, it was applied to
        alchemists.

12   **And thine eye shall not pity; but life shall go for life, eye for
        eye, tooth for tooth, hand for hand, foot for foot.**
        (19:21)

Moses is instructing the people about how to behave in the
Promised Land, where times will be hard and enemies will be many
– hence his reiteration of this implacable-seeming code of justice.

13 **Thou shalt not muzzle the ox when he treadeth out the corn.**
(25:4)
The ox which walks round and round to grind the corn is to be
allowed to eat its fill: this has since come to have the same
proverbial meaning as the later phrase 'the labourer is worthy of his
hire'.

14 **Cursed be he that removeth his neighbour's landmark.**
(27:17)
No doubt of great importance in the time it was written as a
protection of land tenure in the newly settled Promised Land, this
law has been pilloried ever since as typical of the more intractable,
not to say dottier, Old Testament teachings which survive as
sermon-texts – and even so, it is still occasionally so used.

15 **The secret things belong unto the Lord our God.**
(29:29)
Moses is contrasting revealed truth, which is what should guide
God's people, with the secret truth known only to God himself. The
phrase has, however, come to stand for the covenant itself, the
agreement between God and his people: some early Christian cults
even took it to refer to the 'mystery' of Christ's incarnation.

16 **My doctrine shall drop as the rain, my speech shall distil as**
the dew, as the small rain upon the tender herb, and as the
showers upon the grass.
(32:2)
As a statement of the all-pervasiveness of God's word, this passage
found willing ears in rain-soaked Elizabethan England. In
Shakespeare's *The Merchant of Venice*, Portia's mercy-speech for
example, begins with a direct reminiscence: 'The quality of mercy is
not strained. It droppeth as the gentle rain from heaven.'

17 **He found him in a desert land, and in the waste howling**
wilderness.
(32:10)
Moses tells of God's mercy to his people. This is the first literary
use of the phrase 'howling wilderness', as mysterious as it is
evocative. Perhaps what was in the writer's mind was the howling of
desert creatures in the night.

18 **He led him about, he instructed him, he kept him as the apple of his eye.**
(32:10)
Moses is still talking of God's tenderness towards his people. The 'apple of his eye' is the pupil, the tenderest part – thought in Elizabethan times to be apple-shaped. The phrase has since become a metaphor for 'favourite'.

19 **Jeshurun waxed fat, and kicked: thou art waxen fat, thou art grown thick, thou art covered with fatness; then he forsook God which made him, and lightly esteemed the Rock of his salvation.**
(32:15)
Moses chides the Israelites' disobedience to God's commands, especially those about diet. 'Jeshurun' ('upright one'), is an alternative name for Israel, here used ironically. The phrase 'Rock of his salvation', referring to God as the rock on which the foundations of a house are built, has become even more familiar in the form 'Rock of Ages', used of Jesus.

20 **O that they were wise, that they understood this, that they would consider their latter end!**
(32:29)
This is one of the earliest Biblical references to the Day of Judgment. The adjective 'latter' (familiar also in such phrases as 'latter day': see Job 38) was an Elizabethan synonym for 'last'.

21 **To me belongeth vengeance, and recompence.**
(32:35)
In his letter to the Romans (see Ro 40) Paul paraphrased this verse, and set it in the middle of a homily on mercy and loving kindness. Vengeance is God's, and should be left to him; human beings should be loving and forgiving to one another. There are no such instructions here.

22 **Their foot shall slide in due time: for the day of their calamity is at hand.**
(32:35)
Moses explains how God's vengeance will smite the idolaters, against whom he is warning the Israelites.

23 **The eternal God is thy refuge, and underneath are the everlasting arms.**
(33:27)
This is one of the earliest appearances in the Bible of two frequent and comforting metaphors, comparing God to a castle of security, and to a nurse's arms which give sure support.

24   The Lord said unto him, This is the land which I sware unto
      Abraham, unto Isaac, and unto Jacob, saying, I will give it
      unto thy seed: I have caused thee to see it with thine eyes.
      (34:4)
      After forty years in the wilderness, Moses is shown the Promised
      Land at last, though he is not himself allowed to enter it.

25   Moses the servant of the Lord died there in the land of Moab,
      according to the word of the Lord.
      (34:5)
      This unsentimental statement of Moses' death was added to
      Deuteronomy by a later, unknown hand. 'Servant of the Lord'
      became a standard phrase, first for a priest or pastor and then for an
      obedient Christian of any kind.

Joshua

1   As I was with Moses, so I will be with thee: I will not fail thee,
      nor forsake thee.
      (1:5)
      God gives to Joshua, Moses' successor, the same promise of his
      presence as he had given to Moses in the wilderness.

2   Be strong and of a good courage; be not afraid, neither be
      thou dismayed: for the Lord thy God is with thee
      whithersoever thou goest.
      (1:9)
      God continues to support and encourage Joshua.

3   All that thou commandest us we will do, and whithersoever
      thou sendest us, we will go.
      (1:16)
      Originally expressing the Israelites' acceptance of Joshua's rule,
      these words have since been used as a prayer, accepting God's
      presence in human lives.

4   This line of scarlet thread.
      (2:18)
      Rahab, a prostitute, has saved the lives of two of Joshua's spies in
      the enemy city of Jericho. They tell her to put a scarlet thread in her
      window, and she and her family will be spared when the city is
      sacked. The phrase has since come to mean either literally a
      'lifeline', or the carotid artery of the neck, the 'scarlet thread' which
      carries blood to the brain.

5   **Sanctify yourselves: for tomorrow the Lord will do wonders among you.**
        (3:5)
        Joshua prepares his people for the battle of Jericho. His words have
        been used ever since as an injunction to God's people throughout
        the world.

6   **All the Israelites passed over on dry ground.**
        (3:17)
        God checks the waters of the swollen river Jordan, to let the
        Israelites pass into the territory of Jericho – an echo of the parting of
        the Red Sea, the miracle he worked for Moses (see Exod 41).

7   **That all the people of the earth might know the hand of the
        Lord, that it is mighty: that ye might fear the Lord your God
        for ever.**
        (4:24)
        Joshua explains to his people God's purpose in holding back the
        river Jordan to let them pass.

8   **Behold, there stood a man over against him with his sword
        drawn in his hand: and Joshua went unto him, and said unto
        him, Art thou for us, or for our adversaries?**
        (5:13)
        Joshua challenges God's angel outside Jericho. A slightly different
        version of his words, 'Are you for us or against us?', has been used
        as a challenge ever since – and was memorably adapted by St Paul
        (see Rom 32).

9   **So the people shouted when the priests blew with the
        trumpets: and it came to pass, when the people heard the
        sound of the trumpet, and the people shouted with a great
        shout, that the wall fell down flat.**
        (6:20)
        Seven priests with seven ram's-horn trumpets, following the
        tabernacle of God seven times round the walls of Jericho, achieve
        an act of demolition few siege-weapons could have managed more
        efficiently.

10   **Let them be hewers of wood and drawers of water unto all the
        congregation.**
        (9:21)
        Ambassadors from the people of Gibeon have gone to Joshua and
        surrendered their people rather than be destroyed. The warlike
        leaders of the Israelite congregation, despising them for cowardice,
        promptly make their people the lowliest of all servants, in a phrase
        which has become proverbial.

11 **I am going the way of all the earth.**
(23:14)
Joshua tells the people of his impending death.

Judges

1 **I will not drive them out from before you; but they shall be as thorns in your sides, and their gods shall be a snare unto you.**
(2:3)
Instead of driving out all the idolatrous inhabitants of the Promised Land, and throwing down their altars, as God has commanded, the Israelites make peace with some of them – and God sends an angel to announce this punishment, of continued temptation, in a phrase which rapidly became proverbial.

2 **The anger of the Lord was hot against Israel, and he delivered them into the hands of spoilers that spoiled them.**
(2:14)
God punishes the Israelites' idolatry.

3 **They would not hearken unto their judges, but they went a whoring after other gods, and bowed themselves unto them.**
(2:17)
Despite being reprieved, the Israelites continue their idolatrous ways.

4 **Then Jael Heber's wife took a nail of the tent, and took an hammer in her hand, and went softly unto him, and smote the nail into his temples, and fastened it into the ground.**
(4:21)
Jael kills Sisera, captain of the enemy guard, who has taken refuge with her neutral husband Heber, the Kenite.

5 **They fought from heaven; the stars in their courses fought against Sisera.**
(5:20)
Part of the triumph-song made about Sisera's death. 'Stars in their courses' has entered the language. 'Courses' means the stars' fixed paths across the sky, as determined by God.

6 **He asked water, and she gave him milk; she brought forth butter in a lordly dish.**
(5:25)

The triumph-song over Sisera continues. Here Jael is imagined as giving him far more than he ever asked for.

7   **The Lord is with thee, thou mighty man of valour.**
(6:12)
God's angel appears to Gideon, and encourages him to lead his people against the Midianites.

8   **The host of Midian was beneath him in the valley.**
(7:8)
Gideon and three hundred men ambush the enemy army. The phrase 'host of Midian' has often been used since as a synonym for a vast, barbarian army, or for the 'army of unbelievers' generally.

9   **Gideon came to Jordan, and passed over, he, and the three hundred men that were with him, faint, yet pursuing them.**
(8:4)
Gideon's men pursue the fleeing Midianites across the river Jordan. The expression 'faint yet pursuing', or 'faint, but pursuing', became proverbial.

10   **Then said they unto him, Say now Shibboleth: and he said Sibboleth; for he could not frame to pronounce it right. Then they took him, and slew him at the passages of Jordan.**
(12:6)
In the time of Jepthah, anyone trying to cross the river Jordan is given this test, and those who fail, being proved to be from another tribe, suffer for it. *Shibboleth*, simply the Hebrew word for 'ear of grain' or 'stream', has become a standard word for a test to be passed, a difficult and terrifying obstacle.

11   **He said unto them, Out of the eater came forth meat, and out of the strong came forth sweetness.**
(14:14)
Samson poses this riddle to the Philistine oppressors whose sister he has married. It arises from two earlier proofs of God's favour towards him: a lion, a man-eater, he killed with his bare hands, and a swarm of bees who made sweet honey in the lion's carcass. The answer to the riddle implies that God will give Samson strength over his enemies, and will provide sweet nourishment for his people; the Philistines only find out the answer by making Samson's new wife wheedle it out of him.

12   **He smote them hip and thigh.**
(15:8)

Samson deals with the Philistines. No one has ever explained why the phrase should imply enormous slaughter, but so it does.

13 **He found a new jawbone of an ass, and put forth his hand, and took it, and slew a thousand men therewith.**
(15:15)
Samson continues spectacularly slaughtering the Philistines.

14 **With the jawbone of an ass, heaps upon heaps, with the jaw of an ass have I slain a thousand men.**
(15:16)
Samson boasts of his prowess.

15 **He told her all his heart, and said unto her, There hath not come a rasor upon mine head; for I have been a Nazarite unto God from my mother's womb: if I be shaven, then my strength will go from me, and I shall become weak, and be like any other man.**
(16:17)
Samson tells Delilah the secret of his strength: he is a Nazarite, a servant of God, and his unshorn hair is a sign of it.

16 **The Philistines took him, and put out his eyes, and brought him down to Gaza and bound him with fetters of brass; and he did grind in the prison house.**
(16:21)
Samson is captured by the Philistines. 'Eyeless in Gaza' (Milton, *Samson Agonistes* 1.40) is the way his plight is now remembered.

17 **Samson took hold of the two middle pillars upon which the house stood, and on which it was borne up, of the one with his right hand, and of the other with his left. And Samson said, Let me die with the Philistines. And he bowed himself with all his might; and the house fell upon the lords, and upon all the people that were therein. So the dead which he slew at his death were more than they which he slew in his life.**
(16:29–30)
Samson revenges himself on his Philistine captors.

18 **In those days there was no king in Israel, but every man did that which was right in his own eyes.**
(17:6)
This evocative description of anarchy was a quotation beloved by politicians for centuries.

19   **The congregation was gathered together as one man, from Dan even to Beersheba.**
(20:1)
In days of anarchy, an old priest has called all the Israelites together to fight their oppressors. The phrase 'from Dan even to Beersheba' became proverbial, meaning 'without exception'.

20   **All the people arose as one man.**
(20:8)
Originally meant literally, of a gathering of no less than four hundred thousand people jumping up to fight their enemies, this phrase passed into the language as a description of unanimity.

Ruth

1   **The Lord deal kindly with you, as ye have dealt with the dead, and with me.**
(1:8)
Naomi, about to go home to her own country, suggests to her widowed daughters-in-law Ruth and Orpah that they go back to their own parents' homes and make new marriages. This phrase has been used in a wider context since, as the minister's closing words in many funeral services.

2   **Whither thou goest, I will go; and where thou lodgest, I will lodge: thy people shall be my people, and thy God my God: Where thou diest, will I die, and there will I be buried.**
(1:16–17)
Ruth refuses to leave Naomi, in a noble phrase often subsequently used as a lover's declaration.

3   **She gleaned in the field until even, and beat out that she had gleaned.**
(2:17)
Boaz allows Ruth, a stranger from a foreign land, to pick up and keep the grain which the reapers have dropped. The proverbial expression 'gleaning amid the alien corn', meaning both making the best of life in a strange place and pining for home, is a combination of this passage and a line in Keats' 'Ode to a Nightingale', referring to Ruth 'when sick for home, /She stood in tears amid the alien corn'.

4   **He shall be unto thee a restorer of thy life, and a nourisher of thine old age.**
(4:15)

After Ruth marries Boaz and bears the child Obed, the women of Bethlehem tell Naomi the good news. Because Obed grew up to be the ancestor of the house of David, this verse has sometimes been taken as a prophecy not only of David's own greatness but also of that of Jesus, his descendant.

I Samuel

1   **The sons of Eli were sons of Belial; they knew not the Lord. (2:12)**
The meaning here is literal: Eli's sons worshipped a heathen deity. (Belial is no specific god: the word is simply Hebrew for 'wickedness'). Later, Belial came to mean the Devil himself (see II Cor 8), and because of this 'sons of Belial' is a proverbial phrase not for idolaters but for degenerates or criminals of any kind. In Elizabethan English this meaning gained even more strength by the (false) association of Belial with the verb 'to belie'.

2   **All the increase of thine house shall die in the flower of their age. (2:33)**
Eli is warned that his sons' wickedness will be punished by God. The phrase 'in the flower of their age' has entered the language, sometimes in the form 'flower of youth'.

3   **The Lord called Samuel: and he answered, Here am I. (3:4)**
Samuel, a young child, becomes Eli's servant in the temple. Mistaking God's voice for Eli's, he runs to his master with what was once a standard servant's response, 'Here am I'.

4   **The Lord came, and stood, and called as at other times, Samuel, Samuel. Then Samuel answered, Speak; for thy servant heareth. (3:10)**
Eli has told Samuel whose voice he is actually hearing in the temple, and how to answer.

5   **The ears of everyone that heareth it shall tingle. (3:11)**
God tells Samuel how all Israel will be affected by his punishment of Eli's sons' idolatry. Because God was also warning the Israelites against idolatry of their own, the phrase has come to have associations of personal guilt for the hearer: our ears tingle (or 'burn') when we are being talked about.

6   Quit yourselves like men, and fight.
(4:9)
The Philistines' rallying-cry before their first battle with the
Israelites. 'Quit' is an Elizabethan alternative for 'acquit'. The
phrase is echoed in one of Paul's exhortations to the early
Christians (see I Cor 36).

7   All the people shouted, and said, God save the king.
(10:24)
Samuel has shown Saul to the Israelites, and they acknowledge him.
A shout of 'God save the king' (or 'queen') has been a central part
of British coronations for centuries, at the moment just after the
crown is set on the monarch's head.

8   The Lord hath sought him a man after his own heart.
(13:14)
Saul and Samuel have quarrelled, and Samuel tells Saul that he is
no longer God's choice as king.

**9   As the Lord liveth, there shall not one hair of his head fall to
the ground.**
(14:45)
Jonathan has disobeyed the orders of his father Saul, and the people
prevent Saul from killing him. Because the people here claim that
Jonathan did what he did in obedience to God, not man, the phrase
has become symbolic of the safety from harm promised to those
who keep God's word.

**10   Behold, to obey is better than sacrifice, and to hearken than
the fat of rams.**
(15:22)
Samuel, in God's name, has ordered the destruction of every
possession of the Amalekites, but Saul and the people have kept
back the best sheep and cattle for sacrifice. The passage has been
frequently quoted to support the teaching that disobedience, even
for the best of reasons, is always a sin: it was a main part of the
teaching of later Hebrew prophets.

**11   The Lord seeth not as man seeth; for man looketh on the
outward appearance, but the Lord looketh on the heart.**
(16:7)
God has sent Samuel to choose a new king for Israel from among
the sons of Jesse. Samuel picks Eliab, a tall, handsome man – but he
is not God's choice.

12   He was ruddy, and withal of a beautiful countenance, and
      goodly to look to. And the Lord said, Arise, anoint him: for
      this is he.
      (16:12)
      This is the famous description of David, Jesse's youngest son and
      God's chosen king of Israel. The words are lightly dismissive, much
      as we might describe a young man as 'fresh-faced' or 'cherubic'.

13   There went out a champion out of the camp of the Philistines,
      named Goliath, of Gath, whose height was six cubits and a
      span. And he had an helmet of brass upon his head, and he
      was armed with a coat of mail; and the weight of the coat was
      five thousand shekels of brass. And he had greaves of brass
      upon his legs, and a target of brass between his shoulders.
      And the staff of his spear was like a weaver's beam; and his
      spear's head weighed six hundred shekels of iron: and one
      bearing a shield went before him.
      (17:4–7)
      David's future adversary is described. A cubit was about 18 inches
      (45 cms); a shekel – not the unit of currency but the weight – was
      approximately 0.4 ounces (12g).

14   I know thy pride, and the naughtiness of thine heart.
      (17:28)
      David has left his father's sheep and gone to fight the Philistines.
      His elder brother Eliab is furious.

15   Thy servant slew both the lion and the bear.
      (17:36)
      David explains to Saul that even though he is only a shepherd, he is
      fit to fight the Philistines – has he not already faced enemies just as
      fierce?

16   Go, and the Lord be with thee.
      (17:37)
      Saul sends David to fight Goliath, in a phrase which has become a
      familiar part of many religious services.

17   He took his staff in his hand, and chose him five smooth
      stones out of the brook.
      (17:40)
      David prepares to face Goliath, ignoring the difference in their
      sizes, the fact that he is unarmed but for a shepherd's sling, and the
      warnings and jeers of his older brothers.

18   **Am I a dog, that thou comest to me with staves?**
      (17:43)
      Goliath treats the apparently unarmed David with contempt.

19   **Saul hath slain his thousands, and David his ten thousands.**
      (18:7)
      The Israelite women sing this victory-song for David, much to
      Saul's annoyance. The words have been used as a celebration of
      victory ever since, but without the edge of comparison between one
      champion and another.

20   **David arose and went, he and his men, and slew of the**
      Philistines two hundred men; and David brought their
      foreskins, and they gave them in full tale to the king.
      (18:27)
      Saul has demanded what he thinks is an impossible bride-price for
      his daughter's hand in marriage, but David fulfils it not so much to
      the letter (i e 'tale' or total) as twice over. The phrase 'one hundred
      Philistine foreskins' became proverbial for an impossible demand.

21   **Is Saul also among the prophets?**
      (19:24)
      Saul has sent many messengers to arrest David, and all of them
      have been converted into 'prophets', servants of Samuel inspired by
      God. Finally Saul himself goes, is filled with God's spirit in his
      turn, and joins the prophets. Even in Biblical times this phrase
      acquired the proverbial meaning it has had ever since: a description
      of someone acting utterly out of character.

22   **God hath delivered him into mine hand.**
      (23:7)
      Saul in his madness thinks that because David is in a walled town,
      Keilah, he can be besieged there and killed.

23   **Behold, I have played the fool, and have erred exceedingly.**
      (26:21)
      Saul comes to his senses and realises how he has been treating
      David. Like many Biblical phrases, 'played the fool' has become so
      much part of the language that its meaning has changed and the
      original serious context has been forgotten.

II Samuel

1 **The beauty of Israel is slain upon thy high places: how are the mighty fallen!**
(1:19)
This is the beginning of David's lament over his former protector Saul and his friend Jonathan, killed in battle by the Amalekites. It yields nothing in quality compared with David's other poetry in the Bible (see for example Ps 95 or Ps 210).

2 **Tell it not in Gath, publish it not in the streets of Askelon; lest the daughters of the Philistines rejoice, lest the daughters of the uncircumcised triumph.**
(1:20)
These words, from David's lament for Saul and Jonathan, were once widely used in English (for example in nineteenth-century parliamentary speeches, by leader writers in *The Times*) as a heavily ironical warning that some utterly trifling news was about to be announced.

3 **Saul and Jonathan were lovely and pleasant in their lives, and in their death they were not divided: they were swifter than eagles, they were stronger than lions.**
(1:23)
David's lament continues. Here he dwells on two contrasting ideas: the father–son affection between Saul and Jonathan and their prowess in war.

4 **I am distressed for thee, my brother Jonathan: very pleasant hast thou been unto me: thy love to me was wonderful, passing the love of women.**
(1:26)
David's lament continues. The phrase 'passing the love of women' has been taken to imply that David and Jonathan were homosexual lovers – and indeed was used as a synonym for homosexuality in the nineteenth century. But in view of the moral context of the period (see Lev 10) it almost certainly suggests no more than intimate friendship.

5 **How are the mighty fallen, and the weapons of war perished!**
(1:27)
This last verse of David's lament, originally elegiac – he is referring to Saul and Jonathan – has come to be used triumphantly, about the defeat of any proud enemy.

6   **David danced before the Lord with all his might.**
     (6:14)
     David celebrates a double victory over the Philistines. Ecstatic
     religious dancing was common in the early Middle East, and though
     it was frowned on and discouraged by the fathers of the Christian
     Church, still survives in many religious traditions as a legitimate,
     and exuberant, counterpart to ritual.

7   **David arose from off his bed, and walked upon the roof of the**
     king's house: and from the roof he saw a woman washing
     herself; and the woman was very beautiful to look upon.
     (11:2)
     David has his first glimpse of Bathsheba, the wife of Uriah the
     Hittite.

8   **Set ye Uriah in the forefront of the hottest battle, and retire**
     ye from him.
     (11:15)
     David's instructions for the death of Uriah the Hittite in battle have
     been used as a kind of coded message ever since – and the code
     (since Uriah himself carried these orders in a letter) means 'kill the
     messenger'. Equally, the name Uriah came to have associations of
     humble obedience, associations which Dickens took full advantage
     of when he christened the flattering hypocrite of *David Copperfield*
     Uriah Heep.

9   **The poor man had nothing, save one little ewe lamb.**
     (12:3)
     Nathan the prophet tells David, in a parable, that God is angry with
     him for stealing Bathsheba from Uriah the Hittite. The phrase
     'little ewe lamb' became second only to 'apple of the eye' as a
     metaphor for 'favourite person or possession'.

10   **Thou art the man.**
     (12:7)
     Nathan tells David that he is the villain in the parable. The phrase
     became proverbial as a declaration of guilt, until it was cruelly
     parodied by Pilate at Jesus' trial (*Ecce homo*, 'Behold the man': see
     John 67), and became converted into a triumphant assertion of
     Christ as God-made-flesh.

11   **We must needs die, and are as water spilt on the ground,**
     which cannot be gathered up again; neither doth God respect
     any person.
     (14:14)

A wise woman tries to persuade David not to grieve for his murdered son Absalom. The last phrase above was paraphrased by St Peter (see Acts 36) in a form which has become even more widely known.

12   **Come out, come out, thou bloody man, and thou man of Belial.**
(16:7)
Shimei curses David, as a murderer and a blasphemer. For 'man of Belial', compare I Sam 1.

13   **The king said unto Cushi, Is the young man Absalom safe? And Cushi answered, The enemies of my lord the king, and all that rise against thee to do thee hurt, be as that young man is.**
(18:32)
Absalom, leader of a revolt against his father David, has been treacherously murdered. Cushi's grim joke in answer to David's question has often been used in similar circumstances since.

14   **O my son Absalom, my son, my son Absalom! would God I had died for thee, O Absalom, my son, my son!**
(18:33)
David weeps for Absalom.

15   **The Lord is my rock, and my fortress, and my deliverer.**
(22:2)
David's song of thanksgiving when the rebellions are crushed.

16   **Thou art my lamp, O Lord: and the Lord will lighten my darkness.**
(22:29)
This phrase from David's triumph-song was adapted into one of the best-known of all Christian prayers, 'Lighten our darkness, we beseech thee, O Lord.'

17   **The sweet psalmist of Israel.**
(23:1)
This description of David precedes the last of his poems quoted in II Samuel. 'Psalmist' had none of the ritualistic implications it has today: it simply means 'maker of sacred songs'.

18   **Be it far from me, O Lord, that I should do this: is not this the blood of the men that went in jeopardy of their lives?**
(23:17)

David has wished for water from a well in enemy-held Jerusalem, and three of his men have risked their lives to fetch it. David refuses to drink it and pours it out. 'In jeopardy' has lost most of its colouring in contemporary English. To Elizabethan ears, the phrase would have been a powerful metaphor from chess: anyone in 'jeopardy' (from the French *Jeu parti*) had made his or her move and was waiting to see what risks, if any, had been run. At one point chess itself was known as 'jeopardy'.

I Kings

1   **King David was old and stricken in years.**
     (1:1)
     Like much ancient literature, the Bible frequently emphasizes points by repeating them in different words. 'Stricken in years' is no more than an elaboration of 'old'. It has been so used, often ironically or half-jokingly, ever since.

2   **I go the way of all the earth.**
     (2:2)
     David tells his son Solomon that he is dying.

3   **Keep the charge of the Lord thy God, to walk in his ways, to keep his statutes, and his commandments, and his judgments, and his testimonies, as it is written in the law of Moses, that thou mayest prosper in all that thou doest.**
     (2:3)
     David gives Solomon advice which has since become paraphrased in a well-known prayer for obedience.

4   **I am but a little child: I know not how to go out or come in.**
     (3:7)
     Solomon prays to God for help.

5   **The king said, Divide the living child in two, and give half to the one, and half to the other.**
     (3:25)
     This is the 'judgment of Solomon', a phrase which has become even better known than the incident which provoked it.

6   **Now therefore command thou that they hew me cedar trees out of Lebanon.**
     (5:6)

Solomon writes to Hiram king of Tyre, asking for building
materials for the proposed new temple in Jerusalem. Lebanese
cedars were a major export at the time, and indeed well into Roman
times. Their wood was some of the most highly valued in the
ancient world, and their name has become a byword for excellence.

7   **I have surely built thee an house to dwell in, a settled place
     for thee to abide in for ever.**
     (8:13)
     Solomon dedicates the temple to God.

8   **O Lord my God, to hearken unto the cry and to the prayer,
     which thy servant prayeth before thee to day: That thine eyes
     may be open toward this house night and day, even toward
     the place of which thou hast said, My name shall be there.**
     (8:28–9)
     Solomon continues his prayer in the temple.

9   **The Lord our God be with us, as he was with our fathers: let
     him not leave us, nor forsake us: That he may incline our
     hearts unto him, to walk in all his ways, and to keep his
     commandments.**
     (8:57–8)
     Solomon's words to the people at the dedication of the temple have
     become part of many forms of worship.

10   **Behold, the half was not told me: thy wisdom and prosperity
     exceedeth the fame which I heard.**
     (10:7)
     The Queen of Sheba (present-day Yemen), having come to see
     Solomon's glory and wisdom for herself, is impressed.

11   **Once in three years came the navy of Tharshish, bringing
     gold, and silver, ivory, and apes, and peacocks.**
     (10:22)
     Tribute from one single area (perhaps the western Mediterranean,
     modern Spain and Portugal) gives some idea of Solomon's fabulous
     wealth.

12   **King Solomon loved many strange women.**
     (11:1)
     Wise and rich though he was, Solomon's behaviour was not popular
     with all his people. The women here were 'strange' not in their own
     personalities but because they were strangers: Egyptians, Moabites,
     Edomites and others, idolaters all.

13   **My little finger shall be thicker than my father's loins.**
(12:10)
After Solomon's death, his son Rehoboam becomes king. His
young friends advise him not to be a lightweight, God-fearing ruler,
but to govern with a heavy hand. This is the scornful message (since
proverbial) they suggest he gives the Israelites. 'Loins' means
'penis'.

14   **My father hath chastised you with whips, but I will chastise
you with scorpions.**
(12:11)
Rehoboam adds hyperbole to scorn in his message to his people.
Inspired by this verse, torturers in the Middle Ages gave the name
'scorpion' to a particularly brutal whip, whose four or five thongs
were spiked with steel.

15   **To your tents, O Israel.**
(12:16)
The Israelites rebel against Rehoboam.

16   **As the Lord God of Israel liveth, before whom I stand, there
shall not be dew nor rain these years, but according to my
word.**
(17:1)
Elijah warns King Ahab of the punishment for idolatry.

17   **Get thee hence, and turn thee eastward, and hide thyself by
the brook Cherith, that is before Jordan. And it shall be, that
thou shalt drink of the brook; and I have commanded the
ravens to feed thee there.**
(17:2–3)
God gives instructions and reassurance to Elijah.

18   **The barrel of meal wasted not, neither did the cruse of oil fail,
according to the word of the Lord.**
(17:16)
God rewards the widow who shares her last morsel of food with
Elijah. The phrase 'widow's cruse', referring to an earthenware oil-
jug, has become proverbial for the source of any never-ending
supply.

19   **How long halt ye between two opinions?**
(18:21)
Elijah asks the people to choose between God and Baal. 'Halt' here
means 'stumble'.

20 **Cry aloud: for he is a god; either he is talking, or he is pursuing, or he is in a journey, or peradventure he sleepeth, and must be awaked.**
(18:27)
Elijah mocks the prophets of Baal because their god seems unable to hear their prayers in a competition to see whose god can miraculously set fire to a sacrifice. 'Pursuing' means 'hunting'; 'peradventure' means 'possibly'.

21 **Elijah said unto Ahab, Get thee up, eat and drink; for there is a sound of abundance of rain.**
(18:41)
Elijah announces the coming end of the drought. The phrase 'a sound of abundance of rain' was much used in Victorian English, to mean 'prosperity is on the way'.

22 **Behold, there ariseth a little cloud out of the sea, like a man's hand.**
(18:44)
Elijah's servant reports that rain is on the way at last. 'A cloud no bigger than a man's hand' has become proverbial, for the small beginning which may well lead to something big.

23 **He said, Go forth, and stand upon the mount before the Lord: And, behold, the Lord passed by, and a great and strong wind rent the mountains, and brake in pieces the rocks before the Lord; but the Lord was not in the wind: and after the wind an earthquake; but the Lord was not in the earthquake: And after the earthquake a fire; but the Lord was not in the fire; and after the fire a still small voice.**
(19:11–12)
Even after God sends rain and Elijah kills the prophets of Baal, the Israelites keep to their idolatry. Elijah goes in despair into the wilderness, where an angel orders him to go to the mountain-top and appear before God. God speaks to him in none of the expected, portentous ways, but in a 'still, small voice', and tells him what to do.

24 **Elijah passed by him, and cast his mantle upon him.**
(19:19)
Elijah selects Elisha to be his successor. The phrase 'the mantle of the prophet', meaning inherited position or authority, comes from this verse.

25 **Let not him that girdeth on his harness boast himself as he that putteth it off.**
(20:11)

This is King Ahab's proud answer to Benhadad, King of Syria, who has announced that he is invading Israel. The phrase has a proverbial meaning similar to 'Don't count your chickens until they're hatched.' 'Harness' means 'armour'.

26 **Naboth the Jezreelite had a vineyard, which was in Jezreel, hard by the palace of Ahab king of Samaria. And Ahab spake unto Naboth, saying, Give me thy vineyard, that I may have it for a garden of herbs, because it is near unto my house: and I will give thee for it a better vineyard than it; or, if it seem good to thee, I will give thee the worth of it in money. And Naboth said to Ahab, The Lord forbid it me, that I should give the inheritance of my fathers unto thee.**
(21:1–3)
'Naboth's vineyard' came to be a well-understood legal phrase for property one person wanted and another refused to part with.

27 **They carried him forth out of the city, and stoned him with stones, that he died.**
(21:13)
Naboth is punished by King Ahab's soldiers for refusing to sell his vineyard.

28 **Hast thou found me, O mine enemy?**
(21:20)
This is Ahab's greeting to Elijah, who goes to remonstrate with him after Naboth's death.

29 **I will bring evil upon thee, and will take away thy posterity, and will cut off from Ahab him that pisseth against the wall.**
(21:21)
Elijah's curse against Ahab is comprehensive: not even total strangers will have anything to do with him. He 'that pisseth against the wall' is another way of saying 'the man in the street'.

30 **Thus saith the king, Put this fellow in the prison, and feed him with bread of affliction and with water of affliction.**
(22:27)
Micaiah the prophet is punished for speaking unpalatable truth.

31 **A certain man drew a bow at a venture, and smote the king of Israel between the joints of the harness.**
(22:34)
Ahab is killed in battle, almost by accident. 'To draw a bow at a venture' is to do or say something casually which results in a much greater success than intended.

32   He did evil in the sight of the Lord.
(22:52)
Ahaziah, son of King Ahab, was by no means the first or last person
in the Bible to 'do evil in the sight of the Lord', but he is the first of
whom this phrase is used.

II Kings

1   I pray thee, let a double portion of thy spirit be upon me.
(2:9)
This is Elisha's request when he hears that his master, Elijah the
prophet, is about to die.

**2   Behold, there appeared a chariot of fire, and horses of fire,
and parted them both asunder; and Elijah went up by a
whirlwind into heaven.**
(2:11)
Elijah ascends into heaven.

3   Go up, thou bald head; go up, thou bald head.
(2:23)
Street-urchins mock Elisha. In a society where priests never cut
their hair or beards, his baldness must have been particularly
noteworthy.

**4   There came forth two she bears out of the wood, and tare
forty and two children of them.**
(2:24)
The urchins are punished for mocking Elisha by calling out 'Go up,
thou bald head'. 'Tare' means 'tore'.

**5   Is it well with thee? is it well with thy husband? is it well with
the child?**
(4:26)
Because Elisha's landlady comes running to him in broad daylight,
against custom, he senses that something is wrong, and sends a
servant with these questions.

6   The child sneezed seven times, and the child opened his eyes.
(4:35)
Elisha brings his landlady's son back from the dead.

**7   Are not Abana and Pharpar, rivers of Damascus, better than
all the waters of Israel?**
(5:12)

Naaman, an important Syrian, has asked Elisha how he can be cured of leprosy, and has been told to wash in the river Jordan. This is his furious response.

8   **His flesh came again like unto the flesh of a little child, and he was clean.**
(5:14)
Naaman follows instructions and is cured.

9   **He went out from his presence a leper as white as snow.**
(5:27)
Elisha's servant is punished for taking payment for the cure of Naaman, and lying about it to Elisha.

10   **Now, behold, if the Lord should make windows in heaven, might such a thing be?**
(7:19)
An unnamed lord, told by Elisha that famine will lead to two measures of barley, or one of ground flour, being sold for a shekel, makes this unbelieving reply, which became a proverbial expression of amazed disbelief.

11   **Is thy servant a dog, that he should do this great thing?**
(8:13)
Hazael's indignant question to Elisha, who has prophesied that he is to fight and conquer his own people, was a popular expression in the nineteenth century, used by people asked to do something they thought unworthy of them. The wittiest known use of it (described in Brewer's *Dictionary of Phrase and Fable*) was by one Lockhart, when it was suggested that he should have his portrait painted by Landseer, the celebrated painter of pet animals.

12   **The driving is like the driving of Jehu the son of Nimshi; for he driveth furiously.**
(9:20)
Told by Elisha that he was to be king in place of Ahab, Jehu drove furiously about in all directions, eliminating potential opposition. In the eighteenth and nineteenth centuries his name became a synonym, first for a reckless driver and then, ironically, for any kind of coachman.

13   **When Jehu was come to Jezreel, Jezebel heard of it; and she painted her face, and tired her head, and looked out at a window.**
(9:30)

Ever since this comparatively innocent incident, Jezebel has meant a
'painted lady' or harlot. 'Tired' means 'attired'. She was an
unprincipled woman, wife of the wicked King Ahab, but does
nothing in the Bible to justify her subsequent reputation.

14 **They went to bury her: but they found no more of her than
the skull, and the feet, and the palms of her hands.**
(9:35)
Jezebel is thrown from a window for favouring Jehu, and is eaten by
dogs with this result: a solemn warning, perhaps, against over-
indulgence in face-painting.

15 **Now, behold, thou trustest upon the staff of this bruised reed,
even upon Egypt, on which if a man lean, it will go into his
hand, and pierce it: so is Pharaoh king of Egypt unto all that
trust on him.**
(18:21)
The king of Assyria tries to frighten the Israelites into submission
by telling them that they are without allies. The point here (literally)
is that a bruised reed is sharp and dangerous, and in the same way
Pharaoh is an untrustworthy ally. Isaiah (see Isa 58) used the phrase
'broken reed' with the same meaning; nowadays, by contrast, it
suggests someone prone to collapse and therefore useless to lean
on.

16 **He turned his face to the wall, and prayed unto the Lord.**
(20:2)
Hezekiah, sick 'unto death', turns his face to the wall to pray in
private. The phrase has, however, come to mean that someone
realizes that their death is imminent, gives up all hope and turns
away from any further human contact.

I Chronicles

1 **Give thanks unto the Lord, call upon his name, make known
his deeds among the people. Sing unto him, sing psalms unto
him, talk ye of all his wondrous works. Glory ye in his holy
name: let the heart of them rejoice that seek the Lord.**
(16:8–10)
This is the beginning of David's triumph-song after a defeat of the
Philistines, when the ark is carried into Jerusalem.

2 **Sing unto the Lord, all the earth; shew forth from day to day
his salvation.**
(16:23)

David's triumph-song continues. In a common idea in Hebrew poetry, the very earth is invited to join with all its inhabitants in praising God.

3   **Let the sea roar, and the fulness thereof: let the fields rejoice, and all that is therein.**
(16:32)
David's triumph-song continues. He develops the idea that inanimate parts of the earth should take voice and hymn God's praise.

4   **O give thanks unto the Lord; for he is good; for his mercy endureth for ever.**
(16:34)
This verse from David's triumph-song reappears almost word for word in one of the Psalms (see Ps 217).

5   **I am in a great strait: let me fall now into the hand of the Lord; for very great are his mercies: but let me not fall into the hand of man.**
(21:13)
God has offered David the choice between three months' heaven-sent plague, as a punishment for his people's disobedience, or a three-month war against their enemies.

6   **David lifted up his eyes, and saw the angel of the Lord stand between the earth and the heaven, having a drawn sword in his hand stretched out over Jerusalem.**
(21:16)
God's angel appears, to destroy Jerusalem.

7   **Thine, O Lord, is the greatness, and the power, and the glory, and the victory, and the majesty: for all that is in the heaven and in the earth is thine; thine is the kingdom, O Lord, and thou art exalted as head above all.**
(29:11)
David praises God at the start of his son Solomon's coronation. The phrase 'the power and the glory' reappears at the end of the Lord's Prayer.

8   **We are strangers before thee, and sojourners, as were all our fathers: our days on the earth are as a shadow, and there is none abiding.**
(29:15)
David humbles himself and his people before God.

9   He died in a good old age, full of days, riches, and honour.
     (29:28)
     The chronicler gives this epitaph for David – often used since, and
     a source of the expression 'a ripe old age'.

II Chronicles

1   That they may fear thee, to walk in thy ways.
     (6:31)
     Solomon prays to God at the dedication of the temple. 'They' are
     the people.

2   Happy are thy men, and happy are these thy servants, which
     stand continually before thee, and hear thy wisdom.
     (9:7)
     The Queen of Sheba praises Solomon, in words which have since
     frequently been used as praise of God himself.

3   He did evil, because he prepared not his heart to seek the
     Lord.
     (12:14)
     Originally spoken about Solomon's renegade son Rehoboam, these
     words have frequently been used since in denunciation of those of
     whom the Church disapproves.

Ezra

1   The hand of our God was upon us, and he delivered us from
     the hand of the enemy, and of such as lay in wait by the way.
     (8:31)
     Ezra has led 1,700 people from Babylonian exile back to Jerusalem,
     and they have travelled 900 miles (1,440 km) in complete safety,
     despite carrying a fortune in gold, silver and jewels. The phrase 'the
     hand of God was upon us' (or 'over us'), has entered the language.

2   And now for a little space grace hath been shewed from the
     Lord our God.
     (9:8)
     Ezra thanks God for leading the people safely from exile.

Nehemiah

1   Now Tobiah the Ammonite was by him, and he said, Even
that which they build, if a fox go up, he shall even break down
their stone wall.
(4:3)
Encouraged by Nehemiah, the Israelites are rebuilding the
shattered walls of Jerusalem – but their enemies, in this case
Tobiah the Ammonite, sneer to see it.

2   They which builded on the wall, and they that bare burdens,
with those that laded, every one with one of his hands
wrought in the work, and with the other hand held a weapon.
For the builders, every one had his sword girded by his side,
and so builded.
(4:17–18)
Ringed by enemies, Nehemiah's Israelites are forced to carry on
their rebuilding work fully armed.

3   I am doing a great work, so that I cannot come down: why
should the work cease, whilst I leave it, and come down to
you?
(6:3)
Nehemiah refuses his enemies' offer of a parley.

4   Thou, even thou, art Lord alone; thou hast made heaven, the
heaven of heavens, with all their host, the earth, and all things
that are therein, the seas, and all that is therein, and thou
preservest them all; and the host of heaven worshippeth thee.
(9:6)
The Israelites sing in triumph when the building work is safely
done. The verse, and the thoughts behind it, were in the minds of
the authors of two of the most potent of all the utterances of the
Christian Church, the Nicene Creed ('I believe in one God') and
the Te Deum ('To thee Cherubim and Seraphim continually do
cry, "Holy, holy, holy"').

5   Yet thou in thy manifold mercies forsookest them not.
(9:19)
The Israelites' hymn of praise continues. This reference is to God
providing manna in the wilderness (see Exod 46).

Esther

1   If it please the king, let there go a royal commandment from
    him, and let it be written among the laws of the Persians and
    the Medes, that it be not altered.
    (1:19)
    Vashti, wife of King Ahasuerus, has refused to show herself at court
    in all her finery merely because he orders it. The court officials urge
    him to make a decree divorcing her. The phrase 'laws of the Medes
    and Persians' was proverbial, even in Biblical times, for laws which
    could not be altered possibly because they were inscribed on stone
    slabs and set up in every part of the Persian empire, and so must
    have seemed much more permanent than laws kept in books or in
    lawyers' memories.

2   And the king loved Esther above all the women, and she
    obtained grace and favour in his sight.
    (2:17)
    Seeking a new wife in Vashti's place, King Ahasuerus spends time
    with every attractive girl who can be found for him, including Esther
    the Israelite. 'Grace and favour', here used literally, came to have a
    more dismissive, derogatory tone, describing patronage more
    grudging than wholehearted.

3   So will I go in unto the king, which is not according to the law:
    and if I perish, I perish.
    (4:16)
    Ahasuerus, duped by an ambitious courtier, has decreed a
    persecution of every Jew in the kingdom. Esther agrees to try to talk
    him out of it, even though by law the queen is forbidden to
    approach the king unless invited.

4   Then took Haman the apparel and the horse, and arrayed
    Mordecai, and brought him on horseback through the street
    of the city, and proclaimed before him, Thus shall it be done
    unto the man whom the king delighteth to honour.
    (6:11)
    Mordecai, the Israelite who warned Ahasuerus about an
    assassination plot, is rewarded with riches, a fine horse and a
    procession through the city, despite the earlier royal proclamation
    that Jews are to be persecuted.

5   How can I endure to see the evil that shall come unto my
    people? or how can I endure to see the destruction of my
    kindred?
    (8:6)

Esther begs Ahasuerus to end the persecution of the Jews.

6   **On the thirteenth day of the month Adar; and on the
      fourteenth day of the same rested they, and made it a day of
      feasting and gladness.**
      (9:17)
      Thanks to Esther, the Jews have been freed from persecution and
      they now celebrate. This story is the origin of the Feast of Purim,
      held in the twelfth month of the Jewish year (February – March): a
      time of joy, and a reminder that anti-semitism can be changed, that
      it is not a natural human attitude.

Job

1   **That man was perfect and upright, and one that feared God,
      and eschewed evil.**
      (1:1)
      The description of Job as honest and honourable is crucial to the
      whole meaning of his story. If his sufferings had been deserved,
      who would care?

2   **The Lord said unto Satan, Whence comest thou? Then Satan
      answered the Lord, and said, From going to and fro in the
      earth, and from walking up and down in it.**
      (1:7)
      God's sons come before him one by one, including Satan. Satan's
      words have been used ever since to describe the presence of evil
      everywhere in the world.

3   **Hast thou considered my servant Job, that there is none like
      him in the earth, a perfect and an upright man, one that
      feareth God, and escheweth evil?**
      (1:8)
      God suggests to Satan that Job is a paragon among humankind.
      The implication is that because there is no evil in him, he is
      immune from harm.

4   **Doth Job fear God for nought?**
      (1:9)
      Satan suggests that Job's humility is not as innocent as it seems.
      The question has often since been used as a kind of generalized
      political smear, an attack on apparently disinterested loyalty.

5   **Behold, all that he hath is in thy power; only upon himself put not forth thine hand.**
(1:12)
God gives Satan authority to test Job.

6   **Naked came I out of my mother's womb, and naked shall I return thither: the Lord gave, and the Lord hath taken away; blessed be the name of the Lord.**
(1:21)
Despite a chain of disasters (the loss of all his property, and the deaths of all his children and children-in-law), Job's loyalty to God remains unswerving.

7   **Skin for skin, yea, all that a man hath will he give for his life. But put forth thine hand now, and touch his bone and his flesh, and he will curse thee to thy face.**
(2:4–5)
Satan finds a bad interpretation for Job's unswerving piety despite all the suffering heaped on him, and asks God's permission to test him further.

8   **He took him a potsherd to scrape himself withal; and he sat down among the ashes.**
(2:8)
Job is afflicted with boils. A 'potsherd' is simply a piece of broken crockery.

9   **Dost thou still retain thine integrity? curse God, and die.**
(2:9)
Even Job's wife tempts him from his loyalty to God. 'Integrity' means 'single-mindedness'.

10   **Let the day perish wherein I was born.**
(3:3)
Job begins a bitter, lengthy curse, but still avoids cursing God.

11   **As for that night, let darkness seize upon it; let it not be joined unto the days of the year, let it not come into the number of the months.**
(3:6)
Job curses the night of his conception.

12   **Let the stars of the twilight thereof be dark; let it look for light, but have none; neither let it see the dawning of the day.**
(3:9)
Job's curse on the night of his conception continues.

13   **There the wicked cease from troubling; and there the weary be at rest.**
(3:17)
Job talks of the peace beyond the grave.

14   **Wherefore is light given to him that is in misery, and life unto the bitter in soul?**
(3:20)
Job curses the gift of existence.

15   **Shall mortal man be more just than God? shall a man be more pure than his maker?**
(4:17)
Job's friend, Eliphaz the Temanite, says that all human beings are tainted with sin and therefore doomed to suffer.

16   **Yet man is born unto trouble, as the sparks fly upward.**
(5:7)
Eliphaz the Temanite continues his gloomy meditation on the ineluctable misery of the human condition.

17   **Behold, happy is the man whom God correcteth: therefore despise not thou the chastening of the Almighty.**
(5:17)
Eliphaz the Temanite preaches a comfortable obedience to God.

18   **As a servant earnestly desireth the shadow, and as an hireling looketh for the reward of his work: So am I made to possess months of vanity, and wearisome nights are appointed to me.**
(7:2–3)
Job talks of the bitterness of his existence. 'Vanity' means 'emptiness'.

19   **My days are swifter than a weaver's shuttle, and are spent without hope.**
(7:6)
Job's diatribe against his own life continues. However fast the time passes, it is sterile.

20   **What is man, that thou shouldest magnify him? and that thou shouldest set thine heart upon him?**
(7:17)
Job begs God to explain what human beings have done to deserve their uniqueness. Job's own uniqueness here is that he is being

persecuted by God: he has had God's heart 'set on him' in no uncertain terms.

21 **Thou shalt seek me in the morning, but I shall not be.**
(7:21)
Job prays to God to pardon his sins, or else they will destroy him in the night.

22 **God will not cast away a perfect man.**
(8:20)
Bildad the Shuhite, Job's second friend, is urging him not to let transient sufferings weaken his faith in God.

23 **Which removeth the mountains, and they know not: which**
overturneth them in his anger. Which shaketh the earth out of
her place, and the pillars thereof tremble. Which
commandeth the sun, and it riseth not; and sealeth up the
stars.
(9:5–7)
Job talks of God's power, asking how any human being can stand against it or deny it. St Paul developed the image in his sermon on Faith, Hope and Charity (see I Cor 19), and the common proverb 'Faith can move mountains' grew from a combination of both passages.

24 **My soul is weary of my life; I will leave my complaint upon**
myself; I will speak in the bitterness of my soul.
(10:1)
This is one of the earliest literary expressions of the idea of soul-sickness, existential weariness, which has been such a powerful idea in twentieth-century writing and philosophy.

25 **Remember, I beseech thee, that thou hast made me as the**
clay; and wilt thou bring me into dust again? Hast thou not
poured me out as milk, and curdled me like cheese? Thou
hast clothed me with skin and flesh, and hast fenced me with
bones and sinews. Thou has granted me life and favour, and
thy visitation hath preserved my spirit.
(10:9–12)
Job asks God why he should have created him merely for so much misery. The thinking behind this passage is nobly picked up in the prose soliloquy Shakespeare gives to Hamlet (*Hamlet* II.2), in the passage which begins 'What a piece of work is a man!' and ends 'Man delights not me.'

26   Are not my days few? cease then, and let me alone, that I may
take comfort a little, Before I go whence I shall not return,
even to the land of darkness and the shadow of death; A land
of darkness, as darkness itself; and of the shadow of death,
without any order, and where the light is as darkness.
(10:20–2)
Job prays for peace before he dies, in a passage which, once again,
was possibly in Shakespeare's mind as he wrote *Hamlet*. It is
reflected in the III, 1, soliloquy 'To be or not to be' with its image of
the sleep of death as 'the undiscovered country from whose
bourne/no traveller returns'.

27   Canst thou by searching find out God? canst thou find out the
Almighty unto perfection?
(11:7)
Job's third friend, Zophar the Naamathite, asks how any human
being can ever hope to understand God's will.

28   And thou shalt be secure, because there is hope; yea, thou
shalt dig about thee, and thou shalt take thy rest in safety.
(11:18)
Zophar is urging Job to have faith in God, rather than an attempt to
understand him.

29   No doubt but ye are the people, and wisdom shall die with
you.
(12:2)
Job turns on his three friends, with the only moment of sarcasm he
ever allows himself. The point here is that they are *not* 'the people' –
that is, the only wise people in the world – although by their
behaviour they appear to think they are.

30   With the ancient is wisdom; and in length of days
understanding.
(12:12)
The idea that the old are wise reappears frequently in the Bible, as
in much ancient writing. In one form, based on this passage (see
Dan 18), it gave rise to a proverbial description of God himself – all
wisdom personified.

31   But we are forgers of lies.
(13:4)
In a magnificent, often-quoted phrase, Job rounds on his well-
meaning friends.

32   **Though he slay me, yet will I trust in him.**
(**13:15**)
Despite his suffering, and his complaining, Job is still able to say
this, one of the bluntest, most ringing affirmations of faith in the
whole Bible.

33   **Man that is born of a woman is of few days, and full of
trouble. He cometh forth like a flower, and is cut down: he
fleeth also as a shadow, and continueth not.**
(**14:1–2**)
Job reflects on mortality. The first sentence was adapted as part of
the funeral service in the prayer book ('Man that is born of a woman
hath but a short time to live, and is full of misery'); the thought
behind the second sentence is a staple idea in ancient literature,
from grand (Homer reflecting on the death of the heroes at Troy) to
less grand (Catullus bemoaning his suffering at the hands of a
faithless lover).

34   **Art thou the first man that was born?**
(**15:7**)
Job's friends remind him that he is not unique, either in knowledge
or in suffering.

35   **Miserable comforters are ye all.**
(**16:2**)
Ever since this phrase was translated, the expression 'Job's
comforters' has been proverbial for people who blame the person
for his or her own suffering instead of offering true sympathy.

36   **I am escaped with the skin of my teeth.**
(**19:20**)
Job is reflecting not on his misery, but on his luck at escaping death
after the sins he has committed. For all its biological inexactness,
the phrase has been used ever since as a metaphor for a very lucky
escape indeed.

37   **Oh that my words were now written! oh that they were
printed in a book!**
(**19:23**)
Job wants his sufferings written down, as an example to others to
worship God. In view of their context (in the middle of a piece of
writing called 'The Book of Job') these words are a remarkable
piece of authorial intervention, a reminder that what we are reading
was written with a purpose. The practice became common in later
literature – it is ever-present, for example, in nineteenth-century
novels – but was rare indeed in the Bible. (Mark 15 is the best-
known other example).

38   I know that my redeemer liveth, and that he shall stand at the
     latter day upon the earth: And though after my skin worms
     destroy this body, yet in my flesh shall I see God.
     (19:25–6)
     This simple declaration of faith in God had particular resonance for
     later Christians. It is now universally known in its musical setting as
     one of the climactic moments in Handel's *Messiah*.

39   How oft is the candle of the wicked put out! and how oft
     cometh their destruction upon them! God distributeth
     sorrows in his anger. They are as stubble before the wind, and
     as chaff that the storm carrieth away.
     (21:17–18)
     Job reflects on how the wicked are doomed to punishment – an
     extension and variant of one of the earlier remarks of Eliphaz the
     Temanite (see Job 16). 'They' refers to the wicked rather than to the
     sorrows God sends them.

40   Oh that I knew where I might find him! that I might come
     even to his seat! I would order my cause before him, and fill
     my mouth with arguments. I would know the words which he
     would answer me, and understand what he would say unto
     me.
     (23:3–5)
     Job's bitterest regret is not his suffering but his lack of
     understanding of God's purpose; his greatest punishment is not
     poverty, boils or the death of his family, but the absence of God.

41   I go forward, but he is not there; and backward, but I cannot
     perceive him.
     (23:8)
     Job continues to bemoan the lack of God's presence, articulating
     the feeling of existential aloneness which has so often seemed an
     essential part of the human condition (see Job 24).

42   The Almighty troubleth me.
     (23:16)
     Job means this not literally – the deaths, the poverty, the boils – but
     metaphorically, in the modern sense of the phrase. Awareness of
     God is not a comfortable thing: it alarms and unsettles him. The
     answer to existential loneliness (see Job 41) is no easier than the
     problem.

43   But where shall wisdom be found? and where is the place of
     understanding? Man knoweth not the price thereof; neither is
     it found in the land of the living. The depth saith, It is not in
     me: and the sea saith, It is not with me.
     (28:12–14)

Job contrasts the difficulty of finding wisdom, the riches of the mind, with the easy search (by comparison) for the earth's material wealth. By 'wisdom' he means the 'knowledge of good and evil' (see Gen 9) which God alone possesses and to which human beings can only aspire.

44   It cannot be gotten for gold, neither shall silver be weighed for the price thereof. It cannot be valued with the gold of Ophir, with the precious onyx, or the sapphire. The gold and the crystal cannot equal it: and the exchange of it shall not be for jewels of fine gold. No mention shall be made of coral, or of pearls: for the price of wisdom is above rubies. The topaz of Ethiopia shall not equal it, neither shall it be valued with pure gold.
(28:15–19)

Job's poetic flight on the value of wisdom continues. The phrase 'the price of wisdom is above rubies' has become proverbial, and would have had a particular resonance in the Middle Ages, when rubies were regarded as magic stones, able not only to cure physical illness but to turn people's minds from grief to joy and from wickedness to good.

45   I put on righteousness, and it clothed me: my judgment was as a robe and a diadem. I was eyes to the blind, and feet was I to the lame.
(29:14–15)

Job talks of the kind of man he was in the days before God turned from him.

46   But now they that are younger than I have me in derision, whose fathers I would have disdained to have set with the dogs of my flock.
(30:1)

Job contrasts the way he is scorned now with the respect in which he was once held.

47   I am a brother to dragons, and a companion to owls.
(30:29)

Job returns to the theme of his own wickedness. In many ancient communities, owls were regarded as magic creatures, night-flying spirits of darkness and hence of Satan who ruled it; they were the dark counterpart of dragons, whose magic was rooted in brightness, fire and flame.

48   **Great men are not always wise: neither do the aged understand judgement.**
(32:9)
Elihu, the son of Barachel the Buzzite, takes up the argument, angry that his elders have failed to counter Job's continual self-justifications. Although this phrase now seems obviously true, a platitude, it was a startling remark for a young man to make in ancient Israelite society, when to be old was to be an 'elder', a repository of knowledge and understanding (see Job 30 and 46).

49   **For I am full of matter, the spirit within me constraineth me.**
(32:18)
Elihu explains why he can sit quiet no longer.

50   **Thou hast spoken in mine hearing, and I have heard the voice of thy words, saying, I am clean without transgression, I am innocent; neither is there iniquity in me. Behold, he findeth occasions against me, he counteth me for his enemy, He putteth my feet in the stocks, he marketh all my paths. Behold, in this thou art not just: I will answer thee, that God is greater than man.**
(33:8–12)
Elihu summarizes Job's arguments and then counters them in a phrase so simple that it approaches platitude.

51   **What man is like Job, who drinketh up scorning like water?**
(34:7)
Elihu pinpoints Job's 'sin': self-abasement carried well over the brink of pride.

52   **He multiplieth words without knowledge.**
(35:16)
Elihu says that Job is so busy saying how he understands nothing of God, that he gives himself no time to try to understand him.

53   **Hearken unto this, O Job: stand still, and consider the wondrous works of God.**
(37:14)
Elihu prescribes a new genuinely humble lifestyle for Job.

54   **Then the Lord answered Job out of the whirlwind, and said, Who is this that darkeneth counsel by words without knowledge?**
(38:1–2)
At last God speaks directly to Job, and begins the explanation for which Job has so desperately been begging.

55   Gird up now thy loins like a man; for I will demand of thee,
      and answer thou me.
      (38:3)
      God scolds Job out of his self-pitying lethargy. In ancient times,
      when people wore clothes with long skirts, they had to gather them
      up between the legs and hitch them to their belts before starting any
      strenuous job. The phrase became proverbial even in Biblical times,
      and was given a magnificent metaphorical twist by St Peter (see I
      Pet 2), an exact equivalent of its meaning here.

56   Where wast thou when I laid the foundations of the earth?
      declare, if thou hast understanding. Who hath laid the
      measures thereof, if thou knowest? or who hath stretched the
      line upon it? Whereupon are the foundations thereof
      fastened? or who laid the corner stone thereof; When the
      morning stars sang together, and all the sons of God shouted
      for joy?
      (38:4-7)
      God challenges Job directly, apparently asking *him* for answers
      instead of questions.

57   Hath the rain a father? or who hath begotten the drops of
      dew?
      (38:28)
      God continues his challenge.

58   Canst thou bind the sweet influences of Pleiades, or loose the
      bands of Orion?
      (38:31)
      God's assertion of his power continues, in one of the most
      Shakespearean passages in this whole translation of the Bible.

59   Hast thou given the horse strength? hast thou clothed his
      neck with thunder? Canst thou make him afraid as a
      grasshopper? The glory of his nostrils is terrible. He paweth
      in the valley, and rejoiceth in his strength: he goeth on to
      meet the armed men.
      (39:19-21)
      God continues to proclaim his glory, as revealed in every created
      thing. 'The glory of his nostrils' was a well-pilloried phrase in the
      nineteenth century, perhaps because the exaggeration seemed close
      to the flared-nostril romanticism of popular fiction. But in its
      context the image remains magnificent.

60   Behold now Behemoth, which I made with thee; he eateth
      grass as an ox.
      (40:15)

God's greatness is revealed in everything he has made, from the least to the largest. 'Behemoth' (from an old Egyptian word meaning 'water-buffalo') was apparently the Elizabethan word for a hippopotamus, a beast so rarely seen in the northern hemisphere that it remained as fabulous as unicorns or dragons. Later, it became a common word for any large, lumbering and vaguely threatening monster, either living (such as the giant creatures supposed to inhabit unexplored jungle) or made by human hands (such as the earliest military tanks).

61   **He lieth under the shady trees, in the covert of the reed, and fens. The shady trees cover him with their shadow; the willows of the brook compass him about. Behold, he drinketh up a river, and hasteth not.**
(40:21–3)
The description of Behemoth continues.

62   **Canst thou draw out Leviathan with an hook?**
(41:1)
From land monsters, God moves to water beasts. 'Leviathan', from the Hebrew word for 'water beast', probably suggested a crocodile to the original readers of Job; it came to mean a whale, and then, metaphorically, any vast ocean-living thing. To 'draw out Leviathan with an hook' became proverbial for 'to attempt the impossible'.

63   **I know that thou canst do everything, and that no thought can be withholden from thee.**
(42:2)
Job acknowledges God, in true humility at last.

64   **The Lord blessed the latter end of Job more than his beginning.**
(42:12)
Job's long-suffering, and his quest for true understanding of God, are finally rewarded. Ever since this book, his 'patience' (i e long-suffering) has been proverbial.

Psalms

1   **Blessed is the man that walketh not in the counsel of the ungodly, nor standeth in the way of sinners, nor sitteth in the seat of the scornful. But his delight is in the law of the Lord.**
(1:1–2)
The true believer is described.

2 He shall be like a tree planted by the rivers of water, that bringeth forth his fruit in his season; his leaf also shall not wither; and whatsoever he doeth shall prosper. The ungodly are not so: but are like the chaff which the wind driveth away. (1:3–4)

In simple rural metaphors, the happiness of the true believer is contrasted with the futility and sure destruction of idolaters.

3 Why do the heathen rage, and the people imagine a vain thing? The kings of the earth set themselves, and the rulers take counsel together, against the Lord, and against his anointed, saying, Let us break their bands asunder, and cast away their cords from us. (2:1–3)

The temporal powers of the world set up their ephemeral authority against God's. 'Vain' here means 'empty', 'non-existent'. The 'Lord's anointed' is God's appointed king.

4 He that sitteth in the heavens shall laugh: the Lord shall have them in derision. (2:4)

God scorns the fury of heathen potentates.

5 Thou art my Son; this day have I begotten thee. Ask of me, and I shall give thee the heathen for thine inheritance, and the uttermost parts of the earth for thy possession. (2:7–9)

Because these verses are spoken by God to his chosen king, this psalm is known as one of the 'Royal Psalms'. They have also been taken as one of the clearest Old Testament references to Christ.

6 Kiss the Son, lest he be angry, and ye perish from the way, when his wrath is kindled but a little. Blessed are all they that put their trust in him. (2:12)

The people are recommended to worship God's chosen king. The last sentence has become a standard part of many church services.

7 Thou, O Lord, art a shield for me; my glory, and the lifter up of mine head. (3:3)

Written at the time of Absalom's revolt against his father, David, this is David's specific reminder to himself that he is God's chosen king.

8   **Lord, lift thou up the light of thy countenance upon us.**
     (4:6)
     This line, from a psalm to be sung at nightfall, has become a central
     part of many services of evening prayer.

9   **I will both lay me down in peace, and sleep: for thou, Lord,**
     only makest me dwell in safety.
     (4:8)
     This verse, from a psalm of evening prayer, is even better known in
     its prayer-book form 'I will lay me down in peace, and take my rest'.

10   **Give ear to my words, O Lord, consider my meditation.**
     (5:1)
     This is a morning psalm which balances the evening prayer of
     Psalm 4 above (see Ps 8 and 9).

11   **My voice shalt thou hear in the morning, O Lord; in the**
     morning will I direct my prayer unto thee, and will look up.
     (5:3)
     The morning prayer continues.

12   **Lead me, O Lord, in thy righteousness because of mine**
     enemies; make thy way straight before my face.
     (5:8)
     The psalmist prays for God's guidance against the onslaughts of the
     world.

13   **O Lord, rebuke me not in thine anger, neither chasten me in**
     thy hot displeasure. Have mercy upon me, O Lord; for I am
     weak: O Lord, heal me; for my bones are vexed.
     (6:1–2)
     In a mood of anguish and doubt, the psalmist prays for help from
     God.

14   **But thou, O Lord, how long?**
     (6:3)
     This tortured cry, how long must God's people suffer, has often
     been heard from beleaguered believers down the centuries. In a
     memorable, if not very comforting, passage, Isaiah gave God's
     answer (see Isa 14).

15   **For in death there is no remembrance of thee: in the grave**
     who shall give thee thanks?
     (6:5)
     In his despair, the speaker tries to bargain with God: 'Save me from
     death, or who will be left to worship you?'

16   The Lord hath heard my supplication; the Lord will receive
      my prayer.
      (6:9)
      The despairing speaker of the rest of this psalm tries to comfort
      himself with the thought that the God he believes in will not
      abandon him.

17   O Lord my God, in thee do I put my trust: save me from all
      them that persecute me, and deliver me.
      (7:1)
      For all its quiet opening, this psalm is full of military and triumphal
      imagery, about God routing the enemies of the unrighteous (unless,
      that is, they are God's instrument for punishing the sins of God's
      own people). Its fine military phrases and the prayerful repose with
      which it begins and ends, have made it a favourite for musical
      setting, particularly in Renaissance times in its Latin version *In te,
      domine, speravi*.

18   I will praise the Lord according to his righteousness: and will
      sing praise to the name of the Lord most high.
      (7:17)
      This verse rounds off the psalm with a paean of praise, not the least
      of its attractions for musicians (see Ps 17).

19   Out of the mouth of babes and sucklings hast thou ordained
      strength because of thine enemies, that thou mightest still the
      enemy and the avenger.
      (8:2)
      In its Biblical context (a hymn of praise to God the creator) the
      meaning of this phrase is obscure, but perhaps its later proverbial
      use – the idea that the untutored can utter the truth without
      understanding it, and that this unconscious blurting out somehow
      makes the truth even truer – gives a clue to its meaning here: God's
      praise, even on a child's lips, can silence an unbeliever.

20   What is man, that thou art mindful of him? and the son of
      man, that thou visitest him? For thou hast made him a little
      lower than the angels, and hast crowned him with glory and
      honour.
      (8:4–5)
      Comparing the human race with the glories of the rest of creation,
      the psalmist is amazed that God should so honour us.

21   O Lord, our Lord, how excellent is thy name in all the earth!
      (8:9)

This verse is often detached from its own psalm and used as an independent prayer of praise.

22   The Lord also will be a refuge for the oppressed, a refuge in times of trouble.
(9:9)
This verse, from a psalm of praise, picks up and develops an idea common in Jewish religious thought from the time of Moses (see Deut 23).

23   Arise, O Lord; let not man prevail.
(9:19)
The translation of this phrase in the prayer book, 'Up, Lord, and let not man have the upper hand', has given rise to a proverbial expression 'to have (or get) the upper hand'. The general meaning, to win, of the latter is far clearer than whatever sporting or other metaphor was in the translator's mind.

24   Selah.
(9:20)
This word, which closes this particular psalm, occurs seventy-one times in the Book of Psalms and four times in Habbakuk. No one knows its precise meaning, but its position – as here – suggests that it indicated a kind of doxology (e g 'Glory be to the Father'), a pause or an instrumental interlude.

25   Upon the wicked he shall rain snares, fire and brimstone, and an horrible tempest: this shall be the portion of their cup.
(11:6)
In a land as arid as ancient Israel, the idea of God as a provider of drink was particularly potent: he poured water of righteousness for his followers, and less palatable phenomena for those who rejected him.

26   They speak vanity every one with his neighbour: with flattering lips and with a double heart do they speak.
(12:2)
The psalmist is surrounded by cheats and liars on all sides.

27   The words of the Lord are pure words: as silver tried in a furnace of earth, purified seven times.
(12:6)
God's trustworthiness is likened to the finest silver. Each of the seven meltings removed more impurities from the metal.

28   The fool hath said in his heart, There is no God.
       (14:1)
       The psalmist gloomily reflects on the prevalence of unbelievers in
       the world.

29   They are corrupt, they have done abominable works, there is
       none that doeth good. The Lord looked down from heaven
       upon the children of men, to see if there were any that did
       understand, and seek God. They are all gone aside, they are
       all together become filthy: there is none that doeth good, no,
       not one.
       (14:1–3)
       The psalmist's gloom at human unbelief in God continues. 'Filthy'
       was replaced in the prayer book by 'abominable' and 'altogether
       abominable' became a standard expression of dislike in Cromwell's
       time, particularly in denunciation of theatrical entertainment.

30   Lord, who shall abide in thy tabernacle? who shall dwell in thy
       holy hill? He that walketh uprightly, and worketh
       righteousness, and speaketh the truth in his heart.
       (15:1–2)
       This form of prayer, question followed by answer, was not so much
       private communion as a form of teaching. The psalm goes on, in
       less frequently quoted lines, to add to the company of the godly
       those who avoid lending money, making false accusations for
       reward and slandering their neighbours and the prayer book
       ringingly ends the psalm by announcing that anyone who avoids
       these acts 'shall never fall'.

31   The Lord is the portion of mine inheritance and of my cup:
       thou maintainest my lot. The lines are fallen unto me in
       pleasant places; yea, I have a goodly heritage.
       (16:5–6)
       These are the rewards of those who worship God. The complexity
       of the second sentence – in which 'lines' means 'boundary-marks' –
       led to a (somewhat) clearer version in the prayer book, which was
       once well-known: 'The lot is fallen unto me in a fair ground.'

32   For thou wilt not leave my soul in hell; neither wilt thou
       suffer thine Holy One to see corruption. Thou wilt shew me
       the path of life: in thy presence is fulness of joy; at thy right
       hand there are pleasures for evermore.
       (16:10–11)
       These words, about the rescuing of the believer from the darkness
       of death, were repeated by St Paul in a sermon on the meaning of
       Christ's resurrection, the guarantee to Christians that they, too, will
       'see no corruption' (see Acts 40).

33   I will love thee, O Lord, my strength. The Lord is my rock,
and my fortress, and my deliverer; my God, my strength, in
whom I will trust; my buckler, and the horn of my salvation,
and my high tower.
(18:1–2)
This is a revised version of David's song of triumph over the
Philistines (See II Sam 15): here the same expressions of praise and
thanksgiving are given more general, though no less heroic,
application.

34   And he rode upon a cherub, and did fly: yea, he did fly upon
the wings of the wind.
(18:10)
This verse is known chiefly for its use in visual representations of
God riding in triumph through the sky. A *cherub* (plural *cherubim*)
was not the plump small boy of less awesome art, but a symbol of
sacred power, either a stormcloud harnessed to give God a chariot
or a fabulous bridled beast, a bull with eagle's wings and a human
face. The phrase 'wings of the wind' has entered the language.

35   The heavens declare the glory of God; and the firmament
sheweth his handywork. Day unto day uttereth speech, and
night unto night sheweth knowledge. There is no speech nor
language, where their voice is not heard. Their line is gone
out through all the earth, and their words to the end of the
world.
(19:1–4)
All creation, not in words but by its simple existence, praises God
who made it. The passage is even better known in its translation in
the prayer book.
    The heavens declare the glory of God: and the firmament
    sheweth his handywork.
    One day telleth another: and one night certifieth another.
    There is neither speech nor language: but their voices are heard
    among them.
    Their sound is gone out into all lands: and their words unto the
    ends of the world.

36   The fear of the Lord is clean, enduring for ever: the
judgments of the Lord are true and righteous altogether.
More to be desired are they than gold, yea, than much fine
gold: sweeter also than honey and the honeycomb.
(19:9–10)
The psalmist moves from a description of all creation hymning
God's glory to a paean of praise for his laws which guide it.

37   Let the words of my mouth, and the meditation of my heart,
be acceptable in thy sight, O Lord, my strength, and my
redeemer.
(19:14)
This closing verse of the psalm of praise for God's law as shown in
all creation has been detached and made into a favourite Christian
prayer.

38   My God, my God, why hast thou forsaken me?
(22:1)
Christ quoted these words on the cross (see Matt 169), and their
fame has distracted attention from the rest of the psalm, which
moves from desperate appeals for deliverance to a declaration that
all the world will be saved by God and will join in praising him.

39   The Lord is my shepherd; I shall not want. He maketh me to
lie down in green pastures: he leadeth me beside the still
waters. He restoreth my soul: he leadeth me in the paths of
righteousness for his name's sake. Yea, though I walk through
the valley of the shadow of death, I will fear no evil: for thou
art with me; thy rod and thy staff they comfort me. Thou
preparest a table before me in the presence of mine enemies:
thou anointest my head with oil; my cup runneth over. Surely
goodness and mercy shall follow me all the days of my life:
and I will dwell in the house of the Lord for ever.
(23:1–6)
Few translations of this much-loved psalm surpass the dignity and
simplicity of the Authorized Version quoted here. The images
prefigure two of the commonest ideas about Jesus in the New
Testament: that he is a careful shepherd lovingly tending his flock,
and that he is the servant of all who believe in him.

40   The earth is the Lord's, and the fulness thereof; the world,
and they that dwell therein.
(24:1)
This psalm is thought to have been written to accompany the first
entry of the Ark of the Covenant into Jerusalem, and is suitably
festive and processional.

41   Lift up your heads, O ye gates; and be ye lift up, ye everlasting
doors; and the King of glory shall come in. Who is this King of
glory? The Lord strong and mighty, the Lord mighty in battle.
Lift up your heads, O ye gates; even lift them up, ye
everlasting doors; and the King of glory shall come in. Who is
this King of glory? The Lord of hosts, he is the King of glory.
Selah.
(24:7–10)

The repetitions in these verses, like the question-and-answer earlier (see Ps 30), suggests antiphonal singing between one group in the triumphal procession (see Ps 40) and another.

42   **Remember not the sins of my youth, nor my transgressions: according to thy mercy remember thou me for thy goodness' sake, O Lord.**
(25:7)
The psalmist prays that goodness in adult life may outweigh a misspent youth. 'Remember' here means 'consider'.

43   **The Lord is my light and my salvation; whom shall I fear? The Lord is the strength of my life; of whom shall I be afraid?**
(27:1)
From this psalm derives the image of Jesus as the Light of the World, the dawn which scatters the darkness of unbelief.

44   **Wait on the Lord; be of good courage, and he shall strengthen thine heart: wait, I say, on the Lord.**
(27:14)
This exhortation to a life of prayer and meditation was a favourite prayer of St Francis of Assisi, and of his and many other contemplative orders since. 'Wait on' means 'serve'.

45   **Worship the Lord in the beauty of holiness.**
(29:2)
In a predominantly turbulent psalm of praise this verse provides a notable moment of quiet calm.

46   **The voice of the Lord is upon the waters: the God of glory thundereth: the Lord is upon many waters.**
(29:3)
This verse describes God's presence in floodwaters, a particularly striking phenomenon in the dry regions of the river Jordan, which rises spectacularly in spate each spring.

47   **The voice of the Lord breaketh the cedars; yea, the Lord breaketh the cedars of Lebanon. He maketh them also to skip like a calf; Lebanon and Sirion like a young unicorn.**
(29:5–6)
Two images are run together in these lines: the ideas of God's voice as thunder and of his power as floodwater battering trees in a forest. 'Sirion' is the local name for Mount Hermon in Lebanon, whose upper slopes are always snow-covered but whose lower slopes are shaggy with cedars and other trees.

48   Sing unto the Lord, O ye saints of his, and give thanks at the
      remembrance of his holiness. For his anger endureth but a
      moment; in his favour is life: weeping may endure for a night,
      but joy cometh in the morning.
      (30:4–5)
      This psalm was written to celebrate the end of one of David's many
      wars against the Philistines. In the nineteenth century the phrase
      'joy cometh in the morning' was quoted, mistakenly, to mean hope
      deferred, in the same sense as 'jam yesterday and jam tomorrow,
      but never jam today'. Its real meaning is triumphant: joy comes each
      morning, as unfailingly and as dazzlingly as the rising sun.

49   Thou hast turned for me my mourning into dancing: thou
      hast put off my sackcloth, and girded me with gladness; to the
      end that my glory may sing praise to thee, and not be silent. O
      Lord my God, I will give thanks unto thee for ever.
      (30:11–12)
      In the midst of celebration, David remembers – and reminds his
      people – who should be thanked for their success in battle. The
      message was timely, if they had only listened to it: after this
      thanksgiving feast, they disobeyed God's orders and were punished
      by a plague which killed seven thousand people.

50   In thee, O Lord, do I put my trust; let me never be ashamed:
      deliver me in thy righteousness.
      (31:1)
      The prayer book replaces 'ashamed' with 'put to confusion'; the
      best-known English form of this prayer is the one used at the end of
      the Te Deum: 'In thee, O Lord, have I trusted; let me never be
      confounded'.

51   For thou art my rock and my fortress; therefore for thy
      name's sake lead me, and guide me.
      (31:3)
      The psalmist's hymn of confidence continues, picking up an image
      from a previous psalm (see Ps 33).

52   Into thine hand I commit my spirit: thou hast redeemed me,
      O Lord God of truth.
      (31:5)
      The prayer book translates 'commit' as 'commend', and the first
      half of the phrase is best-known as Jesus' dying words on the cross
      (see Luke 68).

53   Blessed is the man unto whom the Lord imputeth not
      iniquity, and in whose spirit there is no guile. When I kept

silence, my bones waxed old through my roaring all the day long.
(32:2–3)
The prayer book translates 'imputeth no sin' and – less memorably – 'my bones consumed away through my daily complaining'. The comparison is between someone in whom God can genuinely find ('imputeth') no guilt and those who refuse to admit their guilt, bottling it up until their bones crumble with the psychic turbulence, the 'roaring' inside the body.

54   I said, I will confess my transgressions unto the Lord; and thou forgavest the iniquity of my sin. Selah.
(32:5)
The only way to ease the heart and the bones (see Ps 53) is to admit one's guilt and so be purged of it.

55   For this shall every one that is godly pray unto thee in a time when thou mayest be found: surely in the floods of great waters they shall not come nigh unto him.
(32:6)
As often (see, for example, Ps 46), the awesomeness of God is described in terms of a river in spate – 'great water-floods', as the prayer book translates it. It is pointless to approach God 'in the floods of great waters' because he is raging not with fury but in his full majesty, far beyond mortal comprehension.

56   Be ye not as the horse, or as the mule, which have no understanding: whose mouth must be held in with bit and bridle, lest they come near unto thee.
(32:9)
Since the Garden of Eden itself (see Gen 15), possession of 'knowledge', that is understanding of God's purposes, has raised human beings above all other created things.

57   Rejoice in the Lord, O ye righteous: for praise is comely for the upright. Praise the Lord with harp: sing unto him with the psaltery and an instrument of ten strings. Sing unto him a new song; play skilfully with a loud noise.
(33:1–3)
A jubilant musical outburst, this psalm is particularly well-known because of the prayer book translation of verse 3 above: 'Sing unto the Lord a new song: sing praises lustily unto him with a good courage' – an instruction which has been eagerly followed, in settings of these very verses, in churches and chapels ever since. In heaven itself, according to John's vision (see Rev 53), a 'new song' is what the 144,000 redeemed souls sing in praise of God.

58 He gathereth the waters of the sea together as an heap: he layeth up the depth in storehouses.
(33:7)
In a remarkably bold metaphor, even for David, God is said to heap floodwater as mortals heap grain in barns: the implication is that for God, even the impossible is easy.

59 O taste and see that the Lord is good: blessed is the man that trusteth in him.
(34:8)
'Taste' here means 'try' or 'experiment': sampling God's presence is the best way to discover it.

60 The young lions do lack, and suffer hunger: but they that seek the Lord shall not want any good thing. Come, ye children, hearken unto me: I will teach you the fear of the Lord.
(34:10–11)
Even lion cubs, protected by the fiercest and noblest parents on earth, die of starvation, unlike the believers who trust in God.

61 What man is he that desireth life, and loveth many days, that he may see good? Keep thy tongue from evil, and thy lips from speaking guile. Depart from evil, and do good; seek peace, and pursue it.
(34:12–14)
Filled with his own certainty and joy, the psalmist tries to draw everyone into the circle of what he has earlier called 'saints', that is those who surrender themselves and sanctify themselves in God.

62 Let them be as chaff before the wind: and let the angel of the Lord chase them. Let their way be dark and slippery: and let the angel of the Lord persecute them.
(35:5–6)
In one of the most uncomprising of all the psalms, David calls on God to treat the enemies of Israel exactly as they have treated the Israelites. The ethical hackles these sentiments have raised in Christians since would hardly have been felt by people of David's own time, steeped in a morality of like for like.

63 Yea, they opened their mouth wide against me, and said, Aha, aha, our eye hath seen it. This thou hast seen, O Lord: keep not silence.
(35:21–2)
The psalmist imagines his enemies jeeringly implying that he is not as God-fearing as he seems – and then imagines God looking at them and judging them, in turn.

64 O continue thy lovingkindness unto them that know thee; and thy righteousness to the upright in heart.
(36:10)
This verse, from a psalm contrasting those who scorn God and those who love him, has been detached from its context and made into a Christian prayer.

65 Fret not thyself because of evildoers, neither be thou envious against the workers of iniquity. For they shall soon be cut down like the grass, and wither as the green herb.
(37:1–2)
David continues to advise his followers to ignore the enemies of God's people and to keep themselves pure for God. The prayer book translates 'evildoers', specifically, as 'the ungodly' – an expression which has become proverbial in its own right for anyone of whose ways or manners the speaker disapproves.

66 The meek shall inherit the earth; and shall delight themselves in the abundance of peace.
(37:11)
In a characteristically heart-easing phrase, the prayer book translates the second half of this verse as 'and shall be refreshed in the multitude of peace'. The earlier part of the verse was quoted by Jesus in the Sermon on the Mount, as the third Beatitude (see Matt 15).

67 I have been young, and now am old; yet have I not seen the righteous forsaken, nor his seed begging bread.
(37:25)
This verse became a somewhat ponderous way of saying 'What nonsense!', favoured in Victorian times in stuffier clubs and committee-rooms.

68 I have seen the wicked in great power, and spreading himself like a green bay tree. Yet he passed away, and, lo, he was not: yea, I sought him, but he could not be found. Mark the perfect man, and behold the upright: for the end of that man is peace.
(37:35–7)
The transcience of wordly success achieved without God is contrasted with the eternal happiness guaranteed to those who trust in God. Stripped of its associations of ungodliness, 'to flourish as the green bay tree' (in the prayer-book version of the first phrase) became a proverb for any kind of exuberant health, prosperity or happiness. As so often in the psalms, the prayer-book version of the last verse, 'Keep innocency, and take heed unto the thing that is right: for that shall bring a man peace at the last', is even better known than its Authorized Version equivalent.

69   O Lord, rebuke me not in thy wrath: neither chasten me in thy hot displeasure.
(38:1)
This prayer for mercy was subtitled 'to bring to remembrance', that is to draw the psalmist's anguish and remorse to God's attention.

70   Lord, make me to know mine end, and the measure of my days.
(39:4)
The religious thinking behind this prayer is that if we know the length of our time on earth, we can stop worrying about sudden death and devote ourselves entirely to worshipping God.

71   Hear my prayer, O Lord, and give ear unto my cry.
(39:12)
This, the best-known version of a prayer repeated in many forms throughout the Bible, is frequently used on its own in modern church services.

72   I waited patiently for the Lord; and he inclined unto me, and heard my cry.
(40:1)
This verse opens a hymn of praise for God's goodness and of prayer that it may continue.

73   Many, O Lord my God, are thy wonderful works which thou hast done, and thy thoughts which are to us-ward.
(40:5)
The psalmist has announced that he will begin a new song of praise to God; this is its opening.

74   Be pleased, O Lord, to deliver me: O Lord, make haste to help me.
(40:13)
A form of this prayer, substituting 'us' for 'me', became a familiar part of the Church of England's Order of Morning Prayer. It is also well-loved in Nahum Tate's metrical version of 1696: 'As pants the hart for cooling streams. / When heated in the chase.'

75   Blessed is he that considereth the poor: the Lord will deliver him in time of trouble.
(41:1)
Although this verse conforms to the general pattern of the Beatitudes (see Matt 15), and so, perhaps, seems more familiar than it is, it was not actually quoted by Jesus. Its ideas, however, are elaborated in the fifth Beatitude and in the later image of God's followers as the salt of the earth (see Matt 16).

76   **Blessed be the Lord God of Israel from everlasting, and to
everlasting. Amen, and Amen.**
(41:13)
This was a standard formula-verse of praise, like our 'Glory be to
the Father' which could be added at will to the end of a psalm or set
of psalms. Here it indicates that the first book of psalms has come to
a close.

77   **As the hart panteth after the water brooks, so panteth my soul
after thee, O God. My soul thirsteth for God, for the living
God.**
(42:1–2)
In exile, the singer prays for a swift return to God's presence. 'Hart'
means 'deer'.

78   **Why art thou cast down, O my soul? and why art thou
disquieted in me? hope thou in God: for I shall yet praise him
for the help of his countenance.**
(42:5)
This verse appears twice in this psalm and once in the next one, as a
kind of refrain, scolding the singer's soul for being troubled despite
the assurances God's presence gives.

79   **Deep calleth unto deep at the noise of thy waterspouts: all thy
waves and thy billows are gone over me.**
(42:7)
God's presence is compared to a torrent, a typhoon, a storm which
echoes over every sea. Curiously the prayer book replaces
'waterspouts' with 'waterpipes', thus replacing the image of
naturally rushing water with one of overflowing gutters after a
storm.

80   **As with a sword in my bones, mine enemies reproach me;
while they say daily unto me, Where is thy God?**
(42:10)
The prayer book expanded this verse, none too felicitously, into
'My bones are smitten asunder as with a sword: while mine enemies
that trouble me cast me in the teeth: Namely, while they say daily
unto me: Where is now thy God?' The phrase 'to cast into
someone's teeth', meaning to remind someone jeeringly of
something they might rather forget, passed into the language.

81   **We have heard with our ears, O God, our fathers have told us,
what work thou didst in their days, in the times of old.**
(44:1)

Written in a time of calamity – the Israelites had just been defeated by one of their many enemies – this psalm contrasts God's apparent desertion of his people with the help he gave their ancestors. This verse has, however, come to be used more as a reminder of God's continuing mercy than as a lament for its disappearance.

82 **Shall not God search this out? for he knoweth the secrets of the heart.**
(44:21)
The singer has been saying that his people have never abandoned faith in God, despite persecution from their enemies – a fact which God will surely acknowledge.

83 **My heart is inditing a good matter: I speak of the things which I have made touching the king: my tongue is the pen of a ready writer.**
(45:1)
This hymn of praise was probably written for the wedding of King Ahab and Queen Jezebel, and is bright with ceremonial language in their honour. It has often been used as a royal anthem since, for example in Handel's resplendent eighteenth-century musical setting, written for the coronation of George II in 1727. 'Inditing' means 'uttering, declaiming'.

84 **Thou lovest righteousness, and hatest wickedness: therefore God, thy God, hath anointed thee with the oil of gladness above thy fellows.**
(45:7)
The psalmist praises Ahab, the royal bridegroom.

85 **The king's daughter is all glorious within: her clothing is of wrought gold. She shall be brought unto the king in raiment of needlework: the virgins her companions that follow her shall be brought unto thee.**
(45:13–14)
The psalmist describes Jezebel, the royal bride.

86 **Instead of thy fathers shall be thy children, whom thou mayest make princes in all the earth.**
(45:16)
The psalmist links the present generation, the royal couple, with the God-fearing generations of the past and the glorious generations to come. The prayer book, slightly less obscurely, reads 'Instead of their fathers thou shalt have children'; 'instead' means 'in place of' and hence 'in your fathers' place', that is in a line of direct descent.

87   **God is our refuge and strength, a very present help in trouble.
Therefore will not we fear, though the earth be removed, and
though the mountains be carried into the midst of the sea;
Though the waters thereof roar and be troubled, though the
mountains shake with the swelling thereof.**
(46:1–3)
These verses, well-known in their own right, are also the inspiration
of Luther's hymn *Ein feste burg*, 'A safe stronghold our God is still,
A trusty shield and weapon.'

88   **There is a river, the streams whereof shall make glad the city
of God, the holy place of the tabernacles of the most High.
God is in the midst of her; she shall not be moved: God shall
help her, and that right early.**
(46:4–5)
These verses may have influenced John's vision of the holy city, the
New Jerusalem (see Rev 76); the river is the Jordan.

89   **The heathen raged, the kingdoms were moved: he uttered his
voice, the earth melted. The Lord of hosts is with us; the God
of Jacob is our refuge. Selah.**
(46:6–7)
God's awesome power, which devastates the ungodly, is the 'refuge
and strength' (see Ps 87) of his chosen people.

90   **He maketh wars to cease unto the end of the earth; he
breaketh the bow, and cutteth the spear in sunder; he
burneth the chariot in the fire.**
(46:9)
God's power as a peacemaker is described. The prayer-book
translation 'knappeth the spear in sunder' is particularly well-
known, though 'knappeth' is no more than a synonym for
'snappeth'.

91   **O clap your hands, all ye people; shout unto God with the
voice of triumph.**
(47:1)
This is another triumphal hymn, popular with composers because
of its musical images (see also Ps 92).

92   **God is gone up with a shout, the Lord with the sound of a
trumpet.**
(47:5)
The prayer book has 'God is gone up with a merry noise'. The
reference is probably to God entering the temple.

93 They saw it, and so they marvelled; they were troubled, and
hasted away. Fear took hold upon them there, and pain, as of
a woman in travail.
(48:5–6)

Mortal pomp is as nothing to the majesty of God, which even mortal
potentates – the 'they' of this quotation – are overawed to see. The
prayer book translates the first verse as 'They marvelled to see such
things: they were astonished, and suddenly cast down' – and
although the 'cast down' here has the literal meaning 'dethroned
from power', it and its derivative 'downcast' have entered the
language as meaning 'depressed'.

94 Walk about Zion, and go round about her: tell the towers
thereof. Mark ye well her bulwarks, consider her palaces; that
ye may tell it to the generation following.
(48:12–13)

This psalm was probably written to celebrate the lifting of an enemy
siege of Jerusalem, and these verses suggest the procession of
thanksgiving that would have followed, accounting for (or 'telling')
every single building, as a miser 'tells' his hoard.

95 The mighty God, even the Lord, hath spoken, and called the
earth from the rising of the sun unto the going down thereof.
(50:1)

God summons the whole world to give an account of itself. The
verse is remembered in English-speaking lands at least, for the
paraphrase in Lawrence Binyon's *For the Fallen*, used at Armistice
Day and other remembrance services:

They shall not grow old, as we that are left grow old:
Age shall not weary them, nor the years condemn.
At the going down of the sun and in the morning
We will remember them.

96 Our God shall come, and shall not keep silence: a fire shall
devour before him, and it shall be very tempestuous round
about him. He shall call to the heavens from above, and to the
earth, that he may judge his people.
(50:3–4)

The psalmist foretells the Day of Judgment.

97 Have mercy upon me, O God, according to thy lovingkindess:
according unto the multitude of thy tender mercies blot out
my transgressions. Wash me throughly from mine iniquity,
and cleanse me from my sin.
(51:1–2)

David is thought to have written this prayer for forgiveness after his adultery with Bathsheba and the death of Uriah. These verses have been adapted into prayers of confession and penitence in many church traditions.

98   **Purge me with hyssop, and I shall be clean: wash me, and I shall be whiter than snow.**
(51:7)
In the form *asperges me, Domine, hyssopo*, 'Sprinkle me with hyssop, O Lord', this verse was used in Catholic and Eastern churches as an anthem at baptism and the sprinkling of holy water. Hyssop is one of the herbs specified for the Jewish ritual of purification.

99   **O Lord, open thou my lips; and my mouth shall shew forth thy praise.**
(51:15)
This verse has been adapted as the beginning of a sequence of prayers and responses in many church traditions.

100   **For thou desirest not sacrifice; else would I give it: thou delightest not in burnt offering.**
(51:16)
David contrasts the true sacrifice required by God, subjugation of self-will, with the burnt offerings and other meat sacrifices which are not appropriate in his situation.

101   **Give ear to my prayer, O God; and hide not thyself from my supplication.**
(55:1)
David is thought to have written this prayer for consolation at the time of the rebellion of his son Absalom.

102   **Fearfulness and trembling are come upon me, and horror hath overwhelmed me.**
(55:5)
Renaissance composers, who liked to fill their church music with imitative sound-effects to 'colour' the words they set, often turned the Latin of this verse, *Timor et tremor conturbant me*, into a series of shudders, trills and panicky runs which are among the most evocative 'illustrations' in all music.

103   **Oh that I had wings like a dove! for then would I fly away, and be at rest.**
(55:6)
The images of shivering and quaking in the previous verse (see Ps 102) run beautifully into this prayer, which became world-famous in the 1920s when the boy treble Ernest Lough recorded

Mendelssohn's setting of them, a piece which has been a standard 'popular classic' ever since.

104 **Evening, and morning, and at noon, will I pray, and cry aloud: and he shall hear my voice.**
(55:17)
Whatever the terrors that surround him, the psalmist vows never to abandon the worship of God in regular, thrice-daily prayer.

105 **The words of his mouth were smoother than butter, but war was in his heart: his words were softer than oil, yet were they drawn swords.**
(55:21)
In addition to overt enemy attacks, the psalmist is suffering from the treachery of a false friend. The evocative phrase describing a plausible rogue, 'butter wouldn't melt in his mouth', derives from this verse.

106 **Cast thy burden upon the Lord, and he shall sustain thee: he shall never suffer the righteous to be moved.**
(55:22).
The psalmist, in the depths of despair, gives himself advice as if he were a third party. God is like a rock, and those who rely on him will not be moved.

107 **In God I have put my trust; I will not fear what flesh can do unto me.**
(56:4)
The thought behind this verse also underlies the end of the *Te Deum*, 'O Lord, in thee have I trusted: let me never be confounded.'

108 **Be merciful unto me, O God, be merciful unto me: for my soul trusteth in thee: yea, in the shadow of thy wings will I make my refuge, until these calamities be overpast.**
(57:1)
In the prayer book, 'calamities' is translated as 'tyranny', which fits the Biblical context better: David wrote the psalm when he was fleeing for his life from Saul.

109 **My soul is among lions: and I lie even among them that are set on fire, even the sons of men, whose teeth are spears and arrows, and their tongue a sharp sword.**
(57:4)
Pursued by Saul, David feels that he can trust no one, and expresses his terror in a series of ever more surreal images. 'Even' here means 'also'.

110   They have prepared a net for my steps; my soul is bowed
down: they have digged a pit before me, into the midst
whereof they are fallen themselves.
(57:6)
Even surrounded by enemies and traps on all sides, David feels
secure because of his trust in God.

111   My heart is fixed, O God, my heart is fixed: I will sing and
give praise. Awake up, my glory; awake, psaltery and harp: I
myself will awake early. I will praise thee, O Lord, among the
people: I will sing unto thee among the nations.
(57:7–9)
Because his 'heart is fixed' and he knows where his salvation lies,
David can sublimate his panic and worship God.

112   Their poison is like the poison of a serpent: they are like the
deaf adder that stoppeth her ear; Which will not hearken to
the voice of charmers, charming never so wisely.
(58:4–5)
In an extraordinary simile, even for the Old Testament, the psalmist
compares evil-doers – in this case, corrupt judges who will not
listen to the voice of God's prophets – with snakes who resist being
charmed.

113   Break their teeth, O God, in their mouth: break out the great
teeth of the young lions, O Lord. Let them melt away as
waters which run continually: when he bendeth his bow to
shoot his arrows, let them be as cut in pieces. As a snail which
melteth, let every one of them pass away: like the untimely
birth of a woman, that they may not see the sun.
(58:6–8)
The psalmist's fury against corrupt judges, and the vehemence of
his language, continue unabated. In ancient times, snails were
thought to melt away by a kind of mysterious internal combustion,
so that their slime-trails were all that was left of them. 'Untimely
birth of a woman' refers to miscarriage.

114   Deliver me from mine enemies, O my God: defend me from
them that rise up against me. Deliver me from the workers of
iniquity, and save me from bloody men. For, lo, they lie in
wait for my soul.
(59:1–3)
David wrote this psalm when he was besieged in his own house by
assassins sent by Saul. Even in these desperate straits, he turns the
thought into a general reflection on the dangers which ambush the
soul of the true believer.

115   The God of my mercy shall prevent me: God shall let me see
my desire upon mine enemies.
(59:10)
David speaks of God as a kind of spiritual 'minder' or bodyguard,
whose function is to go in front of him ('prevent me') and deal with
his enemies as they deserve.

116   At evening let them return; and let them make a noise like a
dog, and go round about the city. Let them wander up and
down for meat, and grudge if they be not satisfied.
(59:14–15)
Instead of death for his enemies, David prays for beggary. 'Grudge'
means 'whine'.

117   Thou hast shewed thy people hard things: thou hast made us
to drink the wine of astonishment.
(60:3)
God's people are beset by enemies, and the psalmist asks if God has
also deserted them, or if he is sending their troubles to increase
their faith. The second half of this verse was once used as a
proverbial expression of amazement.

118   Moab is my washpot; over Edom will I cast out my shoe:
Philistia, triumph thou because of me.
(60:8)
In this verse – once regarded as a real test of sermon-making
ingenuity – the psalmist imagines God scornfully declaring his
power over three of the main tribes hostile to Israel.

119   Truly my soul waiteth upon God: from him cometh my
salvation. He only is my rock and my salvation: he is my
defence; I shall not be greatly moved.
(62:1–2)
These verses of absolute trust in God have been widely
paraphrased, in prayers and liturgies from many traditions. God is
compared, in standard Old Testament images, to the foundation-
stone which supports the house, and to the rock which forms the
defensive tower. The phrase 'greatly moved' has come to have
metaphorical meaning, of the emotions; the psalmist here meant it
literally.

120   He only is my rock and my salvation: he is my defence; I shall
not be moved. In God is my salvation and my glory: the rock
of my strength, and my refuge, is in God.
(62:6–7)

The comparison continues between God and the rock which guarantees safety against all enemies. The repetitions and minute variations of language give a sing-song, regular feeling to the language, a remarkable case of the words themselves symbolizing their own meaning.

121   **Surely men of low degree are vanity, and men of high degree are a lie: to be laid in the balance, they are altogether lighter than vanity.**
(62:9)
The meaning of these somewhat obscure lines is that all human beings, whatever their status in life, are worth nothing in comparison with God. The phrases 'men of low degree' and 'men of high degree' have entered the language. The prayer book paraphrases the verse, memorably but not entirely helpfully, in the form 'As for the children of men, they are but vanity: the children of men are deceitful upon the weights, they are altogether lighter than vanity itself.'

122   **Trust not in oppression, and become not vain in robbery: if riches increase, set not your heart upon them.**
(62:10)
The psalmist gives a clear warning against self-enrichment by crime; the prayer book, by replacing 'robbery' with 'vanity', links the verse to the preceding one, but makes its meaning markedly less clear. The idea of 'setting one's heart' entered the language.

123   **O God, thou art my God; early will I seek thee: my soul thirsteth for thee, my flesh longeth for thee in a dry and thirsty land, where no water is.**
(63:1)
Longing for God is compared to longing for an oasis in the desert, an idea which links this psalm to earlier ones describing God as the provider of drink for his thirsty people.

124   **My soul shall be satisfied as with marrow and fatness; and my mouth shall praise thee with joyful lips.**
(63:5)
The idea that God's presence satisfies the soul as food and drink satisfy the body is memorably extended.

125   **I remember thee upon my bed, and meditate on thee in the night watches.**
(63:6)
Unlike the body, which feeds only by day, the soul will be nourished by God also in the long night hours. The prayer book prosaically

rewrites: 'Have I not remembered thee in my bed, and thought upon thee when I was waking?'

126   **They shall fall by the sword: they shall be a portion for foxes.**
(63:10)
The psalmist, secure in the certainty of God's presence, foretells the end of the enemies of his soul. 'A portion for foxes' became proverbial for something worthless, as cast-off as carrion.

127   **Praise waiteth for thee, O God, in Sion: and unto thee shall the vow be performed.**
(65:1)
This verse, the opening of a triumphal, processional hymn of praise, is even better known in its prayer book form: 'Thou, O God, art praised in Sion: and unto thee shall the vow be performed in Jerusalem.'

128   **Blessed is the man whom thou choosest, and causest to approach unto thee, that he may dwell in thy courts: we shall be satisfied with the goodness of thy house, even of thy holy temple.**
(65:4)
David pictures the true worshipper of God as a kind of royal attendant, waiting in the antechambers of heaven as a courtier might serve in a king's palace on earth.

129   **O God of our salvation; who art the confidence of all the ends of the earth, and of them that are afar off upon the sea: Which by his strength setteth fast the mountains; being girded with power: Which stilleth the noise of the seas, the noise of their waves, and the tumult of the people. They also that dwell in the uttermost parts are afraid at thy tokens: thou makest the outgoings of the morning and evening to rejoice.**
(65:5–8)
David invokes God's universal majesty.

130   **Thou visitest the earth, and waterest it: thou greatly enrichest it with the river of God, which is full of water: thou preparest them corn, when thou hast so provided for it. Thou waterest the ridges thereof abundantly: thou settlest the furrows thereof: thou makest it soft with showers: thou blessest the springing thereof. Thou crownest the year with thy goodness; and thy paths drop fatness. They drop upon the pastures of the wilderness: and the little hills rejoice on every side. The pastures are clothed with flocks; the valleys also are covered over with corn; they shout for joy, they also sing.**
(65:9–13)

David praises God as the bringer of harvest. The phrase 'crown of the year' has become proverbial for harvest-time, and the images of the little hills rejoicing and the cornfields shouting for joy underlie much English metaphysical poetry, and later religious poetry such as Gerard Manley Hopkins' 'Hurrahing in Harvest'.

131   Make a joyful noise unto God, all ye lands: Sing forth the honour of his name: make his praise glorious. Say unto God, How terrible art thou in thy works! through the greatness of thy power shall thine enemies submit themselves unto thee. All the earth shall worship thee, and shall sing unto thee; they shall sing to thy name.
(66:1-4)
This is another 'musical' psalm, an outpouring of praise and joy intended for processional use.

132   God be merciful unto us, and bless us; and cause his face to shine upon us; Selah. That thy way may be known upon earth, thy saving health among all nations. Let the people praise thee, O God; let all the people praise thee.
(67:1-3)
Though at first sight this psalm seems merely to summarize ideas more fully developed elsewhere, it remains an impressively compact statement of two of the main styles of Jewish religious poetry, dignified intercession and unrestrained jubilation.

133   Let God arise, let his enemies be scattered: let them also that hate him flee before him.
(68:1)
Written for ceremonies commemorating the first entry of the Ark into Jerusalem, this psalm is a jubilant processional hymn, and has been used on grand state occasions ever since Elizabethan times.

134   Sing unto God, sing praises to his name: extol him that rideth upon the heavens by his name JAH, and rejoice before him. A father of the fatherless, and a judge of the widows, is God in his holy habitation. God setteth the solitary in families: he bringeth out those which are bound with chains: but the rebellious dwell in a dry land. O God, when thou wentest forth before thy people, when thou didst march through the wilderness; Selah. The earth shook, the heavens also dropped at the presence of God: even Sion itself was moved at the presence of God, the God of Israel.
(68:4-8)
The jubilation of Ps 133 continues. God is a father to orphans, a judge (that is, defender) of widows, a solace for the lonely and a freer of prisoners; only evil-doers are barred from him. The prayer

book replaces 'but the rebellious dwell in a dry land' with the
sonorous phrase 'but letteth the runagates continue in scarceness'.

**135 Why leap ye, ye high hills? this is the hill which God desireth
to dwell in; yea, the Lord will dwell in it for ever.
(68:16)**
The hills shake (or, as the prayer-book engagingly puts it, 'hop') at
God's tread; his chosen hill is Mount Zion in Jerusalem.

**136 Thou hast ascended on high, thou hast led captivity captive.
(68:18)**
'Ascended on high,' (or, in the prayer-book phrase, 'gone up on
high') means 'taken your place on the throne'; 'to lead captivity
captive', once implying the imprisonment of those who imprisoned
the Israelites, was changed in Christian thinking to refer to Christ's
voluntary acceptance of captivity (that is, the prison of mortality)
and his triumph over it (by rising from the dead).

**137 They that hate me without a cause are more than the hairs of
mine head: they that would destroy me, being mine enemies
wrongfully, are mighty.
(69:4)**
Verses like this, from a psalm of terror and despair, were frequently
on the lips of early Christians at the time of the Roman
persecutions, and underlie much Christian teaching of the time, for
example, St Paul's letters.

**138 For the zeal of thine house hath eaten me up; and the
reproaches of them that reproached thee are fallen upon me.
(69:9)**
The righteous person's very devotion to God encourages his or her
enemies in their hostility. The disciples remembered, and quoted,
the first half of this verse when Jesus was arousing hostility by
driving traders from the temple; ever since then it has been taken,
somewhat overzealously, as one of the many Old Testament
references to Christ.

**139 Reproach hath broken my heart; and I am full of heaviness:
and I looked for some to take pity, but there was none; and for
comforters, but I found none. They gave me also gall for my
meat; and in my thirst they gave me vinegar to drink.
(69:20–1)**
The psalmist's misery continues. Two sections are famous in their
prayer-book alternatives: 'Their rebuke has broken my heart' and
'They gave me gall to eat: and when I was thirsty they gave me
vinegar to drink' – the latter often taken as a prophecy of Christ's

suffering and death. 'Gall' is the secretion which gives liver its bitter taste; 'vinegar' is sour wine.

140 **Let them be blotted out of the book of the living, and not be written with the righteous.**
(69:28)
In later times, when 'book' was taken to mean the list of all those to be given eternal life, this verse was quoted as a kind of curse; later still, it was used as a general expression of ironical contempt.

141 **Let them be turned back for a reward of their shame that say, Aha, aha.**
(70:3)
This verse became notorious as one of the Bible's sillier quotations, and particularly in the prayer-book version which changes 'Aha, aha' into 'There, there'. In the original context, the words are jeers spoken by the psalmist's enemies.

142 **In his days shall the righteous flourish; and abundance of peace so long as the moon endureth. He shall have dominion also from sea to sea, and from the river unto the ends of the earth. They that dwell in the wilderness shall bow before him; and his enemies shall lick the dust.**
(72:7–9)
This hymn of praise originally referred to Solomon in all his glory, and the references were specific: 'from sea to sea', for example, meant from the Mediterranean to the Persian Gulf; 'the river' meant the Euphrates and 'the ends of the earth' were located somewhere in the mountains of the Hindu Kush. The words have become much better known, however, as a celebration not of Solomon's golden age but of the kingdom of God on earth. To 'lick the dust' is literal here – the enemies lick the ground as a sign of submission – but this verse also gave rise to the common idea of enemies crashing to the ground, 'biting the dust'.

143 **O deliver not the soul of thy turtledove unto the multitude of the wicked.**
(74:19)
The apparent bizarreness of this image made the verse well-known in nineteenth-century literary circles, often with mockery attached. Its meaning, in context, is however perfectly straightforward. The devout person is close to God's heart, as cherished as a pet dove, and begs not to be overwhelmed by the forces of the ungodly.

144 **I will open my mouth in a parable: I will utter dark sayings of old: Which we have heard and known, and our fathers have told us.**
(78:2–3)

The psalmist proposes to explain God's relationship with his people by quoting historical events, using them as parables. 'Dark sayings', meaning riddles hard to explain, entered the language.

145 **Then the Lord awaked as one out of sleep, and like a mighty man that shouteth by reason of wine.**
(78:65)
God has turned from his people because of their idolatry, but now, seeing them surrounded by enemies, has changed his mind. The prayer book, perhaps disliking the comparison of God with a drunkard, translates 'like a giant refreshed with wine' and ever since, the phrase 'like a giant refreshed' has been proverbial for anyone acting with renewed or remarkable vigour.

146 **Thou feedest them with the bread of tears; and givest them tears to drink in great measure.**
(80:5)
The psalmist is talking of God's anger with his people. As an image of desolation, 'bread of tears' or 'bread of lamentation' became proverbial.

147 **Sing aloud unto God our strength: make a joyful noise unto the God of Jacob.**
(81:1)
This jubilant psalm was written to be sung at Sukkoth, the feast of tabernacles, when people travelled joyfully to Jerusalem to offer the firstfruits of the harvest in the temple.

148 **Blow up the trumpet in the new moon, in the time appointed, on our solemn feast day.**
(81:3)
Much used in anthems, this verse has always been a choirboys' favourite, and Sir Thomas Beecham was often heard to mutter it sarcastically at orchestral rehearsals when the brass played too loud.

149 **God standeth in the congregation of the mighty.**
(82:1)
The purpose of this verse is not to praise God as being like a mortal prince, but to remind mortal rulers that God is among them, watching them. The psalm goes on to advise them to rule with justice and with mercy. 'The congregation of the mighty' became a common expression for British courts and parliaments, stripped of the warning overtones in the rest of the psalm.

150 How amiable are thy tabernacles, O Lord of hosts! My soul
longeth, yea, even fainteth for the courts of the Lord: my
heart and my flesh crieth out for the living God.
(84:1–2)
This psalm, written to describe the joy of worshipping God in the
temple here on earth, has been taken much more generally, as a
vision of Paradise itself. The opening words are best known in their
prayer book form, 'O how amiable are thy dwellings, thou Lord of
hosts'; lovers of classical music know the piece best, perhaps, in the
setting from Brahms' *A German Requiem*.

151 For a day in thy courts is better than a thousand. I had rather
be a doorkeeper in the house of my God, than to dwell in the
tents of wickedness.
(84:10)
Like earlier verses from the psalm this one was intended literally, as
a reference to the keepers of the temple in Jerusalem, but has been
used much more powerfully as a metaphor for the soul's longing to
serve with God's saints in Paradise.

152 Give ear, O Lord, unto my prayer; and attend to the voice of
my supplications.
(86:6)
This verse has been adapted as a standard formula for prayer in
many religious traditions.

153 But thou, O Lord, art a God full of compassion, and gracious,
longsuffering and plenteous in mercy and truth.
(86:15)
Once again a standard formula for prayer is given clear and
memorable expression in this psalm.

154 Glorious things are spoken of thee, O city of God.
(87:3)
Originally meaning Jerusalem, the phrase 'city of God' came to
imply the fellowship of all believers, and was used in that sense as
the title of St Augustine's book defending and expounding the
Christian faith.

155 Lord, thou hast been our dwelling place in all generations.
Before the mountains were brought forth, or ever thou hadst
formed the earth and the world, even from everlasting to
everlasting, thou art God.
(90:1–2)
This psalm was claimed to be a rewording of original words by
Moses himself. Its themes are the puniness of the human race
compared to God, and our need to rely on his strength, and it opens

with a majestic assertion of God's grandeur. The prayer book replaces 'dwelling' with 'refuge'.

156 **For a thousand years in thy sight are but as yesterday when it is past, and as a watch in the night.**
(90:4)
The psalmist reflects on the eternity of God.

157 **They are as a sleep: in the morning they are like grass which groweth up. In the morning it flourisheth, and groweth up; in the evening it is cut down, and withereth.**
(90:5–6)
'They' refers to years, to the pointlessness of human timescales when applied to God.

158 **The days of our years are threescore years and ten; and if by reason of strength they be fourscore years, yet is their strength labour and sorrow; for it is soon cut off, and we fly away.**
(90:10)
The psalmist has been describing God's eternity; now he contrasts it with human shortlivedness, the short span of years we reach with enormous effort and little purpose.

159 **So teach us to number our days, that we may apply our hearts unto wisdom.**
(90:12)
The psalmist finally makes his point: our lives on earth are fleeting and futile unless we learn to devote every moment of them to God.

160 **He that dwelleth in the secret place of the most High shall abide under the shadow of the Almighty.**
(91:1)
The theme of the previous psalm is further developed. 'In the secret place' means 'under the protection'.

161 **I will say of the Lord, He is my refuge and my fortress: my God; in him will I trust.**
(91:2)
The metaphor of God as a safe stronghold, a castle of security, is developed.

162 **Surely he shall deliver thee from the snare of the fowler, and from the noisome pestilence. He shall cover thee with his feathers, and under his wings shalt thou trust: his truth shall be thy shield and buckler.**
(91:3–4)

In a way typical of Hebrew poetry, these verses take very simple metaphorical ideas (God is a mother-bird protecting its young; God's truth is armour) and entwine them with grand abstract thought, to produce an effect as complex as it is brief, as evocative as it is simple. 'Buckler' is simply another word for shield. (Shields are rectangular; bucklers are round.)

163   **Thou shalt not be afraid for the terror by night; nor for the arrow that flieth by day; Nor for the pestilence that walketh in darkness; nor for the destruction that wasteth at noonday. (91:5–6)**
God's presence is the armour of those who believe in him: the metaphors of the previous verses are extended in one of the psalm's best-loved poetic flights.

164   **For he shall give his angels charge over thee, to keep thee in all thy ways. They shall bear thee up in their hands, lest thou dash thy foot against a stone. (91:11–12)**
The idea of God as a castle, a safe place to live, continues. The Devil used these words to tempt Jesus on the temple roof (see Matt 13).

165   **Thou shalt tread upon the lion and adder: the young lion and the dragon shalt thou trample under feet. (91:13)**
From high-flown metaphorical ideas the psalmist returns to straightforward, everyday images. To Elizabethan readers, 'dragon' would have meant not so much the fire-breathing monster of myth and legend as a straightforward lizard – but the Elizabethans regarded all lizards as poisonous.

166   **It is a good thing to give thanks unto the Lord, and to sing praises unto thy name, O most High: To shew forth thy lovingkindness in the morning, and thy faithfulness every night, Upon an instrument of ten strings, and upon the psaltery; upon the harp with a solemn sound. (92:1–3)**
So begins a straightforward psalm of Sabbath rejoicing.

167   **O Lord God, to whom vengeance belongeth; O God, to whom vengeance belongeth, shew thyself. (94:1)**
The idea that 'vengeance belongeth to the Lord', that he will punish those who persecute his people, was strong both in Old Testament times and during the Roman persecution of the early Christians.

St Paul picked up this phrase, in a notably apocalyptic manner, in his letter to the Romans (see Ro 40).

168 **He that planted the ear, shall he not hear? he that formed the eye, shall he not see?**
(94:9)
This reassurance to God's people that their suffering would not go unnoticed became detached, perhaps because of its vigorous language, and was used as a general warning that retribution was sure to follow crime.

169 **O come, let us sing unto the Lord: let us make a joyful noise to the rock of our salvation. Let us come before his presence with thanksgiving, and make a joyful noise unto him with psalms.**
(95:1–2)
These verses begin a group of six jubilant psalms, expressions of straightforward delight in the presence of God.

170 **In his hand are the deep places of the earth: the strength of the hills is his also. The sea is his, and he made it: and his hands formed the dry land. O come, let us worship and bow down: let us kneel before the Lord our maker.**
(95:4–6)
The psalmist's paean of praise continues to God, the creator and Lord of everything on earth.

171 **O sing unto the Lord a new song: sing unto the Lord, all the earth. Sing unto the Lord, bless his name; shew forth his salvation from day to day. Declare his glory among the heathen, his wonders among all people. For the Lord is great, and greatly to be praised: he is to be feared above all gods.**
(96:1–4)
The opening phrase was traditional, even in Old Testament times, as the beginning of a type of musical celebration of which this and the surrounding psalms are typical.

172 **O worship the Lord in the beauty of holiness.**
(96:9)
In the context of its psalm, this verse is a reminder to the people of a standard Old Testament theme, that the best way to celebrate communion with God is to keep his word: obedience itself is a form of prayer. As often, by using the simplest possible language, the psalmist has achieved a verbal effect of the utmost delicacy: the lines *are* their meaning.

173   Let the sea roar, and the fulness thereof; the world, and they
       that dwell therein. Let the floods clap their hands: let the hills
       be joyful together Before the Lord.
       (98:7–9)
       Creation is envisaged, in forceful metaphors, as joining in the noisy
       human celebration of God's glory.

174   Make a joyful noise unto the Lord, all ye lands. Serve the
       Lord with gladness: come before his presence with singing.
       Know ye that the Lord he is God: it is he that hath made us,
       and not we ourselves; we are his people, and the sheep of his
       pasture. Enter into his gates with thanksgiving, and into his
       courts with praise: be thankful unto him, and bless his name.
       For the Lord is good; his mercy is everlasting; and his truth
       endureth to all generations.
       (100:1–5)
       Whether in this version or in that of the prayer book (which begins
       'O be joyful in the Lord'), this short psalm is one of the most
       succinct and frequently quoted of all Biblical outpourings of human
       joy in God.

175   Hear my prayer, O Lord, and let my cry come unto thee. Hide
       not thy face from me in the day when I am in trouble; incline
       thine ear unto me: in the day when I call answer me speedily.
       (102:1–2)
       In contrast to the jubilation of the immediately preceding psalms,
       this is the prayer of a person in spiritual torment, convinced not only
       that enemies press in on all sides, but that God himself has turned
       away.

176   I am like a pelican of the wilderness: I am like an owl of the
       desert. I watch, and am as a sparrow alone upon the house
       top.
       (102:6–7)
       The psalmist uses images of solitary birds to express his own
       feelings of isolation and despair. The idea of a pelican in this
       context must have seemed bizarre to the Elizabethans, for whom
       pelicans were symbols of selfless love (they were thought to nourish
       their young on their own life's blood) and who also used the pelican
       as a metaphor for Christ himself.

177   The Lord is merciful and gracious, slow to anger, and
       plenteous in mercy. He will not always chide: neither will he
       keep his anger for ever. He hath not dealt with us after our
       sins; nor rewarded us according to our iniquities.
       (103:8–10)
       The psalmist remembers God's loving-kindness.

178 As for man, his days are as grass: as a flower of the field, so he flourisheth. For the wind passeth over it, and it is gone; and the place thereof shall know it no more.
(103:15–16)

This is one of the best-known statements of a common Biblical theme, the contrast between the shortness of human existence and the eternity of God. The underlying idea is that we can have no relationship with such a God except obedience, fear and worship.

179 O Lord my God, thou art very great; thou art clothed with honour and majesty. Who coverest thyself with light as with a garment: who stretchest out the heavens like a curtain: Who layeth the beams of his chambers in the waters: who maketh the clouds his chariot: who walketh upon the wings of the wind: Who maketh his angels spirits; his ministers a flaming fire: Who laid the foundations of the earth, that it should not be removed for ever. Thou coveredst it with the deep as with a garment: the waters stood above the mountains.
(104:1–6)

The psalmist praises God in a succession of majestic metaphors.

180 The young lions roar after their prey, and seek their meat from God.
(104:21)

Apart from being the symbol of the tribe of Judah, and hence of the line of King David and of Christ himself, the lion stands throughout the Bible as the very model of a self-sufficient creature. This makes the young lions' reliance on God in this verse a particularly striking idea – one lost on later generations who have used the phrase 'young lions' to mean proud, ambitious troops.

181 He made him lord of his house, and ruler of all his substance: To bind his princes at his pleasure; and teach his senators wisdom.
(105:21–2)

The reference here is to Joseph, whom Pharaoh placed in authority over all his officials. The phrase 'to teach the senators wisdom' has been extracted and used proverbially (perhaps with overtones of the Roman senate, grey-bearded elders needing the emperor's strong hand to guide them); its implication is that even elected rulers can learn from any individual gifted or strong-minded enough to sidestep their discursive deliberations.

182 **Yea, they despised the pleasant land, they believed not his word: But murmured in their tents, and hearkened not unto the voice of the Lord.**
(106:24–5)
The psalmist recalls how the Israelites turned ungratefully on Moses, and scorned the land of milk and honey to which he was leading them from Egypt. The phrase 'murmured in their tents' became a proverbial description of sullen discontent.

183 **Oh that men would praise the Lord for his goodness, and for his wonderful works to the children of men!**
(107:8)
This verse recurs throughout the psalm, a chorus of rejoicing after each specific example of God's generosity to the human race.

184 **They that go down to the sea in ships, that do business in great waters; These see the works of the Lord, and his wonders in the deep.**
(107:23–4)
Few things, for the psalmist, more clearly symbolize God's power than the majesty of the sea: mariners are therefore particularly well-placed to acknowledge him.

185 **They mount up to the heaven, they go down again to the depths: their soul is melted because of trouble. They reel to and fro, and stagger like a drunken man, and are at their wits' end.**
(107:26–7)
The psalmist explains why seafarers are notably likely to sing God's praise. 'At their wits' end' has become an everyday expression, to the point where it even seems to belie these sonorous origins.

186 **The Lord said unto my Lord, Sit thou at my right hand, until I make thine enemies thy footstool.**
(110:1)
This verse begins a so-called 'royal-psalm', which forecasts the Messiah who will save all Israel. Jesus quoted the verse to Pharisees who were discussing with him the nature of the 'Lord's Anointed', and it was subsequently taken by all Christian writers to refer specifically to him. The first 'Lord' is God; the second is the Messiah.

187 **Thy people shall be willing in the day of thy power, in the beauties of holiness from the womb of the morning: thou hast the dew of thy youth.**
(110:3)

The psalmist talks of the time after the coming of the Messiah, when everyone will gladly follow him and will be invigorated by worshipping him as the earth is invigorated by dew.

188 **The fear of the Lord is the beginning of wisdom.**
(111:10)
One of the most frequently recurring thoughts in Hebrew sacred poetry is here given its briefest, clearest utterance.

189 **Blessed is the man that feareth the Lord, that delighteth greatly in his commandments. His seed shall be mighty upon earth: the generation of the upright shall be blessed. Wealth and riches shall be in his house: and his righteousness endureth for ever.**
(112:1–3)
The happiness of true surrender to God is described in material rather than spiritual terms, but the blend of abstract and concrete images makes it clear that the psalmist's real subject is satisfaction of the soul, a theme the rest of the psalm takes up.

190 **A good man sheweth favour, and lendeth: he will guide his affairs with discretion. Surely he shall not be moved for ever: the righteous shall be in everlasting remembrance.**
(112:5–6)
As before in this psalm, material images are used to express abstract ideas. The true believer overflows with knowledge of God, and lavishes it on others; none the less, it is his or her rock-like religious faith which makes the greatest impression. 'Moved' here means 'forgotten'.

191 **The mountains skipped like rams, and the little hills like lambs. What ailed thee, O thou sea, that thou fleddest? thou Jordan, that thou wast driven back?**
(114:4–5)
This verse is from a passover psalm, and celebrates the Israelites' journey to the Promised Land. These verses pose a kind of sacred riddle – what is it that causes mountains, seas, rivers and rocks to behave like this?

192 **Tremble, thou earth, at the presence of the Lord, at the presence of the God of Jacob.**
(114:7)
The psalmist answers the 'riddle' quoted above.

193 **Not unto us, O Lord, not unto us, but unto thy name give glory, for thy mercy, and for thy truth's sake.**
(115:1)

This psalm was used as a marching hymn in Old Testament times, and in its later Latin translation (*Non nobis, domine*) was one of the best-known and most stirring processionals of medieval Christianity.

194 **They have mouths, but they speak not: eyes have they, but they see not. They have ears, but they hear not: noses have they, but they smell not: They have hands, but they handle not: feet have they, but they walk not: neither speak they through their throat.**
(115:5–7)
Heathen idols are denounced in antiphonal verses of powerful, echoing rhythm.

195 **They that make them are like unto them; so is every one that trusteth in them. O Israel, trust thou in the Lord: he is their help and their shield.**
(115:8–9)
Heathen idolators are scathingly contrasted with true believers: the idolaters are as futile as the images of the gods they make, whereas the true believers are protected by a strong and loving God.

196 **The sorrows of death compassed me, and the pains of hell gat hold upon me.**
(116:3)
As often in the psalms, the terrors of the journey through life are depicted; to trust in God, the psalm goes on, is the only guarantee of safety.

197 **The Lord preserveth the simple.**
(116:6)
'Simple' here means pure-hearted, uncomplicatedly devout. The verse has often been used sarcastically as a pious-sounding expression of amazement at someone else's stupidity.

198 **Thou hast delivered my soul from death, mine eyes from tears, and my feet from falling.**
(116:8)
The idea continues of God as a guide through the dangerous journey of life.

199 **I will take the cup of salvation, and call upon the name of the Lord.**
(116:13)
Because of Christ's words at the Last Supper (see Matt 154), this verse, and particularly the idea of a 'cup of salvation', acquired enormous extra resonance in Christian times. To Old Testament

hearers, it related to the standard metaphors of God feeding his followers on the food of righteousness and filling cups to the brim for them to drink.

200 **O give thanks unto the Lord; for he is good: because his mercy endureth for ever.**
(118:1)
This verse begins a processional psalm, sung as the king and people take offerings to the temple at Sukkoth (the feast of tabernacles).

201 **I shall not die, but live, and declare the works of the Lord.**
(118:17)
God's gift to his people is eternal life; their response is an eternal hymn of praise.

202 **The stone which the builders refused is become the head stone of the corner.**
(118:22)
Jesus often used this verse in his teaching, to remind his hearers that God's assessment of human worth is uninfluenced by status in the mortal world. To the psalmist the reference was to the Israelites, the nation chosen by God despite the scorn of all their neighbours; to Christians, it applies to all believers.

203 **This is the day which the Lord hath made; we will rejoice and be glad in it.**
(118:24)
The day in question was the last day of Sukkoth, when gifts symbolizing the firstfruits of harvest were laid at the altar in the heart of the temple. In later times, the phrase has come to be used of the Lord's Day in general: Sunday.

204 **Blessed be he that cometh in the name of the Lord.**
(118:26)
The psalm from which this verse comes was sung to welcome the king and people bringing offerings to the temple; when Jesus rode into Jerusalem on Palm Sunday, the crowds sang the verse to welcome him.

205 **Thy word is a lamp unto my feet, and a light unto my path.**
(119:105)
This verse extends the common Old Testament idea of God as a guide on the dark journey that is human life. Jesus extended it still further, into the now-familiar image of himself as the Light of the World.

206   Woe is me, that I sojourn in Mesech, that I dwell in the tents of Kedar!
(120:5)
Even at the time it was written, this was no more than an obscure way of saying that the Israelites were surrounded by idolaters; in this Authorized Version it became proverbial (meaning something like 'I am the only civilized person here, the rest are barbarians') without losing any of its obscurity.

207   I will lift up mine eyes unto the hills, from whence cometh my help. My help cometh from the Lord, which made heaven and earth. He will not suffer thy foot to be moved: he that keepeth thee will not slumber. Behold, he that keepeth Israel shall neither slumber nor sleep. The Lord is thy keeper: the Lord is thy shade upon thy right hand. The sun shall not smite thee by day, nor the moon by night. The Lord shall preserve thee from all evil: he shall preserve thy soul. The Lord shall preserve thy going out and thy coming in from this time forth, and even for evermore.
(121:1–8)
Standard images of God as an unfailing protector, common throughout the Bible, are here united in outpouring of remarkable poetic intensity; the literary form of the words is not the least part of their power.

208   I was glad when they said unto me, Let us go into the house of the Lord.
(122:1)
Originally the beginning of a pilgrims' hymn, to be sung on the way to Jerusalem, this verse has come to be used as a general introit, an expression of joy at the opportunity to worship God in church.

209   Pray for the peace of Jerusalem.
(122:6)
This pilgrims' prayer, once specific to Jerusalem itself, is now widely taken to refer to the whole congregation of those who believe in God.

210   They that sow in tears shall reap in joy. He that goeth forth and weepeth, bearing precious seed, shall doubtless come again with rejoicing, bringing his sheaves with him.
(126:5–6)
The 'precious seed' is belief in God. The whole passage is a metaphorical statement of the theme, common in the Psalms, that the true believer will emerge unscathed from all mortal suffering. The first sentence of this quotation has been detached and is often

used in funeral services, as a reminder of the promise of eternal life.

211   Except the Lord build the house, they labour in vain that build it: except the Lord keep the city, the watchman waketh but in vain.
(127:1)
A favourite psalm in the Middle Ages, this was adapted as the motto of many of the more god-fearing cities, towns, businesses and families; it is still, for example, the motto of the city of Edinburgh in Scotland.

212   Children are an heritage of the Lord: and the fruit of the womb is his reward. As arrows are in the hand of a mighty man; so are children of the youth. Happy is the man that hath his quiver full of them.
(127:3–5)
In farming communities, and particularly in ancient times when infant mortality was high, a large family was not a penance but a guarantee of prosperity. In Victorian times, the English sometimes used these verses to justify enormous families – a trait Trollope gently mocked in his *Chronicles of Barsetshire* by calling one of his parsons, a man notable only for the sheer number of his offspring, Mr Quiverful.

213   Thy wife shall be as a fruitful vine by the sides of thine house: thy children like olive plants round about thy table.
(128:3)
Fecundity, so essential in a community of high infant mortality, is presented as one of the rewards of the contented householder, secure in the worship of God.

214   Out of the depths have I cried unto thee, O Lord. Lord, hear my voice: let thine ears be attentive to the voice of my supplications.
(130:1–2)
The psalmist, plunged in troubles as if in a stormy sea, prays for help to God.

215   My soul waiteth for the Lord more than they that watch for the morning: I say, more than they that watch for the morning.
(130:6)
The original image, comparing the believer to a nightwatchman eagerly waiting for dawn, seems to have escaped the prayer-book translators, who produced instead an impressive but meaningless

poetic fancy: 'My soul fleeth unto the Lord: before the morning watch, I say, before the morning watch.'

216   **Lord, my heart is not haughty, nor mine eyes lofty.**
(131:1)
The prayer-book version of this passage, beginning 'Lord, I am not high-minded', gave a word to the language, though 'high-minded' now means rather more 'above the hurly-burly of ordinary people's lives' than the original 'ambitious'.

217   **O give thanks unto the Lord; for he is good: for his mercy endureth for ever.**
(136:1)
This verse begins a paean of praise to God, recalling his blessings one by one in the history of his people.

218   **By the rivers of Babylon, there we sat down, yea, we wept, when we remembered Zion. We hanged our harps upon the willows in the midst thereof. For there they that carried us away captive required of us a song; and they that wasted us required of us mirth, saying, Sing us one of the songs of Zion. How shall we sing the Lord's song in a strange land? If I forget thee, O Jerusalem, let my right hand forget her cunning. If I do not remember thee, let my tongue cleave to the roof of my mouth; if I prefer not Jerusalem above my chief joy.**
(137:1–6)
Exiled in Babylon, the Israelites comfort themselves by turning their misery itself into poetry: they soothe themselves not with memories but with the very cadences of despair.

219   **O Lord, thou hast searched me, and known me. Thou knowest my downsitting and mine uprising, thou understandest my thought afar off.**
(139:1–2)
David reflects on God's omniscience.

220   **If I ascend up into heaven, thou art there: if I make my bed in hell, behold, thou art there. If I take the wings of the morning, and dwell in the uttermost parts of the sea; Even there shall thy hand lead me, and thy right hand shall hold me.**
(139:8–10)
David imagines himself like a fugitive from God, discovering God's omnipresence by trying to escape from it.

221   **I will praise thee; for I am fearfully and wonderfully made: marvellous are thy works; and that my soul knoweth right well.**
(139:14)

Humble praise of God, says David picking up a theme which runs through many of his psalms, is the best way to come to terms with his power.

222 **My substance was not hid from thee, when I was made in secret, and curiously wrought in the lowest parts of the earth.** (139:15)

David is imagining the dust which existed before Adam was made, the elements of his own being. 'Curiously' means not so much 'strangely' as 'fascinatingly'.

223 **Search me, O God, and know my heart: try me, and know my thoughts: And see if there be any wicked way in me, and lead me in the way everlasting.** (139:23–4)

David rounds off his praise of the omniscience and omnipresence of God by turning the searchlight, so to speak, on his own soul. The tone of the verses is not so much boastful, an oblique declaration that the speaker is pure-minded beyond reproach, as a prayer for divine mercy, for uncompromising spiritual investigation and correction.

224 **Let my prayer be set forth before thee as incense; and the lifting up of my hands as the evening sacrifice.** (141:2)

The idea David expresses here, that pure-hearted prayer can be as potent an offering as incense or the smoke of sacrifice, was especially influential on later religious thinking: this psalm greatly encouraged the early Christians, who were trying to distance their own religious practices from the barbarism and bloodthirstiness of Roman pagan ritual.

225 **Hear my prayer, O Lord, give ear to my supplications.** (143:1)

The psalmist begins his prayer with words which have been a standard formula down the ages. This psalm is thought to have been written when David was in hiding from Saul's hired assassins.

226 **Enter not into judgment with thy servant: for in thy sight shall no man living be justified.** (143:2)

David's prayer for mercy continues, asking God to answer his need and not his deservings.

227 **Man is like to vanity: his days are as a shadow that passeth away.**
(144:4)
In a more robustly poetic version of this phrase, the prayer-book replaces 'vanity' with 'a thing of nought'.

228 **That our oxen may be strong to labour; that there be no breaking in, nor going out; that there be no complaining in our streets.**
(144:14)
David is praying for future blessings for his people. The prayer book replaces 'breaking in' and 'going out' with the more comprehensible 'decay' and 'leading into captivity', respectively. 'Complaining in the streets' means crying like beggars.

229 **The Lord is gracious, and full of compassion; slow to anger, and of great mercy.**
(145:8)
This verse, from a psalm of praise in which each verse begins with a different letter of the Hebrew alphabet, is often used separately. It comes from one of the oldest of all Hebrew religious traditions: Exodus recounts that angels sang it when God appeared to Moses on Mount Sinai.

230 **The Lord is good to all: and his tender mercies are over all his works.**
(145:9)
'Tender mercies' has become proverbial. 'Tender' here means fond, as parents are fond of their children.

231 **The eyes of all wait upon thee; and thou givest them their meat in due season.**
(145:15)
The psalmist praises God the provider, linking his generosity – as would be standard practice in a mainly agricultural community – with the rhythm of the seasons. 'Meat' here means 'food'.

232 **The Lord is nigh unto all them that call upon him, to all that call upon him in truth. He will fulfil the desire of them that fear him: he also will hear their cry, and will save them.**
(145:18–19)
The psalmist reiterates the terms of the long-standing covenant between God and his people: God gives ever-present help and protection, and in return the people give obedience and grateful praise.

233 **Praise ye the Lord, Praise the Lord, O my soul.**
(146:1)
These phrases were often used by the more extreme Puritan sects in Cromwell's time, as exclamations of agreement during sermons and services. Some even went so far as to christen their children with these texts; the christian name of one of Cromwell's own officers was 'Praise-the-Lord'.

234 **Put not your trust in princes, nor in the son of man, in whom there is no help.**
(146:3)
No mortal is to be relied on, however powerful: only God can be trusted. The prayer-book translators, avoiding a problem which the pre-Christian writers of the psalms never envisaged, changed 'son of man' to 'child of man'.

235 **Praise ye the Lord: for it is good to sing praises unto our God; for it is pleasant; and praise is comely.**
(147:1)
This bidding prayer is even better known in its prayer-book form, 'A joyful and pleasant thing it is to be thankful.'

236 **He telleth the number of the stars, he calleth them all by their names.**
(147:4)
The idea behind this famous image is that God alone knows the names of every star in the sky, and so has power over them. In Genesis, God shows Abraham the stars in the night sky, and promises him that his offspring will be just as numerous – a connection unstated here, but likely to be both in the psalmist's and his hearers' thoughts. 'Telleth' means 'tells over', 'counts'.

237 **He giveth snow like wool: he scattereth the hoarfrost like ashes. He casteth forth his ice like morsels: who can stand before his cold?**
(147:16–17)
The splendour of the images has made these verses better known, perhaps, than their subtlety or depth of religious thought might suggest.

238 **Praise ye the Lord. Praise ye the Lord from the heavens: praise him in the heights. Praise ye him, all his angels: praise ye him, all his hosts. Praise ye him, sun and moon: praise him, all ye stars of light. Praise him, ye heavens of heavens, and ye waters that be above the heavens.**
(148:1–4)

All nature is exhorted to praise God its creator. The echoes of the account of the creation in Genesis are surely intentional.

239   **Praise the Lord from the earth, ye dragons, and all deeps: Fire, and hail; snow, and vapour; stormy wind fulfilling his word: Mountains, and all hills; fruitful trees, and all cedars: Beasts, and all cattle; creeping things, and flying fowl: Kings of the earth, and all people; princes, and all judges of the earth: Both young men, and maidens; old men, and children: Let them praise the name of the Lord: for his name alone is excellent; his glory is above the earth and heaven.**
   (148:7–13)
   The exhortation to praise God extends to every person and thing in creation, until the summons itself becomes a litany of praise.

240   **Sing unto the Lord a new song, and his praise in the congregation of saints.**
   (149:1)
   The psalmist calls on all God's creation to join in praising him.

241   **Let the saints be joyful in glory: let them sing aloud upon their beds. Let the high praises of God be in their mouth, and a two-edged sword in their hand; To execute vengeance upon the heathen, and punishments upon the people.**
   (149:5–7)
   The psalmist uses powerful language to evoke the idea of an invincible, singing army of the godly. 'Two-edged sword' nowadays suggests one that harms the striker as well as the struck; there is no such equivocation in the word's use here. It implies 'of double strength'.

242   **Praise ye the Lord. Praise God in his sanctuary: praise him in the firmament of his power. Praise him for his mighty acts: praise him according to his excellent greatness. Praise him with the sound of the trumpet: praise him with the psaltery and harp. Praise him with the timbrel and dance: praise him with stringed instruments and organs. Praise him upon the loud cymbals: praise him upon the high sounding cymbals. Let every thing that hath breath praise the Lord. Praise ye the Lord.**
   (150:1–6)
   The Book of Psalms ends with a resounding summons to all creation to join in making music in praise of God. Its imagery, as well as its magnificence, have inspired more musical settings than for any other psalm. A psaltery is a plucked-string instrument; a timbrel is a drum used to give the beat for dancing.

Proverbs

1   **To know wisdom and instruction; to perceive the words of understanding.**
(1:2)
Proverbs begins by announcing that its purpose is to increase understanding in those who hear or read it. 'Wisdom' here, as often in Old Testament writing, means belief in or obedience to God (see Ps 188).

2   **To give subtilty to the simple, to the young man knowledge and discretion.**
(1:4)
Proverbs continues to state its authors' aims, of which this is one of the most resonant for twentieth-century educators. The phrase 'knowledge and discretion' has entered the language as a synonym for maturity, sometimes in the form 'years of (knowledge and) discretion'.

3   **Surely in vain the net is spread in the sight of any bird.**
(1:17)
The analogy is with the snares of the ungodly, set to trap the true believer. Knowledge of God allows us to avoid moral danger as a bird avoids the net it sees being set.

4   **Be not wise in thine own eyes: fear the Lord, and depart from evil.**
(3:7)
One of the chief charges levelled by the Israelites against idolators was arrogance: they did the most presumptuous thing a human being could do – invented gods. True believers, by contrast, are taught humility by their very obedience to God – as this verse declares.

5   **My son, despise not the chastening of the Lord; neither be weary of his correction: For whom the Lord loveth he correcteth; even as a father the son in whom he delighteth.**
(3:11–12)
The wise person learns even from the hardships and punishments God sends.

6   **Happy is the man that findeth wisdom, and the man that getteth understanding. For the merchandise of it is better than the merchandise of silver, and the gain thereof than fine gold. She is more precious than rubies: and all the things thou canst desire are not to be compared unto her.**
(3:13–15)

The fear of the Lord, 'understanding', is set above the riches of the
world. The idea, though not the exact form of words, also occurs in
Job (see Job 44).

7   **Length of days is in her right hand; and in her left hand riches
and honour. Her ways are ways of pleasantness, and all her
paths are peace.**
(3:16–17)
Praise of understanding (that is, fear of the Lord) continues. The
original word for understanding was feminine – hence the use of
'she' and 'her' in this translation.

8   **The Lord by wisdom hath founded the earth: by
understanding hath he established the heavens.**
(3:19)
This verse links human wisdom, fear of the Lord, with that
'knowledge' which enabled God to begin creation, and which he
later embodied in the tree of knowledge of good and evil in the
Garden of Eden.

9   **The wise shall inherit glory: but shame shall be the
promotion of fools.**
(3:35)
This verse has been taken as a promise of eternal life to true
believers. The Salvation Army phrase 'promoted to glory', meaning
that someone has died in the fear of God and gone to heaven, is
derived from it.

10 **Wisdom is the principal thing; therefore get wisdom: and
with all thy getting get understanding.**
(4:7)
This verse reiterates the teaching that the fear of God – 'wisdom' –
is the basis of all human intelligence, the quality which
distinguishes human beings from animals.

11 **She shall give to thine head an ornament of grace: a crown of
glory shall she deliver to thee.**
(4:9)
From Roman times onwards, painters trying to represent the 'crown
of glory' mentioned in this verse, the belief in God that is the
ornament of all true believers, have shown it as a halo.

12 **But the path of the just is as the shining light, that shineth
more and more unto the perfect day.**
(4:18)

The image in the writer's mind is one of enlightenment gradually irradiating the believer's life, as dawn irradiates the sky to full daylight ('perfect day'). Later teachers have developed its meaning into a description of the soul's journey towards the Day of Judgment itself, when all things will be revealed and human knowledge will exactly coincide with God's. This interpretation has led to 'perfect day' being used as a synonym for Day of Judgment.

13 **For the lips of a strange woman drop as an honeycomb, and her mouth is smoother than oil: But her end is bitter as wormwood, sharp as a two-edged sword. Her feet go down to death; her steps take hold on hell.**
(5:3–5)
The warning here is partly against sexual promiscuity, but also develops a standard Old Testament idea, that devotion to God is like a true marriage, and that idolatry, 'whoring after strange gods', is a sin against that marriage. The fanciful description of the 'strange woman' in these lines has led to them being widely quoted, usually without reference to these religious overtones.

14 **Let thy fountain be blessed: and rejoice with the wife of thy youth. Let her be as the loving hind and pleasant roe; let her breasts satisfy thee at all times; and be thou ravished always with her love.**
(5:18–19)
As in the previous quotation, the implications here are not only secular, but also concern the 'marriage' between God and his true believers. Later Christian images of the Church as the Bride of Christ extend the thought still further.

15 **Go to the ant, thou sluggard; consider her ways, and be wise: Which having no guide, overseer, or ruler, Provideth her meat in the summer, and gathereth her food in the harvest.**
(6:6–8)
Just as the ant needs no encouragement towards good housekeeping, the human being should avoid idleness, not only in daily life but in religious observance.

16 **Yet a little sleep, a little slumber, a little folding of the hands to sleep: So shall thy poverty come as one that travelleth, and thy want as an armed man.**
(6:10–11)
The warning continues against even the slightest yielding to idleness. Poverty, which here includes the idea of poverty of the soul, will come on the spiritually idle as a stranger or a soldier arrives unexpectedly in the night while the householder dozes. The idea of spiritual vigilance, of watching and waiting, became a central

part of Jewish teaching about the Messiah, and also of Christian
teaching about the Second Coming.

17   **Can a man take fire in his bosom, and his clothes not be
burned? Can one go upon hot coals, and his feet not be
burned?**
(6:27–28)
The teacher is still warning against adultery. The excitement, as
with holding or walking on fire, is high, but the risks are great.

18   **Come, let us take our fill of love until the morning: let us
solace ourselves with loves. For the goodman is not at home,
he is gone a long journey.**
(7:18–19)
Idolatry, in the preacher's imagination, seduces the unwary believer
as a harlot seduces a fool in the street. The 'goodman' is the honest
householder – and stands here for God.

19   **He goeth after her straightway as an ox goeth to the slaughter.**
(7:22)
The fool, in the preacher's parable, is taken in by the harlot's wiles
(that is, the charms of false religion) and goes without thinking to
his own destruction.

20   **Whoso findeth me findeth life, and shall obtain favour of the
Lord.**
(8:35)
Wisdom herself, true knowledge of the true God, is speaking.

21   **Wisdom hath builded her house, she hath hewn out her seven
pillars.**
(9:1)
In contrast to Folly, who seduces people from true knowledge as a
harlot seduces men in the street, Wisdom is depicted as an honest,
self-sufficient householder, with a notably well-made house. Seven
roof-pillars denotes considerable substance; seven is also a mystical
number, associated with spiritual perfection. The phrase 'the seven
pillars of wisdom' became proverbial, and led to the pillars
themselves being identified as such qualities as Faith, Honesty,
Deliberation and Long-Suffering. (There are many, varied lists.)

22   **Stolen waters are sweet, and bread eaten in secret is pleasant.
But he knoweth not that the dead are there; and that her
guests are in the depths of hell.**
(9:17–18)

Folly is trying to seduce true believers by offering them illicit entertainment; Wisdom points out that the doorway at which Folly beckons is the doorway to destruction. The phrase 'stolen waters are sweet' became proverbial as advice against illicit pleasures: the addition 'but dangerous' was always in the speaker's mind. 'There' means in the house of Folly.

23 **A wise son maketh a glad father: but a foolish son is the heaviness of his mother.**
(10:1)
As well as subtler teaching, Proverbs is studded with remarks as banal and obvious as this one, which is attributed to no less an authority than Solomon.

24 **The rich man's wealth is his strong city: the destruction of the poor is their poverty.**
(10:15)
'Wealth' in the speaker's mind is identified with wisdom, fear of God; 'poverty' includes idolatry. The last phrase of the quotation was given a sociological, rather than a religious, turn by Engels in the course of his description and denunciation of nineteenth-century urban poverty in Britain.

25 **Riches profit not in the day of wrath: but righteousness delivereth from death.**
(11:4)
The contrast between the wealth of the world and spiritual wealth, made throughout Proverbs, is here pointedly, and chillingly, related to the Day of Judgment.

26 **As a jewel of gold in a swine's snout, so is a fair woman which is without discretion.**
(11:22)
The vigour of its expression has plucked this verse from the many male chauvinistic remarks in the Old Testament, and given it continued currency. 'Fair' means pretty; 'discretion' means a kind of bashful reticence, thought appropriate in a society where 'decent' women avoided letting themselves be seen in public.

27 **He that troubleth his own house shall inherit the wind.**
(11:29)
The meaning here is that those who make trouble at home are ruining their own future inheritance, fouling their own nest. 'Inherit the wind' has become proverbial.

28   A virtuous woman is a crown to her husband: but she that
      maketh ashamed is as rottenness in his bones.
      (12:4)
      This uncompromising notion has been quoted with approval (by
      men) down the centuries.

29   A righteous man regardeth the life of his beast: but the tender
      mercies of the wicked are cruel.
      (12:10)
      Even the kindness of a wicked person, because it is tainted by his or
      her wickedness, is no better than cruelty. The second half of this
      verse, for all its obscurity, became proverbial.

30   Hope deferred maketh the heart sick: but when the desire
      cometh, it is a tree of life.
      (13:12)
      The beauty of its expression has made this a favourite proverb,
      although it does no more than state the obvious. 'When the desire
      cometh' means 'when we get what we long for'.

31   He that spareth his rod hateth his son: but he that loveth him
      chasteneth him betimes.
      (13:24)
      Best known in the form 'spare the rod and spoil the child', this
      proverb would have had spiritual overtones for its original audience
      (see Prov 5).

32   In all labour there is profit: but the talk of the lips tendeth
      only to penury.
      (14:23)
      Despite all kinds of later perversions and adaptations of this proverb
      – culminating, perhaps, in the notorious *Arbeit macht Frei*, 'Work
      Frees', the motto of the Auschwitz concentration camp – the
      original meaning is clear and innocently apolitical: a wise person
      gets on with the meaningful activities of life, and a fool squanders
      time in profitless babble.

33   Righteousness exalteth a nation: but sin is a reproach to any
      people.
      (14:34)
      This is less of a platitude than it sounds: to the audience,
      'righteousness' implied worship of the true God, and 'sin' implied
      idolatry.

34   A soft answer turneth away wrath.
      (15:1)

This verse not only foreshadows the Christian idea of turning the other cheek, but is also an example of the tendency in Proverbs to contradict itself: a later, much more belligerent, Old Testament proverb reads 'a soft tongue breaketh the bone'.

35   **A merry heart maketh a cheerful countenance.**
(15:13)
Throughout the ages, nuggets of moral wisdom have been expressed in mottoes like this, designed perhaps to make the hearers nod in agreement rather than to provoke deep thought.

36   **Better is a dinner of herbs where love is, than a stalled ox and hatred therewith.**
(15:17)
The contrast is between eating sparse, meatless fare and feasting on an ox fattened in its stall. In an earlier English version of the Bible (Matthew's Bible, 1535), the verse was even more succinctly translated 'Better a dinner of herbs where love is, than a fat ox with evil will.'

37   **A word spoken in due season, how good is it!**
(15:23)
Timely advice is the best advice of all.

38   **Pride goeth before destruction, and an haughty spirit before a fall.**
(16:18)
This proverb is best known in its abbreviated form 'Pride goes before a fall.' The context here is not so general as that suggests: as often in Proverbs, pride is associated with idolatry, and is contrasted with the humble obedience of the true believer.

39   **He that is slow to anger is better than the mighty; and he that ruleth his spirit than he that taketh a city.**
(16:32)
The meekness of the true believer, and the idea of belief as the armour of righteousness, are here implicitly linked.

40   **A merry heart doeth good like a medicine: but a broken spirit drieth the bones.**
(17:22)
As often with Old Testament sayings, pithiness and striking expression have made this observation better known than its obviousness perhaps deserves.

41   Wine is a mocker, strong drink is raging: and whosoever is
      deceived thereby is not wise.
      (20:1)
      This verse begins a selection of moral precepts about
      abstemiousness of all kinds. The phrase 'strong drink', so well-
      known as to seem straightforward, standard English, actually comes
      from here.

42   Even a child is known by his doings, whether his work be
      pure, and whether it be right.
      (20:11)
      As God's nature is revealed in his works (that is, in the wonders of
      creation), and grown men's and women's by the way they spend
      their days, so even a child's behaviour declares its moral stature.
      The verse occurs in the middle of a long piece of teaching against
      idleness, either of body or of spirit.

43   The hearing ear, and the seeing eye, the Lord hath made even
      both of them.
      (20:12)
      The implication is that God uses our human faculties to perceive
      the world: this means that he is aware both of our perceptions and
      of the effect they have on us.

44   It is better to dwell in a corner of the housetop, than with a
      brawling woman in a wide house.
      (21:9)
      This widely quoted verse contrives to be both unexceptionably true
      – as can be seen if we simply replace the word 'woman' with 'man' –
      and gratuitously offensive to half the human race.

45   A good name is rather to be chosen than great riches, and
      loving favour rather than silver and gold.
      (22:1)
      This verse begins a series of teachings on people's relationships
      with their community. 'Good name' is the regard people earn from
      their neighbours; 'loving favour', that is affectionate
      openhandedness, is how they earn it.

46   Train up a child in the way he should go: and when he is old,
      he will not depart from it.
      (22:6)
      This simple thought underlies both the Jesuitic idea that the most
      lasting religious teaching is that absorbed before the age of seven,
      and Wordsworth's succinct line 'The child is father of the man.'

47 Foolishness is bound in the heart of a child; but the rod of correction shall drive it far from him.
(22:15)
Proverbs' rather stern view of childrearing continues.

48 Rob not the poor, because he is poor: neither oppress the afflicted in the gate: For the Lord will plead their cause, and spoil the soul of those that spoiled them.
(22:22–3)
The somewhat frigid, self-interested procedure advocated here, not harming the poor for fear of God's retaliation, was developed by Jesus into a policy of direct help and affection for the poor, and became a central part of Christian teaching.

49 Look not thou upon the wine when it is red.
(23:31)
'Red' is the colour of unmixed wine. In most of the ancient world wine was thick and potent, and was usually drunk diluted with three, four or even five times as much water. The instruction here is therefore to be abstemious rather than teetotal, and the quotation which follows gives the reason.

50 At the last it biteth like a serpent, and stingeth like an adder. Thine eyes shall behold strange women, and thine heart shall utter perverse things. Yea, thou shalt be as he that lieth down in the midst of the sea, or as he that lieth upon the top of a mast.
(23:32–4)
The effects of drinking 'red' or unmixed wine are eloquently described. The first of these sentences was a particular favourite in Victorian times.

51 A word fitly spoken is like apples of gold in pictures of silver.
(25:11)
As often, Solomon – to whom this section of Proverbs is credited – has irradiated a platitude with poetry.

52 If thine enemy be hungry, give him bread to eat; and if he be thirsty, give him water to drink: For thou shalt heap coals of fire upon his head, and the Lord shall reward thee.
(25:21–2)
The morality of mortifying others with charity seems somewhat dubious. The idea of heaping coals of fire on someone's head has outlived the rest of the quotation.

53   As cold waters to a thirsty soul, so is good news from a far
      country.
      (25:25)
      This is another demonstration that Solomon's gift was as much for
      memorable phrasemaking as for depth of thought.

54   A whip for the horse, a bridle for the ass, and a rod for the
      fool's back.
      (26:3)
      The vehemence of Old Testament denunciation of folly is
      explained by the religious overtones of the idea of folly: the fool is
      one who refuses to believe in God.

55   Answer not a fool according to his folly, lest thou also be like
      unto him. Answer a fool according to his folly, lest he be wise
      in his own conceit.
      (26:4–5)
      There has been much furrowing of brows over why two consecutive
      sentences should give apparently contradictory advice. The
      favourite answer is that the first sentence normally applies – since
      no true believer would want, even for a moment, to appear to agree
      with the fools who disbelieve in God – but that there are occasions
      when seeming to agree with fools will show them how foolish they
      are. The phrase 'Wise in his own conceit', rather than any nit-
      picking about meaning, is the reason why the lines have lived.

56   As a dog returneth to his vomit, so a fool returneth to his
      folly.
      (26:11)
      Solomon's denunciation of fools, that is the ungodly, continues.

57   She looketh well to the ways of her household, and eateth not
      the bread of idleness.
      (31:27)
      Proverbs closes with a poem in praise of the virtuous wife, of which
      this is one of the least sanctimonious verses. 'Bread of idleness'
      became proverbial.

Ecclesiastes

1   Vanity of vanities, saith the Preacher, vanity of vanities; all is
      vanity.
      (1:2)

'The Preacher' (*Ecclesiastes* in Greek) is a translation of the Hebrew word *Quoholeth*, which more accurately means 'state philosopher' and indicates a position of religious importance in the Jewish court, akin to that of the 'chief musician' who oversaw the music in the temple and to whom many of the psalms are dedicated. The Preacher was in charge of moral education and of the books of teachings (Leviticus, Proverbs, etc) which guided it. To judge by the tone of many of the remarks in the book which bears his name, his teaching was uncompromising and to the point. He is referring here, for example, to the emptiness ('vanity') of human life lived without God.

2   **What profit hath a man of all his labour which he taketh under the sun? One generation passeth away, and another generation cometh: but the earth abideth for ever. The sun also ariseth, and the sun goeth down, and hasteth to his place where he arose.**
(1:3–4)
Human mortality, the impermanence of our existence, is contrasted with the permanence of the earth and the endless circuit of the sun.

3   **All the rivers run into the sea; yet the sea is not full; unto the place from whence the rivers come, thither they return again.**
(1:7)
The image here, of the ceaseless circle between sea, rainclouds and rivers, gives the Preacher a powerful metaphor for the restlessness of human life on earth.

4   **The thing that hath been, it is that which shall be; and that which is done is that which shall be done: and there is no new thing under the sun.**
(1:9)
All invention, all discovery, is illusion. The implication at the back of the Preacher's mind is that only God and his worship are permanent.

5   **There is no remembrance of former things; neither shall there be any remembrance of things that are to come with those that shall come after.**
(1:11)
The true believer's relationship with God puts him or her in a kind of timeless state to which human past, present and future have no relevance. The novelist Proust robustly disagreed with this view. He thought that our memory of the past, our historical sense, is what validates our present and guarantees our future, and called his book accordingly *À la recherche du temps perdu*, 'In search of lost time' or,

in the more common English translation, 'Remembrance of things past'.

6   I the Preacher was King over Israel in Jerusalem. And I gave my heart to seek and search out by wisdom concerning all things that are done under heaven: this sore travail hath God given to the sons of man to be exercised therewith. I have seen all the works that are done under the sun; and, behold, all is vanity and vexation of spirit.
(1:12–14)
Scholars identify this King, and therefore the pseudonymous Preacher, as Solomon, who is also credited with the authorship of Proverbs. His jaded view of human pomp now includes the idea that restlessness, activity for its own vain sake, is a burden laid on the human race by God – an implicit reference to God's punishment of Adam in Eden (see Gen 18). The last verse quoted is the origin of the phrase 'everything under the sun'.

7   That which is crooked cannot be made straight: and that which is wanting cannot be numbered.
(1:15)
'Making the crooked straight' became proverbial for doing the impossible. The prophet Isaiah (see Isa 61) used this phrase for his memorable vision of the day of the coming of the Messiah, the day when all worldly crookedness, all imperfection, will be corrected.

8   In much wisdom is much grief: and he that increaseth knowledge increaseth sorrow.
(1:18)
The words 'wisdom' and 'knowledge' here have none of their usual Old Testament overtones of obedience to God: the Preacher is talking of worldly wisdom only.

9   I said of laughter, It is mad: and of mirth, What doeth it?
(2:2)
'Mad' here carries the idea of pointlessness – the 'vanity' which the Preacher has been ascribing to all human activity. The ancients believed that laughter was one of the few uncontrollable human activities, a spontaneous eruption caused by God or the Devil. Wild, unbridled laughter was a sign that the Devil had taken full control, that the person was insane.

10   I saw that wisdom excelleth folly, as far as light excelleth darkness. The wise man's eyes are in his head; but the fool walketh in darkness: and I myself perceived also that one event happeneth to them all.
(2:13–14)

Because 'one event' (that is, death) happens to all human beings, there is in the end no difference between the wise man and the fool, and hence worldly wisdom is pointless.

11 To every thing there is a season, and a time to every purpose under the heaven: A time to be born, and a time to die; a time to plant, and a time to pluck up that which is planted; A time to kill, and a time to heal; a time to break down, and a time to build up; A time to weep, and a time to laugh; a time to mourn, and a time to dance; A time to cast away stones, and a time to gather stones together; a time to embrace, and a time to refrain from embracing; A time to get, and a time to lose; a time to keep, and a time to cast away; A time to rend, and a time to sew; a time to keep silence, and a time to speak; A time to love, and a time to hate; a time of war, and a time of peace.
(3:1–8)
The underlying thought, that there is a season for human pomp as for everything else in life, is prefaced by a poem on seasonableness, the balance of the phrases reflecting the order time brings to human existence.

12 For that which befalleth the sons of men befalleth beasts; even one thing befalleth them.
(3:19)
The 'one thing', the one season common to all earthly creatures, is death.

13 I perceive that there is nothing better, than that a man should rejoice in his own works; for that is his portion: for who shall bring him to see what shall be after him?
(3:22)
Because there is a season for everything people do, there is also a season for pride in human achievement. The idea that we should enjoy the present because we have no insight into the future is close to other ancient philosophies, notably Epicureanism with its teaching of 'Live for today, for tomorrow you die.'

14 I praised the dead which are already dead more than the living which are yet alive.
(4:2)
The miseries of life are so great that we would be better dead. This is the conclusion Ecclesiastes reaches after a characteristically glum survey of human wickedness in the world.

15   **A threefold cord is not quickly broken.**
(4:12)
The Preacher uses a homely metaphor – which has since continued
to be proverbial – to make his point that human beings are better
working together than individually.

16   **Better is a poor and a wise child than an old and foolish king,
who will no more be admonished.**
(4:13)
The idea continues that human pomp and circumstance are 'vanity'.
The child still has an ability the king has not: the ability to learn
more about God.

17   **The sleep of a labouring man is sweet, whether he eat little or
much: but the abundance of the rich will not suffer him to
sleep.**
(5:12)
This verse is part of a diatribe against riches. The contrast between
honest toil and idle wealth was a favourite with Victorian hymn-
writers, who broadened it to include the notion that the labourer's
work was done in God's service, whereas the rich person's wealth
was nothing but distraction and delusion.

18   **As the crackling of thorns under a pot, so is the laughter of
the fool.**
(7:6)
The fool's laughter is like the noise made by thorn-tree branches
when on a cooking-fire: loud but useless for the purpose (in this
case, of heating the food).

19   **Better is the end of a thing than the beginning thereof: and
the patient in spirit is better than the proud in spirit.**
(7:8)
The wise person remembers that death is the end of all human
undertakings, and lives therefore in a state of sober-minded, patient
expectation.

20   **My soul seeketh, but I find not: one man among a thousand
have I found.**
(7:28)
The Preacher claims that he has considered the human race one by
one, looking for someone who is spontaneously good, without need
of moral help from God. The phrase 'one man in a thousand'
became proverbial for someone of outstanding merit.

21   A man hath no better thing under the sun, than to eat, and to
     drink, and to be merry.
     (8:15)
     Gloomily, the Preacher says that since there is so much evil in the
     world, and since we are all bound for death, we may as well enjoy
     ourselves while we can. The idea of desperate gaiety which the
     verse suggests, of the dance before the tomb, was polished by Isaiah
     into an epigram (see Isa 32), which was much quoted in Biblical
     times, and was later amalgamated with this verse to make the
     proverb 'Eat, drink and be merry, for tomorrow we die.'

22   For a living dog is better than a dead lion.
     (9:4)
     Life, however lowly our state, is preferable to death, because it
     allows the possibilities of hope and of moral improvement.

23   Eat thy bread with joy, and drink thy wine with a merry heart;
     for God now accepteth thy works.
     (9:7)
     For the first time, the Preacher brings God fully into his teaching.
     Life may be troublesome and pointless, but God takes what we do
     as an offering, blesses it, and so justifies both our existence and our
     activity.

24   Whatsoever thy hand findeth to do, do it with thy might; for
     there is no work, nor device, nor knowledge, nor wisdom, in
     the grave, whither thou goest.
     (9:10)
     Just as God's approval is the justification for human activity, so what
     we do is the justification of our lives. The circle is as complete as
     that of sea, clouds and rivers (see Eccles 3), but the purpose of the
     circle is at last explained.

25   The race is not to the swift, nor the battle to the strong.
     (9:11)
     God's approval of human endeavour makes everyone equal: his
     favour is without favouritism.

26   Dead flies cause the ointment of the apothecary to send forth
     a stinking savour.
     (10:1)
     The 'dead flies' in this robust metaphor are the remnants of folly
     (that is, disobedience to God) in an otherwise sensible person; the
     'ointment' is the healing acceptance of God's will. The expression
     'flies in the ointment', meaning drawbacks, comes from this verse.

27   He that diggeth a pit shall fall into it; and whoso breaketh an
      hedge, a serpent shall bite him.
      (10:8)
      These two random proverbs, both advising against 'foolish'
      behaviour, are memorably if somewhat implausibly linked. Jaques,
      in Shakespeare's *As You Like It*, found 'sermons in stones'; the
      Preacher here, one feels, could make a moral out of anything.

28   Woe to thee, O land, when thy king is a child.
      (10:16)
      The Old Testament's view of children, however highly born, was
      that they were morally unformed and that their role in life was to
      learn: a child ruling others, therefore, is as ludicrous an idea as that
      of the blind leading the blind (see Matt 100). The phrase has been
      used with approval in many subsequent cultures and kingdoms, but
      with political rather than moral overtones.

29   Cast thy bread upon the waters: for thou shalt find it after
      many days.
      (11:1)
      The Preacher's whole moral argument comes to a point. If life is
      difficult, dangerous and long, but is warmed by God's approval of
      the way we spend it, we should regard everything we do as
      purposeful and do it with a will. This applies even to actions
      apparently as pointless as throwing bread out to sea. (The phrase
      sounds grander than it is: it is probably a homely metaphor from
      fishing).

30   Remember now thy Creator in the days of thy youth, while
      the evil days come not, nor the years draw nigh, when thou
      shalt say, I have no pleasure in them; While the sun, or the
      light, or the moon, or the stars, be not darkened, nor the
      clouds return after the rain: In the day when the keepers of
      the house shall tremble, and the strong men shall bow
      themselves, and the grinders cease because they are few, and
      those that look out of the windows be darkened, And the
      doors shall be shut in the streets, when the sound of the
      grinding is low, and he shall rise up at the voice of the bird,
      and all the daughters of musick shall be brought low; Also
      when they shall be afraid of that which is high, and fears shall
      be in the way, and the almond tree shall flourish, and the
      grasshopper shall be a burden, and desire shall fail: because
      man goeth to his long home, and the mourners go about the
      streets: Or ever the silver cord be loosed, or the golden bowl
      be broken, or the pitcher be broken at the fountain, or the
      wheel broken at the cistern. Then shall the dust return to the

earth as it was: and the spirit shall return unto God who gave it.
(12:1–7)

The simple instruction 'Obey God all your life' is worked up into a description of the seasons of human existence in as poetic and potent a way as Shakespeare's 'Seven ages of man' speech in *As You Like It*, II, 7. ('At first, the infant, mewling and puking in the nurse's arms.')

31   **The words of the wise are as goads.**
(12:11)

Like goads, the words of the wise encourage us in the right direction, while leaving it up to us whether we go or stay. Free will is ours.

32   **And further, by these, my son, be admonished: of making many books there is no end; and much study is a weariness of the flesh.**
(12:12)

Continual study of and commentary on 'wisdom' (obedience to God) are not the same thing as wisdom itself.

33   **Let us hear the conclusion of the whole matter: Fear God, and keep his commandments: for this is the whole duty of man.**
(12:13)

The Preacher's final advice is as pithy as the analysis of 'vanity' which began his teaching. God is the arbiter of all human life, and living in obedience to him is our reason for existence.

Song of Solomon

1   **The song of songs, which is Solomon's.**
(1:1)

This book is literally a 'song of songs', a single poetic utterance made from a series of love songs. It is set in the countryside and chiefly celebrates the physical rapture of a village girl and her shepherd lover. The attribution to Solomon has led some scholars to think that the poems celebrate his love for the girl Abishag, and her refusal to leave her shepherd lover, even for the king. Others see the book as a religious allegory, the two ecstatic lovers standing for God and his people Israel. This interpretation earned the Song of Solomon its place in the Bible.

2   **I am black, but comely, O ye daughters of Jerusalem, as the tents of Kedar, as the curtains of Solomon.**
     (1:5)
     The girl is speaking. The Kedar were a nomadic tribe, and their tents were woven from black goat's wool, the best colour to reduce the sun's glare.

3   **I am the rose of Sharon, and the lily of the valleys.**
     (2:1)
     These two phrases became proverbial as descriptions of perfect, untouched beauty; Sharon indeed (originally the name of a fertile region of flowers and orchards) became a favourite girl's name. The 'rose of Sharon' was nothing like the modern, cultivated hybrid: it was either a wild rose or some completely different flower, such as a crocus or a narcissus.

4   **Stay me with flagons, comfort me with apples: for I am sick of love.**
     (2:5)
     The girl's every waking thought is of her beloved. She cries less for cure than for distraction, in a lover's conceit common in literature, when complaining about love's anguish is really a way of savouring it still further. 'Stay' means 'cure'; 'flagons' are cups of wine, used in ancient medicine to cure fever.

5   **Rise up, my love, my fair one, and come away. For, lo, the winter is past, the rain is over and gone; The flowers appear on the earth; the time of the singing of birds is come, and the voice of the turtle is heard in our land.**
     (2:10–12).
     The girl's beloved is calling her to come to him. 'Turtle' means turtledove or lovebird.

6   **Take us the foxes, the little foxes, that spoil the vines: for our vines have tender grapes.**
     (2:15)
     'Take' here means trap. 'Little foxes' are jackals, who must be prevented from nibbling the blossom and killing the vines. 'Tender' means young. The girl is saving herself for her beloved, and wants nothing to do with other lovers.

7   **My beloved is mine, and I am his.**
     (2:16)
     In mystical Christian literature of the Middle Ages, this phrase was used specifically of the relationship between Christ, the bridegroom, and the Church, his bride.

8   Behold, thou art fair, my love; behold, thou art fair; thou hast doves' eyes within thy locks: thy hair is as a flock of goats, that appear from mount Gilead. Thy teeth are like a flock of sheep that are even shorn, which came up from the washing; whereof every one bear twins, and none is barren among them. Thy lips are like a thread of scarlet, and thy speech is comely: thy temples are like a piece of a pomegranate within thy locks. Thy neck is like the tower of David builded for an armoury, whereon there hang a thousand bucklers, all shields of mighty men. Thy two breasts are like two young roes that are twins, which feed among the lilies. Until the day break, and the shadows flee away, I will get me to the mountain of myrrh, and to the hill of frankincense. Thou art all fair, my love; there is no spot in thee.
(4:1–7)
In an outburst of rapturous poetry, the young man describes his beloved.

9   A garden inclosed is my sister, my spouse.
(4:12)
'Garden inclosed' is a walled or secret garden, used often in the literature of this period as a symbol of the site or source of mystical or sexual ecstasy. 'Sister' here means 'beloved'.

10   Awake, O north wind; and come, thou south; blow upon my garden, that the spices thereof may flow out. Let my beloved come into his garden, and eat his pleasant fruits.
(4:16)
This verse, developing the idea of the beloved as a secret garden, a place of mystical delight, was used in medieval allegories. Christ was the gardener and the Church, his Eden of the senses, was his garden.

11   My beloved is white and ruddy, the chiefest among ten thousand. His head is as the most fine gold, his locks are bushy, and black as a raven. His eyes are as the eyes of doves by the rivers of waters, washed with milk, and fitly set. His cheeks are as a bed of spices, as sweet flowers: his lips like lilies, dropping sweet smelling myrrh. His hands are as gold rings set with the beryl: his belly is as bright ivory overlaid with sapphires. His legs are as pillars of marble, set upon sockets of fine gold: his countenance is as Lebanon, excellent as the cedars. His mouth is most sweet: yea, he is altogether lovely.
(5:10–16)
The girl rapturously describes her lover.

12   **Set me as a seal upon thine heart.**
(8:6)
The meaning of this is both literal (the beloved's picture, engraved
on a sealstone, is to be worn round the neck so that it hangs above
the heart) and meltingly poetic. Like other verses from the Song of
Solomon, this came to have mystical Christian overtones: Christ
says it to his devoted worshipper.

Isaiah

1   **The ox knoweth his owner, and the ass his master's crib: but
Israel doth not know, my people doth not consider.**
(1:3)
Isaiah's intention is to pull the chosen people back from worldliness
to the strict obedience to God which is their only safeguard in a
hostile world. He begins by denouncing their backsliding, in what
he says are God's own words.

2   **The daughter of Zion is left as a cottage in a vineyard, as a
lodge in a garden of cucumbers, as a besieged city.**
(1:8)
Because the chosen people have turned from God, Israel's enemies
have plundered the kingdom, leaving dereliction and poverty. 'A
lodge in a garden of cucumbers', which a modern writer might
render as 'a shed on an allotment', became a proverbial metaphor
for tumbledown subsistence. 'Daughter of Zion' means the city of
Jerusalem.

3   **Come now, and let us reason together, saith the Lord: though
your sins be as scarlet, they shall be as white as snow.**
(1:18)
God calls his people to repent, and promises forgiveness. The
associations of the colour scarlet with sinfulness, with the work of
the devil, and of white with purity, were traditional to the Middle
East and have spread, via Bible verses such as this, to the rest of the
world.

4   **How is the faithful city become an harlot! it was full of
judgment; righteousness lodged in it; but now murderers.**
(1:21)
The idea of Jerusalem, God's own bride, becoming like a prostitute
with open house to thieves, murderers and idolators, was first stated
here with Isaiah's typical feeling for the pungent metaphor. It was

eagerly taken up and used by later writers of all kinds, until the idea of any large city as a welcoming whore became proverbial.

5   **And it shall come to pass in the last days, that the mountain of the Lord's house shall be established in the top of the mountains, and shall be exalted above the hills; and all nations shall flow unto it.**
(2:2)
Isaiah prophesies the day, far in the future – in the 'last days' – when Jerusalem, with God's temple on its holy hill, will be a place of religious renewal for all the world's people. The phrase which begins the prophecy was a standard form of words, used to give moral impact to what followed. It has become better known than most of the prophecies it introduced.

6   **They shall beat their swords into plowshares, and their spears into pruninghooks: nation shall not lift up sword against nation, neither shall they learn war any more.**
(2:4)
Isaiah is prophesying total harmony between the world's peoples, beginning on the Day of Judgment when God's presence is everywhere acknowledged on earth.

7   **What mean ye that ye beat my people to pieces, and grind the faces of the poor?**
(3:15)
Isaiah prophesies God's words to harsh rulers on the Day of Judgment.

8   **My wellbeloved hath a vineyard in a very fruitful hill.**
(5:1)
The 'wellbeloved' is God and the vineyard is the city of Jerusalem.

9   **He looked that it should bring forth grapes, and it brought forth wild grapes.**
(5:2)
For all God's care of his vineyard (the holy city of Jerusalem), its fruit (the nation of Israel) is degenerate and sour.

10   **He looked for judgment, but behold oppression; for righteousness, but behold a cry.**
(5:7)
Isaiah explains what God expected from his chosen people, and what he got. 'Righteousness' means 'rule of law'; 'cry' means 'hue and cry', mob rule.

11 In the year that king Uzziah died I saw also the Lord sitting
    upon a throne, high and lifted up, and his train filled the
    temple. Above it stood the seraphims: each one had six wings;
    with twain he covered his face, and with twain he covered his
    feet, and with twain he did fly. And one cried unto another,
    and said, Holy, holy, holy, is the Lord of hosts: the whole
    earth is full of his glory.
    (6:1–3)
    Isaiah recounts a vision of God's majesty. A *seraph* (plural *seraphim*)
    is a winged fiery serpent; seraphim formed the first of nine angelic
    choirs which sang God's praise. Their antiphonal chant, 'Holy,
    holy, holy', became part of many human liturgies of praise.

12 Then said I, Woe is me! for I am undone.
    (6:5)
    This is Isaiah's reaction to the vision of the seraphim hymning God.

13 Then flew one of the seraphims unto me, having a live coal in
    his hand, which he had taken with the tongs from off the
    altar: And he laid it upon my mouth, and said, Lo, this hath
    touched thy lips; and thine iniquity is taken away, and thy sin
    purged.
    (6:6–7)
    Isaiah has said that he is a sinner, and that his sinner's lips are not
    fit to speak God's prophecies. This is God's response.

14 Then said I, Lord, how long? And he answered, Until the
    cities be wasted without inhabitant, and the houses without
    man, and the land be utterly desolate.
    (6:11)
    Isaiah asks when spiritual enlightenment will be granted to God's
    people; God's answer is both unexpected and alarming.

15 Behold, a virgin shall conceive, and bear a son, and shall call
    his name Immanuel.
    (7:14)
    God promises to confirm, by this sign, that he will redeem the
    human race. The prophecy was repeated to Joseph of Nazareth to
    soothe his anger when he discovered that his betrothed, Mary, was
    pregnant (see Matt 4). 'Immanuel' means 'God with us'.

16 Sanctify the Lord of hosts himself; and let him be your fear,
    and let him be your dread. And he shall be for a sanctuary;
    but for a stone of stumbling and for a rock of offence to both
    the houses of Israel, for a gin and for a snare to the
    inhabitants of Jerusalem.
    (8:13–14)

Isaiah is told to follow God, and not to associate himself with the godless ways of the Israelites. A 'gin' is a trap. 'Stone of stumbling' or 'stumbling-block' sounds more spectacular than it is: it is merely an imaginative translator's rendering of the Greek word *problema*, 'obstacle'.

17   **Wizards that peep, and that mutter.**
      (8:19)
      This is Isaiah's scornful description of the spiritual guides of the
      Israelites in their godlessness.

18   **The people that walked in darkness have seen a great light:**
      they that dwell in the land of the shadow of death, upon them
      hath the light shined.
      (9:2)
      Isaiah prophesies the end of spiritual darkness, the coming of the
      redeemer.

19   **For unto us a child is born, unto us a son is given: and the**
      government shall be upon his shoulder: and his name shall be
      called Wonderful, Counsellor, The mighty God, The
      everlasting Father, The Prince of Peace. Of the increase of his
      government and peace there shall be no end, upon the throne
      of David, and upon his kingdom, to order it, and to establish
      it with judgment and with justice from henceforth even for
      ever. The zeal of the Lord of hosts will perform this.
      (9:6–7)
      Isaiah, in God's words, prophesies the coming of the Messiah, the
      priest-king who will rescue the human race from sin.

20   **And there shall come forth a rod out of the stem of Jesse, and**
      a Branch shall grow out of his roots.
      (11:1)
      Isaiah gives more details about the Messiah. Jesse was the father of
      King David.

21   **The wolf also shall dwell with the lamb, and the leopard shall**
      lie down with the kid; and the calf and the young lion and the
      fatling together; and a little child shall lead them. And the
      cow and the bear shall feed; their young ones shall lie down
      together: and the lion shall eat straw like the ox. And the
      sucking child shall play on the hole of the asp, and the
      weaned child shall put his hand on the cockatrice' den.
      (11:6–8)
      In a series of remarkable images, reversing the perceived order of
      nature, Isaiah prophesies universal peace after the coming of the
      Messiah.

22   **With joy shall ye draw water out of the wells of salvation.**
(12:3)
The idea that God's goodness to his people is like a cup brimming
with water, a favourite Old Testament metaphor, is here broadened
to describe the people's delight at the coming of the Messiah.

23   **Howl ye; for the day of the Lord is at hand.**
(13:6)
Unlike true believers, who will be filled with joy by the coming of
the Day of Judgment, the ungodly will cry like dogs.

24   **The day of the Lord cometh, cruel both with wrath and fierce
anger, to lay the land desolate.**
(13:9)
This description of the Day of Judgment was worked into a
magnificent medieval poem, *Dies Irae* ('Day of Wrath'), which
became part of the liturgy and thence a resplendent utterance used
by many composers in the requiem mass.

25   **Wild beasts of the desert shall lie there; and their houses shall
be full of doleful creatures; and owls shall dwell there, and
satyrs shall dance there. And the wild beasts of the islands
shall cry in their desolate houses, and dragons in their
pleasant palaces: and her time is near to come, and her days
shall not be prolonged.**
(13:21–2)
Isaiah prophesies the downfall of even the most sumptuous
kingdom known to the Jews, Babylon, on the Day of Judgment.
'Dragons in their pleasant palaces', referring to lizards rather than
firebreathing monsters, became a common image for ruined pomp.

26   **How hath the oppressor ceased! the golden city ceased!**
(14:4)
These words, Isaiah says, will be the hymn of the righteous over the
ruins of Babylon on the Day of Judgment. 'Golden city', here meant
literally – Babylon was made of mudbricks which glowed yellow in
the sun, and its walls and roofs were topped with gold – came to be
proverbial for any place of decadent, ostentatious luxury.

27   **How art thou fallen from heaven, O Lucifer, son of the
morning!**
(14:12)
The people rejoice over the fall of evil on the Day of Judgment.
'Lucifer' means literally 'light-bringer': he was the morning star,
the brightest of all stars in the sky, and the most dazzling of all
God's angels, until he defied his creator and was hurled from
heaven to hell.

28   Behold, Damascus is taken away from being a city, and it
     shall be a ruinous heap.
     (17:1)
     This splendid phrase begins the lament which Isaiah says will be
     sung over Damascus on the Day of Judgment.

29   At that day shall a man look to his Maker.
     (17:7)
     From the destruction of mortal pomp on the Day of Judgment,
     Isaiah says, people will turn their eyes to God. Temporal
     dissolution will lead to spiritual regeneration.

30   It shall be for a sign and for a witness unto the Lord of hosts
     in the land of Egypt.
     (19:20)
     Isaiah is prophesying that the pillar of God's wrath will appear on
     the borders of Egypt on the Day of Judgment.

31   Watchman, what of the night? Watchman, what of the night?
     The watchman said, The morning cometh, and also the night:
     if ye will inquire, inquire ye: return, come.
     (21:11–12)
     Isaiah prophesies the nervous questions and riddling answers on
     Israel's borders on the Day of Judgment, after news is brought of
     the fall of Babylon.

32   And behold joy and gladness, slaying oxen, and killing sheep,
     eating flesh, and drinking wine: let us eat and drink; for to
     morrow we shall die.
     (22:13)
     God has called Israel to repentance – and instead, Isaiah caustically
     points out, the people turn to hedonism, and justify it with this well-
     known tag of pagan philosophy.

33   The world languisheth and fadeth away, the haughty people
     of the earth do languish.
     (24:4)
     Isaiah prophesies a sickly, dying world after the Day of Judgment.

34   The earth shall reel to and fro like a drunkard, and shall be
     removed like a cottage.
     (24:20)
     Even the earth itself, apparently so solid, will be shaken on the Day
     of Judgment.

35   **The moon shall be confounded, and the sun ashamed.**
     (24:23)
     The coming of the Day of Judgment will affect even the sun and
     moon, once regarded as unshakable fixtures in the sky.

36   **He will swallow up death in victory; and the Lord God will**
     wipe away tears from off all faces; and the rebuke of his
     people shall he take away from off all the earth.
     (25:8)
     Isaiah reiterates his theme that the end of evil on the Day of
     Judgment will mean the rebirth of all true believers. The first part
     of the verse was memorably expanded, and given specific Christian
     overtones, by St Paul (see I Cor 34).

37   **In that day shall the Lord of hosts be for a crown of glory, and**
     for a diadem of beauty, unto the residue of his people.
     (28:5)
     Isaiah continues to prophesy the joy of God's true worshippers on
     the Day of Judgment. The 'crown of glory' is the halo depicted on
     many paintings of this scene, the radiance of those who truly
     worship God.

38   **The priest and the prophet have erred through strong drink,**
     they are swallowed up of wine, they are out of the way
     through strong drink; they err in vision, they stumble in
     judgment.
     (28:7)
     The idea of drunken priests, profoundly shocking to orthodox Jews,
     symbolizes the debauchery of the ungodly – in this case the
     Samaritans – which will be punished on the Day of Judgment. The
     implication is that the 'strong drink' which intoxicates the priests is
     not alcohol but idolatry.

39   **The word of the Lord was unto them precept upon precept,**
     precept upon precept; line upon line, line upon line; here a
     little, and there a little.
     (28:13)
     Scrupulous understanding of and obedience to God's word, Isaiah
     is implying, is the way to salvation, unlike the idolatrous laxity he
     sees all around him.

40   **We have made a covenant with death, and with hell are we at**
     agreement.
     (28:15)
     The idolators boast that they will be immune on the Day of
     Judgment. Their decadence and orgies are like a calculated gamble
     with the Devil, an attempt to buy off death.

41 The hail shall sweep away the refuge of lies, and the waters shall overflow the hiding place. And your covenant with death shall be disannulled, and your agreement with hell shall not stand; when the overflowing scourge shall pass through, then ye shall be trodden down by it.
(28:17–18)
God answers those who think that they have bought off death. Isaiah's prophesy unites images of the Day of Judgment, when all accounts will be paid in full, and of the flood which God sent in Noah's time to cleanse the world.

42 They are drunken, but not with wine; they stagger, but not with strong drink.
(29:9)
Isaiah reiterates his vision of idolators, intoxicated with false religion.

43 I will proceed to do a marvellous work among this people, even a marvellous work and a wonder.
(29:14)
God promises to reward his true worshippers.

44 Shall the work say of him that made it, He made me not?
(29:16)
With mock astonishment, Isaiah compares human beings who deny God's existence with the idea of clay pots denying the existence of the potter.

45 Woe to the rebellious children, saith the Lord.
(30:1)
Originally referring to those of the children of Israel who allied with Egypt and followed Egyptian religion, this outcry has been applied much more generally since, as an exclamation of despair at the unruliness of the younger generation.

46 Their strength is to sit still.
(30:7)
Isaiah is talking of the Egyptians, who will do nothing to help the Israelites in trouble – and he means at the Day of Judgment. The phrase has been used proverbially since, referring to politicians or nations who practise masterly inactivity.

47 Speak unto us smooth things, prophesy deceits.
(30:10)
The idolaters who are the allies of the wayward Israelites instruct their priests and prophets to avoid discomforting them with truth.

48   **The bread of adversity, and the water of affliction.**
(30:20)
There is no way, says Isaiah, for God's true worshippers to avoid
suffering on earth; he compares it, however, to prison diet, thus
implying that one day release will come.

49   **Thine ears shall hear a word behind thee, saying, This is the**
way, walk ye in it, when ye turn to the right hand, and when ye
turn to the left.
(30:21)
God's word will guide his people. This verse is the Biblical origin of
the idea, much used by later thinkers, writers and preachers, that
God's word is a 'way'.

50   **Behold a king shall reign in righteousness, and princes shall**
rule in judgment.
(32:1)
Isaiah prophesies the coming of the Messiah.

51   **A man shall be as an hiding place from the wind, and a covert**
from the tempest; as rivers of water in a dry place, as the
shadow of a great rock in a weary land.
(32:2)
In the time after the Messiah's coming, human beings will no longer
be puny and helpless: they will become strong when they are cured
of sin.

52   **O Lord, be gracious unto us; we have waited for thee.**
(33:2)
Isaiah prays on behalf of the godly on the Day of Judgment.

53   **The wilderness and the solitary place shall be glad for them;**
and the desert shall rejoice, and blossom as the rose.
(35:1)
Isaiah prophesies blessings for true believers when the Messiah
comes. The blossoming of the desert is paralleled with the
healthiness of human souls freed from the blight of sin.

54   **Then the eyes of the blind shall be opened, and the ears of the**
deaf shall be unstopped.
(35:5)
On the Day of Judgment, all normal human conditions will be
transformed. Christians later took this verse as a specific reference
to Jesus' healing miracles.

55   Then shall the lame man leap as an hart, and the tongue of
the dumb sing: for in the wilderness shall waters break out,
and streams in the desert. And the parched ground shall
become a pool, and the thirsty land springs of water: in the
habitation of dragons, where each lay, shall be grass with
reeds and rushes.
(35:6–7)
Isaiah prophesies the blossoming of the desert when the Messiah
comes. 'Dragons' are sandlizards.

56   An highway shall be there, and a way, and it shall be called
The way of holiness; the unclean shall not pass over it.
(35:8)
Where there was once the desert of idolatry, the Messiah will create
the fertile land of true belief, and the path of God will be plain for
all to follow.

57   And the ransomed of the Lord shall return, and come to Zion
with songs and everlasting joy upon their heads: they shall
obtain joy and gladness, and sorrow and sighing shall flee
away.
(35:10)
The souls saved from destruction on the Day of Judgment, like
prisoners ransomed from jail, will walk joyfully along the way of
God's word into the eternal city.

58   Now on whom dost thou trust, that thou rebellest against me?
Lo, thou trustest in the staff of this broken reed, on Egypt;
whereon if a man lean, it will go into his hand, and pierce it.
(36:5–6)
The king of Assyria's messenger Rabshakeh is inviting the Israelites
to surrender to his master, and is claiming that Egypt, however
powerful, will be worthless as an ally, untrustworthy, or both. This
is Isaiah's account of events also narrated in the Book of Kings (see
II Kgs 15), and he picks up the evocative phrase 'this broken reed'
from there.

59   Set thine house in order: for thou shalt die, and not live.
(38:1)
Isaiah breaks the news to King Hezekiah that he is about to die.
The phrase 'set thine house in order', ostensibly to do with goods
and chattels, is used here and has been used ever since as an
exhortation to spiritual self-cleansing.

60   Comfort ye, comfort ye my people, saith your God. Speak ye
comfortably to Jerusalem, and cry unto her, that her warfare
is accomplished, that her iniquity is pardoned.
(40:1–2)

Isaiah tells the Israelites that whatever their sins have been, and however much they have neglected God, they are still the chosen people.

61 The voice of him that crieth in the wilderness, Prepare ye the way of the Lord, make straight in the desert a highway for our God. Every valley shall be exalted, and every mountain and hill shall be made low: and the crooked shall be made straight, and the rough places plain: And the glory of the Lord shall be revealed, and all flesh shall see it together: for the mouth of the Lord hath spoken it.
(40:3–5)
Isaiah tells the people to prepare for the coming of the Messiah. John the Baptist later used these words, thus identifying himself as the 'voice crying in the wilderness' and Jesus as the Messiah.

62 All flesh is grass, and all the goodliness thereof is as the flower of the field: The grass withereth, the flower fadeth: because the spirit of the Lord bloweth upon it: surely the people is grass. The grass withereth, the flower fadeth: but the word of our God shall stand for ever.
(40:6–8)
Isaiah meditates on human mortality. We are as prone to die as grass; our only hope of eternal life is obedience to the undying word of God. Peter quoted these words, specifying that the enduring word of the Lord was the Christian gospel (see I Pet 3).

63 He shall feed his flock like a shepherd: he shall gather the lambs with his arm, and carry them in his bosom, and shall gently lead those that are with young.
(40:11)
The familiar metaphor of Christ as the good shepherd (see John 38), originates in this verse.

64 The nations are as a drop of a bucket, and are counted as the small dust of the balance: behold, he taketh up the isles as a very little thing.
(40:15)
Isaiah reflects on the awesomeness of God.

65 Have ye not known? have ye not heard? hath it not been told you from the beginning? have ye not understood from the foundations of the earth?
(40:21)

'What is God like?' the people have asked, lacking the reassurance provided by the statues and likenesses of other, heathen faiths. Isaiah's answer begins with a somewhat impatient rhetorical flourish.

66 **It is he that sitteth upon the circle of the earth, and the inhabitants thereof are as grasshoppers; that stretcheth out the heavens as a curtain, and spreadeth them out as a tent to dwell in.**
(40:22)
Isaiah describes God's nature and power for the people, giving them images not in stone or brass, but in words.

67 **Hast thou not known? hast thou not heard, that the everlasting God, the Lord, the Creator of the ends of the earth, fainteth not, neither is weary? there is no searching of his understanding.**
(40:28)
Isaiah exalts God above human frailty.

68 **Even the youths shall faint and be weary, and the young men shall utterly fall: But they that wait upon the Lord shall renew their strength; they shall mount up with wings as eagles; they shall run, and not be weary; and they shall walk, and not faint.**
(40:30–1)
Mortal strength is nothing unaided; only those who serve and obey God are truly strong.

69 **Fear not: for I am with thee.**
(43:5)
This verse was written to give specific comfort at a specific time. The Israelites were about to be taken as slaves to Babylon, and the prophet reminds them that God is their strength. The prophet is not necessarily Isaiah, into whose account of the Day of Judgment and coming of the Messiah several chapters about the Babylonian exile have been interpolated. The phrase gained great currency immediately after Jesus' crucifixion, when his dismayed and scattered followers took it as a comforting assertion of his continued presence in the world. It has been taken so ever since.

70 **I am the Lord, and there is none else, there is no God beside me: I girded thee, though thou hast not known me: That they may know from the rising of the sun, and from the west, that there is none beside me. I am the Lord, and there is none else.**
(45:5–6)

God reminds the Israelites, in terrified Babylonian exile, that they are his chosen people. The words echo those of the First Commandment (see Exod 47); their form is that of a legal contract, a covenant.

71 **Woe unto him that striveth with his Maker! Let the potsherd strive with the potsherds of the earth. Shall the clay say to him that fashioneth it, What makest thou? or thy work, He hath no hands?**
(45:9)
God has made men and women as a potter moulds clay. This is God's part of the covenant. Human beings' part should begin by their acknowledging the fact of their creation. If they want to argue, they should argue not with the potter but with the other pots. A 'potsherd' is a piece of broken pottery.

72 **I have sworn by myself, the word is gone out of my mouth in righteousness, and shall not return, That unto me every knee shall bow, every tongue shall swear.**
(45:23)
This prophecy is even better known in St Paul's paraphrase (see Phil 4).

73 **I have chosen thee in the furnace of affliction.**
(48:10)
God reminds his chosen people that the suffering he sends is a way of testing them, of purifying their faith.

74 **O that thou hadst hearkened to my commandments! then had thy peace been as a river, and thy righteousness as the waves of the sea.**
(48:18)
God's promise to his people remains as it always has been; the backsliding has been theirs, not his.

75 **There is no peace, saith the Lord, unto the wicked.**
(48:22)
God points out to the Israelites that their present suffering (in this case, exile in Babylon) is their own fault. The phrase has entered the language, to the point where its Biblical origins and overtones are almost entirely lost.

76 **The redeemed of the Lord shall return, and come with singing unto Zion; and everlasting joy shall be upon their head: they shall obtain gladness and joy; and sorrow and mourning shall flee away.**
(51:11)

The context of this verse clearly relates it to the Israelites' return from exile in Babylon. Its wider surroundings, however, are Isaiah's prophecies about the joy of true believers entering the city of God after the coming of the Messiah, and it is in that light that it is usually read today.

77 **How beautiful upon the mountains are the feet of him that bringeth good tidings, that publisheth peace.**
(52:7)
Isaiah describes God's messenger who will bring news of the coming of redemption. 'How beautiful ... are the feet' is a common archaic literary formula for 'how welcome'. 'Publisheth' means 'announces'.

78 **Thy watchmen shall lift up the voice; with the voice together shall they sing: for they shall see eye to eye, when the Lord shall bring again Zion.**
(52:8)
The watchmen are God's faithful in the holy city, alert for the return of his people. Originally referring to the return of the Jews from exile in Babylon, this verse has always had far deeper spiritual overtones – and Isaiah certainly meant it so. To see 'eye to eye', here meaning to glance at one another in excitement, has entered the language as a metaphor for total agreement.

79 **Break forth into joy, sing together, ye waste places of Jerusalem: for the Lord hath comforted his people, he hath redeemed Jerusalem.**
(52:9)
The very rocks and dust of the sacked city of Jerusalem rejoice at news of the redeemer. The city had been literally laid waste by the Babylonians, but Isaiah's idea is also of spiritual desolation.

80 **For he shall grow up before him as a tender plant, and as a root out of a dry ground: he hath no form nor comeliness; and when we shall see him, there is no beauty that we should desire him.**
(53:2)
The messenger of God's mercy, the redeemer, is no prince, riding in manifest glory, but an ordinary person unnoticeable in a crowd. 'Tender' here means 'young'.

81 **He is despised and rejected of men; a man of sorrows, and acquainted with grief.**
(53:3)

Eight-hundred years before the coming of Jesus, Isaiah is describing the scapegoat-like human weakness of the redeemer, the despised figure who carries the whole burden of human guilt. This was a very different view of the saving of humanity from the idea, prevalent in the Old Testament, of the Messiah as a prince riding in triumph while all people bowed in homage.

82   **Surely he hath borne our griefs, and carried our sorrows: yet we did esteem him stricken, smitten of God, and afflicted. But he was wounded for our transgressions, he was bruised for our iniquities: the chastisement of our peace was upon him; and with his stripes we are healed.**
(53:4–5)
Isaiah's vision of the redeemer as a scapegoat continues. 'Stripes' are the wounds caused by whipping.

83   **All we like sheep have gone astray; we have turned every one to his own way; and the Lord hath laid on him the iniquity of us all. He was oppressed, and he was afflicted, yet he opened not his mouth: he is brought as a lamb to the slaughter, and as a sheep before her shearers is dumb, so he openeth not his mouth.**
(53:6–7)
These verses make an unexpected and powerful link between the idea of God's people as lost sheep and that of the redeemer not as a shepherd but as one of the sheep himself, a voluntary sacrifice. The theological implications, familiar and comforting to us today, must have seemed bizarre to Isaiah's original hearers.

84   **He was taken from prison and from judgment: and who shall declare his generation? for he was cut off out of the land of the living: for the transgression of my people was he stricken.**
(53:8)
This verse vigorously describes the human isolation of the redeemer: a criminal whose very ancestry is forgotten or ignored, someone cut from human society like a discarded limb. 'The land of the living' has entered the language.

85   **For thy Maker is thine husband; the Lord of hosts is his name; and thy Redeemer the Holy One of Israel.**
(54:5)
Isaiah has been comparing the godly to a lonely widow, outcast or set apart from the bustling society around her. Now he compares the redeemer with the husband who will restore her to full life, and identifies the redeemer uncompromisingly as one aspect of God himself. The passage gives a new perspective to the familiar Old

Testament view that the relationship between God and the human race is like a marriage.

86 **The mountains shall depart, and the hills be removed; but my kindness shall not depart from thee, neither shall the covenant of my peace be removed, saith the Lord that hath mercy on thee.**
(54:10)
The coming of the redeemer, which is the context of this passage, is linked here with the covenant God made with the patriarchs in ancient times. Human beings may falter, but God's promise is eternal and unchanging – and the coming of the redeemer is its fulfilment.

87 **Ho, every one that thirsteth, come ye to the waters, and he that hath no money; come ye, buy, and eat; yea, come, buy wine and milk without money and without price. Wherefore do ye spend money for that which is not bread? and your labour for that which satisfieth not? hearken diligently unto me, and eat ye that which is good, and let your soul delight itself in fatness.**
(55:1–2)
Isaiah is reworking and amalgamating two standard Old Testament themes: that God offers his true believers the bread of righteousness and the water of forgiveness, and that the coming of the redeemer will sweep away all the usual constraints of human society (for example those separating poor and rich).

88 **Incline your ear, and come unto me: hear, and your soul shall live; and I will make an everlasting covenant with you, even the sure mercies of David.**
(55:3)
As so often in the Old Testament, the human part of the covenant with God is no more than obedient belief: all blessings flow from that.

89 **Seek ye the Lord while he may be found, call ye upon him while he is near.**
(55:6)
The tone of Isaiah's prophecy moves from promises of redemption to imperatives. The coming of the redeemer is imminent, and the need for belief – which alone will guarantee redemption – is urgent.

90 **For my thoughts are not your thoughts, neither are your ways my ways, saith the Lord. For as the heavens are higher than the earth, so are my ways higher than your ways, and my thoughts than your thoughts.**
(55:8–9)

These words have been wrenched out of context, and used to reinforce the idea of God as stern, remote and awesome. In fact Isaiah means them to be comforting, a statement that God, unlike his chosen people, keeps to his word and will not be distracted from his covenant with the human race.

91   **For ye shall go out with joy, and be led forth with peace: the mountains and the hills shall break forth before you into singing, and all the trees of the field shall clap their hands. (55:12)**
Isaiah describes the fulfilment of God's promise, in the standard metaphors of the whole created world rejoicing in its creator.

92   **Instead of the thorn shall come up the fir tree, and instead of the brier shall come up the myrtle tree. (55:13)**
In joy at the fulfilment of God's promise, and as a living, lasting proof of it, the desert will bloom.

93   **I will give them an everlasting name, that shall not be cut off. (56:5)**
'Them' refers to strangers and eunuchs, outcasts from conventional society. If they believe in and obey God, they will be given an equal share of his redemption. Jesus Christ took up this theme, and it was an aspect of his teaching which outraged not only the strictest Jews (with their ideas of strict, lifelong adherence to the law and that a person should be without blemish) but also the Roman overlords of the early Christians (who had a strictly hierarchical view of society).

94   **They are greedy dogs which can never have enough, and they are shepherds that cannot understand: they all look to their own way, every one for his gain, from his quarter. (56:11)**
Isaiah is attacking strict spiritual guides whose zeal is more for forbidding than forgiveness. God's mercy is available to everyone who asks; in his eyes, whatever human beings may do or say, there are no classes or hierarchies of the devout. 'Greedy dogs', stripped of this theological context, has become a proverbial description of importunate and inconsiderate gluttons.

95   **The righteous perisheth, and no man layeth it to heart: and merciful men are taken away, none considering that the righteous is taken away from the evil to come. (57:1)**

The grim message of this verse is that over-strict devotion to the outward forms of piety can prevent us caring for true believers who do not conform to our standards: mistaking form for substance, in short, will end in tears.

96   Is it such a fast that I have chosen? a day for a man to afflict his soul? is it to bow down his head as a bulrush, and to spread sackcloth and ashes under him? wilt thou call this a fast, and an acceptable day to the Lord?
(58:5)
Isaiah continues his denunciation of those who mistake the outward show of piety for the real thing – which he goes on to define (see Isa 97). 'An acceptable day unto the Lord', originally meaning no more than a day of good omen, superstitiously impeccable, became widely used, out of this sarcastic context, as a description of a day of pure-hearted, genuine worship.

97   Is not this the fast that I have chosen? to loose the bands of wickedness, to undo the heavy burdens, and to let the oppressed go free, and that ye break every yoke? Is it not to deal thy bread to the hungry, and that thou bring the poor that are cast out to thy house? when thou seest the naked, that thou cover him; and that thou hide not thyself from thine own flesh?
(58:6–7)
In contrast to those who define 'fasts', holy days, in terms of obsessive obedience to the forms of ritual, Isaiah defines true godliness.

98   Then shall thy light break forth as the morning, and thine health shall spring forth speedily.
(58:8)
These are the rewards of those who practise true godliness instead of a parade of ritualistic and moral impeccability.

99   He put on righteousness as a breastplate, and an helmet of salvation upon his head; and he put on the garments of vengeance for clothing, and was clad with zeal as a cloke.
(59:17)
Isaiah has been describing God's horror at the evil of the human race; now he imagines him arming himself for redemption, an image which was taken up by St Paul (see Eph 19) and then became proverbial.

100   Arise, shine; for thy light is come, and the glory of the Lord is risen upon thee.
(60:1)

God speaks to his chosen people. The light is the radiance brought to them by the redeemer. This verse is the origin of the colloquial expression 'rise and shine'.

101 **The Lord hath anointed me to preach good tidings unto the meek; he hath sent me to bind up the brokenhearted, to proclaim liberty to the captives, and the opening of the prison to them that are bound; To proclaim the acceptable year of the Lord, and the day of vengeance of our God; to comfort all that mourn; To appoint unto them that mourn in Zion, to give unto them beauty for ashes, the oil of joy for mourning, the garment of praise for the spirit of heaviness.**
(61:1–3)
God's redeemer, the Messiah, is speaking.

102 **And they shall call them, The holy people, The redeemed of the Lord.**
(62:12)
Isaiah is describing the procession of saints into the holy city, both literally, of the Israelites returning from exile, and metaphorically, of all human beings redeemed by the Messiah. 'Redeemed' means literally ransomed from captivity.

103 **I have trodden the winepress alone; and of the people there was none with me: for I will tread them in mine anger, and trample them in my fury.**
(63:3)
Isaiah sees the Lord riding into Jerusalem and asks why his clothes are red. This is God's answer. The metaphor of the people as grapes and of God as treading them into wine is one of the most startling and apocalyptic even from Isaiah's powerful pen, a far cry from Jesus' entwining of the ideas of blood, wine and redemption at the Last Supper.

104 **Oh, that thou wouldest rend the heavens, that thou wouldest come down, that the mountains might flow down at thy presence.**
(64:1)
Isaiah prays for the coming of the Messiah.

105 **But we are all as an unclean thing, and all our righteousnesses are as filthy rags; and we all do fade as a leaf; and our iniquities, like the wind, have taken us away.**
(64:6)
The chosen people are at the lowest ebb, with no hope in them: there is no better moment, Isaiah is implying, for the coming of the redeemer.

106   Stand by thyself, come not near to me; for I am holier than
      thou.
      (65:5)
      God is listing all the kinds of sinners who are in the ascendance on
      earth. He is particularly angered by those who make their own
      holiness – their own strict adherence to the law – a kind of idolatry.
      Here he imagines the words they speak to 'lesser men'.

107   I create new heavens and a new earth: and the former shall
      not be remembered, nor come into mind.
      (65:17)
      Isaiah imagines not only the human race but every part of creation
      remade by the coming of the Messiah.

108   The Lord will come with fire, and with his chariots like a
      whirlwind, to render his anger with fury, and his rebuke with
      flames of fire. For by fire and by his sword will the Lord plead
      with all flesh: and the slain of the Lord shall be many.
      (66:15–16)
      Isaiah's apocalyptic vision of the Day of Judgment returns. The
      complex theological idea of using fire and the sword to 'plead' with
      the human race has become obscured by the general vividness of its
      context as a description of total war.

Jeremiah

1   Then the word of the Lord came unto me, saying, Before I
      formed thee in the belly I knew thee; and before thou camest
      forth out of the womb I sanctified thee, and I ordained thee a
      prophet unto the nations.
      (1:4–5)
      Jeremiah describes God calling him to be a prophet.

2   Ah, Lord God! behold, I cannot speak: for I am a child.
      (1:6)
      Jeremiah's horrified response to God's call echoes both Moses' (see
      Exod 15) and Solomon's (see I Kgs 4).

3   The Lord put forth his hand, and touched my mouth. And the
      Lord said unto me, Behold, I have put my words in thy
      mouth.
      (1:9)
      God gives Jeremiah the power to prophesy. 'To put words in
      someone's mouth' has acquired sinister overtones of meaning, quite
      unlike those here.

4   **To root out, and to pull down, and to destroy, and to throw down, to build, and to plant.**
(1:10)
Perhaps disingenuously, Jeremiah reports the effects that God promises his power of prophecy will have.

5   **Thine own wickedness shall correct thee, and thy backslidings shall reprove thee.**
(2:19)
Jeremiah is thundering against the Israelites' idolatry. 'Backsliding' is literal: it refers to the habit of slithering into an idol's presence, or backsliding out of it on one's belly, a religious practice thought to be favoured by the heathen peoples whose gods attracted the weaker brethren among the Israelites. 'Backsliding Israel' was one of Jeremiah's favourite themes, and he used the image constantly.

6   **Saying to a stock, Thou art my father; and to a stone, Thou hast brought me forth.**
(2:27)
This is Jeremiah's evocative description of idolatry. Instead of the true creator, God, the people worship blocks of wood (stocks) and stones, as if they were their parents.

7   **Can a maid forget her ornaments, or a bride her attire? yet my people have forgotten me days without number.**
(2:32)
The idea is that God, for his chosen people, is as much a confirmation of their status as the girl's ornaments or the bride's dress. This verse was a favourite text for nineteenth-century sermons.

8   **Why gaddest thou about so much to change thy way?**
(2:36)
The phrase 'gadding about', meaning restless busyness, derives from this verse. The context here concerns the Israelites' apparent dissatisfaction with God, which makes them trot from one idolatrous religion to another.

9   **Circumcise yourselves to the Lord, and take away the foreskins of your heart.**
(4:4)
Jeremiah is advocating a return from idolatry to true religion. His somewhat startling metaphor – he has none of Isaiah's feeling for a telling phrase – was widely used in hell-fire sermons in Puritan Britain; its effect on the congregation is not recorded.

10   **My bowels, my bowels! I am pained at my very heart.**
     (4:19)
     Jeremiah's reputation as a bilious misery derives from frequent
     exclamations of this kind. In fact here he is putting words into
     God's own mouth, suggesting that the Israelites' backsliding and
     idolatry cause their creator actual physical discomfort.

11   **They were as fed horses in the morning: every one neighed**
     after his neighbour's wife.
     (5:8)
     This strange simile comes in the middle of a denunciation of the
     Israelites' corruptness. The people are so comfortable, like fed
     horses, that they can turn their attention from making a living to
     adultery, which in this case also stands for idolatry – whoring after
     strange gods. The connection with horses has no theological
     significance, but is what has made the quotation popular.

12   **Fear ye not me? saith the Lord: will ye not tremble at my**
     presence, which have placed the sand for the bound of the sea
     by a perpetual decree, that it cannot pass it: and though the
     waves thereof toss themselves, yet can they not prevail;
     though they roar, yet can they not pass over it?
     (5:22)
     Jeremiah reminds the backsliding Israelites of the power of God the
     creator.

13   **But this people hath a revolting and a rebellious heart; they**
     are revolted and gone.
     (5:23)
     Jeremiah sees God's people as a mutinous army deserting its
     commander.

14   **A wonderful and horrible thing is committed in the land: The**
     prophets prophesy falsely, and the priests bear rule by their
     means; and my people love to have it so.
     (5:30–1)
     Everyone in Israel is enthusiastically idolatrous. Jeremiah saw these
     verses as part of a final warning: he went on to say that there was
     still time for the people to come to their senses before God
     destroyed them all.

15   **Reprobate silver shall men call them, because the Lord hath**
     rejected them.
     (6:30)
     Jeremiah pronounces God's terrible judgement on his people.
     'Reprobate' means 'counterfeit' – and counterfeit coins were
     melted down to be purified and reminted.

16   Is this house, which is called by my name, become a den of
robbers in your eyes? Behold, even I have seen it, saith the
Lord.
(7:11)
Jeremiah is talking generally of the degeneration of the temple and
those who worship in it. When Jesus adapted the words (see Matt
122), he was referring specifically to hucksters' and money-
changers' stalls.

17   The stork in the heaven knoweth her appointed times; and
the turtle and the crane and the swallow observe the time of
their coming; but my people know not the judgment of the
Lord.
(8:7)
The meaning is that the birds of the air – 'turtle' means turtledove –
know their place in the scheme of things and keep to it; human
beings, by contrast, refuse to obey ('know not') their creator.

18   Is there no balm in Gilead; is there no physician there? why
then is not the health of the daughter of my people recovered?
(8:22)
'Balm' is healing ointment, made from the resin of a tree which
grew profusely in Gilead. Jeremiah's meaning is that the means for
the Israelites to cure their idolatry are readily available, but they
refuse to use them. 'Balm in Gilead' came to be used proverbially
for consolation rather than cure, and 'balm' itself is still regularly so
used. In Coverdale's 1535 translation of the Bible 'balm' was
splendidly replaced by 'treacle', since the healing resin trickled
from the tree.

19   They are altogether brutish and foolish: the stock is a
doctrine of vanities.
(10:8)
Worshipping idols – a 'stock' is a block of wood – makes the people
no better than imbeciles or animals. Jeremiah is making the usual
Old Testament links between 'knowledge' and obedience to God,
and between 'vanity' and idolatry.

20   Give glory to the Lord your God, before he cause darkness,
and before your feet stumble upon the dark mountains.
(13:16)
Jeremiah turns from denunciation to clear advice.

21   Can the Ethiopian change his skin, or the leopard his spots?
then may ye also do good, that are accustomed to do evil.
(13:23)

Although the Israelites have turned to sin, goodness is as much a part of them as an African's skin or a leopard's spots, and cannot be changed.

22 It shall come to pass, if they say unto thee, Whither shall we go forth? then thou shalt tell them, Thus saith the Lord; Such as are for death, to death; and such as are for the sword, to the sword; and such as are for the famine, to the famine; and such as are for the captivity, to the captivity.
(15:2)
Even if the people turn from their false prophets and ask Jeremiah for help, there is no comfort for them.

23 Their widows are increased to me above the sand of the seas: I have brought upon them against the mother of the young men a spoiler at noonday: I have caused him to fall upon it suddenly, and terrors upon the city. She that hath borne seven languisheth: she hath given up the ghost.
(15:8–9)
God speaks his terrible punishment for the Israelites' backsliding. 'A spoiler at noonday' became proverbial for an overwhelming, implacable army. To 'give up the ghost' also became proverbial.

24 The heart is deceitful above all things, and desperately wicked: who can know it?
(17:9)
In most ancient cultures, the heart and not the brain was regarded as the seat of intelligence – hence Jeremiah's question, which implies 'Who is to know what a person truly believes, or if they are as honest as they claim?'

25 I the Lord, search the heart, I try the reins, even to give every man according to his ways, and according to the fruit of his doings.
(17:10)
Jeremiah answers his own question (see Jer 24): God knows the truth, and people are judged not by what they say but by what they do. 'Reins' ('kidneys') here stands for the internal organs which ancient peoples believed to be the seat of emotion and moral judgment.

26 As the partridge sitteth on eggs, and hatcheth them not; so he that getteth riches, and not by right, shall leave them in the midst of his days, and at his end shall be a fool.
(17:11)

This verse has become famous because of the unlikeliness of the comparison. Partridges were regarded in ancient times as the stupidest of all birds, because they would unhesitatingly incubate eggs laid by other birds. The implication of the comparison seems to be that a rich man, who sits on money earned by the sweat of others' brows, is wasting effort he could more profitably spend on good works of his own.

27 **Shall evil be recompensed for good? for they have digged a pit for my soul. Remember that I stood before thee to speak good.**
(18:20)
The idea of repaying good with evil was proverbial. Jeremiah is here giving it an apocalyptic twist, asking God to pay the Israelites back with suffering for the suffering they have caused him (Jeremiah): he was not the most popular of holy men.

28 **I will make this city desolate, and an hissing; every one that passeth thereby shall be astonished and hiss because of all the plagues thereof.**
(19:8)
God prophesies the destruction of Jerusalem. 'An hissing' means an object of scorn.

29 **Cursed be the day wherein I was born: let not the day wherein my mother bare me be blessed. Cursed be the man who brought tidings to my father, saying, A man child is born unto thee; making him very glad.**
(20:14–15)
Jeremiah has been thrown into the stocks because of his violent prophecies, and is plunged into despair. The first verse is a variant of one of Job's bleakest curses (see Job 10).

30 **Is not my word like as a fire? saith the Lord; and like a hammer that breaketh the rock in pieces?**
(23:29)
This verse is the warning climax of a denunciation of false prophets and the wilful fools who ignore God's word and follow them.

31 **Thus saith the Lord; A voice was heard in Ramah, lamentation and bitter weeping; Rahel weeping for her children refused to be comforted for her children, because they were not.**
(31:15)
Jeremiah is talking of Jacob's wife Rachel (or Rahel), the mother of Joseph and Benjamin. He makes her grief at their death stand for the grief of all the bereft mothers of Israel. St Matthew later

referred to this verse as a prophecy of the grief in Israel after Herod's slaughter of the innocents.

32   I have satiated the weary soul, and I have replenished every sorrowful soul.
(31:25)
God speaks to Jeremiah in a dream, promising an end to his and Israel's grief.

33   Behold, the days come, saith the Lord, that I will make a new covenant with the house of Israel, and with the house of Judah.
(31:31)
This prophecy was taken up by the writer of Hebrews (see Heb 3) and referred directly by him to the kingdom of Christ on earth. Christ's coming marks the 'new covenant' between God and his people, replacing the old covenant made in the time of Moses.

34   In those days, and at that time, will I cause the Branch of righteousness to grow up unto David; and he shall execute judgment and righteousness in the land.
(33:15)
God prophesies the coming of the Messiah.

35   Their Redeemer is strong; the Lord of hosts is his name: he shall throughly plead their cause, that he may give rest to the land, and disquiet the inhabitants of Babylon.
(50:34)
Jeremiah promises the Israelites God's comfort in their Babylonian exile. 'Throughly' means thoroughly.

36   In their heat I will make their feasts, and I will make them drunken, that they may rejoice, and sleep a perpetual sleep, and not wake, saith the Lord.
(51:39)
God is talking of the idolatrous Babylonians. The image behind this verse is the sleep of death, from which true believers, but not idolaters, will one day awake to bask in God's glory as in the dawn.

Lamentations

1   How doth the city sit solitary that was full of people! how is she become as a widow! she that was great among the nations, and princess among the provinces, how is she become

tributary! She weepeth sore in the night, and her tears are on her cheeks.
(1:1–2)

The Lamentations, ascribed in the Greek Bible to Jeremiah, are a set of five poems lamenting the capture of Jerusalem by Nebuchadnezzar's Babylonian army in 587 BC and the sacking of the temple. They are read in synagogues on the anniversary each year. This one begins by comparing the deserted city of Jerusalem to a bereft woman weeping on her own ruined doorstep.

2   Is it nothing to you, all ye that pass by? behold, and see if there be any sorrow like unto my sorrow which is done unto me, wherewith the Lord hath afflicted me in the day of his fierce anger.
(1:12)

Like a weeping woman in a war-torn town, Jerusalem holds out her hands for pity to every passing stranger.

3   The yoke of my transgressions is bound by his hand: they are wreathed, and come up upon my neck: he hath made my strength to fall, the Lord hath delivered me into their hands, from whom I am not able to rise up.
(1:14)

The city of Jerusalem, personified, continues her lament. The Israelites have brought their punishment on themselves, and God has yoked them to their own sin as an ox is yoked to a cart. The phrase 'yoke of my transgressions' became proverbial, simply meaning guilt.

4   All that pass by clap their hands at thee; they hiss and wag their head at the daughter of Jerusalem, saying, Is this the city that men call The perfection of beauty, The joy of the whole earth?
(2:15)

Because the Israelites have deserved their punishment, there is no comfort for them and they are a lesson and a mockery to the whole world.

5   And I said, My strength and my hope is perished from the Lord: Remembering mine affliction and my misery, the wormwood and the gall.
(3:18–19)

Jeremiah laments on behalf of his people. 'From the Lord' means 'at the Lord's hand'. 'Gall and wormwood' has become proverbial for something which is incurably bitter. Gall is the secretion of the liver; wormwood is the herb *absinthium* (called wormwood because

it was thought to cure intestinal worms, and used today to make the
French liqueur *absinthe*); both cause nausea.

6   **It is of the Lord's mercies that we are not consumed, because
his compassions fail not. They are new every morning: great
is thy faithfulness.**
(3:22–3)
Even while God punishes his people, he is still merciful: his
relationship with them is unchanged.

7   **It is good that a man should both hope and quietly wait for
the salvation of the Lord.**
(3:26)
The desolation of Jerusalem and the enslavement of the Jews in
Babylon both teach submission: that is, quiet obedience to God who
will reward them with deliverance.

8   **He giveth his cheek to him that smiteth him.**
(3:30)
This image of gentle submission was developed by Jesus in the
course of his Sermon on the Mount (see Matt 22).

9   **They that did feed delicately are desolate in the streets: they
that were brought up in scarlet embrace dunghills.**
(4:5)
In two memorable images, human wealth and pomp – both, in the
author's eyes, bad things because they seduce people from the true
worship of God – are cut down to size.

10 **Thou, O Lord, remainest for ever; thy throne from generation
to generation. Wherefore dost thou forget us for ever, and
forsake us so long time?**
(5:19–20)
In the anguish of their capture, the Israelites can find no comfort
even in the idea that God and his mercy are eternal. Why does he
take so long, in that case, to help them?

11 **Thou hast utterly rejected us; thou art very wroth against us.**
(5:22)
The Israelites answer their own question (see Lam 10), heaping
coals of fire on their own heads in the process.

Ezekiel

1 Above the firmament that was over their heads was the
likeness of a throne, as the appearance of a sapphire stone:
and upon the likeness of the throne was the likeness as the
appearance of a man above upon it. And I saw as the colour of
amber, as the appearance of fire round about within it, from
the appearance of his loins even upward, and from the
appearance of his loins even downward, I saw as it were the
appearance of fire, and it had brightness round about. As the
appearance of the bow that is in the cloud in the day of rain,
so was the appearance of the brightness round about. This
was the appearance of the likeness of the glory of the Lord.
(1:26–8)
Ezekiel is describing the apocalyptic vision which led him to begin
his prophetic mission. He is one of the very few Old Testament
visionaries to see God himself, and describes the experience in
language matched only by the words of Revelation or the mystical
pictures of William Blake. Some readers take his words as literal
descriptions, true in every detail; others take them as figurative, a
kind of poetic attempt to describe the indescribable; others again
have based all kinds of fantasies on them, for example that in this
passage Ezekiel was describing the arrival on earth of colonist-
astronauts from outer space.

2 And he said unto me, Son of man, I send thee to the children
of Israel, to a rebellious nation that hath rebelled against me:
they and their fathers have transgressed against me, even
unto this very day.
(2:3)
This verse gives the reason for the second kind of writing in
Ezekiel. His visions were matched, every time, by a feeling that the
Israelites were doomed unless they changed their ways, and he
preached sermons of denunciation and repentance as hard-hitting
as any by Jeremiah. 'Son of Man', familiar in the Christian context,
is simply here a formula meaning 'mortal'.

3 He said unto me, Son of man, cause thy belly to eat, and fill
thy bowels with this roll that I give thee. Then did I eat it; and
it was in my mouth as honey for sweetness.
(3:3)
God gives Ezekiel the roll (that is, book) of his prophecy. The
description of 'eating the roll' has been taken both literally,
concerning the papyrus scroll containing God's word, or
figuratively, absorbing God's word into the mind as the body takes
in nourishment. Our view of which is more likely colours our

reception of all similar uses of language in Ezekiel. The image of the roll's sweetness being like honey was memorably extended by the author of Revelation (see Rev 42).

4   **Thou art not sent to a people of a strange speech and of an hard language, but to the house of Israel.**
    (3:5)
    Ezekiel's mission from God should be an easy one, as he will be talking to fellow-members of the Chosen People.

5   **But the house of Israel will not hearken unto thee; for they will not hearken unto me: for all the house of Israel are impudent and hardhearted.**
    (3:7)
    The very fact that Ezekiel's future hearers are the Chosen People will make his task far harder than if they had been Gentiles. Foreigners, God has just remarked, would have been far readier to listen.

6   **Son of man, I have made thee a watchman unto the house of Israel: therefore hear the word at my mouth, and give them warning from me.**
    (3:17)
    From this verse originates the familiar idea of the prophet as a watchman of the Almighty, one whose roles are to mediate between God and mortals and to keep watch for God's coming to judge the mortal world.

7   **And I will make thy tongue cleave to the roof of thy mouth, that thou shalt be dumb.**
    (3:26)
    The temporary removal of some ordinary faculty often accompanied the acceptance of a prophetic vision. In Ezekiel's case it was dumbness; in St Paul's case, later, it was blindness. The idea was a powerful variant of the standard ancient view that all bodily changes, for good or bad, were caused by the presence of spirits or by the touch of God. In the case of prophets, the lifting of the affliction was a sign that the mission should begin.

8   **Thus saith the Lord God; Behold, I, even I, am against thee, and will execute judgments in the midst of thee in the sight of the nations.**
    (5:8)
    Ezekiel speaks God's denunciation of the Israelites. The phrase 'I, even I', was regularly used by rulers pronouncing sentence on evildoers; here it is linked to 'I am', the name of God, with chilling effect.

9   The king shall mourn, and the prince shall be clothed with
     desolation.
     (7:27)
     Not even high rank will be a protection against God's anger.

10   Son of man, hast thou seen what the ancients of the house of
     Israel do in the dark, every man in the chambers of his
     imagery? for they say, The Lord seeth us not; the Lord hath
     forsaken the earth.
     (8:12)
     Ezekiel has seen a vision of a roomful of idols, reeking with incense
     in the darkness, and in front of each of them an Israelite elder with a
     censer, leading prayers. The elders proceed to add blasphemy to
     idolatry, claiming that God has abandoned his own creation.

11   Behold, in the firmament that was above the head of the
     cherubims there appeared over them as it were a sapphire
     stone, as the appearance of the likeness of a throne. And he
     spake unto the man clothed with linen, and said, Go in
     between the wheels, even under the cherub, and fill thine
     hand with coals of fire from between the cherubims, and
     scatter them over the city. And he went in in my sight.
     (10:1–2)
     In Ezekiel's vision, God orders the destruction of Jerusalem.

12   Thus saith the Lord God; Although I have cast them far off
     among the heathen, and although I have scattered them
     among the countries, yet will I be to them as a little sanctuary
     in the countries where they shall come.
     (11:16)
     Despite the destruction of Jerusalem and the dispersion of the
     Chosen People, God still offers them a crumb of hope.

13   I will give them one heart, and I will put a new spirit within
     you; and I will take the stony heart out of their flesh, and will
     give them an heart of flesh.
     (11:19)
     The survivors of the Chosen People will be reborn in true
     obedience to God. The idea of a heart of stone was proverbial even
     in Ezekiel's time.

14   Son of man, eat thy bread with quaking, and drink thy water
     with trembling and with carefulness.
     (12:18)
     God tells Ezekiel, and by implication every member of the human
     race, to live each moment in anticipation of the Day of Judgment.

15   **Woe to the women that sew pillows to all armholes, and make kerchiefs upon the head of every stature to hunt souls!**
(13:18)
Ezekiel speaks God's denunciation of witches, in words as powerful as they are obscure.

16   **Son of man, What is the vine tree more than any tree, or than a branch which is among the trees of the forest?**
(15:2)
God asks Ezekiel why the Israelites should expect special treatment just because they are the Chosen People. The vine was a common symbol for Israel.

17   **Behold, when it was whole, it was meet for no work: how much less shall it be meet yet for any work, when the fire hath devoured it, and it is burned?**
(15:5)
God pronounces his terrible sentence on the vine, that is the Israelites, who have thought themselves immune from divine wrath because they are his Chosen People.

18   **Wherefore, O harlot, hear the word of the Lord: Thus saith the Lord God; Because thy filthiness was poured out, and thy nakedness discovered through thy whoredoms with thy lovers, and with all the idols of thy abominations, and by the blood of thy children, which thou didst give unto them; Behold, therefore I will gather all thy lovers, with whom thou hast taken pleasure, and all them that thou hast loved, with all them that thou hast hated; I will even gather them round about against thee, and will discover thy nakedness unto them, that they may see all thy nakedness.**
(16:35-7)
Ezekiel thunders God's sentence against Jerusalem, using a metaphor common to all the prophets, that the city was like a whore, with a smile and a welcome for every foreign god.

19   **As is the mother, so is her daughter.**
(16:44)
This proverb, says Ezekiel, has been proved true by the behaviour of the Israelites. Jerusalem is the daughter, and her mother is every other people, from Sodomites to Samaritans, who have ever practised idolatry.

20   **The fathers have eaten sour grapes, and the children's teeth are set on edge.**
(18:2)

The 'sour grapes' are idolatry, and Ezekiel uses the proverb to imply that Israel has been corrupt for generations. There is nothing here of the modern idea of 'sour grapes', derived from an Aesop fable: something scorned because it is unattainable. These Old Testament grapes, false religion, are all too accessible, but they are sour and therefore both sterile and unnourishing.

21   **When the wicked man turneth away from his wickedness that he hath committed, and doeth that which is lawful and right, he shall save his soul alive.**
(18:27)
The idea of repentance leading to forgiveness, so common in Old Testament moral teaching, is once again hammered home. The reason for its frequency is that it was unique: no other religion of the time described its deity in terms of a loving father, chastising but caring, stern but always ready to forgive.

22   **For the king of Babylon stood at the parting of the way, at the head of the two ways.**
(21:21)
In its context, this phrase refers to the king preparing to consult oracles and omens about how best to destroy Israel. Its proverbial meaning since, referring to people about to separate and go their different ways, has developed utterly apart from this Biblical origin, to the point where the basic meaning now seems obscure. Even more obscurely, the Hebrew word here translated 'parting' actually means 'mother'.

23   **Aholah played the harlot when she was mine; and she doted on her lovers, on the Assyrians her neighbours, Which were clothed with blue, captains and rulers, all of them desirable young men, horsemen riding upon horses.**
(23:5–6)
Ezekiel tells a parable about two sisters, both of whom turned to prostitution. The first sister, Aholah, stands for Samaria, and her 'desirable young men' are heathen gods.

24   **They lay with her, and they bruised the breasts of her virginity, and poured their whoredom upon her. Wherefore I have delivered her into the hand of her lovers, into the hand of the Assyrians, upon whom she doted.**
(23:8–9)
Aholah (that is, Samaria) is punished for her whoredom (that is idolatry). Ezekiel is referring to the Assyrian sacking of Samaria in 722 BC.

25 Thou shalt be filled with drunkenness and sorrow, with the cup of astonishment and desolation, with the cup of thy sister Samaria. Thou shalt even drink it and suck it out, and thou shalt break the sherds thereof, and pluck off thine own breasts: for I have spoken it, saith the Lord God.
(23:33-4)
Ezekiel brings to a point his parable about the two sisters (that is, nations) who practised whoredom (that is idolatry). The lesson is clear for the Israelites to learn.

26 Then all the princes of the sea shall come down from their thrones, and lay away their robes, and put off their broidered garments: they shall clothe themselves with trembling; they shall sit upon the ground, and shall tremble at every moment, and be astonished at thee.
(26:16)
Ezekiel is prophesying the destruction, one by one, of the heathen peoples who surround the Israelites. This verse describes the mourners horror-struck at the fate of Tyre.

27 Thy riches, and thy fairs, thy merchandise, thy mariners, and thy pilots, thy calkers, and the occupiers of thy merchandise, and all thy men of war, that are in thee, and in all thy company which is in the midst of thee, shall fall into the midst of the seas in the day of thy ruin.
(27:27)
Ezekiel itemizes the destruction of Tyre on the Day of Judgment.

28 I will send into her pestilence, and blood into her streets; and the wounded shall be judged in the midst of her by the sword upon her on every side; and they shall know that I am the Lord.
(28:23)
God foretells the punishment of Sidon for idolatry.

29 There shall be no more a pricking brier unto the house of Israel, nor any grieving thorn of all that are round about them, that despised them; and they shall know that I am the Lord God.
(28:24)
The destruction of Israel's enemies is proof that God is on the side of his Chosen People, and is an encouragement to them to give up their own idolatry.

30 Behold, I am against thee, Pharaoh king of Egypt, the great dragon that lieth in the midst of his rivers, which hath said,

My river is mine own, and I have made it for myself.
(29:3)
God denounces the Pharaoh of Egypt. 'Dragon' here means
crocodile. The Pharaohs' crime was that they insisted on being
worshipped as gods.

31   Ye eat the fat, and ye clothe you with the wool, ye kill them
that are fed: but ye feed not the flock.
(34:3)
Ezekiel denounces the corrupt leaders of Israel.

32   The hand of the Lord was upon me, and carried me out in the
spirit of the Lord, and set me down in the midst of the valley
which was full of bones.
(37:1)
In a vision, God takes Ezekiel to the desolation which is all that is
left of Jerusalem, a dry desert full of skeletons. The phrase 'valley of
dry bones' became proverbial for any place devoid of the spark of
inspiration: it was scornfully applied by Trollope, for example, to
the senior common rooms of Oxbridge colleges, and by Anthony
Powell to the arid society of post-second-world-war Britain.

33   He said unto me, Son of man, can these bones live? And I
answered, O Lord God, thou knowest.
(37:3)
The implication is that God can do anything, even create life from
death.

34   He said unto me, Prophesy upon these bones, and say unto
them, O ye dry bones, hear the word of the Lord.
(37:4)
God sends Ezekiel to arouse the skeletons, to tell them that he will
put flesh on them and put breath in them to demonstrate his power.

35   So I prophesied as I was commanded: and as I prophesied,
there was a noise, and behold a shaking, and the bones came
together, bone to his bone.
(37:7)
God's word, spoken by Ezekiel to the skeletons in the valley of dry
bones which is all that is left of Jerusalem, works a miracle.

36   Then he said unto me, Son of man, these bones are the whole
house of Israel: behold, they say, Our bones are dried, and
our hope is lost: we are cut off for our parts. Therefore
prophesy and say unto them, Thus saith the Lord God;
Behold, O my people, I will open your graves, and cause you

to come up out of your graves, and bring you into the land of
Israel.
(37:11–12)
Ezekiel explains the vision of the valley of bones.

37   Son of man, set thy face against Gog, the land of Magog, the
chief prince of Meshech and Tubal, and prophesy against
him.
(38:2)
Gog, prince of Magog, is here identified as a specific person.
('Land' here means 'ruler'. Queen Elizabeth I used similarly to call
herself 'England'.) In later Biblical times, Gog and Magog (the
latter now a person not a place) stood for all the enemies of God's
people; in British legend Gogmagog (now a single person) was one
of the fiercest of all the giants.

38   The glory of the God of Israel came from the way of the east:
and his voice was like a noise of many waters: and the earth
shined with his glory.
(43:2)
God appears to Ezekiel in glory, to show that he will lead his chosen
people from exile into the New Jerusalem.

39   It shall come to pass, that every thing that liveth, which
moveth, whithersoever the rivers shall come, shall live: and
there shall be a very great multitude of fish, because these
waters shall come thither: for they shall be healed; and every
thing shall live whither the river cometh.
(47:9)
Ezekiel prophesies that godliness will flow from the New Jerusalem
like rivers of water, teeming with life, bringing the parched land to
life and making the desert of the soul burst into blossom.

Daniel

1   Children in whom was no blemish, but well favoured, and
skilful in all wisdom, and cunning in knowledge, and
understanding science, and such as had ability in them to
stand in the king's palace, and whom they might teach the
learning and the tongue of the Chaldeans.
(1:4)
This is the description of a group taken from the Jewish exiles in
Babylon, selected to be trained as royal courtiers and priests of the
Babylonian religion. Daniel was one of them; three of his
companions were Shadrach, Meshach and Abednego; none of them
was willing to give up the Jewish belief and custom.

2   **O king, live for ever.**
       (2:4)
       This phrase was used by every Babylonian subject before every
       remark made to the king. Daniel and the other Jews would have
       nothing to do with it because it suggested that a mortal ruler might
       share immortality – which belonged to God alone.

3   **Blessed be the name of God for ever and ever: for wisdom**
       and might are his: And he changeth the times and the
       seasons: he removeth kings, and setteth up kings: he giveth
       wisdom unto the wise, and knowledge to them that know
       understanding: He revealeth the deep and secret things: he
       knoweth what is in the darkness, and the light dwelleth with
       him.
       (2:20–2)
       Daniel praises God. His words refer to a specific piece of wisdom,
       God's revealing of a prophetic dream; they have, however, been
       taken more generally ever since.

4   **This image's head was of fine gold, his breast and his arms of**
       silver, his belly and his thighs of brass, His legs of iron, his
       feet part of iron and part of clay.
       (2:32–3)
       King Nebuchadnezzar of Babylon has dreamed of a mysterious,
       awesome statue, and none of his wise men can explain the dream.
       The problem is that a sculpture so solidly made should have feet of
       perishable materials, quite apart from the fact that iron and clay
       cannot be mixed at all. 'Feet of clay', meaning the human
       weaknesses which destroy a person's pretensions to grandeur,
       became proverbial.

5   **Then an herald cried aloud, To you it is commanded, O**
       people, nations, and languages, That at what time ye hear the
       sound of the cornet, flute, harp, sackbut, psaltery, dulcimer,
       and all kinds of musick, ye fall down and worship the golden
       image that Nebuchadnezzar the king hath set up: And whoso
       falleth not down and worshippeth shall the same hour be cast
       into the midst of a burning fiery furnace.
       (3:4–6)
       King Nebuchadnezzar has made a huge golden statue – the Bible
       gives its dimensions as 60 cubits or 90ft (25 m) high and 6 cubits or
       9ft (2.5 m) wide; twice as large as the gold-and-ivory statue of Zeus
       at Olympia, for centuries one of the Seven Wonders of the World.
       Now he orders his people, including those of Jewish origin, to
       worship it as a god.

6   **Who is that God that shall deliver you out of my hands?**
    (3:15)
    Shadrach, Meshach and Abednego have refused to bow down to
    King Nebuchadnezzar's golden statue, and claim that their God
    will save them from punishment in the burning fiery furnace.
    Nebuchadnezzar scornfully questions them.

7   **Lo, I see four men loose, walking in the midst of the fire, and**
    they have no hurt; and the form of the fourth is like the Son of
    God.
    (3:25)
    King Nebuchadnezzar has had Shadrach, Meshach and Abednego
    thrown into a burning fiery furnace, and is now astounded by what
    he sees. 'Son of God' here means 'servant of god', that is an angel.

8   **The same hour was the thing fulfilled upon Nebuchadnezzar:**
    and he was driven from men, and did eat grass as oxen, and
    his body was wet with the dew of heaven, till his hairs were
    grown like eagles' feathers, and his nails like birds' claws.
    (4:33)
    God punishes King Nebuchadnezzar for idolatry. The behaviour
    was that of a madman, and its cure was to abandon idols and
    worship God alone.

9   **Belshazzar the king made a great feast to a thousand of his**
    lords, and drank wine before the thousand.
    (5:1)
    King Belshazzar does not follow his father Nebuchadnezzar's
    conversion to the Jewish God, but persists in idolatry – for which
    drinking wine is a standard Old Testament metaphor.

10 **Then they brought the golden vessels that were taken out of**
    the temple of the house of God which was at Jerusalem; and
    the king, and his princes, his wives, and his concubines,
    drank in them.
    (5:3)
    Belshazzar adds sacrilege to his idolatry. Apart from anything else,
    no mortal lips were allowed to touch the sacred vessels of the Jewish
    temple.

11 **They drank wine, and praised the gods of gold, and of silver,**
    of brass, of iron, of wood, and of stone.
    (5:4)
    Babylonian idolatry consists not merely in worshipping dozens of
    gods instead of the one true God, but in worshipping them in the
    form of lumps of metal, wood and stone, something abhorred by the

Jews since the days of the First Commandment and the Golden Calf.

12   In the same hour came forth fingers of a man's hand, and wrote over against the candlestick upon the plaister of the wall of the king's palace: and the king saw the part of the hand that wrote.
(5:5)
God sends King Belshazzar a warning. This event is the origin of the proverbial expression 'the writing on the wall', meaning a portent of unavoidable disaster.

13   And this is the writing that was written, MENE, MENE, TEKEL, UPHARSIN.
(5:25)
The words are all the names of weights: 'Mene' is a *mina*, 'tekel' a *shekel* and 'upharsin' a half-*shekel*.

14   Thou art weighed in the balances, and art found wanting.
(5:27)
Daniel interprets the meaning of the writing on the wall. 'Thou' is the idolatrous King Belshazzar; the measurer is God.

15   Then said these men, We shall not find any occasion against this Daniel, except we find it against him concerning the law of his God.
(6:5)
The officials of King Darius, jealous of Daniel's power and authority, have been trying to find some flaw in his character so that they can pull him down. Their only hope, they say, is in his devout religious observance, the 'law of his God'. The idea of 'a Daniel' (or, in Shylock's words in Shakespeare's *Merchant of Venice*, 'a Daniel come to judgment'), meaning someone incorruptible and pure, derives from this verse.

16   Then the king commanded, and they brought Daniel, and cast him into the den of lions. Now the king spake and said unto Daniel, Thy God whom thou servest continually, he will deliver thee.
(6:16)
Daniel is punished for breaking a law of King Darius, that no favours are to be asked of anyone but the king. (Daniel has broken it by praying three times a day to God.) The proverbial phrase 'Daniel in the lions' den', meaning an innocent person surrounded by implacable and apparently deadly adversaries, comes from this story.

17   **Four great beasts came up from the sea, diverse one from another.**
      (7:3)
      This passage begins an account of Daniel's prophetic vision of the future. The four beasts symbolize four empires – Babylonian, Syrian, Egyptian and Greek – all of which will give way in the end to the kingdom of God. The ancient Hebrews regarded the sea as the home of all uncleanness, and its creatures all as evil or pestilential.

18   **The Ancient of days did sit, whose garment was white as snow, and the hair of his head like the pure wool: his throne was like the fiery flame, and his wheels as burning fire.**
      (7:9)
      Daniel's vision sees God in familiar Old Testament terms, as a patriarch sitting on a fiery throne. His images are meant symbolically, but they have since been taken literally, and result in the idea many people have of God as an old man with a long white beard: the figure, for example, in William Blake's illustrations to the Book of Job.

19   **I saw in the night visions, and, behold, one like the Son of man came with the clouds of heaven, and came to the Ancient of days, and they brought him near before him. And there was given him dominion, and glory, and a kingdom, that all people, nations, and languages, should serve him: his dominion is an everlasting dominion, which shall not pass away, and his kingdom that which shall not be destroyed.**
      (7:13–14)
      Daniel's vision of the Day of Judgment continues. These verses were later taken as a prophecy of the coming of Christ: the phrase 'Son of Man' was how Jesus frequently described himself.

20   **Many of them that sleep in the dust of the earth shall awake, some to everlasting life, and some to shame and everlasting contempt. And they that be wise shall shine as the brightness of the firmament; and they that turn many to righteousness as the stars for ever and ever.**
      (12:2–3)
      Daniel prophesies the Day of Judgment. No previous Old Testament prophet ever mentioned resurrection – hence the importance of these verses in the eyes of early Christians.

Hosea

1   **I gave her corn, and wine, and oil, and multiplied her silver and gold, which they prepared for Baal.**
(2:8)
Through Hosea, God accuses Israel of idolatry. Corn, wine and oil were the offerings traditionally made to heathen idols.

2   **They have sown the wind, and they shall reap the whirlwind.**
(8:7)
Hosea prophesies the destruction of Samaria as a punishment for idolatry. The metaphor, one of the most original and powerful in the whole Bible, seems to be Hosea's own and not a proverb – but its power very soon made it proverbial, referring to wrongdoers whose actions bring them completely unforeseen disaster.

3   **Ye have plowed wickedness, ye have reaped iniquity; ye have eaten the fruit of lies.**
(10:13)
Hosea develops further his metaphor that idolatry is false farming. Jesus extended the idea in his parable of the sower and the seed (see Matt 90).

4   **I drew them with cords of a man, with bands of love: and I was to them as they that take off the yoke on their jaws, and I laid meat unto them.**
(11:4)
God describes his fatherly kindness to the Israelites – which they have ungratefully repaid with idolatry. Hosea's images are to do with ploughing: the bands and cords are the harness which links the ploughman and the beast which pulls the plough. 'Yoke on their jaws' means the bit rather than the wooden yoke itself; 'meat' here (since draught-animals ate corn and straw, not flesh) simply means food. Out of the whole bizarre verse, 'bands of love' passed most readily into the language, referring in a concrete way to the affection which unites parents and children.

5   **O Israel, thou hast destroyed thyself; but in me is thine help.**
(13:9)
God speaks to his people through Hosea. Despite the Israelites' self-lacerating idolatry, they can still rely on God's mercy, if only they turn to him.

6   **I will ransom them from the power of the grave; I will redeem them from death: O death, I will be thy plagues; O grave, I will be thy destruction.**
(13:14)

Death and the grave here, to Hosea's audience, would have meant
the destructive results of idolatry. In early Christian times, however,
the verse was taken to refer to the Day of Judgment.

7   **An east wind shall come, the wind of the Lord shall come up
      from the wilderness.**
      (13:15)
      The east wind was notoriously hot and parching, disastrous to
      crops. Hosea is prophesying the anger of God against idolaters; the
      phrase has been taken since to refer to the whirlwind of God on the
      Day of Judgment.

Joel

1   **That which the palmerworm hath left hath the locust eaten.**
      (1:4)
      Joel is warning the Israelites of the power of God's anger, which he
      compares to a plague of locusts. 'Palmerworm' is an Elizabethan
      word for caterpillar.

2   **Awake, ye drunkards, and weep; and howl, all ye drinkers of
      wine, because of the new wine; for it is cut off from your
      mouth.**
      (1:5)
      The drunkards are idolators and the new wine they drink is idolatry.

3   **A fire devoureth before them; and behind them a flame
      burneth: the land is as the garden of Eden before them, and
      behind them a desolate wilderness; yea, and nothing shall
      escape them.**
      (2:3)
      Joel continues his vision of the Day of Judgment.

4   **I will restore to you the years that the locust hath eaten, the
      cankerworm, and the caterpiller, and the palmerworm, my
      great army which I sent among you. And ye shall eat in plenty,
      and be satisfied, and praise the name of the Lord your God.**
      (2:25-6)
      God promises to help his people despite their idolatry and its
      terrible punishment. The phrase 'the locust years' became
      proverbial for times of natural disaster, especially crop failure.

5   And it shall come to pass afterward, that I will pour out my
     spirit upon all flesh; and your sons and your daughters shall
     prophesy, your old men shall dream dreams, your young men
     shall see visions.
     (2:28)
     By the Day of Judgment, the blindness of idolatry will be stripped
     away, and every human being will see God truly, face to face.

6   I will shew wonders in the heavens and in the earth, blood,
     and fire, and pillars of smoke. The sun shall be turned into
     darkness, and the moon into blood, before the great and the
     terrible day of the Lord come. And it shall come to pass, that
     whosoever shall call on the name of the Lord shall be
     delivered.
     (2:30–2)
     Joel continues to develop his theme that redemption, even on the
     Day of Judgment, can only follow an apocalyptic purification of the
     earth and everything in it.

7   Beat your plowshares into swords, and your pruninghooks
     into spears: let the weak say, I am strong.
     (3:10)
     God advises the idolatrous Gentiles to prepare for war on the Day
     of Judgment. Their effort is a direct reversal of what was
     recommended to true believers (see Isa 6) and it is doomed.

8   Multitudes, multitudes in the valley of decision: for the day of
     the Lord is near in the valley of decision.
     (3:14)
     The idolators gather for war on the Day of Judgment. 'Valley of
     decision' became proverbial.

9   And it shall come to pass in that day, that the mountains shall
     drop down new wine, and the hills shall flow with milk, and
     all the rivers of Judah shall flow with waters, and a fountain
     shall come forth of the house of the Lord, and shall water the
     valley of Shittim.
     (3:18)
     In a traditional metaphor, of the blossoming of the desert, Joel
     promises God's favour to his Chosen People on the Day of
     Judgment. The valley of Shittim is a desert area north-east of the
     Dead Sea.

Amos

1 Can two walk together, except they be agreed?
(3:3)
Amos is reminding the Israelites that there are two parties to any
agreement, even to the covenant between them and God.

2 Shall a trumpet be blown in the city, and the people not be
afraid? shall there be evil in a city, and the Lord hath not done
it?
(3:6)
Every disaster which comes on the Israelites, every enemy attack, is
God's punishment because they have broken their covenant with
him.

3 I have overthrown some of you, as God overthrew Sodom and
Gomorrah, and ye were as a firebrand plucked out of the
burning: yet have ye not returned unto me, saith the Lord.
(4:11)
God has saved the Israelites time and time again, and still they turn
from him to idolatry.

4 Prepare to meet thy God, O Israel. For, lo, he that formeth
the mountains, and createth the wind, and declareth unto
man what is his thought, that maketh the morning darkness,
and treadeth upon the high places of the earth, The Lord,
The God of hosts, is his name.
(4:12–14)
God warns the Israelites that even they will not escape examination
on the Day of Judgment.

5 Woe unto you that desire the day of the Lord! to what end is it
for you? the day of the Lord is darkness, and not light.
(5:18)
It is no use looking smugly forward to the Day of Judgment,
confident in one's own 'good life'; before there is joy there will be
sorrow, and no one will escape.

6 Thus he shewed me: and, behold, the Lord stood upon a wall
made by a plumbline, with a plumbline in his hand. And the
Lord said unto me, Amos, what seest thou? And I said, A
plumbline. Then said the Lord, Behold, I will set a plumbline
in the midst of my people Israel: I will not again pass by them
any more.
(7:7–8)

Amos has asked God how the Israelites can escape punishment, and is granted this vision in reply. The plumbline is God's law, and strict adherence to it will produce safety, as strict following of the plumbline guarantees a straight, strong wall.

7   **Though they dig into hell, thence shall mine hand take them; though they climb up to heaven, thence will I bring them down.**
(9:2)
There will be no hiding places for evildoers on the Day of Judgment.

8   **I will sift the house of Israel among all nations, like as corn is sifted in a sieve, yet shall not the least grain fall upon the earth.**
(9:9)
God's people will be separated from nonbelievers on the Day of Judgment: they will be punished but they will not be destroyed.

Obadiah

1   **Though thou exalt thyself as the eagle, and though thou set thy nest among the stars, thence will I bring thee down, saith the Lord.**
(1:4)
Obadiah's slender book (one chapter, twenty-one verses altogether) is a denunciation of the Edomites, a desert people who thought themselves impregnable in their mountain city (Petra, carved in the rocks south-east of the Dead Sea). They took advantage of the Babylonian sacking of Jerusalem in 587 BC to attack Judah – and hence this book. 'Nest among the stars' refers to the Edomites' mountain stronghold.

2   **For the day of the Lord is near upon all the heathen: as thou hast done, it shall be done unto thee: thy reward shall return upon thine own head.**
(1:15)
The Edomites will be swept away on the Day of Judgment, together with all Israel's other idolatrous persecutors. The idea that by evil-doing you chose to run the risk of punishment, that you gambled with fate, was enshrined in the proverb 'on your own head be it', even in Obadiah's time.

Jonah

1   **And they said every one to his fellow, Come, and let us cast lots, that we may know for whose cause this evil is upon us. So they cast lots, and the lot fell upon Jonah.**
(1:7)
Jonah, ordered by God to denounce the powerful rulers of Nineveh, is trying to hide. He has taken ship to Tarshish (in Spain), but it is storm-tossed and foundering. The phrase 'a Jonah', meaning a person believed to bring bad luck, derives from this story.

2   **Now the Lord had prepared a great fish to swallow up Jonah. And Jonah was in the belly of the fish three days and three nights.**
(1:17)
God spares Jonah's life, but is not reluctant to make him look ridiculous.

3   **Then Jonah prayed unto the Lord his God out of the fish's belly. And said, I cried by reason of mine affliction unto the Lord, and he heard me; out of the belly of hell cried I, and thou heardest my voice.**
(2:1–2)
'Out of the belly of hell' became proverbial.

4   **But I will sacrifice unto thee with the voice of thanksgiving; I will pay that that I have vowed. Salvation is of the Lord.**
(2:9)
Saved from the whale, Jonah promises obedience to God.

Micah

1   **Behold, the Lord cometh forth out of his place, and will come down, and tread upon the high places of the earth. And the mountains shall be molten under him, and the valleys shall be cleft, as wax before the fire, and as the waters that are poured down a steep place.**
(1:3–4)
Micah prophesies the Messiah's coming in terms of God striding from hilltop to hilltop, a king coming to judge his people.

2   **Woe to them that devise iniquity, and work evil upon their beds!**
(2:1)

The image of people lying in bed in the dark, plotting wickedness, is common in Old Testament writing. The prophets contrasted night, the time of devils and idols, with the bright daylight of God in which no evil could be hidden.

3   **They shall sit every man under his vine and under his fig tree; and none shall make them afraid: for the mouth of the Lord of hosts hath spoken it.**
(4:4)
God's coming will scatter Israel's enemies and bring peace and prosperity – here depicted in a standard Old Testament moral image – to his Chosen People.

4   **But thou, Bethlehem Ephratah, though thou be little among the thousands of Judah, yet out of thee shall he come forth unto me that is to be ruler in Israel; whose goings forth have been from of old, from everlasting.**
(5:2)
Micah prophesies the birth of the Messiah. Bethlehem, at the time of this prophecy, was so obscure a place that Micah adds the name of its surrounding district, Ephratah, to make it clear where he means.

5   **Will the Lord be pleased with thousands of rams, or with ten thousands of rivers of oil? shall I give my firstborn for my transgression, the fruit of my body for the sin of my soul? He hath shewed thee, O man, what is good; and what doth the Lord require of thee, but to do justly, and to love mercy, and to walk humbly with thy God?**
(6:7–8)
The frightened sinner asks what he or she must give God to be saved; Micah answers.

Nahum

1   **The shield of his mighty men is made red, the valiant men are in scarlet: the chariots shall be with flaming torches in the day of his preparation, and the fir trees shall be terribly shaken.**
(2:3)
Nahum is prophesying the fall of Nineveh, capital of the Assyrian empire. His words have, however, been taken as a more general prophecy of the Day of Judgment.

2   **The chariots shall rage in the streets, they shall justle one against another in the broad ways: they shall seem like torches, they shall run like the lightnings.**
(2:4)
Nahum's vision of the siege of Nineveh continues.

3   **Woe to the bloody city! it is all full of lies and robbery.**
(3:1)
Originally cried against Nineveh, these words were used by Cromwell's hell-fire preachers to denounce royalist London.

4   **Thy crowned are as the locusts, and thy captains as the great grasshoppers, which camp in the hedges in the cold day, but when the sun ariseth they flee away, and their place is not known where they are.**
(3:17)
Nahum continues to fulminate against the people of Nineveh. 'Cold day' means the chill before dawn; the contrast is between the darkness of idolatry and the bright daylight brought by the coming of God.

Habakkuk

1   **The Lord answered me, and said, Write the vision, and make it plain upon tables, that he may run that readeth it.**
(2:2)
Habakkuk has asked God how long evil is to remain in the world. 'Tables' are stone tablets, like those which Moses once brought down from Sinai. The phrase 'he may run that readeth it' has been widely imitated, notably in nineteenth-century hymns, but never satisfactorily explained. 'He may run' perhaps means no more than 'the man or woman in the street', someone going about their daily affairs.

2   **I will rejoice in the Lord, I will joy in the God of my salvation.**
(3:18)
This verse, from a hymn of praise to God, is like that of the Virgin Mary when Gabriel told her that she would conceive (see Luke 6).

Zephaniah

1   Hold thy peace at the presence of the Lord God: for the day of
the Lord is at hand: for the Lord hath prepared a sacrifice, he
hath bid his guests.
(1:7)
Zephaniah prophesies the coming of the Day of Judgment.

2   Their blood shall be poured out as dust, and their flesh as the
dung.
(1:17)
There will be no comfort for the wicked on the Day of Judgment.

3   Seek ye the Lord, all ye meek of the earth, which have
wrought his judgment; seek righteousness, seek meekness: it
may be ye shall be hid in the day of the Lord's anger.
(2:3)
Zephaniah preaches about the only way to avoid punishment on the
Day of Judgment – and even so he makes no promises.

Haggai

1   Then came the word of the Lord by Haggai the prophet,
saying, Is it time for you, O ye, to dwell in your cieled houses,
and this house lie waste? Now therefore thus saith the Lord of
hosts; Consider your ways. Ye have sown much, and bring in
little; ye eat, but ye have not enough; ye drink, but ye are not
filled with drink; ye clothe you, but there is none warm; and
he that earneth wages earneth wages to put it into a bag with
holes.
(1:3–6)
Haggai's prophecy dates from the Jews' return from exile in
Babylon. They were so relieved to be home that they spent years
restoring their farms and reorganizing their family life, without
taking time to rebuild God's house, the temple in Jerusalem. The
purpose of Haggai's book was to remind them of this duty, and he
did so in fine, vigorous language like this passage, expanding the
traditional Biblical message that spiritual concerns should outweigh
domestic ones, that 'man does not live by bread alone'. 'Cieled'
means panelled or wainscoted – a sign of domestic prosperity in
days when most farm buildings were wattle-and-daub or wooden
frames filled with rough plaster.

2　The glory of this latter house shall be greater than of the former, saith the Lord of hosts: and in this place will I give peace, saith the Lord of hosts.
(2:9)
Haggai is talking of the temple which he wants to see rebuilt. The verse has been used more generally, however, of the place where the blessed will be united with God after the Last Judgment; the 'latter house' is the place for the communion of all the saints.

Zechariah

1　Be ye not as your fathers, unto whom the former prophets have cried, saying, Thus saith the Lord of hosts; Turn ye now from your evil ways, and from your evil doings: but they did not hear, nor hearken unto me, saith the Lord. Your fathers, where are they? and the prophets, do they live for ever?
(1:4–5)
Zechariah begins his call to the people to repent with a splendid dismissal of all his own predecessors and the congregation whose hearts they failed to change.

2　I lifted up mine eyes again, and looked, and behold a man with a measuring line in his hand. Then said I, Whither goest thou? And he said unto me, To measure Jerusalem, to see what is the breadth thereof, and what is the length thereof.
(2:1–2)
These verses repeat a traditional Old Testament metaphor, that God's word is a measure, a straightedge or plumbline, against which all human constructions should be judged. The metaphor is particularly apposite here, as Zechariah's mission, like Haggai's, was to persuade the Israelites to rebuild the temple in Jerusalem destroyed by the Babylonians.

3　Then I turned, and lifted up mine eyes, and looked, and behold a flying roll.
(5:1)
Zechariah's vision is of an enormous scroll of paper 31 yds (10m) long, 15 yds (5m) wide. It moves through the sky above the earth, and hovers above sinners' heads. On it is written God's curse on sin. The roll's presence engulfs the sinner, his house and his family in flames.

4　And I turned, and lifted up mine eyes, and looked, and, behold, there came four chariots out from between two mountains; and the mountains were mountains of brass. In

the first chariot were red horses; and in the second chariot
black horses; And in the third chariot white horses; and in the
fourth chariot grisled and bay horses.
(6:1–3)
The four chariots carry God's angels, riding through the world and
reporting on humankind before the Day of Judgment. The idea
foreshadows, but is not so devasting as, the vision of the Four
Horsemen of the Apocalypse in Revelation. 'Grisled' means
piebald; 'in' the chariots means yoked to them.

5   Rejoice greatly, O daughter of Zion; shout, O daughter of
      Jerusalem: behold, thy King cometh unto thee: he is just, and
      having salvation; lowly, and riding upon an ass, and upon a
      colt the foal of an ass.
      (9:9)
      Zechariah prophesies the entry of the Messiah into Jerusalem. This
      was one of the many Old Testament prophecies fulfilled by Jesus
      (see Matt 120).

6   Turn you to the strong hold, ye prisoners of hope.
      (9:12)
      'Prisoners of hope' later became proverbial, with a changed
      meaning: those imprisoned by their own hopes, forever yearning for
      the unattainable. Zechariah means prisoners who *have* hope; he is
      referring to the Chosen People, persecuted and imprisoned during
      their lives on earth, but still warmed with hope of deliverance on the
      Day of Judgment.

7   Howl, fir tree; for the cedar is fallen; because the mighty are
      spoiled: howl, O ye oaks of Bashan; for the forest of the
      vintage is come down.
      (11:2)
      The 'pathetic fallacy', a literary device in which rocks, plants, seas
      and clouds are given human emotions, is seldom better used in the
      Old Testament than here. Zechariah imagines the forest trees
      bewailing the destruction of their kinsfolk, the cedars of Lebanon
      and oaks of Bashan, on the Day of Judgment. The forests here
      stand for the states themselves, whose wealth they represented. The
      'forest of the vintage' means trees of great age and rare
      magnificence.

8   I said unto them, If ye think good, give me my price; and if
      not, forbear. So they weighed for my price thirty pieces of
      silver.
      (11:12)

God himself is speaking. Thirty pieces of silver was the price of a slave: Zechariah's meaning here is that the Israelites are so underrating the covenant, that they treat God no better than the lowest member of the household.

9 **And one shall say unto him, What are these wounds in thine hands? Then he shall answer, Those with which I was wounded in the house of my friends.**
(13:6)
At the second coming, Zechariah has been saying, all the prophets will be confounded. The man described in this verse, however, will be vindicated, for he is not a professional prophet but an ordinary workman. Though Zechariah was probably doing no more than preaching against professional holy men who never cut their hands by doing an honest day's work in their lives, the verse has not unnaturally been taken by Christians as a specific reference to Jesus' stigmata, despite the problems this causes in explaining what it means here in this context.

10 **And it shall be in that day, that living waters shall go out from Jerusalem; half of them toward the former sea, and half of them toward the hinder sea: in summer and in winter shall it be. And the Lord shall be king over all the earth: in that day shall there be one Lord, and his name one.**
(14:8-9)
Zechariah rounds off his vision of the day of the coming of the Messiah with a message of resounding hope.

Malachi

1 **For from the rising of the sun even unto the going down of the same my name shall be great among the Gentiles; and in every place incense shall be offered unto my name, and a pure offering: for my name shall be great among the heathen, saith the Lord of hosts.**
(1:11)
In the eighty years since Haggai and Zechariah urged the rebuilding of the temple and a state of constant readiness for the coming of the Messiah, the Chosen People have become restless and cynical. Malachi's mission was to restore their zeal for God. Here he quotes from earlier sacred writings, running together ideas from the Psalms and the prophecy of Isaiah to remind the people that although the day of the Second Coming is later than they expected, it is sure to dawn.

2   Behold, I will send my messenger, and he shall prepare the
     way before me: and the Lord, whom ye seek, shall suddenly
     come to his temple, even the messenger of the covenant,
     whom ye delight in.
     (3:1)
     Malachi prophesies the coming of the Messiah. The verse has been
     taken to refer first to John the Baptist and then to Christ, but the
     'messenger' and the 'messenger of the covenant' are here one
     person, the Messiah himself.

3   But who may abide the day of his coming? and who shall
     stand when he appeareth? for he is like a refiner's fire, and
     like fullers' soap: And he shall sit as a refiner and purifier of
     silver: and he shall purify the sons of Levi, and purge them as
     gold and silver, that they may offer unto the Lord an offering
     in righteousness.
     (3:2-3)
     Malachi reminds the people, and especially the 'sons of Levi',
     professional priests, that the Second Coming will be a time of
     judgment as well as of joy.

4   But unto you that fear my name shall the Sun of
     righteousness arise with healing in his wings.
     (4:2)
     The Messiah is envisaged as the Sun, rising to drive the darkness of
     unbelief from the world, and as a dove of peace (a bird traditionally
     associated with healing).

APOCRYPHA

I Esdras

1   Let every one of us speak a sentence: he that shall overcome, and whose sentence shall seem wiser than the others, unto him shall the king Darius give great gifts, and great things in token of victory: As, to be clothed in purple, to drink in gold, and to sleep upon gold, and a chariot with bridles of gold, and an headtire of fine linen, and a chain about his neck.
(3:5–6)
Three young men, Jewish exiles at the court of King Darius of Persia, decide to hold a contest in wisdom, by writing wise remarks on pieces of paper which they then put under the king's pillow for him to choose from. This story dates from a time (early fifth century BC) when this kind of writing was used for transmitting spells; the story therefore has overtones not only of a contest or lottery, but of magic.

2   The first wrote, Wine is the strongest. The second wrote, The king is strongest. The third wrote, Women are strongest: but above all things Truth beareth away the victory.
(3:10–12)
These are the contents of the three pieces of paper put under King Darius' pillow. The question they are all answering – a favourite in such contests even down to medieval times – is 'What is the strongest force on earth?'

3   And he said thus, O ye men, how exceeding strong is wine! it causeth all men to err that drink it.
(3:18)
When King Darius wakes up and finds the three pieces of paper put under his pillow, he calls their authors to council and asks each in turn to explain what he wrote. The first young man is here defending the view 'Wine is the strongest.'

4   And when they are in their cups, they forget their love both to friends and brethren, and a little after draw out swords: But when they are from the wine, they remember not what they have done.
(3:22–3)

The first of the young men continues to defend his view that wine is the strongest force on earth. The phrase 'in their cups', which here makes one of its earliest appearances in English, is a translation of a common idiom in both Greek and Latin, 'among the wine-cups', meaning at the end of a banquet when the eating was over and the conversation, and serious drinking, had begun.

5   **O ye men, do not men excel in strength, that bear rule over sea and land, and all things in them?**
(4:2)
The second of the three young men defends the view that kings are the strongest force on earth.

6   **And yet he is but one man: if he command to kill, they kill; if he command to spare, they spare; If he command to smite, they smite; if he command to make desolate, they make desolate; if he command to build, they build; If he command to cut down, they cut down; if he command to plant, they plant.**
(4:7–9)
The second young man continues to expound the power of a king.

7   **Yea, and if men have gathered together gold and silver, or any other goodly thing, do they not love a woman which is comely in favour and beauty? And letting all those things go, do they not gape, and even with open mouth fix their eyes fast on her; and have not all men more desire unto her than unto silver or gold, or any goodly thing whatsoever?**
(4:18–19)
The third young man, Zerobabel, says that women are the strongest force on earth.

8   **Do ye not labour and toil, and give and bring all to the woman? Yea, a man taketh his sword, and goeth his way to rob and to steal, to sail upon the sea and upon rivers; And looketh upon a lion, and goeth in the darkness; and when he hath stolen, spoiled, and robbed, he bringeth it to his love.**
(4:22–4)
Zerobabel continues to prove the power of women over men.

9   **Great is the earth, high is the heaven, swift is the sun in his course, for he compasseth the heavens round about, and fetcheth his course again to his own place in one day. Is he not great that maketh these things? therefore great is the truth, and stronger than all things.**
(4:34–5)

From defending women, Zerobabel suddenly switches to an assertion that 'truth' (that is, belief in God) is the strongest power on earth.

10   With her there is no accepting of persons or rewards; but she doeth the things that are just, and refraineth from all unjust and wicked things; and all men do well like of her works. Neither in her judgment is any unrighteousness; and she is the strength, kingdom, power, and majesty, of all ages. Blessed be the God of truth.
(4:39–40)
Zerobabel concludes his praise of truth, that is true religion. The original word for 'truth' was feminine; hence 'her' and 'she' in this translation.

11   Great is Truth, and mighty above all things.
(4:41)
Zerobabel's hearers, convinced by his arguments, shout their agreement. In the time of the Crusaders, the Latin form of this phrase (*Magna est veritas, et praevalet*, or MVP) was often used as a motto on flags and shields.

12   From thee cometh victory, from thee cometh wisdom, and thine is the glory, and I am thy servant. Blessed art thou, who hast given me wisdom: for to thee I give thanks, O Lord of our fathers.
(4:59–60)
Zerobabel, having won the contest and been rewarded by being allowed to lead his people from exile and rebuild the temple in Jerusalem, praises God.

13   By their secret plots, and popular persuasions and commotions, they hindered the finishing of the building all the time that king Cyrus lived.
(5:73)
The heathen of the area around Jerusalem, annoyed that the Israelites have returned from exile, offer at first to help them rebuild the temple, and then, when the offer is refused, hinder the work by both overt and covert attacks. 'Popular persuasions and commotions' was quoted, by Milton among others, to describe plots and counterplots at the time of the English Civil War.

14   Mightest not thou be angry with us to destroy us, till thou hadst left us neither root, seed, nor name?
(8:88)

Asked to find a reason why God is preventing the rebuilding of the temple, Esdras (the same man as the Old Testament Ezra) says it is because the Israelites, and specifically the Levites, or priests, have married idolaters. If this is so, if God's covenant has been broken, why should God not be angry?

15   **Go then, and eat the fat, and drink the sweet, and send part to them that have nothing; For this day is holy unto the Lord: and be not sorrowful; for the Lord will bring you to honour.**
(9:51–2)
The Israelites promise to divorce their heathen wives, and Esdras declares a day of thanksgiving and praise of God.

II Esdras

1   **I led you through the sea, and in the beginning gave you a large and safe passage; I gave you Moses for a leader, and Aaron for a priest. I gave you light in a pillar of fire, and great wonders have I done among you; yet have ye forgotten me, saith the Lord.**
(1:13–14)
In a vision, Esdras hears God rebuke the Chosen People for their breaking of the covenant, despite continuing divine favour.

2   **Ye have not as it were forsaken me, but your own selves, saith the Lord.**
(1:27)
In Esdras' vision, God continues to rebuke the Israelites.

3   **They shall have the tree of life for an ointment of sweet savour; they shall neither labour, nor be weary. Go, and ye shall receive; pray for few days unto you, that they may be shortened: the kingdom is already prepared for you: watch.**
(2:12–13)
Esdras' vision continues. God promises to forgive his people, and to continue his favour towards them. The Christian overtones of this and subsequent sections of Esdras – here references to watching for the Day of Judgment – are explained by the fact that although the book deals with events of the fifth century BC, this section was probably written in Christian Alexandria in about AD 90.

4   **Mother, embrace thy children, and bring them up with gladness, make their feet as fast as a pillar: for I have chosen thee, saith the Lord.**
(2:15)

'Mother' means the Church (probably, in the writer's mind, the Christian Church) which will re-educate the people in God's true faith as a mother educates her children.

5   Be not weary: for when the day of trouble and heaviness cometh, others shall weep and be sorrowful, but thou shalt be merry and have abundance. The heathen shall envy thee, but they shall be able to do nothing against thee, saith the Lord. (2:27–8)
Esdras' vision continues with God's reassurance to his people about their fate on the Day of Judgment.

6   I Esdras saw upon the mount Sion a great people, whom I could not number, and they all praised the Lord with songs. And in the midst of them there was a young man of a high stature, taller than all the rest, and upon every one of their heads he set crowns, and was more exalted; which I marvelled at greatly. So I asked the angel, and said, Sir, what are these? He answered and said unto me, These be they that have put off the mortal clothing, and put on the immortal, and have confessed the name of God: now are they crowned, and receive palms. Then said I unto the angel, What young person is it that crowneth them, and giveth them palms in their hands? So he answered and said unto me, It is the Son of God. (2:42–7)
Esdras sees a vision of the New Jerusalem on the Day of Judgment, thronged with those born again in Christ.

7   And he said unto me, If I should ask thee how great dwellings are in the midst of the sea, or how many springs are in the beginning of the deep, or how many springs are above the firmament, or which are the outgoings of paradise: Peradventure thou wouldest say unto me, I never went down into the deep, nor as yet into hell, neither did I ever climb up into heaven. (4:7–8)
Esdras, in his vision, has asked how God can be so merciful to his erring people. The angel answers by reminding him of his ignorance of tangible, earthly matters, let alone of the ways of heaven.

8   He answered me, and said, I went into a forest into a plain, and the trees took counsel, And said, Come, let us go and make war against the sea, that it may depart away before us, and that we may make us more woods. The floods of the sea also in like manner took counsel, and said, Come, let us go up and subdue the woods of the plain, that there also we may

make us another country. The thought of the wood was in
vain, for the fire came and consumed it. The thought of the
floods of the sea came likewise to nought, for the sand stood
up and stopped them. If thou wert judge now betwixt these
two, whom wouldest thou begin to justify? or whom wouldest
thou condemn?
(4:13–18)
Esdras has asked the angel to explain why, if God is just, there is
still violence in the world. The angel answers with a parable,
designed to show that human beings are as different from one
another as trees are from water and water is from fire, and that they
will quarrel because of their natures; this has nothing to do with
God, who sees all things impartially.

9   We pass away out of the world as grasshoppers, and our life is
     astonishment and fear, and we are not worthy to obtain
     mercy.
     (4:24)
     Convinced by the angel's parable, Esdras marvels at the
     insignificance of the human race.

10   Behold, the days come, that I will begin to draw nigh, and to
     visit them that dwell upon the earth, And will begin to make
     inquisition of them, what they be that have hurt unjustly with
     their unrighteousness, and when the affliction of Sion shall be
     fulfilled; And when the world, that shall begin to vanish away,
     shall be finished, then will I shew these tokens: the books
     shall be opened before the firmament, and they shall see all
     together: And the children of a year old shall speak with their
     voices, the women with child shall bring forth untimely
     children of three or four months old, and they shall live, and
     be raised up. And suddenly shall the sown places appear
     unsown, the full storehouses shall suddenly be found empty:
     And the trumpet shall give a sound, which when every man
     heareth, they shall be suddenly afraid.
     (6:18–23)
     God's angel tells Esdras, in God's words, of the coming Day of
     Judgment.

11   Evil shall be put out, and deceit shall be quenched. As for
     faith, it shall flourish, corruption shall be overcome, and the
     truth, which hath been so long without fruit, shall be
     declared.
     (6:27–8)
     God's angel prophesies the new age of faith which will follow the
     Day of Judgment.

12 And now, O Lord, behold, these heathen, which have ever
been reputed as nothing, have begun to be lords over us, and
to devour us. But we thy people (whom thou hast called thy
firstborn, thy only begotten, and thy fervent lover) are given
into their hands. If the world now be made for our sakes, why
do we not possess an inheritance with the world? how long
shall this endure?
(6:57–9)

Esdras asks God how long his faithful are to be tormented by evil
oppressors. The thought was relevant both to Esdras' own time, and
to the Roman persecution of Christians current when the book was
being written.

13 Then were the entrances of this world made narrow, full of
sorrow and travail: they are but few and evil, full of perils, and
very painful. For the entrances of the elder world were wide
and sure, and brought immortal fruit. If then they that live
labour not to enter these strait and vain things, they can never
receive those that are laid up for them.
(7:12–14)

God answers Esdras' anguished questions about why there should
be suffering in the world and how long it should last. Originally, the
world was paradisal, and had no gates, but after Adam's expulsion
from Paradise the gates were made narrow and difficult to pass.
The idea is the traditional one of the 'straight and narrow' path of
faith leading to eternal life.

14 I will tell thee a similitude, Esdras; As when thou askest the
earth, it shall say unto thee, that it giveth much mould
whereof earthen vessels are made, but little dust that gold
cometh of: even so is the course of this present world. There
be many created, but few shall be saved.
(8:2–3)

Esdras, in his vision, has asked God how every single being in the
world can possibly be saved. This is God's uncomfortable answer.

15 And every one that shall be saved, and shall be able to escape
by his works, and by faith, whereby ye have believed, Shall be
preserved from the said perils, and shall see my salvation in
my land, and within my borders: for I have sanctified them
for me from the beginning.
(9:7–8)

God explains to Esdras which members of the human race are to be
saved from the perils of the Day of Judgment.

16   So I considered the world, and, behold, there was peril
     because of the devices that were come into it. And I saw, and
     spared it greatly, and have kept me a grape of the cluster, and
     a plant of a great people. Let the multitude perish then, which
     was born in vain; and let my grape be kept, and my plant; for
     with great labour have I made it perfect.
     (9:20–2)
     The idea of God's Chosen People as a cluster of choice grapes is a
     common Old Testament metaphor. Vines are pruned of the
     second-rate grapes, to leave the best bunches room to improve still
     further.

17   For the world hath lost his youth, and the times begin to wax
     old. For the world is divided into twelve parts, and the ten
     parts of it are gone already, and half of a tenth part.
     (14:10–11)
     In another vision, God warns Esdras that the end of the world is
     imminent. 'World' here means 'time of fleshly existence', and the
     image is one of passing hours, here called 'parts'.

18   Come hither, and I shall light a candle of understanding in
     thine heart, which shall not be put out, till the things be
     performed which thou shalt begin to write.
     (14:25)
     God has told Esdras to write down his visions, to share with others
     the understanding he has been given.

Tobit

1   O Lord, thou art just, and all thy works and all thy ways are
    mercy and truth, and thou judgest truly and justly for ever.
    Remember me, and look on me, punish me not for my sins
    and ignorances, and the sins of my fathers, who have sinned
    before thee.
    (3:2–3)
    Tobit, an honest but stubborn man, has been miraculously blinded
    by God, and now prays for forgiveness. 'Remember' means
    'consider'.

2   My son, be mindful of the Lord our God all thy days, and let
    not thy will be set to sin, or to transgress his commandments:
    do uprightly all thy life long, and follow not the ways of
    unrighteousness.
    (4:5)

Tobit is speaking to his son Tobias. He says that he (Tobit) will soon die, and urges the young man to keep the faith – necessary advice, as they are exiles in heathen Nineveh.

3   **If thou hast abundance, give alms accordingly: if thou have but a little, be not afraid to give according to that little: For thou layest up a good treasure for thyself against the day of necessity.**
    (4:8–9)
Tobit continues to advise his son about the godly life.

4   **Bless the Lord thy God alway, and desire of him that thy ways may be directed, and that all thy paths and counsels may prosper: for every nation hath not counsel; but the Lord himself giveth all good things, and he humbleth whom he will, as he will.**
    (4:19)
Tobit's advice to his son continues.

5   **I am the only son of my father, and I am afraid.**
    (6:14)
Tobias, Tobit's son, has been taken by the angel Raphael to meet his future wife, and is terrified to discover that she has had seven previous husbands, all of whom died on the wedding night. The sentence quoted became a Christian prayer for help: it was put into Christ's mouth in the mystical writings of the early Church, and was subsequently echoed for devotional purposes, with no recollection of its simple origin here.

6   **Be of good comfort, my daughter; the Lord of heaven and earth give thee joy for this thy sorrow: be of good comfort, my daughter.**
    (7:18)
The mother of Tobias' future wife comforts her daughter, who is afraid to marry again in view of what happened to her seven previous husbands. (They died on the wedding night.) Like the previous verse quoted, this one was dissociated from Tobit in early mystical Christian writings, and was addressed by God to his daughter the Church in her affliction (the Roman persecution of the early Christians).

7   **If ye turn to him with your whole heart, and with your whole mind, and deal uprightly before him, then will he turn unto you, and will not hide his face from you.**
    (13:6)

Tobit has learned his lesson, to trust God, and his sight has been restored. Full of delight at this, and at the successful marriage of his son Tobias, he now praises God.

Judith

1   **Then every man of Israel cried to God with great fervency, and with great vehemency did they humble their souls: Both they, and their wives, and their children, and their cattle, and every stranger and hireling, and their servants bought with money, put sackcloth upon their loins.**
(4:9–10)
Nebuchadnezzar, king of Babylon, has sent his general Holofernes with an army to destroy every temple and shrine, and to replace all other gods with the statue of Nebuchadnezzar his master. As Holofernes comes nearer and nearer to Jerusalem, the people pray to God for help.

2   **Let my lord now pass by, lest their Lord defend them, and their God be for them, and we become a reproach before all the world.**
(5:21)
Holofernes' lieutenant, Achoir, advises Holofernes that the Jews are protected by their God and should not be meddled with. 'Reproach' here means 'laughing-stock'.

3   **We will tread them under foot, and their mountains shall be drunken with their blood, and their fields shall be filled with their dead bodies, and their footsteps shall not be able to stand before us, for they shall utterly perish.**
(6:4)
Holofernes, quoting the words of his master Nebuchadnezzar as if they are the prophecy of a god, scornfully rejects Achior's advice to leave the Jews alone.

4   **Therefore their young children were out of heart, and their women and young men fainted for thirst, and fell down in the streets of the city, and by the passages of the gates.**
(7:22)
Holofernes has besieged the town of Bethuliah, and cut off the water supply.

5   **Who are ye that have tempted God this day, and stand instead of God among the children of men?**
(8:12)

Judith, a widow from Bethuliah, has heard that the leaders of the town are proposing to surrender to Holofernes rather than see the people die of thirst. She tells them sharply not to put themselves in place of God, who is perfectly well able to look after his people. 'Tempted' here means 'questioned the power of'.

6 O God, O my God, hear me also a widow.
(9:4)
Judith prays to God to give her strength against her enemies, as he strengthened so many people in the past.

7 O Lord God of all power, look at this present upon the works of mine hands for the exaltation of Jerusalem.
(13:4)
Judith has gone to Holofernes, the enemy commander, has made him fall in love with her, and is now alone with him as he lies in a drunken sleep. She prays to God for strength.

8 Begin unto my God with timbrels, sing unto my Lord with cymbals: tune unto him a new psalm: exalt him, and call upon his name. For God breaketh the battles: for among the camps in the midst of the people he hath delivered me out of the hands of them that persecuted me.
(16:2–3)
Having beheaded Holofernes and caused the rout of his army, Judith sings a psalm of praise to God.

Additions to Esther

1 Remember, O Lord, make thyself known in time of our affliction, and give me boldness, O King of the nations, and Lord of all power.
(14:2)
The Additions to Esther are an attempt to add religious meaning to the Old Testament book of Esther, which is otherwise bare of it: even the word 'God' is absent. It consists of short interpolations intended for insertion at appropriate places. Here, for example, Esther prays to God for help before she goes to King Ahasuerus to plead for her people.

Wisdom of Solomon

1   **Love righteousness, ye that be judges of the earth: think of the Lord with a good heart, and in simplicity of heart seek him. For he will be found of them that tempt him not; and sheweth himself unto such as do not distrust him.**
(1:1–2)
Wisdom of Solomon is a collection of proverbs and pieces of moral teaching, on the lines of Ecclesiastes or Proverbs in the Old Testament. Although it is attributed to Solomon here, it is really much later, and is more in the style of Greek philosophy than of Hebrew religious teaching. The early Christians, and Paul in particular, made much use of it, and passages such as this one closely echo Paul's own teaching style.

2   **For the ear of jealousy heareth all things: and the noise of murmurings is not hid. Therefore beware of murmuring, which is unprofitable; and refrain your tongue from backbiting: for there is no word so secret, that shall go for nought: and the mouth that belieth slayeth the soul.**
(1:10–11)
The 'ear of jealousy' is God's own ear: he is a 'jealous' God, ever alert for people backsliding from his worship. The phrase became proverbial, of human jealousy in general, without these religious overtones. 'Backbiting', meaning 'blaming in secret', is a metaphor from eating, chewing with the grinding teeth at the back of the jaw.

3   **Let us crown ourselves with rosebuds, before they be withered.**
(2:8)
The ungodly tell each other to enjoy life while it is there, because there is no certainty about tomorrow. The phrase 'crowned with rosebuds' or 'with roses in his hair' became a standard metaphor for riotous living. The idea of present gratification arising out of pessimism for the future is frequently denounced in the Old Testament, as blasphemy against the caring power of God (see, for example, Isa 32).

4   **But the souls of the righteous are in the hand of God, and there shall no torment touch them. In the sight of the unwise they seemed to die: and their departure is taken for misery, And their going from us to be utter destruction: but they are in peace.**
(3:1–3)

Those who truly worship God will be rewarded: their apparent suffering, even to death, is merely their purification for eternal life, as gold is purified in a furnace. Once again, a standard Old Testament idea is given a markedly Christian flavour.

5 **And in the time of their visitation they shall shine, and run to and fro like sparks among the stubble.**
(3:7)
The 'visitation' is the Second Coming, and the image is of the fire of true worship blazing up to consume the stubble of ungodliness.

6 **For the bewitching of naughtiness doth obscure things that are honest; and the wandering of concupiscence doth undermine the simple mind.**
(4:12)
This verse develops the Old Testament idea that false religion is like a prostitute, seducing the unwary or the weak-willed from the true faith. 'Concupiscence', that is lust, stands for any cravings of the flesh instead of those of the spirit, another Old Testament symbol for idolatry.

7 **He, being made perfect in a short time, fulfilled a long time: For his soul pleased the Lord: therefore hasted he to take him away from among the wicked.**
(4:13–14)
The context of this proverb, which came to be much quoted, is that for a just person, a true worshipper, there is no shame in dying young. A short life, if it is spent in worship, is as worthwhile as one of many years.

8 **We fools accounted his life madness, and his end to be without honour: How is he numbered among the children of God, and his lot is among the saints!**
(5:4–5)
Seeing how the just person is rewarded by God, sinners realize that they were fools to mock him.

9 **What hath pride profited us? or what good hath riches with our vaunting brought us? All those things are passed away like a shadow, and as a post that hasted by; And as a ship that passeth over the waves of the water, which when it is gone by, the trace thereof cannot be found, neither the pathway of the keel in the waves; Or as when a bird hath flown through the air, there is no token of her way to be found, but the light air being beaten with the stroke of her wings, and parted with the violent noise and motion of them, is passed through, and therein afterwards no sign where she went is to be found; Or**

like as when an arrow is shot at a mark, it parteth the air,
which immediately cometh together again, so that a man
cannot know where it went through: Even so we in like
manner, as soon as we were born, began to draw to our end,
and had no sign of virtue to shew; but were consumed in our
own wickedness.
(5:8–13)

In contrast to the 'just', who are united with God after death, the
wicked reflect, in a series of fine poetic similes, that their lives have
been spiritually pointless.

10   For the hope of the ungodly is like dust that is blown away
with the wind; like a thin froth that is driven away with the
storm; like as the smoke which is dispersed here and there
with a tempest, and passeth away as the remembrance of a
guest that tarrieth but a day.
(5:14)

The wicked continue to realize that the pleasures of life are no
consolation in the face of death.

11   Love is the keeping of her laws; and the giving heed unto her
laws is the assurance of incorruption.
(6:18)

This is a close parallel to Paul's teaching about Christian love. 'Her'
is wisdom, that is faith in God; 'incorruption' is eternal, spiritual
life.

12   For she is the breath of the power of God, and a pure
influence flowing from the glory of the Almighty: therefore
can no defiled thing fall into her. For she is the brightness of
the everlasting light, the unspotted mirror of the power of
God, and the image of his goodness.
(7:25–6)

The context of these fine lines is a mystical poem in praise of
'wisdom', that is faith and joy in God. The word is feminine in
Greek: hence the 'she' of this passage.

13   I loved her, and sought her out from my youth, I desired to
make her my spouse, and I was a lover of her beauty. In that
she is conversant with God, she magnifieth her nobility: yea,
the Lord of all things himself loved her.
(8:2–3)

Praise of wisdom continues.

14   For her sake I shall have estimation among the multitude,
and honour with the elders, though I be young. I shall be

found of a quick conceit in judgment, and shall be admired in the sight of great men.
(8:10–11)
The man who marries 'wisdom', that is the true believer, will be like a ruler among mortals. This idea combines the Hebrew metaphor of wisdom, the bride, with the Greek philosophical view that a person at peace with himself or herself was a 'king', because he or she was not the slave of worldly pressures or passions.

15 The corruptible body presseth down the soul, and the earthy tabernacle weigheth down the mind that museth upon many things. And hardly do we guess aright at things that are upon earth, and with labour do we find the things that are before us: but the things that are in heaven who hath searched out? And thy counsel who hath known, except thou give wisdom, and send thy Holy Spirit from above?
(9:15–17)
The pressures of the world are like a weight, and our earthly nature enfolds us like a tent (or 'tabernacle'). We spend our time diligently trying to understand the world; how much better to spend it on contemplating the mystery of God.

16 Also the singular diligence of the artificer did help to set forward the ignorant to more superstition. For he, peradventure willing to please one in authority, forced all his skill to make the resemblance of the best fashion. And so the multitude, allured by the grace of the work, took him now for a god, which a little before was but honoured as a man.
(14:18–20)
The writer has in mind the glories of Greek sculpture. Although the 'artificer' (or sculptor) was a man of genius, the statues he made were idols, gods made in the image of human beings, and are therefore worthless compared to the true God.

17 To know thee is perfect righteousness: yea, to know thy power is the root of immortality.
(15:3)
In the middle of a long description of how faith in God, the 'wisdom' which leads to 'understanding', helped the sages and patriarchs of Hebrew history, the writer breaks off and prays to God to grant perfect knowledge to all his people.

Ecclesiasticus

1   It containeth therefore wise sayings, dark sentences, and
     parables, and certain particular ancient godly stories of men
     that pleased God.
     (Prologue)
     As these words imply, Ecclesiasticus is an anthology of religious
     aphorisms, stories and poetry, along the lines of Proverbs or
     Ecclesiastes in the Old Testament. It was originally compiled in 180
     BC by a Jerusalem religious author called Jesus Ben Sira, and was
     translated into Greek by his grandson. It was widely popular in early
     Christian times, especially with Gentile Christians, who found it an
     easier way into Jewish religious teaching than some of the Old
     Testament. The title 'Ecclesiasticus' means 'book of the church',
     and refers to its use as an instruction book in the early Christian
     Church, the *ecclesia*.

2   The Lord is full of compassion and mercy, longsuffering, and
     very pitiful, and forgiveth sins, and saveth in time of
     affliction.
     (2:11)
     God is a sure protector in the difficulties and dangers of the world.

3   We will fall into the hands of the Lord, and not into the hands
     of men: for as his majesty is, so is his mercy.
     (2:18)
     Given a choice between matters spiritual and temporal, human
     beings, if they are 'wise' (that is God-fearing), have no choice.

4   Be not curious in unnecessary matters: for more things are
     shewed unto thee than men understand.
     (3:23)
     Unlike Greek moral thinking, which involved indefatigable enquiry,
     Hebrew teaching says we should recognize that our moral sense
     centres on a mystery. If we accept that mystery and behave
     accordingly, what we do is far more important than future moral
     enquiry: this behaviour is the 'understanding' which faith in God
     involves.

5   Be not as a lion in thy house, nor frantick among thy servants.
     (4:30)
     Moderation is a moral quality, one of the signs of a truly 'wise' or
     God-fearing person.

6   **If thou hast understanding, answer thy neighbour; if not, lay thy hand upon thy mouth. Honour and shame is in talk: and the tongue of man is his fall.**
(5:12–13)
Thinking before you speak is an example of the moderation which the author consistently advises: a sign of true moral 'wisdom'.

7   **Be not ignorant of any thing in a great matter or a small.**
(5:15)
For the original hearers and readers, 'ignorant' in this verse carried the overtone 'neglectful of God's teaching'.

8   **A faithful friend is the medicine of life; and they that fear the Lord shall find him.**
(6:16)
The implication is that from faith come all things, including the friendships which ease our lives.

9   **Justify not thyself before the Lord; and boast not of thy wisdom before the king.**
(7:5)
Spiritual and temporal humility are compared.

10   **Laugh no man to scorn in the bitterness of his soul: for there is one which humbleth and exalteth.**
(7:11)
'Laugh to scorn' – which entered the language – simply means 'jeer at'. Only God can see who is morally superior, the jeerer or the jeered.

11   **Open not thine heart to every man, lest he requite thee with a shrewd turn.**
(8:19)
'Requite' means 'repay'; 'a shrewd turn' means 'a cunning trick'. The author continues his advocation of moderation, both temporal and spiritual: the Old Testament is full of cautionary stories of people who exposed the limit of their spiritual resources, regretted it, and were rescued in the end only by God.

12   **Forsake not an old friend; for the new is not comparable to him: a new friend is as new wine; when it is old, thou shalt drink it with pleasure.**
(9:10)
As often in 'wisdom literature', a homely, not to say obvious, thought is given both vigorous expression and a faintly moral tinge: in Jewish religious teaching, the idea of immoderate or unusual drinking always implied ungodliness.

13 **Many kings have sat down upon the ground; and one that was
never thought of hath worn the crown.**
(11:5)
To 'sit on the ground', a metaphor for falling from power (perhaps
the contrast is with sitting on high, on a throne) was used by
Shakespeare, when the deposed Richard II begins a sad reflection
on his fate: 'In God's name, let us sit upon the ground/And tell sad
stories of the death of kings.' 'One that was never thought of '
means 'someone never highly regarded'. The author here is talking
of the pointlessness of human ambition: our earthly promotion and
demotion are in the hands of God. Although in context the phrase
seems a general-enough truth, some early Christians took it as a
prophecy of the Messiah.

14 **Judge none blessed before his death: for a man shall be
known in his children.**
(11:28)
The first half of this verse is identical to a morose Greek proverb,
attributed to the Athenian lawgiver Solon on the hollowness of life.
The Hebrew adds a common Old Testament rider, that we live on
in our children and grandchildren: we are (in part) what we create.

15 **He that toucheth pitch shall be defiled therewith; and he that
hath fellowship with a proud man shall be like unto him.**
(13:1)
The author is advising us to choose our company carefully, and in
particular to avoid anyone who is morally ambitious or self-satisfied,
as these attributes are infectious.

16 **Have no fellowship with one that is mightier and richer than
thyself: for how agree the kettle and the earthen pot together?
for if the one be smitten against the other, it shall be broken.**
(13:2)
The author's advice against foolish friendships continues. 'Kettle' is
any metal cooking container. The point is that the weaker vessel,
that is the person the author is addressing, will always suffer if the
two come into conflict.

17 **Be not made a beggar by banqueting upon borrowing, when
thou hast nothing in thy purse: for thou shalt lie in wait for
thine own life, and be talked on.**
(18:33)
To 'banquet upon borrowing' means, literally, to use borrowed
money to enjoy oneself – but there are also spiritual overtones of
living on borrowed time, squandering moral capital that is only lent,
not our own. To 'lie in wait for one's own life' means to mistake

shadow for substance, to waste time on futile matters instead of concentrating on the realities of one's existence.

18   **He that contemneth small things shall fall by little and little.**
(19:1)
'Contemneth' means 'pays no attention to'.

19   **Wine and women will make men of understanding to fall away: and he that cleaveth to harlots will become impudent.**
(19:2)
The author's somewhat censorious view of the true path of life continues. 'Men of understanding' implies God-fearing people; 'impudent' means shameless, that is (in a context where harlotry is a symbol for false religion) idolatrous.

20   **Whoso teacheth a fool is as one that glueth a potsherd together, and as he that waketh one from a sound sleep.**
(22:7)
This is not as censorious as it sounds. A favourite Old Testament metaphor for human beings was clay pots moulded by the hands of God: the teacher here is thus mending, morally speaking, someone who has erred from true piety. Waking someone from sleep carries the same implication.

21   **As the turpentine tree I stretched out my branches, and my branches are the branches of honour and grace.**
(24:16)
The author suddenly breaks off his anthology of proverbs and moral maxims and includes a long poem in praise of wisdom. It is envisaged as a beautiful woman, singing its own distinction. The 'turpentine tree' in this verse is the terebinth, a sweet-smelling conifer.

22   **All wickedness is but little to the wickedness of a woman.**
(25:14)
Reflections on the moral stature of women, lower than that of men, were common in Hebrew religious teaching because of the story of Eve in the Garden of Eden. This fact explains their existence, but not their frequent tone of lip-smacking relish.

23   **As the climbing up a sandy way is to the feet of the aged, so is a wife full of words to a quiet man.**
(25:20)
The author's sour view of women continues.

24 **A merchant shall hardly keep himself from doing wrong; and an huckster shall not be freed from sin.**
(26:29)
The idea is that there is a true price for everything, ordained by God: to bargain, therefore, is to question his authority.

25 **Many have fallen by the edge of the sword: but not so many as have fallen by the tongue.**
(28:18)
The context is a collection of moral maxims advocating silence above rash speech, patience above anger, praise above blame.

26 **Envy and wrath shorten the life, and carefulness bringeth age before the time.**
(30:24)
'Carefulness' is not a good quality here: it means constant fault-finding.

27 **Wine is as good as life to a man, if it be drunk moderately: what life is then to a man that is without wine? for it was made to make men glad.**
(31:27)
The last part of this verse became proverbial; the first part was quickly and conveniently discarded.

28 **Honour a physician with the honour due unto him for the uses which ye may have of him: for the Lord hath created him. For of the most High cometh healing.**
(38:1-2)
The high regard shown to doctors in all Hebrew literature arises from the fact that they were thought to work, so to speak, in God's footsteps: as God healed the soul, so they healed the body.

29 **The wisdom of a learned man cometh by opportunity of leisure: and he that hath little business shall become wise. How can he get wisdom that holdeth the plough, and that glorieth in the goad, that driveth oxen, and is occupied in their labours and whose talk is of bullocks?**
(38:24-5)
The point of these verses is not to dispraise ploughmen. Their work is taken as one example only of 'business' (that is, 'busyness'), the bustle of daily activity which can distract our minds from the true worship of God. The verses are advocating meditation, spiritual busyness.

30   **Let us now praise famous men, and our fathers that begat us.**
(44:1)
This verse begins a sequence of several chapters literally doing what
the words suggest: praising such patriarchs of Jewish history as
Noah, Abraham and Jacob.

31   **Such as did bear rule in their kingdoms, men renowned for**
their power, giving counsel by their understanding, and
declaring prophecies: Leaders of the people by their
counsels, and by their knowledge of learning meet for the
people, wise and eloquent in their instructions: Such as found
out musical tunes, and recited verses in writing: Rich men
furnished with ability, living peaceably in their habitations:
All these were honoured in their generations, and were the
glory of their times.
(44:3-7)
Each of these categories of 'famous men', in the author's eyes, has
been used by God to show a different facet of his glory on earth.

32   **There be of them, that have left a name behind them, that**
their praises might be reported. And some there be, which
have no memorial; who are perished, as though they had
never been; and are become as though they had never been
born; and their children after them. But these were merciful
men, whose righteousness hath not been forgotten.
(44:8-10)
Earthly fame, the 'name' which famous people leave behind after
death, is not the only criterion of merit. The measure of excellence
is a spiritual and not a temporal quality: 'righteousness', obedience
to and faith in God.

33   **Their bodies are buried in peace; but their name liveth for**
evermore.
(44:14)
At first sight this verse appears to contradict the earlier statement
that these people leave no 'name' behind them. But the author is in
fact developing his thought. In the earlier passage (Ecclus 32) he
used the word 'name' more or less literally: we know the names of
such God-fearing people of the past as Isaac or David. Here he
means it more generally, in the sense of 'reputation'. The idea of
the unknown person, faithful unto death, who has no other
memorial, led to this passage being much used in remembrance
services, honouring the unknown soldiers who died for their
countries.

34   He was as the morning star in the midst of a cloud, and as the
moon at the full: As the sun shining upon the temple of the
most High, and as the rainbow giving light in the bright
clouds: And as the flower of roses in the spring of the year, as
lilies by the rivers of waters, and as the branches of the
frankincense tree in the time of summer: As fire and incense
in the censer, and as a vessel of beaten gold set with all
manner of precious stones: And as a fair olive tree budding
forth fruit, and as a cypress tree which groweth up to the
clouds.
(50:6–10)
These verses, about Simon the high priest who extended the
temple, are typical of the magnificent praise-poetry of this section of
Ecclesiasticus. It is in the tradition of the Psalms, and though its
subject is less grand it matches their eloquence phrase for phrase.

35   When I was yet young, or ever I went abroad, I desired
wisdom openly in my prayer. I prayed for her before the
temple, and will seek her out even to the end. Even from the
flower till the grape was ripe hath my heart delighted in her:
my foot went the right way, from my youth up sought I after
her. I bowed down mine ear a little, and received her, and gat
much learning.
(51:13–16)
The grandson of the author of Ecclesiasticus rounds off the book
with a prayer of his own for 'wisdom', and takes the opportunity to
write in its praise. 'Or ever I went abroad' means 'before I ever went
outside the house', that is 'when I was still a very young child'.

Baruch

1   Learn where is wisdom, where is strength, where is
understanding; that thou mayest know also where is length of
days, and life, where is the light of the eyes, and peace.
(3:14)
Baruch, secretary of the prophet Jeremiah, is thought to have
written this book at the time of the Jews' exile in Babylon in sixth-
century BC. It is a reflection on the reason for their punishment –
backsliding from true faith in God – and a prayer for mercy. Here
Baruch combines the two ideas in a recommendation to his hearers
and readers to seek for 'wisdom', that is faith.

2   Put off, O Jerusalem, the garment of thy mourning and
affliction, and put on the comeliness of the glory that cometh
from God for ever. Cast about thee a double garment of the

righteousness which cometh from God; and set a diadem on thine head of the glory of the Everlasting.
(5:1–2)
Baruch imagines the city of Jerusalem rejoicing at the return of the exiles – both from Babylonian slavery and from the snares of ungodliness. The city is dressed in faith and crowned with glory as a queen dresses in her finery.

Baruch/Epistle of Jeremy

1   Sometimes also the priests convey from their gods gold and silver, and bestow it upon themselves. Yea, they will give thereof to the common harlots, and deck them as men with garments, [being] gods of silver, and gods of gold, and wood. Yet cannot these gods save themselves from rust and moths, though they be covered with purple raiment.
(6:10–12; 1:10–12)
The prophet Jeremiah is writing to the exiled Jews in Babylon, advising them against the idolatry they will find there. Here his point is that although the Babylonian 'gods' appear to give gifts to their worshippers, their alms are as fake, and as ephemeral, as they are themselves. (Note: as well as being known as Baruch, chapter 6, this section is often separately printed as The Epistle of Jeremy.)

2   They are as one of the beams of the temple, yet they say their hearts are gnawed upon by things creeping out of the earth; and when they eat them and their clothes, they feel it not. Their faces are blacked through the smoke that cometh out of the temple. Upon their bodies and heads sit bats, swallows, and birds, and the cats also. By this ye may know that they are no gods: therefore fear them not.
(6:20–3; 1:20–3)
In a few brisk phrases, Jeremiah dismisses the divine pretensions of the idols of Babylon.

Song of the Three Holy Children

1   O all ye works of the Lord, bless ye the Lord: praise and exalt him above all for ever.
(1:35)
This short work was written to be inserted in the Book of Daniel in the Old Testament. It consists of a prayer for mercy and the song Shadrach, Meshach and Abednego sang in the burning fiery furnace. This verse begins a section of the song which was adapted for Christian liturgical use, the *Benedicite*.

2   O give thanks unto the Lord, because he is gracious: for his mercy endureth for ever. O all ye that worship the Lord, bless the God of gods, praise him, and give him thanks: for his mercy endureth for ever.
(1:67–8)
These verses end the hymn of praise sung to God by Shadrach, Meshach and Abednego in the burning fiery furnace.

Susanna

1   O thou that art waxen old in wickedness, now thy sins which thou hast committed aforetime are come to light.
(1:52)
This story, intended for the beginning of the Book of Daniel, tells how the prophet saved a young woman from the false accusation of two church elders with whom she had refused to make love. Here Daniel has taken one of the elders aside, and accuses him, in God's name, of dishonesty. 'Waxen' means 'grown'.

Bel and the Dragon

1   And Daniel said, Thou hast remembered me, O God: neither hast thou forsaken them that seek thee and love thee.
(1:38)
This short book tells three legends about the prophet Daniel in Babylon: how he exposed the trickery of the priests of Bel (Baal), who were secretly eating the offerings to pretend that their idol was a real live god; how he killed a dragon which the people were worshipping; how God sent him comfort when he was thrown into

the lions' den by angry enemies. Here he is in the lions' den, thanking God for a sign of his mercy.

Prayer of Manasses

1   **Thou, O Lord, according to thy great goodness hast promised repentance and forgiveness to them that have sinned against thee: and of thine infinite mercies hast appointed repentance unto sinners, that they may be saved.**
Manasses (Manasseh in Hebrew) was a king of Judah in the seventh century BC who turned his people from true worship to idolatry. God punished them by sending the Babylonians to enslave them. This prayer, written for insertion in the story of Manasseh in the Second Book of Kings, is the king's prayer to God for forgiveness.

2   **I have sinned above the number of the sands of the sea. My transgressions, O Lord, are multiplied: my transgressions are multiplied, and I am not worthy to behold and see the height of heaven for the multitude of mine iniquities.**
Manasses' prayer for mercy continues. This section was well known in New Testament times, and was later much used in Christian acts of contrition. (Manasses' own story ends happily. God forgave him and sent him and his people back to Judah, where Manasses ruled a God-fearing and prosperous nation for 55 years.)

I Maccabees

1   **They set up the abomination of desolation upon the altar, and builded idol altars throughout the cities of Juda on every side. (1:54)**
After the death of Alexander the Great, in 323 BC, his vast empire was divided among his generals. Seleucus took command of that part of the Mediterranean and Aegean shores which included Israel, and began enthusiastically converting the people to Greek religion and the Greek way of life. The Jews resisted for generations – and the incident mentioned in this verse, the setting up of a heathen image (a statue of Zeus) on the altar in the temple of Jerusalem, was the flashpoint of a revolt in the 160s BC, led by Judas the Maccabee.

2   **In his acts he was like a lion, and like a lion's whelp roaring for his prey. For he pursued the wicked, and sought them out, and burnt up those that vexed his people. Wherefore the**

wicked shrunk for fear of him, and all the workers of iniquity
were troubled, because salvation prospered in his hand.
(3:4–6)
The Greeks saw Judas as a dangerous revolutionary, an 'unstable
element' to be eliminated; to his followers, and to the excited writer
of these verses, he was more like an angel dispensing the wrath of
God.

3   I perceive therefore that for this cause these troubles are
come upon me, and, behold, I perish through great grief in a
strange land.
(6:13)
The heathen king, defeated and on the point of death, realizes that
all his sufferings began when he defiled the temple in Jerusalem.

4   Whom they would help to a kingdom, those reign; and whom
again they would, they displace: finally, that they were greatly
exalted: Yet for all this none of them wore a crown, or was
clothed in purple, to be magnified thereby: Moreover how
they had made for themselves a senate house, wherein three
hundred and twenty men sat in council daily, consulting
alway for the people, to the end they might be well ordered.
(8:13–15)
Still fighting the Greeks, Judas proposes to make an alliance with
the Romans, and tries to find out more about them. This is part of
the report his ambassadors bring back – a view of Rome in marked
contrast to the Jews' later opinion of that city, as expressed in the
Letters and Acts of the New Testament.

5   Then Judas said, God forbid that I should do this thing, and
flee away from them: if our time be come, let us die manfully
for our brethren, and let us not stain our honour.
(9:10)
Judas is trapped and outnumbered, but rejects his followers' pleas
that he should surrender.

6   How is the valiant man fallen, that delivered Israel!
(9:21)
Judas' followers mourn him, killed in battle after six years' brave
campaigning.

II Maccabees

1   Here then will we begin the story: only adding thus much to that which hath been said, that it is a foolish thing to make a long prologue, and to be short in the story itself.
(2:32)
This verse comes at the end of a long prologue, setting the Maccabean uprising in its historical context and describing how the author of this book proposes to abridge an earlier account.

2   And then it happened, that through all the city, for the space almost of forty days, there were seen horsemen running in the air, in cloth of gold, and armed with lances, like a band of soldiers, And troops of horsemen in array, encountering and running one against another, with shaking of shields, and multitude of pikes, and drawing of swords, and casting of darts, and glittering of golden ornaments, and harness of all sorts.
(5:2–3)
Portents and omens are seen in Jerusalem, heralding the defilement of the temple.

3   For the temple was filled with riot and revelling by the Gentiles, who dallied with harlots, and had to do with women within the circuit of the holy places, and besides that brought in things that were not lawful. The altar also was filled with profane things, which the law forbiddeth.
(6:4–5)
The Greeks defile the temple in Jerusalem by treating it as a brothel – a common practice, or so the Jews maintained, in heathen temples, where ritual prostitution was accepted – and by putting statues of their own gods on the altar.

4   And when he was at the last gasp, he said, Thou like a fury takest us out of this present life, but the King of the world shall raise us up, who have died for his laws, unto everlasting life.
(7:9)
A young orthodox Jew is being martyred by the Greeks because he refuses to eat pig meat. 'At the last gasp' became proverbial.

5   And thus he that a little afore thought he might command the waves of the sea, (so proud was he beyond the condition of man) and weigh the high mountains in a balance, was now cast on the ground, and carried in an horse litter, shewing forth unto all the manifest power of God. So that the worms

rose up out of the body of this wicked man, and whiles he lived in sorrow and pain, his flesh fell away, and the filthiness of his smell was noisome to all his army.
(9:8–9)
God punishes the Greek king for his ill-treatment of the Jews.

6   And if I have done well, and as is fitting the story, it is that which I desired: but if slenderly and meanly, it is that which I could attain unto. For as it is hurtful to drink wine or water alone; and as wine mingled with water is pleasant, and delighteth the taste: even so speech finely framed delighteth the ears of them that read the story. And here shall be an end.
(15:38–9)
The writer rounds off his account with a piece of prose as self-consciously graceful as that which began it (see II Macc 1). Either the story is well told as it deserves, he says, or it is poorly done but the best he can manage. His concern is as much with elegant language ('speech finely framed') as with his subject – a judgment echoed, in sterner tones, by later Bible scholars, who have condemned his book as a fanciful farrago, graceful but historically inept.

NEW TESTAMENT

St Matthew

1   **Abraham begat Isaac; and Isaac begat Jacob; and Jacob begat Judas and his brethen.**
(1:2)
Matthew begins by tracing the descent, person by person, of Jesus from Abraham himself. The fifteen verses of 'X begat Y', of which this is the first, have been much ridiculed, but they served a serious, not to say mystical purpose: a demonstration that Jesus was the Messiah, and that he was descended both from Abraham, with whom God renewed the covenant, and from the royal house of Israel, the family of Abraham's descendant King David. The Judas mentioned here is no relation of Judas Iscariot.

2   **Then Joseph her husband, being a just man, and not willing to make her a publick example, was minded to put her away privily.**
(1:19)
Until he learns that the father of Mary's child is the Holy Ghost, Joseph intends to divorce her quietly, rather than have her publicly denounced as an adulteress, the usual course prescribed by law.

3   **And she shall bring forth a son, and thou shalt call his name Jesus, for he shall save his people from their sins.**
(1:21)
The child's Hebrew name was Joshua. Jesus is a form of the Greek word *iesos*, meaning 'healer'.

4   **Now all this was done, that it might be fulfilled which was spoken of the Lord by the prophet saying, Behold, a virgin shall be with child, and shall bring forth a son, and they shall call his name Emmanuel, which being interpreted is, God with us.**
(1:22–3)
Matthew is referring to Isaiah (see Isa 15).

5   Now when Jesus was born in Bethlehem of Judaea in the days
     of Herod the king, behold, there came wise men from the east
     to Jerusalem, Saying, Where is he that is born King of the
     Jews? for we have seen his star in the east, and are come to
     worship him.
     (2:1–2)
     The wise men, or *Magi* in Greek, were astrologers, trained in
     finding portents in the sky. Modern scientists have suggested that if
     the miraculous star has a scientific explanation, it may have been
     Halley's Comet, which passed over the Middle Eastern sky at about
     the time of Jesus' birth, and is mentioned in Roman and other non-
     Christian writings of the time.

6   And when they were come into the house, they saw the young
     child with Mary his mother, and fell down, and worshipped
     him: and when they had opened their treasures, they
     presented unto him gifts; gold, and frankincense, and myrrh.
     (2:11)
     The wise men give Jesus symbolic gifts. Gold stands for kingship,
     frankincense (an aromatic gum used as incense) for divinity and
     myrrh (a resin used in embalming bodies) for mortality.

7   Repent ye: for the kingdom of heaven is at hand. For this is he
     that was spoken of by the prophet Esaias, saying, The voice of
     one crying in the wilderness, Prepare ye the way of the Lord,
     make his paths straight.
     (3:2–3)
     John the Baptist proclaims the coming of the Messiah. Esaias is the
     prophet Isaiah (see Isa 6).

8   And the same John had his raiment of camel's hair, and a
     leathern girdle about his loins; and his meat was locusts and
     wild honey.
     (3:4)
     'Meat' here means food. 'Locusts and wild honey' became
     proverbial for help and support which came to someone by chance
     (or by God's providence), not as the result of their own efforts.

9   O generation of vipers, who hath warned you to flee from the
     wrath to come?
     (3:7)
     John the Baptist scornfully greets the Pharisees and Sadducees
     (strict religionists, sure of their own uprightness) who have come to
     be baptized.

10   I indeed baptize you with water unto repentance: but he that
cometh after me is mightier than I, whose shoes I am not
worthy to bear: he shall baptize you with the Holy Ghost, and
with fire.
(3:11)
Baptism with water was a form of ritual cleansing, a symbolic
washing away of sin. John the Baptist here predicts purgation of a
more apocalyptic kind when the Messiah comes. 'Baptism of fire'
became proverbial.

11   And Jesus, when he was baptized, went up straightway out of
the water: and, lo, the heavens were opened unto him, and he
saw the Spirit of God descending like a dove, and lighting
upon him: And lo a voice from heaven, saying, This is my
beloved Son, in whom I am well pleased.
(3:16–17)
Jesus allows himself to be baptized, not to be cleansed of sin but to
declare his sharing of the human condition. He is then miraculously
confirmed as the Son of God as well as the son of man (that is, a
mortal).

12   And when the tempter came to him, he said, If thou be the
Son of God, command that these stones be made bread. But
he answered and said, It is written, Man shall not live by
bread alone, but by every word that proceedeth out of the
mouth of God.
(4:3–4)
The Devil tempts Jesus in the wilderness, and is answered by a
quotation from Old Testament scripture (see Deut 8).

13   Jesus said unto him, it is written again, Thou shall not tempt
the Lord thy God.
(4:7)
The Devil has carried Jesus to the temple roof and invited him to
throw himself off, so that angels will carry him safely to the ground
and prove him to be the Son of God. 'Tempt', in Jesus' answer,
means 'test' (see Deut 7).

14   And he saith unto them, Follow me, and I will make you
fishers of men.
(4:19)
Jesus calls Peter and Andrew, who were fishermen on the Sea of
Galilee, to be his disciples.

15   And he opened his mouth and taught them, saying, Blessed
are the poor in spirit: for theirs is the kingdom of heaven.
Blessed are they that mourn: for they shall be comforted.

Blessed are the meek: for they shall inherit the earth. Blessed are they which do hunger and thirst after righteousness: for they shall be filled. Blessed are the merciful: for they shall obtain mercy. Blessed are the pure in heart: for they shall see God. Blessed are the peacemakers: for they shall be called the children of God. Blessed are they which are persecuted for righteousness' sake: for theirs is the kingdom of heaven. Blessed are ye, when men shall revile you, and persecute you, and shall say all manner of evil against you falsely, for my sake.
(5:2–11)
These verses, the beginning of Jesus' Sermon on the Mount, have come to be known as the Beatitudes, that is Blessings.

16   Ye are the salt of the earth: but if the salt have lost his savour, wherewith shall it be salted?
(5:13)
Jesus is referring to the Chosen People, reminding them that before they can sharpen up other people's awareness of God they must sharpen up their own.

17   Ye are the light of the world. A city that is set on an hill cannot be hid. Neither do men light a candle, and put it under a bushel, but on a candlestick; and it giveth light unto all that are in the house.
(5:14–15)
In another domestic metaphor, Jesus reminds the Chosen People that secret obedience to God is pointless. The idea of godliness as a light, scattering the darkness of unbelief, is standard throughout the Old Testament. A 'bushel' is a pot able to hold a bushel's-weight of grain.

18   Think not that I am come to destroy the law, or the prophets: I am not come to destroy, but to fulfil. For verily I say unto you, Till heaven and earth pass, one jot or one tittle shall in no wise pass from the law, till all be fulfilled.
(5:17–18)
Jesus explicitly links himself to the Messianic prophecies in the Old Testament.

19   For I say unto you, That except your righteousness shall exceed the righteousness of the scribes and Pharisees, ye shall in no case enter into the kingdom of heaven.
(5:20)
The righteousness of the scribes and Pharisees was really self-righteousness: because they followed scriptural law to the letter, they were convinced that no one was holier, or closer to God, than

themselves. This façade of religiosity was a favourite target of the Old Testament prophets, and Jesus gives it the same context as they did, a call to the people to obey God not superficially but genuinely.

20 Ye have heard that it was said by them of old time, Thou shalt not commit adultery: But I say unto you. That whosoever looketh on a woman to lust after her hath committed adultery with her already in his heart.
(5:27–8)
Jesus continues his teaching that superficial obedience to scriptural law (in this case, the seventh of the Ten Commandments) is not enough.

21 And if thy right eye offend thee, pluck it out, and cast it from thee: for it is profitable for thee that one of thy members should perish, and not that thy whole body should be cast into hell. And if thy right hand offend thee, cut it off, and cast it from thee: for it is profitable for thee that one of thy members should perish, and not that thy whole body should be cast into hell.
(5:29–30)
In a metaphor drawn from the somewhat drastic medical practices of his day (lopping off infected parts of the body), Jesus advocates absolute moral and ethical integrity. The context is a set of teachings about adultery, which Jesus' audiences would also take as a symbol for idolatry.

22 Ye have heard that it hath been said, An eye for an eye, and a tooth for a tooth: But I say unto you, That ye resist not evil: but whosoever shall smite thee on thy right cheek, turn to him the other also.
(5:38–9)
Jesus continues to modify the teaching of the Old Testament (see Deut 12). 'Turn the other cheek' has become proverbial.

23 I say unto you, Love your enemies, bless them that curse you, do good to them that hate you, and pray for them which despitefully use you, and persecute you; That ye may be the children of your Father which is in heaven: for he maketh his sun to rise on the evil and on the good, and sendeth rain on the just and on the unjust.
(5:44–5)
Jesus refutes the Old Testament teaching that friends should be loved but enemies hated.

24   Be ye therefore perfect, even as your Father which is in
      heaven is perfect.
      (5:48)
      In context – Jesus is preaching against insincerity – 'perfect' means
      completely genuine, whole and without reservation.

25   When thou doest alms, let not thy left hand know what thy
      right hand doeth.
      (6:3)
      'To do alms' is to give charity. The phrase about right and left
      hands has become proverbial for stealthy or deliberately deceptive
      behaviour; here, by contrast, it implies unstinting, unostentatious
      generosity.

26   And when thou prayest, thou shalt not be as the hypocrites
      are: for they love to pray standing in the synagogues and in
      the corners of the streets, that they may be seen of men.
      Verily I say unto you, They have their reward.
      (6:5)
      Jesus is still preaching against insincerity. He often uses the phrase
      'Verily I say unto you' to introduce a summary of his teaching on a
      specific point – but what followed was seldom as drily ironical as
      what follows here.

27   But thou, when thou prayest, enter into thy closet, and when
      thou hast shut thy door, pray to thy Father which is in secret;
      and thy Father which seeth in secret shall reward thee openly.
      (6:6)
      Jesus advocates inner sincerity in prayer rather than the self-
      advertising of hypocrites praying on street corners.

28   After this manner therefore pray ye: Our Father which art in
      heaven, Hallowed be thy name. Thy kingdom come. Thy will
      be done in earth, as it is in heaven. Give us this day our daily
      bread. And forgive us our debts, as we forgive our debtors.
      And lead us not into temptation, but deliver us from evil: For
      thine is the kingdom, and the power, and the glory, for ever.
      (6:9–13)
      Jesus' teaching on prayer culminates in what has become a central
      utterance of the whole Christian Church, the Lord's Prayer.

29   Lay not up for yourselves treasures upon earth, where moth
      and rust doth corrupt, and where thieves break through and
      steal: But lay up for yourselves treasures in heaven, where
      neither moth nor rust doth corrupt, and where thieves do not
      break through nor steal: For where your treasure is, there will
      your heart be also.
      (6:19–21)

Jesus is drawing the distinction between worldly and spiritual
wealth familiar from much of the Old Testament, where
concentration on the accumulation of worldly goods was regarded
as a distraction from the true worship of God, almost as a form of
idolatry.

30 **No man can serve two masters: for either he will hate the one,
and love the other; or else he will hold to the one, and despise
the other. Ye cannot serve God and mammon.**
(6:24)
Jesus' preaching on worldly and spiritual wealth continues.
'Mammon' is the Syriac word for wealth; it has been personified
ever since this passage as if it were the name of a heathen idol.

31 **Behold the fowls of the air: for they sow not, neither do they
reap, nor gather into barns; yet your heavenly Father feedeth
them. Are ye not much better than they?**
(6:26)
The ancients believed that birds were among the lowliest and least
significant of all 'God's creatures'; worms, lizards, insects and other
lower creatures belonged to the Devil, not to God. Frequently,
therefore, when Biblical teaching concerns God's care for even the
humblest parts of his creation, his care for tiny birds is described.

32 **Which of you by taking thought can add one cubit unto his
stature?**
(6:27)
Jesus means that we are what we are, what God has made us; to try
to change one's physical self by 'thinking' is a form of magic, a
religious practice favoured in idolatrous Persia or Babylon, and
featured in the Greek and Roman mystery cults popular in Jesus'
own time.

33 **And why take ye thought for raiment? Consider the lilies of
the field, how they grow; they toil not, neither do they spin:
And yet I say unto you, that even Solomon in all his glory was
not arrayed like one of these.**
(6:28–9)
Jesus' teaching continues on the theme 'leave your welfare in God's
hands'. He is still contrasting the relaxed trust of the true believer
with idolaters' restlessness and anxiety.

34 **Take therefore no thought for the morrow: for the morrow
shall take thought for the things of itself. Sufficient unto the
day is the evil thereof.**
(6:34)

As often, Jesus sums up a long piece of teaching with a pithy, aphoristic exhortation, designed to carry the full weight of the preceding thought but also to be easily remembered.

35   **Judge not, that ye be not judged.**
(7:1)
A kind of holier-than-thou censoriousness was prevalent among the stricter Jewish sects of Jesus' time. It had always been a target of the prophets; now Jesus begins an uncompromising attack on it.

36   **Why beholdest thou the mote that is in thy brother's eye, but considerest not the beam that is in thine own eye?**
(7:3)
Jesus' teaching against hypocritical censoriousness continues. A 'mote' is a dust-speck; a 'beam' is a substantial length of wood.

37   **Give not that which is holy unto the dogs, neither cast ye your pearls before swine, lest they trample them under their feet, and turn again and rend you.**
(7:6)
There is a traditional overtone to this passage: 'pearls', to Jesus' hearers, would have included the idea of knowledge of the true God, the wisdom whose price is 'above rubies'; indeed, ever since this passage, the phrase 'pearls of wisdom' has been proverbial, often in a slightly mocking sense. In a similar way 'swine', as well as being the most unclean of all unclean animals in Jewish law, would also have implied unbelievers to Jesus' audience.

38   **Ask, and it shall be given you; seek, and ye shall find; knock, and it shall be opened unto you.**
(7:7)
Jesus is thinking particularly of prayer, for which knocking on God's door was a recognized metaphor even in his day.

39   **Or what man is there of you, whom if his son ask for bread, will he give him a stone? Or if he ask a fish, will he give him a serpent? If ye then, being evil, know how to give good gifts unto your children, how much more shall your Father which is in heaven give good things to them that ask him?**
(7:9–11)
Jesus' teaching about unhesitating, regular prayer continues. If human fathers will respond to their children's needs, why should God refuse?

40   **Wide is the gate, and broad is the way, that leadeth to destruction, and many there be which go in thereat.**
(7:13)

For Jews, in a country swarming with people who worshipped other gods, this must have seemed an almost literal statement: the true believer was outnumbered by a huge crowd of idolaters, pouring towards perdition as crowds pour through city gates.

41 **Strait is the gate, and narrow is the way, which leadeth unto life, and few there be that find it.**
(7:14)
In contrast to the way of idolatry which leads to perdition, the path of faith is cramped ('strait') and narrow.

42 **Beware of false prophets, which come to you in sheep's clothing, but inwardly they are ravening wolves.**
(7:15)
As a result of this verse, the phrase 'a wolf in sheep's clothing', originally a remarkably powerful moral metaphor, became proverbial, and so familiar that its force is all but lost.

43 **By their fruits ye shall know them.**
(7:20)
Jesus has been comparing the prophets of false religions to thistles and thorns, which bear no good fruit and are eventually torn up and thrown into the fire.

44 **Therefore whosoever heareth these sayings of mine, and doeth them, I will liken him unto a wise man, which built his house upon a rock: And the rain descended, and the floods came, and the winds blew, and beat upon that house; and it fell not: for it was founded upon a rock. And every one that heareth these sayings of mine, and doeth them not, shall be likened unto a foolish man, which built his house upon the sand: And the rain descended, and the floods came, and the winds blew, and beat upon that house; and it fell: and great was the fall of it.**
(7:24–7)
Jesus ends the Sermon on the Mount by elaborating a favourite Biblical idea, that unreserved obedience to God is a stronghold, well-founded and able to withstand all assaults.

45 **For he taught them as one having authority, and not as the scribes.**
(7:29)
The scribes were experts in Old Testament law, and their 'teaching' consisted of applying it to the events and problems of modern life. It was a teaching based on precedents, interpreting the present in terms of the past: hence the contrast with Jesus' pragmatic, undogmatic words.

46   **Lord, I am not worthy that thou shouldest come under my roof: but speak the word only, and my servant shall be healed. (8:8)**
A Roman centurion asks Jesus to heal his sick servant, but is embarrassed when Jesus offers to visit the man at home.

47   **I say to this man, Go, and he goeth; and to another, Come, and he cometh; and to my servant, Do this, and he doeth it. (8:9)**
The centurion describes the authority of his rank.

48   **I have not found so great faith, no, not in Israel. (8:10)**
Jesus marvels at the centurion's faith in him, remarkable not only because of the man's high rank but also because he is a Roman, not a follower of the Jewish God.

49   **But the children of the kingdom shall be cast out into outer darkness: there shall be weeping and gnashing of teeth. (8:12)**
Startlingly for his hearers, Jesus predicts a time when 'heathen' from every corner of the world – such as the centurion whose servant he has been asked to heal – will come to share the kingdom of heaven, and those who think they are secure in it because of their orthodox belief will find that adherence to the letter of religious law is not enough.

50   **The foxes have holes, and the birds of the air have nests; but the Son of man hath not where to lay his head. (8:20)**
This is Jesus' enigmatic answer to a scribe (a Jewish religious expert) who offers to follow him wherever he goes.

51   **Follow me; and let the dead bury their dead. (8:22)**
One of Jesus' disciples has asked permission to bury his dead father. This is Jesus' reply.

52   **Why are ye fearful, O ye of little faith? (8:26)**
Caught in a storm at sea, the disciples have woken Jesus in their terror, and he rebukes them.

53   **And, behold, the whole herd of swine ran violently down a steep place into the sea, and perished in the waters. (8:32)**

Jesus has been abused by two men possessed by devils, and has ordered the devils out of them into a nearby herd of pigs. Pigs were regarded as unclean animals, devil's meat, from Old Testament times: the feeling that hearers of this story would have had is less that of cruelty to animals than that both the pigs and the devils got their just deserts. The miracle happened near the town of Gergesa or Gadara, and ever since then 'Gadarene swine' has been proverbial for a crowd of people who rush brainlessly into disaster, and 'Gadarene rush' or 'Gadarene descent' has been proverbial for any frenzied, unstoppable and suicidal impetus.

54   **And as Jesus passed forth from thence, he saw a man, named Matthew, sitting at the receipt of custom: and he saith unto him, Follow me. And he arose, and followed him.**
(9:9)
This verse has been taken ever afterwards as autobiographical: the disciple (and later gospel-writer) Matthew, who worked collecting tolls on the coast road from Damascus, is describing his own call to faith.

55   **Why eateth your Master with publicans and sinners?**
(9:11)
Matthew the tax-collector has invited Jesus to a meal at his house, and a group of Pharisees mutter to Jesus' disciples about the low company he keeps. 'Publicans' were tax-gatherers' agents for the Roman state, and, like modern bailiffs, had the power to seize the goods of people who refused to pay: hence their unpopularity.

56   **They that be whole need not a physician, but they that are sick. But go ye and learn what that meaneth, I will have mercy, and not sacrifice: for I am not come to call the righteous, but sinners to repentance.**
(9:12–13)
Jesus answers the Pharisees who object to his eating with 'publicans and sinners'.

57   **Neither do men put new wine into old bottles: else the bottles break, and the wine runneth out, and the bottles perish: but they put new wine into new bottles, and both are preserved.**
(9:17)
As often, Jesus dissociates himself from those whose piety consisted in strict adherence to ancient Jewish law. The metaphor is more easily understood if we take 'bottles' to mean not glass containers but wineskins, which would crack and split with age. The idea that Jesus' teaching was 'wine' would have been shocking to Old Testament dogmatists, who used wine-drinking as a symbol for worshipping false gods.

58   And, behold, a woman, which was diseased with an issue of blood twelve years, came behind him, and touched the hem of his garment: For she said within herself, If I may but touch his garment, I shall be whole. But Jesus turned him about, and when he saw her, he said, Daughter, be of good comfort; thy faith hath made thee whole. And the woman was made whole from that hour.
(9:20–2)
Jesus works a healing miracle on his way to cure Jairus' daughter. 'Hem of his garment', coming to mean the aura which surrounds a great man, and 'Thy faith hath made thee whole', have entered the language.

59   He said unto them, Give place: for the maid is not dead, but sleepeth. And they laughed him to scorn.
(9:24)
Jesus has been asked to go to Jairus' house and bring Jairus' dead daughter back to life. He finds musicians and professional mourners there, making all the noise and confusion of a funeral, and rebukes them.

60   He casteth out devils through the prince of the devils.
(9:34)
The Pharisees mutter in disapproval of Jesus' healing miracles, and say that he must have the help of Satan.

61   The harvest truly is plenteous, but the labourers are few; Pray ye therefore the Lord of the harvest, that he will send forth labourers into his harvest.
(9:37–8)
Jesus comments on the huge crowds who follow him, hungry to believe.

62   Now the names of the twelve apostles are these; The first, Simon, who is called Peter, and Andrew his brother; James the son of Zebedee, and John his brother; Philip, and Bartholomew; Thomas, and Matthew the publican; James the son of Alphaeus, and Lebbaeus, whose surname was Thaddaeus; Simon the Canaanite, and Judas Iscariot, who also betrayed him.
(10:2–4)
Jesus has assembled his chosen 'disciples', literally 'pupils', to prepare them for their mission. 'Apostles' means 'those sent out'.

63   But go rather to the lost sheep of the house of Israel.
(10:6)

Jesus instructs his disciples about their mission. They are not to preach yet to the Gentiles but to the 'lost sheep' of their own people. The image of God as a shepherd and the people as his flock had been a favourite one since Moses' time.

64 **And as ye go, preach, saying, The kingdom of heaven is at hand.**
(10:7)
Jesus' disciples are to begin their teaching with the same apocalyptic message as John the Baptist (see Matt 7).

65 **Freely ye have received, freely give.**
(10:8)
The purpose of the disciples' mission is unstintingly to share with everyone the good news, that is the presence of Christ in their hearts. They have learned – this is the meaning of the word 'disciple' – and now it is time to teach.

66 **And whosoever shall not receive you, nor hear your words, when ye depart out of that house or city, shake off the dust of your feet.**
(10:14)
There is no time to waste trying to persuade the recalcitrant: the message is urgent and the whole world is waiting to hear it.

67 **Behold, I send you forth as sheep in the midst of wolves: be ye therefore wise as serpents, and harmless as doves.**
(10:16)
This verse begins a passage of clear warning to the disciples about the hostility and violence they will face, and about how they should respond to it.

68 **And ye shall be hated of all men for my name's sake: but he that endureth to the end shall be saved.**
(10:22)
Jesus reassures the disciples that their apostolic mission will succeed despite violent opposition.

69 **The disciple is not above his master, nor the servant above his lord.**
(10:24)
This is less a reminder to the disciples about humility than reassurance. They are carrying out their master's orders, and he is with them to protect them; they are not alone.

70   What I tell you in darkness, that speak ye in light: and what ye
hear in the ear, that preach ye upon the housetops.
(10:27)
The underlying feeling is of the message growing insidiously and
irresistibly, until it becomes a clarion-call: in times of war the call to
arms was delivered from city towers and flat housetops.

71   Are not two sparrows sold for a farthing? and one of them
shall not fall on the ground without your Father. But the very
hairs of your head are all numbered. Fear ye not therefore, ye
are of more value than many sparrows.
(10:29–31)
After his dire warnings about persecution, Jesus reassures the
disciples that God is protecting them. Sparrows were sold for food,
and were among the cheapest and least valued of all meats.

72   Think not that I am come to send peace on earth: I came not
to send peace, but a sword.
(10:34)
Jesus has been saying that he is an intercessor between God and
mortals, but that he will treat people as they treat him, accepting or
rejecting them before God. The effect of his teaching will be to
divide the world. These words have been sometimes thought to be
at variance with the general pacific and all-embracing thrust of
Christian teaching. But there is no conflict: often in Biblical prose,
words implying *result* ('I mean that this will happen') are expressed
as *purpose* (I mean for this to happen').

73   And a man's foes shall be they of his own household. He that
loveth father or mother more than me is not worthy of me:
and he that loveth son or daughter more than me is not
worthy of me. And he that taketh not his cross, and followeth
after me, is not worthy of me. He that findeth his life shall
lose it: and he that loseth his life for my sake shall find it.
(10:36–9)
Jesus develops the idea that one result of his teaching will be
dissension in the world. 'He that findeth his life' means someone
who saves their life by denying his or her new faith when challenged
by the authorities: under Roman law, to do this was a sufficient
defence for anyone accused of preferring other gods to those of
Rome.

74   He that receiveth you receiveth me, and he that receiveth me
receiveth him that sent me.
(10:40)

These words served both to reinforce the disciples' zeal and to reassure them: as messengers, they spoke not with their own authority but with the authority of those who sent them, that is both Jesus and God.

75   **And whosoever shall give to drink unto one of these little ones a cup of cold water only in the name of a disciple, verily I say unto you, he shall in no wise lose his reward.**
      (10:42)
      This simple statement was later developed into a long piece of teaching on charity and the Last Judgment (see Matt 147).

76   **Art thou he that should come, or do we look for another?**
      (11:3)
      John the Baptist has been thrown into prison, and sends servants anxiously to Jesus to ask not for rescue but for confirmation that Jesus is the Messiah. John has been foretelling a king riding in awesome glory, and Jesus hardly conforms to this prophecy.

77   **Jesus answered and said unto them, Go and shew John again those things which ye do hear and see: The blind receive their sight, and the lame walk, and lepers are cleansed, and the deaf hear, the dead are raised up, and the poor have the gospel preached to them.**
      (11:4–5)
      This is Jesus' answer to John the Baptist's question quoted above.

78   **And as they departed, Jesus began to say unto the multitudes concerning John, What went ye out into the wilderness to see? A reed shaken with the wind? But what went ye out for to see? A man clothed in soft raiment? behold, they that wear soft clothing are in kings' houses. But what went ye out for to see? A prophet? yea, I say unto you, and more than a prophet. For this is he, of whom it is written, Behold, I send my messenger before thy face, which shall prepare thy way before thee.**
      (11:7–10)
      Jesus talks to the people about John the Baptist. He was no ordinary sight, no pampered house-servant, but the forerunner of the Messiah himself, the last of the prophets before the coming of the Lord.

79   **He that hath ears to hear, let him hear.**
      (11:15)
      Jesus often used these words to round off a piece of particularly forceful teaching – in this case, that John the Baptist was no eccentric, but a true messenger of the coming of the Messiah.

80   But whereunto shall I liken this generation? It is like unto
children sitting in the markets, and calling unto their fellows,
And saying, We have piped unto you, and ye have not danced;
we have mourned unto you, and ye have not lamented.
(11:16–17)
Jesus compares the Jews with children refusing to join in the
activities he and John the Baptist provide for them.

81   For John came neither eating nor drinking, and they say, He
hath a devil. The Son of man came eating and drinking, and
they say, Behold a man gluttonous, and a winebibber, a friend
of publicans and sinners. But wisdom is justified of her
children.
(11:18–19)
The Jews, says Jesus, could neither accept John the Baptist's
apartness from ordinary people nor Jesus' own ordinariness. The
last sentence is a warning, on the lines of the proverb 'a word to the
wise'.

82   Come unto me, all ye that labour and are heavy laden, and I
will give you rest. Take my yoke upon you, and learn of me;
for I am meek and lowly in heart: and ye shall find rest unto
your souls. For my yoke is easy, and my burden is light.
(11:28–30)
Jesus rounds off a passage of teaching about the nature of the
Second Coming. He has been talking of the humiliation of the
proud and the punishment of those who reject his teaching; now he
promises comfort to the poor and the oppressed.

83   The Son of man is Lord even of the sabbath day.
(12:8)
Jesus rebukes Pharisees who have seen his disciples plucking corn-
ears on the Sabbath and rubbing them between their palms to eat,
and who have complained that they are breaking the Fifth
Commandment.

84   He that is not with me is against me; and he that gathereth
not with me scattereth abroad.
(12:30)
Jesus frequently makes this remark in the course of his teaching, as
reported in the first three Gospels. It is a blunt statement of one of
his central themes, that belief in him must be wholehearted and
unequivocal, or it is no belief.

85   Either make the tree good, and his fruit good; or else make
the tree corrupt, and his fruit corrupt: for the tree is known
by his fruit.
(12:33)

Jesus is developing his teaching that people must be either wholeheartedly for him or against him. The metaphor of trees and fruit was a favourite of St Matthew's, perhaps based on a traditional proverb along the lines of the last phrase quoted here.

86   **O generation of vipers, how can ye, being evil, speak good things? for out of the abundance of the heart the mouth speaketh.**
(12:34)
The ancients believed that the heart, not the brain, was the seat of intelligence: if your heart, therefore, was crammed with evil thoughts, you had no option but to speak evil. Jesus is talking to the Pharisees who have rebuked his disciples for 'working' (eating corn-grains) on the Sabbath. His point is that they (the Pharisees) will one day be called to account for the words they speak, which are the outward sign of their innermost beliefs.

87   **An evil and adulterous generation seeketh after a sign; and there shall no sign be given to it, but the sign of the prophet Jonas: For as Jonas was three days and three nights in the whale's belly; so shall the Son of man be three days and three nights in the heart of the earth.**
(12:39–40)
One of the Pharisees has asked Jesus to prove that he is the Messiah, and this is Jesus' answer, appropriately (for his questioner) based on interpretation of the Old Testament and in riddle-form.

88   **The queen of the south shall rise up in the judgment with this generation, and shall condemn it: for she came from the uttermost parts of the earth to hear the wisdom of Solomon; and, behold, a greater than Solomon is here.**
(12:42)
Jesus' answer continues to the person who asked him for a sign that he was the Messiah. The 'queen of the south' is Sheba (see I Kgs 10).

89   **And he stretched forth his hand toward his disciples, and said, Behold my mother and my brethren! For whosoever shall do the will of my Father which is in heaven, the same is my brother, and sister, and mother.**
(12:49–50)
Jesus has been told that his mother and brothers are waiting to speak to him, and makes this reply.

90   Behold, a sower went forth to sow; And when he sowed, some seeds fell by the way side, and the fowls came and devoured them up: Some fell upon stony places, where they had not much earth: and forthwith they sprung up, because they had no deepness of earth: And when the sun was up, they were scorched; and because they had no root, they withered away. And some fell among thorns; and the thorns sprung up, and choked them: But other fell into good ground, and brought forth fruit, some an hundredfold, some sixtyfold, some thirtyfold.
(14:3–8)
Jesus begins to teach by parables.

91   But he that received seed into the good ground is he that heareth the word, and understandeth it.
(13:23)
Jesus explains the parable of the sower and the seed.

92   But while men slept, his enemy came and sowed tares among the wheat, and went his way.
(13:25)
These words come from another of Jesus' parables, likening God's kingdom to a cornfield sown by a careful farmer. 'Tares' are darnels, poisonous weeds hard to distinguish from growing corn. They are not to be gathered, he goes on to say, before the corn is ripe, in case good grain is gathered with them; when the harvest comes, they are to be plucked up and burned.

93   The kingdom of heaven is like to a grain of mustard seed, which a man took, and sowed in his field: Which indeed is the least of all seeds: but when it is grown, it is the greatest among herbs, and becometh a tree, so that the birds of the air come and lodge in the branches thereof.
(13:31–2)
Jesus continues to teach by parables.

94   Again, the kingdom of heaven is like unto a merchant man, seeking goodly pearls: Who, when he had found one pearl of great price, went and sold all that he had, and bought it.
(13:45–6)
The 'pearl of great price' is the kingdom of heaven itself, and it is worth exchanging everything else we value to possess it.

95   But Jesus said unto them, A prophet is not without honour, save in his own country, and in his own house.
(13:57)

Jesus has been preaching in Nazareth, to the astonishment of local people who think of him only as 'the carpenter's son'.

96 **Give me here John Baptist's head in a charger.**
(14:8)
Salome, the stepdaughter of King Herod, has danced for Herod and been offered any reward she cares to name. A 'charger' is a silver serving-dish. The phrase 'to bring someone's head on a charger', meaning to betray someone in order to oblige a third party, derives from this verse.

97 **And they say unto him, We have here but five loaves, and two fishes.**
(14:17)
Five thousand men, and an uncounted number of women and children, have followed Jesus into the desert by the Sea of Galilee, and these loaves and fishes are all the food they have. On Jesus' instructions the disciples divide them among the crowd, and later gather twelve basketfuls of scraps.

98 **And in the fourth watch of the night Jesus went unto them, walking on the sea. And when the disciples saw him walking on the sea, they were troubled, saying, It is a spirit; and they cried out for fear. But straightway Jesus spake unto them, saying, Be of good cheer; it is I; be not afraid.**
(14:25–7)
Jesus has told his disciples to cross the Sea of Galilee in a boat and wait for him on the other side.

99 **Not that which goeth into the mouth defileth a man; but that which cometh out of the mouth, this defileth a man.**
(15:11)
Pharisees have objected that Jesus' disciples eat without first washing their hands, as strict Jewish law prescribes. This is his answer – delivered not to the Pharisees themselves but to the crowd which stood in awe of them. His point is that the false doctrine issuing from the Pharisees' mouths is more harmful than the honest dirt entering the disciples' mouths.

100 **Let them alone: they be blind leaders of the blind. And if the blind lead the blind, both shall fall into the ditch.**
(15:14)
Jesus' disciples have urged him not to offend the Pharisees, who have wide power and influence. His reply throws even more scorn on the Pharisees' authority, based as it is on a blinkered adherence to the minutiae of Old Testament law.

101 But he answered and said, It is not meet to take the children's bread, and to cast it to dogs. And she said, Truth, Lord: yet the dogs eat of the crumbs which fall from their masters' table.
(15:26–7)
A Canaanite woman, an idolater, has asked Jesus to heal her sick daughter. He refuses, saying that his mission is to the 'lost sheep' of Israel. Her answer melts his heart, and he cures her daughter.

102 He answered and said unto them, When it is evening, ye say, It will be fair weather: for the sky is red. And in the morning, It will be foul weather to day: for the sky is red and lowring. O ye hypocrites, ye can discern the face of the sky; but can ye not discern the signs of the times?
(16:2–3)
A group of Pharisees and Sadducees have asked Jesus for proof that he is the Messiah.

103 And Simon Peter answered and said, Thou art the Christ, the Son of the living God. And Jesus answered and said unto him, Blessed art thou, Simon Barjona: for flesh and blood hath not revealed it unto thee, but my Father which is in heaven. And I say also unto thee, That thou art Peter, and upon this rock I will build my church; and the gates of hell shall not prevail against it. And I will give unto thee the keys of the kingdom of heaven: and whatsoever thou shalt bind on earth shall be bound in heaven: and whatsoever thou shalt loose on earth shall be loosed in heaven.
(16:16–19)
The disciples have told Jesus that the people have many theses about his identity: perhaps he is Elijah, or John the Baptist, or Jeremiah. He asks them who they (the disciples) think he is. 'Peter' is close to the Greek word *petra*, meaning a rock.

104 Get thee behind me, Satan.
(16:23)
Jesus has told the disciples about his forthcoming trial, death and resurrection, and Peter has begged him to avoid them by staying out of Jerusalem. Jesus rebukes him in these words, implying that it is not Peter, the rock, speaking, but the Devil usurping his mouth.

105 Then said Jesus unto his disciples, If any man will come after me, let him deny himself, and take up his cross, and follow me. For whosoever will save his life shall lose it: and whosoever will lose his life for my sake shall find it. For what is a man profited, if he shall gain the whole world, and lose his own soul?
(16:24–6)

Jesus reminds his disciples, as he has often done before, that following him requires total obedience, even beyond death. The phrase 'take up his cross and follow me' has become so tinged, for modern readers, with overtones of Jesus' own crucifixion that its power here, its startling force, is hard to recapture. St Matthew wrote the words after the crucifixion, and their impact may be partly due to hindsight.

106 **Verily I say unto you, If ye have faith as a grain of mustard seed, ye shall say unto this mountain, Remove hence to yonder place; and it shall remove; and nothing shall be impossible unto you.**
(17:20)
Jesus' disciples have tried and failed to drive devils from a sick child. Jesus drives out the devils, and when his disciples ask why they could not, he first answers that their faith was not great enough, and then amplifies his teaching in these words. The proverb 'faith can move mountains' derives from this incident.

107 **Except ye be converted, and become as little children, ye shall not enter into the kingdom of heaven.**
(18:3)
The disciples have asked Jesus about ranks and privileges in the kingdom of heaven. His answer not only reminds them that there are no hierarchies in heaven, but also reiterates another of his teachings, that true faith in God is a state of perfection, analogous to childhood innocence.

108 **And whoso shall receive one such little child in my name receiveth me. But whoso shall offend one of these little ones which believe in me, it were better for him that a millstone were hanged about his neck, and that he were drowned in the depth of the sea.**
(18:5–6)
Jesus has set a child among the disciples, and is both preaching against the idea of position and privilege in the kingdom of heaven and repeating his teaching that the innocence of the truly faithful is like that of a child.

109 **For where two or three are gathered together in my name, there am I in the midst of them.**
(18:20)
Jesus tells the disciples that the Church is not anything tangible, like buildings or rituals, but an accord in the hearts of true believers.

110   Then came Peter to him, and said, Lord, how oft shall my
brother sin against me, and I forgive him? till seven times?
Jesus saith unto him, I say not unto thee, Until seven times:
but, Until seventy times seven.
(18:21–2)
Peter is trying to interpret Christian teaching in the same terms as
Pharisaical Jewish law, which depended on precise calculations of
guilt, penance and punishment.

111   But the same servant went out, and found one of his
fellowservants, which owed him an hundred pence: and he
laid hands on him, and took him by the throat, saying, Pay me
that thou owest.
(18:28)
In Jesus' parable, God is compared to a man who frees one of his
servants from debt, only to find the man harassing a third party who
owes *him* money. The whole parable is another of Jesus' preachings
against those who affected moral superiority over everyone else.

112   What therefore God hath joined together, let not man put
asunder.
(19:6)
The Pharisees are questioning Jesus on Jewish law. This is his
answer about divorce.

113   There is none good but one, that is, God.
(19:17)
A young man, anxious to find out the way to salvation, addresses
Jesus as 'Good Master' and is scolded for it.

114   Jesus said, Thou shalt do no murder, Thou shalt not commit
adultery, Thou shalt not steal, Thou shalt not bear false
witness, Honour thy father and thy mother: and, Thou shalt
love thy neighbour as thyself.
(19:18–19)
Jesus paraphrases the commandments for a young man who has
asked what he should do to have everlasting life.

115   If thou wilt be perfect, go and sell that thou hast, and give to
the poor, and thou shalt have treasure in heaven: and come
and follow me.
(19:21)
The rich young man anxious to have everlasting life, who has been
told to keep the commandments, has asked for more instruction
than merely keep the commandments; this is Jesus' answer.

116 **It is easier for a camel to go through the eye of a needle, than for a rich man to enter into the kingdom of God.**
(19:24)
Jesus comments to the disciples on the crestfallen departure of the rich young man unwilling to sell everything and give the proceeds to the poor.

117 **When his disciples heard it, they were exceedingly amazed, saying, Who then can be saved? But Jesus beheld them, and said unto them, With men this is impossible; but with God all things are possible.**
(19:25-6)
Jesus has just said that it is difficult for the rich to enter the kingdom of heaven. The disciples' amazement arises from their belief – common in the hierarchical society of the time – that people of wealth and position must necessarily also be morally superior to ordinary men and women. Jesus indicates that God's criteria in these matters are not the same as ours.

118 **So the last shall be first, and the first last: for many be called, but few chosen.**
(20:16)
In a parable comparing God to a vineyard-owner who hires labourers at different times of the day and gives the same pay to them all regardless of the hours worked, this is the farmer's answer to workmen who complain that they have worked longest and should be best rewarded. In the kingdom of heaven there are no hierarchies of deserving or reward.

119 **And if any man say ought unto you, ye shall say, The Lord hath need of them; and straightway he will send them.**
(21:3)
Preparing to ride into Jerusalem on Palm Sunday, Jesus sends two disciples to fetch an ass and a colt from a nearby village.

120 **All this was done, that it might be fulfilled which was spoken by the prophet, saying, Tell ye the daughter of Sion, Behold, thy King cometh unto thee, meek, and sitting upon an ass, and a colt the foal of an ass.**
(21:4-5)
Matthew specifically links Jesus' entry into Jerusalem on Palm Sunday with Old Testament prophecy (see Zech 5).

121 **And a very great multitude spread their garments in the way; others cut down branches from the trees, and strawed them in the way. And the multitudes that went before, and that followed, cried, saying, Hosanna to the Son of David: Blessed**

is he that cometh in the name of the Lord; Hosanna in the
highest.
(21:8–9)
As Jesus rides into Jerusalem, the onlookers strew palm-leaves at
his ass's feet and sing a psalm-verse in his honour (see Ps 204).
'Hosanna', meaning 'Praise be!', was a traditional cry of joy at the
Feast of Tabernacles, when the events of Palm Sunday took place.

122   **And said unto them, It is written, My house shall be called the
house of prayer; but ye have made it a den of thieves.**
(21:13)
Jesus throws money-changers and hucksters out of the temple
courtyard, quoting Isaiah and Jeremiah as scriptural authority.

123   **Now in the morning as he returned into the city, he hungered.
And when he saw a fig tree in the way, he came to it, and
found nothing thereon, but leaves only, and said unto it, Let
no fruit grow on thee henceforward for ever. And presently
the fig tree withered away.**
(21:18–19)
Jesus curses the barren fig tree. This is a kind of parable-in-action,
showing the disciples what they could do if they had sufficient faith
– as Jesus explained it to them later – and also making the fig tree
symbolize all those who refused to welcome (that is, feed) God
when they had him in their midst. The idea of the bleakly
ungenerous person as a 'barren fig tree' became proverbial.

124   **Go ye therefore into the highways, and as many as ye shall
find, bid to the marriage. So those servants went out into the
highways, and gathered together all as many as they found,
both bad and good: and the wedding was furnished with
guests.**
(22:9–10)
These instructions come from Jesus' parable comparing God to a
king holding a wedding, who calls people from the streets to be
guests and then ejects a man who comes without a wedding
garment. The implication of the parable is that being called is not
enough in itself: a wholehearted response to the call is also
necessary.

125   **And he saith unto them, Whose is this image and
superscription? They say unto him, Caesar's. Then saith he
unto them, Render therefore unto Caesar the things which
are Caesar's; and unto God the things that are God's.**
(22:20–1)

The Pharisees try to trap Jesus by getting him to say that God is above the Roman emperor, a crime under Roman law. Jesus sends for a coin and asks them whose head is shown on it. He means that worldly tribute (that is, in this context, cash; but the Jews traditionally associated financial riches with false gods) should be paid to worldly authority, and that it has no necessary connection with things spiritual. The answer uses the same hair-splitting logic with which the Pharisees themselves interpreted matters of law, and it silences them.

126 **In the resurrection they neither marry, nor are given in marriage, but are as the angels of God in heaven.**
(22:30)
A group of Sadducees (sectarians who did not believe in resurrection) have tried to trap Jesus by asking what happens after death to a woman who has been married seven times on earth: is she just one man's husband in heaven, or an adulterer? Jesus' mild answer is in fact a rebuke: the Sadducees are completely misunderstanding heaven by assuming that it has the same laws, preoccupations and gradations as on earth.

127 **Jesus said unto him, Thou shalt love the Lord thy God with all thy heart, and with all thy soul, and with all thy mind. This is the first and great commandment. And the second is like unto it, Thou shalt love thy neighbour as thyself. On these two commandments hang all the law and the prophets.**
(22:37–40)
A Pharisee tries to make Jesus say which is the most important of the Ten Commandments – a statement which would immediately ally him with one sect or another, and infuriate the rest. Jesus sidesteps the problem, reiterates his own frequent teaching, and finally, by pointing out that what he says is part of the law of Moses and of the prophets' teaching, leaves his interlocutor speechless.

128 **But be not ye called Rabbi: for one is your Master, even Christ; and all ye are brethren. And call no man your father upon the earth: for one is your Father, which is in heaven. Neither be ye called masters: for one is your Master, even Christ. But he that is greatest among you shall be your servant.**
(23:8–11)
Jesus preaches against the Pharisees, with their love of their own social distinction. 'Rabbi', in the first verse quoted, means 'teacher'.

129 **Ye blind guides, which strain at a gnat, and swallow a camel.**
(23:24)

Jesus' preaching against the Pharisees' hypocrisy continues. The metaphors here are analogous to his earlier teaching about motes and beams in the eye (see Matt 36).

130   Woe unto you, scribes and Pharisees, hypocrites! for ye are like unto whited sepulchres, which indeed appear beautiful outward, but are within full of dead men's bones, and of all uncleanness.
(23:27)
Jesus continues to preach against the Pharisees' hypocrisy, their façade of righteousness masking inner corruption. A sepulchre is a tomb: it stood above ground, was dome-shaped or barrel-roofed, and was coated with whitewash. 'Whited sepulchre', meaning 'hypocrite', became proverbial.

131   O Jerusalem, Jerusalem, thou that killest the prophets, and stonest them which are sent unto thee, how often would I have gathered thy children together, even as a hen gathereth her chickens under her wings, and ye would not!
(23:37)
Jesus' complaint against Jerusalem, the holy city, is that whereas it should be a refuge for all God's people, it has become so obsessed with legalism and the minutiae of religious observance that it is incapable of recognizing true spirituality (symbolized by the prophets) when it comes.

132   Verily I say unto you, There shall not be left here one stone upon another, that shall not be thrown down.
(24:2)
Jesus' disciples have invited him to admire the temple buildings, but he is in no mood for sightseeing. He is still preaching against the obsessive formalism which has replaced true religion in people's hearts, and now foretells the destruction of the temple.

133   Ye shall hear of wars and rumours of wars: see that ye be not troubled: for all these things must come to pass, but the end is not yet.
(24:6)
Jesus' disciples, troubled by his prediction that the temple will be destroyed stone by stone, ask what the signs will be of the end of the world. This is part of his answer.

134   For nation shall rise against nation, and kingdom against kingdom: and there shall be famines, and pestilences, and earthquakes, in divers places.
(24:7)
Jesus continues to talk of the end of the world.

135 **When ye therefore shall see the abomination of desolation, spoken of by Daniel the prophet, stand in the holy place, (whoso readeth, let him understand).**
(24:15)
Some scholars take this as a carefully obscure reference to the future destruction of Jerusalem by the Romans (AD 70). The 'abomination' is the standard their armies bear, which is a symbol of coming desolation, and the last phrase of this quotation is a signal that Jesus is speaking a kind of coded political message. The explanation is not farfetched in one way: people often spoke in such guarded, if lurid, terms of the occupying Romans. But there are no other examples in the Gospels of Jesus himself being politically mealy mouthed.

136 **For as the lightning cometh out of the east, and shineth even unto the west; so shall also the coming of the Son of man be.**
(24:27)
Jesus continues to talk of the Day of Judgment.

137 **For wheresoever the carcase is, there will the eagles be gathered together.**
(24:28)
The reference is to the 'eagles' (the standards) of the Roman army, glutting themselves on the loot of Jerusalem.

138 **Verily I say unto you, This generation shall not pass, till all these things be fulfilled. Heaven and earth shall pass away, but my words shall not pass away.**
(24:34–5)
The first verse refers to the fall of Jerusalem, which took place forty years after this prediction, in the lifetime of many of Jesus' hearers. The second verse contrasts Jesus' own teaching, which is eternal, with the impermanence of everything else which governs his hearers' experience.

139 **But of that day and hour knoweth no man, no, not the angels of heaven, but my Father only.**
(24:36)
Jesus refuses to answer his disciples' question about the exact date of the Day of Judgment – a sobering refusal for them, as he has just been outlining a series of devastating and imminent earthly disasters, including the sack of Jerusalem itself.

140 Watch therefore: for ye know not what hour your Lord doth
come. But know this, that if the goodman of the house had
known in what watch the thief would come, he would have
watched, and would not have suffered his house to be broken
up.
(24:42–3)
Jesus, still preaching about the Second Coming, uses a familiar
metaphor for spiritual vigilance: that of a prudent householder,
eternally on watch so as not to be taken by surprise.

141 And at midnight there was a cry made, Behold, the
bridegroom cometh; go ye out to meet him.
(25:6)
These words come from the parable of the wise and foolish virgins.
All ten are waiting for the bridegroom to come to the evening
wedding feast, but only five have prudently brought oil for their
lamps. The foolish virgins hear this cry and rush off to buy oil; when
they come back, the bridegroom and the wise virgins have gone into
the wedding, and the doors are locked.

142 Watch therefore, for ye know neither the day nor the hour
wherein the Son of man cometh.
(25:13)
Jesus explains the point of the parable of the wise and foolish
virgins: spiritual vigilance.

143 For the kingdom of heaven is as a man travelling into a far
country, who called his own servants, and delivered unto
them his goods. And unto one he gave five talents, to another
two, and to another one; to every man according to his several
ability; and straightway took his journey.
(25:14–15)
Jesus begins the parable of the talents. A 'talent' was a large sum of
money, a weight of silver coins. Its more usual English meaning is
actually a metaphor, and that metaphorical meaning derives from
this parable.

144 His lord said unto him, Well done, thou good and faithful
servant: thou hast been faithful over a few things, I will make
thee ruler over many things: enter thou into the joy of thy
lord.
(25:21)
In the parable of the talents, the master praises the servants who
have used, not buried, the talents he gave them.

145 Then he which had received the one talent came and said,
Lord, I knew thee that thou art an hard man, reaping where
thou hast not sown, and gathering where thou hast not
strawed: And I was afraid, and went and hid thy talent in the
earth: lo, there thou hast that is thine.
(25:24–5)
The last servant of the lord in the parable of the talents comes to
give an account of his stewardship. From these verses, the
metaphorical idea of burying one's talents has entered the language.

146 For unto every one that hath shall be given, and he shall have
abundance: but from him that hath not shall be taken away
even that which he hath. And cast ye the unprofitable servant
into outer darkness: there shall be weeping and gnashing of
teeth.
(25:29–30)
The lord in the parable of the talents punishes the servant who hid
his talent instead of exploiting it. The parable's moral, a
denunciation of spiritual cowardice, is uncompromising and
inescapable.

147 When the Son of man shall come in his glory, and all the holy
angels with him, then shall he sit upon the throne of his glory:
And before him shall be gathered all nations: and he shall
separate them one from another, as a shepherd divideth his
sheep from the goats: And he shall set the sheep on his right
hand, but the goats on the left.
(25:31–3)
Jesus talks of the Day of Judgment. Unlike the prophets, who were
concerned more with the awesome trappings of the royal judge, or
with the results of his judgment, Jesus deals with the actual moment
of judgment itself.

148 Come, ye blessed of my Father, inherit the kingdom prepared
for you from the foundation of the world: For I was an
hungred, and ye gave me meat: I was thirsty, and ye gave me
drink: I was a stranger, and ye took me in: Naked, and ye
clothed me: I was sick, and ye visited me: I was in prison, and
ye came unto me.
(25:34–6)
The king of heaven rewards the righteous on the Day of Judgment.

149 Inasmuch as ye have done it unto one of the least of these my
brethren, ye have done it unto me.
(25:40)

Bewildered, the righteous on the Day of Judgment ask when it was that they helped, clothed or visited the king of heaven (see Matt 148). He answers them.

150 There came unto him a woman having an alabaster box of very precious ointment, and poured it on his head, as he sat at meat. But when his disciples saw it, they had indignation, saying, To what purpose is this waste? For this ointment might have been sold for much, and given to the poor.
(26:7–9)
The pouring of ointment, or anointing, was one of the main events in the coronation ritual.

151 Why trouble ye the woman? for she hath wrought a good work upon me. For ye have the poor always with you; but me ye have not always. For in that she hath poured this ointment on my body, she did it for my burial.
(26:10–12)
The disciples have scolded the woman who 'wasted' her ointment by anointing Jesus' head with it. Jesus in turn scolds them.

152 Then one of the twelve, called Judas Iscariot, went unto the chief priests, And said unto them, What will ye give me and I will deliver him unto you? And they covenanted with him for thirty pieces of silver.
(26:14–15)
Events begin to move towards the betrayal and trial of Christ. 'Thirty pieces of silver' has become synonymous for modern readers with the price of betrayal; in St Matthew's time the phrase had another significance entirely, being the price of a none-too-expensive slave, a household or farmyard drudge.

153 The Son of man goeth as it is written of him: but woe unto that man by whom the Son of man is betrayed! it had been good for that man if he had not been born.
(26:24)
At the Last Supper, Jesus talks to his disciples about the coming betrayal.

154 And as they were eating, Jesus took bread, and blessed it, and brake it, and gave it to the disciples, and said, Take, eat: this is my body. And he took the cup, and gave thanks, and gave it to them, saying, Drink ye all of it; For this is my blood of the new testament, which is shed for many for the remission of sins.
(26:26–8)

These simple events from the Last Supper were symbolically
re-enacted by Christians from the very earliest days after Jesus'
death and resurrection, and have become sacraments at the heart of
Christian worship. In Roman times it was they, more than anything
else Christians did or said, which led to popular revulsion and
persecution: they were misinterpreted by the authorities, and
described at Christian trials, as cannibalism.

155   **Jesus said unto him, Verily I say unto thee, That this night,
before the cock crow, thou shalt deny me thrice.**
(26:34)
Jesus has warned the disciples that they will all suffer for his sake,
and Peter has hotly insisted that he will never be disloyal to Jesus.

156   **Then saith he unto them, My soul is exceeding sorrowful,
even unto death: tarry ye here, and watch with me.**
(26:38)
Jesus has gone with his disciples to Gethsemane, and has taken
Peter, James and John aside from the others.

157   **O my Father, if it be possible, let this cup pass from me:
nevertheless, not as I will, but as thou wilt.**
(26:39)
Jesus prays in Gethsemane: the first time in the Bible that he prays
on his own behalf.

158   **And he cometh unto the disciples, and findeth them asleep,
and saith unto Peter, What, could ye not watch with me one
hour? Watch and pray, that ye enter not into temptation: the
spirit indeed is willing, but the flesh is weak.**
(26:40–1)
After praying in Gethsemane, Jesus goes back to Peter and the
others.

159   **Behold, the hour is at hand, and the Son of man is betrayed
into the hands of sinners.**
(26:45)
Jesus has seen Judas approaching with soldiers and rouses Peter,
James and John.

160   **And forthwith he came to Jesus, and said, Hail, master; and
kissed him.**
(26:49)
Judas betrays Jesus' identity to the soldiers. Ever since this event,
the expression 'Judas kiss' has been proverbial for a show of feigned
affection.

161 Then said Jesus unto him, Put up again thy sword into his place: for all they that take the sword shall perish with the sword.
(26:52)
Peter has drawn a sword to defend Jesus, and has cut off the ear of one of the high priest's servants.

162 But Jesus held his peace. And the high priest answered and said unto him, I adjure thee by the living God, that thou tell us whether thou be the Christ, the Son of God. Jesus saith unto him, Thou hast said.
(26:63–4)
Jesus is examined by Caiaphas the high priest of Jerusalem.

163 And after a while came unto him they that stood by, and said to Peter, Surely thou also art one of them; for thy speech bewrayeth thee. Then began he to curse and to swear, saying, I know not the man. And immediately the cock crew. And Peter remembered the word of Jesus, which said unto him, Before the cock crow, thou shalt deny me thrice. And he went out, and wept bitterly.
(26:73–5)
Peter, sitting in a courtyard of the high priest's palace, has been asked three times if he is a follower of Jesus, and has denied it three times.

164 Have thou nothing to do with that just man: for I have suffered many things this day in a dream because of him.
(27:19)
Pilate's wife urges him to take no more part in Jesus' death.

165 He took water, and washed his hands before the multitude.
(27:24)
Pilate symbolically cleanses himself from complicity in Jesus' death. The phrase 'to wash one's hands' of a matter became proverbial.

166 Then answered all the people, and said, His blood be on us, and on our children.
(27:25)
The people gladly accept the responsibility for Jesus' death which Pilate has just disowned.

167 THIS IS JESUS THE KING OF THE JEWS.
(27:37)
Traditionally, every Roman prisoner executed on the cross had a piece of paper nailed above his head outlining his crime. In Jesus' case, there being no crime under Roman law, the soldiers ironically

write their version of the claim that he is the Messiah, the saviour-king of the Jewish people. The initial letters of the Latin words IESUS NAZARENUS REX IUDAEORUM ('Jesus of Nazareth King of the Jews') often appear and are often worked into the ornamentation or embroidery in Christian churches.

168 He saved others; himself he cannot save.
(27:42)
The scribes and elders mock Jesus on the cross.

169 And about the ninth hour Jesus cried with a loud voice, saying, Eli, Eli, lama sabachthani? that is to say, My God, my God, why hast thou forsaken me?
(27:46)
Jesus' last words on the cross are a quotation from one of the Psalms (see Ps 38).

170 He is not here; for he is risen, as he said. Come, see the place where the Lord lay.
(28:6)
An angel in the empty tomb announces the Resurrection to Mary Magdalene and Mary, Jesus' mother.

171 Lo, I am with you alway, even unto the end of the world. Amen.
(28:20)
These words of reassurance, from the risen Christ to his disciples, end St Matthew's gospel.

St Mark

1 There cometh one mightier than I after me, the latchet of whose shoes I am not worthy to stoop down and unloose. I indeed have baptized you with water: but he shall baptize you with the Holy Ghost.
(1:7–8)
John the Baptist prophesies the coming of the Messiah.

2 And they come unto him, bringing one sick of the palsy, which was borne of four. And when they could not come nigh unto him for the press, they uncovered the roof where he was: and when they had broken it up, they let down the bed wherein the sick of the palsy lay.
(2:3–4)

Jesus, preaching in a house in Capernaum, is surrounded by such a throng that the only way a sick man can be brought to him for healing is through the roof. 'Palsy' is a medieval word, a near-miss at pronouncing the Greek word *paralysis*.

3 **And he said unto them, The sabbath was made for man, and not man for the sabbath.**
(2:27)
Jesus rebukes Pharisees who have objected to his disciples 'working' (that is, rubbing the husks from corn-grains before eating them) on the Sabbath.

4 **And if a kingdom be divided against itself, that kingdom cannot stand. And if a house be divided against itself, that house cannot stand.**
(3:24–5)
This is Jesus' answer to the accusation that he casts out devils by the power of Beelzebub king of devils. Devils' work is to fight good; why should they fight one another instead?

5 **My name is Legion: for we are many.**
(5:9)
A madman (that is 'one possessed by devils') has begged Jesus to cure him, and Jesus asks the name of the devils who plague him. The answer – the phrase quoted here – is a grim joke: a legion was a division of the Roman army, and consisted of 6,000 soldiers plus at least an equal number of camp-followers.

6 **And they come to Jesus, and see him that was possessed with the devil, and had the legion, sitting, and clothed, and in his right mind: and they were afraid.**
(5:15)
Jesus drives the legion of devils into a herd of pigs, which run into the sea and drown. The villagers rush out to see what all the commotion is. 'Clothed and in his right mind' became proverbial.

7 **And straightway his ears were opened, and the string of his tongue was loosed, and he spake plain.**
(7:35)
A deaf and dumb man has come to Jesus, and Jesus has put his fingers into his ears, touched his tongue and said 'Be opened'.

8 **And he looked up, and said, I see men as trees, walking.**
(8:24)
Jesus has cured a blind man, and has asked him what he sees. This answer shows that the man's eyes are still blurred, and Jesus touches them and clears them.

9   Jesus said unto him, If thou canst believe, all things are
     possible to him that believeth. And straightway the father of
     the child cried out, and said with tears, Lord, I believe; help
     thou mine unbelief.
     (9:23–4)
     A man has asked Jesus to cure his son of epilepsy. The last phrase
     quoted became one of the best-known of all Christian prayers.

10   Suffer the little children to come unto me, and forbid them
     not: for of such is the kingdom of God. Verily I say unto you,
     Whosoever shall not receive the kingdom of God as a little
     child, he shall not enter therein. And he took them up in his
     arms, put his hands upon them, and blessed them.
     (10:14–16)
     People have brought their children for Jesus to bless, and the
     disciples, concerned about the size of the crowd, are trying to keep
     them away from him. 'Suffer' means 'allow'.

11   Ye know not what ye ask: can ye drink of the cup that I drink
     of? and be baptized with the baptism that I am baptized with?
     (10:38)
     The disciples James and John have asked Jesus if they can sit on his
     left and right, in glory, in the kingdom of heaven. This is his answer.

12   The Son of man came not to be ministered unto, but to
     minister, and to give his life a ransom for many.
     (10:45)
     The other disciples are angry with James and John for asking
     special privileges in the kingdom of heaven. Jesus points out that
     there are no hierarchies in heaven: a development of his theme that
     'the first shall be last, and the last shall be first'.

13   And there came a certain poor widow, and she threw in two
     mites, which make a farthing.
     (12:42)
     Jesus sits by the treasury of the temple, watching people make
     offerings. The rich give large offerings, and the widow gives two
     tiny coins, the smallest there are. But because she has given all she
     has, Jesus says that her gift far exceeds the donations of the rich: it
     is a parable of spiritual dedication. 'Widow's mite', meaning an
     apparently small amount which is none the less all one can give,
     became proverbial.

14   Watch ye therefore: for ye know not when the master of the
     house cometh, at even, or at midnight, or at the cockcrowing,
     or in the morning: Lest coming suddenly he find you
     sleeping. And what I say unto you I say unto all, Watch.
     (13:35–7)

Jesus is recommending spiritual vigilance, since no one knows when
the Day of Judgment will come.

15   **And there followed him a certain young man, having a linen
cloth cast about his naked body; and the young men laid hold
on him: And he left the linen cloth, and fled from them
naked.**
(14:51–2)
Most scholars say that this young man in Gethsemane with Jesus'
disciples is Mark himself, and that the point of putting in this
anecdote is to authenticate his account of Jesus' arrest.

16   **And when the centurion, which stood over against him, saw
that he so cried out, and gave up the ghost, he said, Truly this
man was the Son of God.**
(15:39)
The centurion in charge of Jesus' execution is the first person to be
converted after Jesus' death.

17   **And he said unto them, Go ye into all the world, and preach
the gospel to every creature.**
(16:15)
Jesus appears to the disciples after the Resurrection and orders
them to preach his gospel to the whole world. It is from this
command that they were given the name 'apostles', that is 'those
sent out'.

St Luke

1   **For he shall be great in the sight of the Lord, and shall drink
neither wine nor strong drink; and he shall be filled with the
Holy Ghost, even from his mother's womb.**
(1:15)
God's angel prophesies the birth and nature of John the Baptist. To
drink wine and strong drink was a symbol for idolatry.

2   **Hail, thou that art highly favoured, the Lord is with thee:
blessed art thou among women.**
(1:28)
This is the angel Gabriel's salutation to Mary, the future mother of
Jesus.

3   And the angel said unto her, Fear not, Mary: for thou hast found favour with God. And, behold, thou shalt conceive in thy womb, and bring forth a son, and shalt call his name JESUS.
(1:30–1)
Gabriel, God's messenger, reassures Mary.

4   And Mary said, Behold the handmaid of the Lord; be it unto me according to thy word. And the angel departed from her.
(1:38)
Mary accepts the message of the angel Gabriel.

5   Blessed art thou among women, and blessed is the fruit of thy womb.
(1:42)
Elizabeth, Mary's cousin and the future mother of John the Baptist, responds with joy to Mary's news that she, too, is pregnant.

6   And Mary said, My soul doth magnify the Lord, And my spirit hath rejoiced in God my Saviour. For he hath regarded the low estate of his handmaiden: for, behold, from henceforth all generations shall call me blessed. For he that is mighty hath done to me great things; and holy is his name. And his mercy is on them that fear him from generation to generation. He hath shewed strength with his arm; he hath scattered the proud in the imagination of their hearts. He hath put down the mighty from their seats, and exalted them of low degree. He hath filled the hungry with good things; and the rich he hath sent empty away. He hath holpen his servant Israel, in remembrance of his mercy; As he spake to our fathers, to Abraham, and to his seed for ever.
(1:46–55)
Mary's hymn of praise and thanks to God has become a main prayer of the Christian Church, the *Magnificat* (from *Magnificat anima mea*, 'my soul magnifies'). 'Holpen' means 'helped'.

7   And thou, child, shalt be called the prophet of the Highest: for thou shalt go before the face of the Lord to prepare his ways; To give knowledge of salvation unto his people by the remission of their sins, Through the tender mercy of our God; whereby the dayspring from on high hath visited us, To give light to them that sit in darkness and in the shadow of death, to guide our feet into the way of peace.
(1:76–9)
Zacharias speaks with joy of his son who is soon to be born, John the Baptist.

8   And it came to pass in those days, that there went out a
decree from Caesar Augustus, that all the world should be
taxed.
(2:1)
One of the main goals of Augustus, the first Roman emperor, was to
make his empire politically stable as well as militarily secure. To do
this, and to regulate the flow of taxes to the imperial treasury, he
ordered a census throughout the empire some time between the
years we now number as 4 BC and AD 1 – the exact date, like many in
Augustus' reign, is imprecise. This event involved Mary and Joseph
in going from Nazareth to Bethlehem, since everyone had to
register for the census in the place of their birth. It involved them in
a journey of 70 miles (110 km), not as far as some people must have
had to travel, but hazardous for a woman in the last weeks of
pregnancy.

9   And she brought forth her firstborn son, and wrapped him in
swaddling clothes, and laid him in a manger; because there
was no room for them in the inn.
(2:7)
Mary gives birth to Jesus in the stable, where she and Joseph have
been quartered because the inn is full.

10   And, lo, the angel of the Lord came upon them, and the glory
of the Lord shone round about them: and they were sore
afraid.
(2:9)
God's angel appears to shepherds in the fields near Bethlehem.

11   And the angel said unto them, Fear not: for, behold, I bring
you good tidings of great joy, which shall be to all people. For
unto you is born this day in the city of David a Saviour, which
is Christ the Lord.
(2:10–11)
The angel announces to the shepherds that Jesus is born.

12   Glory to God in the highest, and on earth peace, good will
toward men.
(2:14)
The shepherds see a choir of angels hymning God. The last words
of this verse are often translated 'peace to men of good will' or,
closest of all to the original Greek, 'peace to the men he favours'.

13   But Mary kept all these things, and pondered them in her
heart.
(2:19)

The meaning of this famous phrase has been much disputed. The favourite explanation is that Mary, a simple village girl, was brought to spiritual maturity by watching the growth of her son, as Christians have been fulfilled by him ever since.

14   **Lord, now lettest thou thy servant depart in peace, according to thy word: For mine eyes have seen thy salvation, Which thou hast prepared before the face of all people; A light to lighten the Gentiles, and the glory of thy people Israel.**
(2:29–32)
When the infant Jesus was presented in the temple, forty days after his birth, the old man Simeon welcomed him with rapture as the Lord's anointed. He was the first person to acknowledge Jesus as the Messiah, and his words have been used ever since as a prayer and as part of many services, both in English and in Latin (*Nunc dimittis*).

15   **And he said unto them, How is it that ye sought me? wist ye not that I must be about my Father's business?**
(2:49)
Jesus, twelve years old, has disappeared, and Mary and Joseph have at last found him in the temple in Jerusalem, discussing religious matters with textual scholars, and astonishing them with his knowledge. Mary and Joseph scold him, and this is his reply.

16   **Physician, heal thyself.**
(4:23)
Jesus, preaching in the synagogue at Nazareth to people who know him only as the carpenter's son, says that they will quote this proverb at him, meaning 'who are you to preach to us?'

17   **And Simon answering said unto him, Master, we have toiled all the night, and have taken nothing: nevertheless at thy word I will let down the net.**
(5:5)
Jesus, besieged by eager crowds, has stood to preach in Simon Peter's boat, just offshore. Afterwards he tells Simon to sail into deep water and let down his nets to fish. Simon protests.

18   **When Simon Peter saw it, he fell down at Jesus' knees, saying, Depart from me; for I am a sinful man, O Lord. For he was astonished, and all that were with him, at the draught of the fishes which they had taken.**
(5:8–9)
Simon's nets, and the nets of all the fishermen who go to help him, are filled with fish to bursting. 'Draught' means 'catch'.

19   Woe unto you, when all men shall speak well of you! for so did
their fathers to the false prophets.
(6:26)
Jesus is preaching against people who are content with the world's
praise, who are satisfied with the façade of life.

20   Give, and it shall be given unto you; good measure, pressed
down, and shaken together, and running over, shall men give
into your bosom.
(6:38)
Jesus advocates not so much charity as spiritual openhandedness.

21   She hath washed my feet with tears, and wiped them with the
hairs of her head.
(7:44)
Jesus praises the woman who anointed him with ointment and
washed his feet in an ecstacy of religious fervour.

22   Her sins, which are many, are forgiven; for she loved much.
(7:47)
Jesus is speaking of the woman whose ecstatic belief made her
anoint him and wash his feet, as if he were a king.

23   For whosoever hath, to him shall be given; and whosoever
hath not, from him shall be taken even that which he seemeth
to have.
(8:18)
This verse ends the parable of the sower and the seed. The message
is that we should all be fertile soil for the seed of God's word; if we
are not, if we are spiritually barren, we shall have nothing to comfort
us when the Day of Judgment comes.

24   And Jesus said unto him, No man, having put his hand to the
plough, and looking back, is fit for the kingdom of God.
(9:62)
Jesus rebukes a man who says he will follow Jesus but must first go
home and say goodbye to his family.

25   And into whatsoever house ye enter, first say, Peace be to this
house. And if the son of peace be there, your peace shall rest
upon it: if not, it shall turn to you again.
(10:5–6)
Jesus sends seventy people out to preach in the towns and villages.

26   And in the same house remain, eating and drinking such
things as they give: for the labourer is worthy of his hire. Go
not from house to house.
(10:7)

Jesus tells the preachers he is sending out that they should behave like guests, not beggars: their message will repay their hosts.

27   And Jesus answering said, A certain man went down from Jerusalem to Jericho, and fell among thieves, which stripped him of his raiment, and wounded him, and departed, leaving him half dead. And by chance there came down a certain priest that way: and when he saw him, he passed by on the other side.
(10:30–1)
A young man, hearing Jesus' instruction 'Love thy neighbour as thyself', has asked 'Who is my neighbour?' Jesus answers with the parable of the Good Samaritan. For all the priest's ostensible holiness, he will have nothing to do with the victim; a Levite (another kind of priest) is equally disdainful; in the end it is a Samaritan, someone Jesus' hearers would have despised as a low-caste sinner and idolator, who shows genuine compassion.

28   Go, and do thou likewise.
(10:37)
Jesus rounds off the story of the Good Samaritan with the kind of pithy moral instruction he favoured after each of his parables.

29   But Martha was cumbered about much serving, and came to him, and said, Lord, dost thou not care that my sister hath left me to serve alone? bid her therefore that she help me.
(10:40)
Martha's sister Mary has gone to listen to Jesus' preaching, and Martha complains that she needs help in the house.

30   Mary hath chosen that good part, which shall not be taken away from her.
(10:42)
Jesus answers Martha's complaints: his message is more important than housework.

31   When a strong man armed keepeth his palace, his goods are in peace: But when a stronger than he shall come upon him, and overcome him, he taketh from him all his armour wherein he trusted, and divideth his spoils.
(11:21–2)
Jesus is answering the Pharisees who say that he can only be casting out devils by the power of Beelzebub himself, king of devils. He is stronger than Satan, and needs no help.

32   **Beware ye of the leaven of the Pharisees, which is hypocrisy.**
(12:1)
Jesus has earlier compared true belief to yeast, that is 'leaven',
which gives life to the whole personality. The Pharisees replace true
belief with a self-righteous parade of godliness, which is both
illusion and delusion, he now says. 'Hypocrisy' in Greek means
play-acting.

33   **And he said, This will I do: I will pull down my barns, and
build greater; and there will I bestow all my fruits and my
goods. And I will say to my soul, Soul, thou hast much goods
laid up for many years; take thine ease, eat, drink, and be
merry. But God said unto him, Thou fool, this night thy soul
shall be required of thee: then whose shall those things be,
which thou hast provided?**
(12:18–20)
Preaching on the theme that spiritual wealth beggars all earthly
treasure, Jesus tells a parable of a rich fool who builds huge
treasuries and then revels in his possessions, not realizing that he
could be called to spiritual account tomorrow. Most Biblical
comparisons of worldly and spiritual wealth have the implied
subtext that worldly wealth is a symbol for idolatry; there seems to
be no such implication here.

34   **Fear not, little flock; for it is your Father's good pleasure to
give you the kingdom.**
(12:32)
Jesus is preaching to his disciples about the security of true
godliness.

35   **Let your loins be girded about, and your lights burning.**
(12:35)
Jesus advocates spiritual vigilance, since no one knows when the day
of the kingdom of heaven will dawn.

36   **But he shall say, I tell you, I know you not whence ye are;
depart from me, all ye workers of iniquity.**
(13:27)
Those who are not spiritually vigilant will find themselves shut out
from the kingdom of heaven when the Messiah comes.

37   **Friend, go up higher.**
(14:10)
Jesus preaches humility, saying that those who take the higher place
at God's table will be asked to move down, and those who take the
lower place will be promoted. The speaker of the quoted words, the
host in the parable, stands for God himself.

38 **For whosoever exalteth himself shall be abased; and he that humbleth himself shall be exalted.**
(14:11)
Jesus pithily sums up his teaching about spiritual humility.

39 **I pray thee have me excused.**
(14:18)
In a parable, Jesus compares the coming of the kingdom of God to a feast. The host issues invitations, saying that everything is ready, only to be met by all kinds of excuses from prospective guests.

40 **And another said, I have married a wife, and therefore I cannot come.**
(14:20)
One of the invited guests to the feast which symbolizes the kingdom of heaven declines to come: he puts worldly concerns before spiritual.

41 **Go out quickly into the streets and lanes of the city, and bring in hither the poor, and the maimed, and the halt, and the blind.**
(14:21)
The host in the parable, giving a feast to which none of the invited guests come, throws his doors – which symbolize the gates of the kingdom of heaven – wide to the world's dispossessed.

42 **Go out into the highways and hedges, and compel them to come in, that my house may be filled.**
(14:23)
The host giving the feast – symbolizing God offering people a place in the kingdom of heaven – is driven to compel people to be his guests.

43 **For which of you, intending to build a tower, sitteth not down first, and counteth the cost, whether he have sufficient to finish it?**
(14:28)
Jesus is advising would-be followers to think the matter through before rushing to join him. 'To count the cost' became proverbial.

44 **Rejoice with me; for I have found my sheep which was lost.**
(15:6)
In answer to Pharisees who grumble when he eats with 'publicans and sinners', Jesus has told the parable of the lost sheep. These are the words of the shepherd in the story when he brings the lost sheep back to the fold.

45   I say unto you, that likewise joy shall be in heaven over one
sinner that repenteth, more than over ninety and nine just
persons, which need no repentance.
(15:7)
Jesus points the moral of the parable of the shepherd and the lost
sheep.

46   The younger son gathered all together, and took his journey
into a far country, and there wasted his substance with
riotous living.
(15:13)
Still responding to Pharisaical grumbles that he associates with
sinners instead of with the righteous, Jesus tells the parable of the
prodigal son.

47   I will arise and go to my father, and will say unto him, Father,
I have sinned against heaven, and before thee, And am no
more worthy to be called thy son: make me as one of thy hired
servants.
(15:18–19)
The prodigal son in the parable, starving and friendless, decides to
throw himself on his father's mercy.

48   Bring hither the fatted calf, and kill it; and let us eat, and be
merry: For this my son was dead, and is alive again: he was
lost, and is found.
(15:23–4)
The father in the parable unreservedly welcomes home his prodigal
son.

49   As soon as this thy son was come, which hath devoured thy
living with harlots, thou hast killed for him the fatted calf.
(15:30)
The brother of the prodigal in the parable objects when his wastrel
brother is better treated than he is himself, for all his years of
devotion and blamelessness. 'To devour someone's living with
harlots' became proverbial.

50   It was meet that we should make merry, and be glad: for this
thy brother was dead, and is alive again; and was lost, and is
found.
(15:32)
In the parable, the father of the prodigal son answers the 'good'
son's objections that the prodigal is welcomed home with open
arms.

51 Then the steward said within himself, What shall I do? for my
lord taketh away from me the stewardship: I cannot dig; to
beg I am ashamed.
(16:3)
Jesus is telling a parable about honest and dishonest service. The
master in the story has told his dishonest steward that he is to be
dismissed.

52 And the lord commended the unjust steward, because he had
done wisely: for the children of this world are in their
generation wiser than the children of light.
(16:8)
The dishonest steward in the parable, hearing that he is to be
sacked, has gone round his master's debtors reducing the amounts
they owe. Jesus praises him for being true to his own nature.

53 And I say unto you, Make to yourselves friends of the
mammon of unrighteousness; that, when ye fail, they may
receive you into everlasting habitations.
(16:9)
Jesus explains the meaning of the parable of the unjust steward.
'Mammon' is the Syriac word for wealth, but was used in the New
Testament as if it was an idol, a heathen god of profit. Certainly this
meaning, the idea of worshipping ill-gotten gains as a god, has stuck
to the phrase 'mammon of unrighteousness' ever since.

54 He that is faithful in that which is least is faithful also in
much: and he that is unjust in the least is unjust also in much.
If therefore ye have not been faithful in the unrighteous
mammon, who will commit to your trust the true riches?
(16:10–11)
The point of this parable has been much disputed – why is the
dishonest manager rewarded for what he does? These verses
suggest an answer. He is true to himself in the comparatively small
issue of worldly dishonesty (he goes on cheating his master, even
when he is found out); this suggests that in more important matters,
such as the true worship of God in the kingdom of heaven, he will
also be consistent. The context is a rebuke from Jesus to Pharisees
who objected to him associating with 'publicans and sinners'; he
means that sinners or not, at least his associates make no pretence
to be anything but what they are.

55 There was a certain rich man, which was clothed in purple
and fine linen, and fared sumptuously every day: And there
was a certain beggar named Lazarus, which was laid at his
gate, full of sores, And desiring to be fed from the crumbs

which fell from the rich man's table: moreover the dogs came
and licked his sores.
(16:19–21)
Pursuing his teaching to the Pharisees, that a self-righteous façade
of goodness on earth is no guarantee of a place in the kingdom of
heaven, Jesus tells this parable.

56　And it came to pass, that the beggar died, and was carried by
the angels into Abraham's bosom: the rich man also died, and
was buried; And in hell he lift up his eyes, being in torments,
and seeth Abraham afar off, and Lazarus in his bosom.
(16:22–3)
Jesus continues his parable of the self-righteous rich man and the
beggar Lazarus.

57　Between us and you there is a great gulf fixed.
(16:26)
The rich man in the parable, tormented by thirst in hell, has begged
Abraham to send Lazarus from heaven with a drop of water on the
end of his finger. Abraham refuses.

58　Abraham saith unto him, They have Moses and the prophets;
let them hear them. And he said, Nay, father Abraham: but if
one went unto them from the dead, they will repent. And he
said unto him, if they hear not Moses and the prophets,
neither will they be persuaded, though one rose from the
dead.
(16:29–31)
The rich man in the parable, tormented in hell, has asked Abraham
to send the beggar Lazarus with word of his plight to his fine rich
friends on earth, so that they can avoid the sins for which he is being
punished. Abraham refuses, saying that they have the teaching of
Moses and the prophets, and have ignored it. These last verses
gained particular force in view both of Jesus' raising from the dead
of the real-life Lazarus later on, and of his own death and
resurrection. The moral, about true devotion to the true God, is
blunt and clear.

59　The kingdom of God cometh not with observation: Neither
shall they say, Lo here! or, lo there! for, behold, the kingdom
of God is within you.
(17:20–1)
Jesus answers Pharisees who have asked for the exact date of the
coming of the kingdom of heaven.

60 Two men went up into the temple to pray; the one a Pharisee, and the other a publican. The Pharisee stood and prayed thus with himself, God, I thank thee, that I am not as other men are, extortioners, unjust, adulterers, or even as this publican. I fast twice in the week, I give tithes of all that I possess. And the publican, standing afar off, would not lift up so much as his eyes unto heaven, but smote upon his breast, saying, God be merciful to me a sinner. I tell you, this man went down to his house justified rather than the other: for every one that exalteth himself shall be abased; and he that humbleth himself shall be exalted.
(18:10–14)
Jesus tells a parable about true honesty of soul.

61 This day is salvation come to this house, forsomuch as he also is a son of Abraham.
(19:9)
Jesus has gone to eat with Zacchaeus, a rich tax-collector, and the crowd have grumbled that Zacchaeus is unworthy because of his profession. Jesus reminds them that, sinner or not, Zacchaeus is as much one of the chosen as they are.

62 And some of the Pharisees from among the multitude said unto him, Master, rebuke thy disciples. And he answered and said unto them, I tell you that, if these should hold their peace, the stones would immediately cry out.
(19:39–40)
Jesus is riding into Jerusalem on an ass, and his followers are shouting and singing that he is the king who comes in God's name. Outraged Pharisees object to this, and Jesus rebukes them.

63 And he beheld them, and said, What is this then that is written, The stone which the builders rejected, the same is become the head of the corner? Whosoever shall fall upon that stone shall be broken; but on whomsoever it shall fall, it will grind him to powder.
(20:17–18)
Shortly after telling the parable of the vineyard – in which wicked labourers kill all messengers sent by their master to tell them to mend their ways, and end by killing the master's son himself – Jesus quotes this passage from the Psalms (see Ps 202). The image would have reminded his hearers of the frequent Old Testament analogy between God and a building securely built; now Jesus fits himself, the cornerstone, into that edifice, to the fury of his Pharisaical hearers, who at once plot to have him arrested for blasphemy.

64   **In your patience possess ye your souls.**
      (21:19)
      Jesus' disciples have asked how long they will have to wait for the
      Day of Judgment, and this is the heart of his answer. 'Possess your
      soul in patience' became proverbial.

65   **And when they were come to the place, which is called**
      Calvary, there they crucified him, and the malefactors, one on
      the right hand, and the other on the left.
      (23:33)
      The place of Jesus' crucifixion, the Roman execution-ground in
      Jerusalem, was a low hill called Golgotha ('Skull hill') by the locals
      and *Calvaria* (hence Calvary) in Latin.

66   **Then said Jesus, Father, forgive them; for they know not what**
      they do.
      (23:34)
      Jesus prays for the soldiers who have just nailed him to the cross.

67   **And he said unto Jesus, Lord, remember me when thou**
      comest into thy kingdom. And Jesus said unto him, Verily I
      say unto thee, To day shalt thou be with me in paradise.
      (23:42–3)
      One of the two thieves crucified with Jesus has cursed him, telling
      him that if he is truly the Christ he should save all three of them.
      The other thief, by contrast, shows both contrition and belief, and
      Jesus comforts him.

68   **And when Jesus had cried with a loud voice, he said, Father,**
      into thy hands I commend my spirit: and having said thus, he
      gave up the ghost.
      (23:46)
      Jesus' last words on the cross, a quotation from one of the Psalms
      (see Ps 52), have been widely paraphrased since as a Christian
      prayer of dedication to God.

69   **He was a good man, and a just.**
      (23:50)
      This is Luke's description of Joseph of Arimathea, the man who
      provided Jesus' tomb.

70   **Why seek ye the living among the dead? He is not here, but is**
      risen.
      (24:5–6)
      Angels speak to the women who have come to Jesus' tomb to wash
      and lay out his body.

71 **And their words seemed to them as idle tales, and they believed them not.**
(24:11)
The women have rushed from Jesus' tomb to tell the disciples news of his Resurrection. At first the disciples are incredulous. 'Idle tales' has entered the language; in Greek the phrase has approximately the same overtone of meaning as our 'fairy tales'.

72 **Behold my hands and my feet, that it is I myself: handle me, and see; for a spirit hath not flesh and bones, as ye see me have.**
(24:39)
Jesus appears to his disciples after the Resurrection.

73 **And they gave him a piece of a broiled fish, and of an honeycomb. And he took it, and did eat before them.**
(24:42–3)
Jesus eats ordinary food, to show that he is risen in the flesh and is not a spirit. The phrase 'a piece of broiled fish and a honeycomb' was once proverbial for 'proof positive'.

74 **That repentance and remission of sins should be preached in his name among all nations, beginning at Jerusalem.**
(24:47)
Jesus explains to the disciples the purpose of his crucifixion and Resurrection.

St John

1 **In the beginning was the Word, and the Word was with God, and the Word was God. The same was in the beginning with God. All things were made by him; and without him was not any thing made that was made.**
(1:1–3)
John begins his gospel with a philosophical prologue reflecting on the nature of God. He uses the Greek *logos* (which means both 'word' and 'order, rationality') to draw together all the images of God using words to bring order out of chaos at the moment of creation (see Gen 2). This passage is also widely taken to refer to the absolute literal authority of God's word as enshrined in the Bible.

2 **In him was life; and the life was the light of men. And the light shineth in darkness; and the darkness comprehended it not.**
(1:4–5)

John is using traditional Old Testament imagery, contrasting the
light of true belief with the darkness of idolatry. 'Him' is God.

3   **That was the true Light, which lighteth every man that
cometh into the world. He was in the world, and the world
was made by him, and the world knew him not.**
(1:9–10)
John identifies the Light of the World as Jesus, and then links Jesus
with God the creator.

4   **And the Word was made flesh, and dwelt among us, (and we
beheld his glory, the glory as of the only begotten of the
Father,) full of grace and truth.**
(1:14)
John identifies Jesus with the creative power of God, the Word
which brings all life into existence.

5   **The law was given by Moses, but grace and truth came by
Jesus Christ. No man hath seen God at any time; the only
begotten Son, which is in the bosom of the Father, he hath
declared him.**
(1:17–18)
Moses revealed only outward signs of God's authority; Jesus reveals
his inner reality.

6   **The next day John seeth Jesus coming unto him, and saith,
Behold the Lamb of God, which taketh away the sin of the
world.**
(1:29)
John the Baptist identifies Jesus with the Passover Lamb, the
symbol of God's deliverance of his Chosen People (see Exod 34).

7   **And Nathanael said unto him, Can there any good thing come
out of Nazareth? Philip saith unto him, Come and see.**
(1:46)
Philip has run to Nathanael, a devout man (whom some identify
with the disciple Bartholomew), with news that they have found the
Messiah: Jesus of Nazareth. 'Can any good thing come out of
Nazareth?' became proverbial.

8   **Jesus saith unto her, Woman, what have I to do with thee?
mine hour is not yet come.**
(2:4)
At a wedding feast in Cana, the wine runs out and Jesus' mother
asks him for a miracle. This is his response. The brusqueness is
spiritual rather than personal: he means that revelation of his true
nature, at Cana, will be premature.

9   **This beginning of miracles did Jesus in Cana of Galilee, and manifested forth his glory; and his disciples believed on him.**
(2:11)

Despite his professed reluctance (see John 8), Jesus has turned water into wine for the wedding feast at Cana. This is the first of seven of his miracles reported by John, each of a different type.

10   **Jesus answered and said unto him, Verily, verily, I say unto thee, Except a man be born again, he cannot see the kingdom of God. Nicodemus saith unto him, How can a man be born when he is old? can he enter the second time into his mother's womb, and be born? Jesus answered. Verily, verily, I say unto thee, Except a man be born of water and of the Spirit, he cannot enter into the kingdom of God.**
(3:3–5)

Nicodemus the Pharisee, impressed by Jesus' teaching and his miracles, has come to him privately and offered to follow him. Jesus prescribes a complete spiritual regeneration.

11   **The wind bloweth where it listeth, and thou hearest the sound thereof, but canst not tell whence it cometh, and whither it goeth: so is every one that is born of the Spirit.**
(3:8)

Like the movements of the wind, the movements of the Holy Spirit in our lives are beyond our understanding, but we should still take heed of them. 'The wind bloweth where it listeth' became proverbial, an expression of the idea that we need have no idea of the reasons why we are chosen, so long as we accept the fact of choice itself. 'Listeth' simply means 'likes'.

12   **How can these things be?**
(3:9)

Bewildered by Jesus' teaching that we must all be born again in spirit, and must answer the call of the Spirit whenever it comes, Nicodemus asks for further instruction.

13   **For God so loved the world, that he gave his only begotten Son, that whosoever believeth in him should not perish, but have everlasting life.**
(3:16)

Jesus answers Nicodemus' questions about the nature of spiritual rebirth with a plain statement – so plainly Christian in fact, that many scholars think that the verse is not Jesus' own words to Nicodemus, but John's explanation of Jesus' meaning, written long afterwards to enlighten the audience of his own gospel.

14   For God sent not his Son into the world to condemn the
      world; but that the world through him might be saved. He
      that believeth on him is not condemned: but he that believeth
      not is condemned already, because he hath not believed in
      the name of the only begotten Son of God. And this is the
      condemnation, that light is come into the world, and men
      loved darkness rather than light, because their deeds were
      evil.
      (3:17–19)
John reiterates his earlier teaching, that Jesus is the Light of the
World, and that those who prefer the darkness of unbelief are
choosing their own perdition.

15   Whosoever drinketh of this water shall thirst again: But
      whosoever drinketh of the water that I shall give him shall
      never thirst; but the water that I shall give him shall be in him
      a well of water springing up into everlasting life.
      (4:13–14)
Jesus contrasts the water he has just been given by a Samaritan
woman with the water of life which he offers all who believe in him.

16   God is a Spirit: and they that worship him must worship him
      in spirit and in truth.
      (4:24)
Jesus is still speaking to the woman at the well in Samaria. He
means his words literally, for the Samaritans were idolaters who had
very tangible, visible gods to worship. The verse's wider theological
resonances are, however, what have made it live.

17   The woman saith unto him, I know that Messias cometh,
      which is called Christ: when he is come, he will tell us all
      things. Jesus saith unto her, I that speak unto thee am he.
      (4:25–6)
This is the only place in the Gospels where Jesus identifies himself
as the Messiah in so many words.

18   Except ye see signs and wonders, ye will not believe.
      (4:48)
Jesus has been asked to perform a miracle, and to heal a man's sick
son. His point is that people consistently put belief and miracles in
the wrong order: belief should precede the consequences, not
follow them.

19   Jesus saith unto him, Rise, take up thy bed, and walk.
      (5:8)

To the annoyance of the Pharisees, Jesus heals a man who has been crippled for thirty-eight years. They object to the man 'working' – that is, carrying his bed – on the Sabbath.

20   I can of mine own self do nothing: as I hear, I judge: and my judgment is just; because I seek not mine own will, but the will of the Father which hath sent me.
(5:30)
Jesus describes his relationship with God. It involves not only the quest for humility, but a state of true humility itself.

21   Search the scriptures; for in them ye think ye have eternal life: and they are they which testify of me.
(5:39)
Jesus preaches against those – for example the Pharisees – who rigorously accept the authority of only those parts of scripture they choose. The Pharisees' claim to righteousness, and therefore to blessings in the kingdom of heaven, was based on a narrow interpretation of the law (that is, the first five books of the Old Testament) and the prophets – and Jesus' objection to this, as so often, is that they concentrate so much on the letter of the law that they fail to see the teaching of the law and the prophets being fulfilled before their eyes.

22   But what are they among so many?
(6:9)
The disciples, faced with a hungry crowd of over five thousand people, look for food and find only five loaves and two fishes. Their dismayed reaction has become proverbial, more often in the sense of a handful of people facing overwhelming odds than in the context of this Gospel.

23   And Jesus said unto them, I am the bread of life: he that cometh to me shall never hunger; and he that believeth on me shall never thirst.
(6:35)
Jesus preaches on the meaning of the feeding of the five thousand. The idea of Jesus' teaching as a 'staff of life' (that is, a staple diet of existence) also derives from this verse.

24   Verily, verily, I say unto you, He that believeth on me hath everlasting life. I am that bread of life. Your fathers did eat manna in the wilderness, and are dead. This is the bread which cometh down from heaven, that a man may eat thereof, and not die. I am the living bread which came down from heaven: if any man eat of this bread, he shall live for ever: and

the bread that I will give is my flesh, which I will give for the life of the world.
(6:47–51)
Jesus takes further his teaching on the meaning of the feeding of the five thousand. His words must have seemed baffling and prophetic at the time, but after his death and resurrection they became a clear statement of one of the central 'mysteries' of Christian belief.

25   I am the living bread which came down from heaven: if any man eat of this bread, he shall live for ever: and the bread that I will give is my flesh, which I will give for the life of the world.
(6:51)
Jesus' preaching continues on the meaning of the feeding of the five thousand. The analogy is with the manna in the wilderness: he has been sent by God to nourish the world with the promise of eternal life.

26   It is the spirit that quickeneth; the flesh profiteth nothing: the words that I speak unto you, they are spirit, and they are life.
(6:63)
Jesus' disciples still fail to understand his teaching about himself as the Bread of Life. He warns them not to believe because of tangible signs, like miracles: the spirit, the word of God, is what gives eternal life (that is 'quickeneth'). He is thinking partly of God's 'word' which brought all things into existence at the moment of creation.

27   Then said Jesus unto them, Yet a little while am I with you, and then I go unto him that sent me.
(7:33)
Jesus speaks these words to soldiers sent by the authorities to arrest him. The words baffle those hearers who think that they mean that he can escape arrest at will.

28   And the scribes and Pharisees brought unto him a woman taken in adultery; and when they had set her in the midst, They say unto him, Master, this woman was taken in adultery, in the very act.
(8:3–4)
The scribes and Pharisees use this incident to test Jesus. There is a prescribed Mosaic punishment for adultery – death by stoning. Does Jesus agree with it?

29   He that is without sin among you, let him first cast a stone at her.
(8:7)

Jesus answers those who want him to follow Mosaic law to the letter
and agree to the stoning of the woman taken in adultery.

30   **When Jesus had lifted up himself, and saw none but the
woman, he said unto her, Woman, where are those thine
accusers? hath no man condemned thee? She said, No man,
Lord. And Jesus said unto her, Neither do I condemn thee:
go, and sin no more.**
(8:10–11)
Having invited anyone who is without guilt to be the first to stone
the woman taken in adultery, Jesus has bent down to write in the
sand while they make up their minds. Now he turns back and finds
that they have all slipped away.

31   **Then spake Jesus again unto them, saying, I am the light of
the world: he that followeth me shall not walk in darkness,
but shall have the light of life.**
(8:12)
Jesus preaches about his true nature. The meaning behind the
words is explored in the philosophical meditation which begins this
Gospel (see John 2).

32   **Ye shall know the truth, and the truth shall make you free.**
(8:32)
Jesus is speaking to his disciples, and those others who believed in
him. He explains that they are slaves of sin, and it is from this that
their true belief will free them.

33   **Verily, verily, I say unto you, If a man keep my saying, he shall
never see death.**
(8:51)
Jesus continues his teaching that those who believe in him, who
'keep his saying', will be rewarded by eternal life.

34   **They say unto the blind man again, What sayest thou of him,
that he hath opened thine eyes? He said, He is a prophet.**
(9:17)
The Pharisees question a man healed of blindness by Jesus. The
phrase 'to have one's eyes opened' came to be proverbial for 'to
begin to believe'.

35   **He is of age; ask him: he shall speak for himself.**
(9:21)
The parents of the once-blind man, when asked how he has
recovered his sight, are afraid to answer because the healing took
place on the Sabbath, against Jewish law as interpreted by the

authorities. In view of the man's verbal dexterity under questioning (see John 36), their reluctance to speak for him is amply justified.

36   **He answered and said, Whether he be a sinner or no, I know not: one thing I know, that, whereas I was blind, now I see. (9:25)**

The Pharisees are trying to get the man who has been healed of blindness to deny that it was Jesus who healed him. Their point is that Jesus is a sinner, and therefore cannot be the Son of God – and if the healed man could be persuaded to give the glory to God, not Jesus, their point would be proved. With a verbal cunning easily the match for theirs, however, the healed man sidesteps legalistic niceties in favour of what really matters.

37   **And Jesus said, For judgment I am come into this world, that they which see not might see; and that they which see might be made blind. (9:39)**

Jesus explains the meaning of the healing of the blind man: it is a parable-in-action about the spiritually blind.

38   **I am the good shepherd: the good shepherd giveth his life for the sheep. But he that is an hireling, and not the shepherd, whose own the sheep are not, seeth the wolf coming, and leaveth the sheep, and fleeth: and the wolf catcheth them, and scattereth the sheep. (10:11–12)**

In a parable, Jesus develops the familar Biblical metaphor of God as a shepherd. He is making the point here that he is 'genuine': a false prophet – which is what the Pharisees have accused him of being – would have abandoned his flock and run at the first sign of danger, like a hired hand running when wolves attack the sheep.

39   **And other sheep I have, which are not of this fold: them also I must bring, and they shall hear my voice; and there shall be one fold, and one shepherd. (10:16)**

Jesus develops the metaphor of the shepherd and the sheep, to include Gentiles in his care: the only people excluded, as he says later, are those who hear but reject his words.

40   **And whosoever liveth and believeth in me shall never die. Believest thou this? She saith unto him, Yea, Lord: I believe that thou art the Christ, the Son of God, which should come into the world. (11:26–7)**

Jesus is talking to Martha, whose brother Lazarus has died and lain
four days in the tomb.

41   **Jesus wept.**
      (11:35)
      Martha and Mary have taken Jesus to the tomb of their brother
      Lazarus. Jesus weeps not for Lazarus, as they imagine, but out of
      compassion for their grief. The phrase 'Jesus wept' has been
      proverbial for centuries, as a slang expression of amazed disbelief
      which has nothing whatsoever to do with this gospel context. These
      two words also constitute the shortest verse in the whole Bible.

42   **And when he thus had spoken, he cried with a loud voice,
      Lazarus, come forth.**
      (11:43)
      Jesus summons the dead Lazarus back to life. This was the last of
      the seven miracles reported by John, and its purpose is to prefigure
      Jesus' own Resurrection, his triumph over death.

43   **The hour is come, that the Son of man should be glorified.**
      (12:23–4)
      For many months, Jesus has been telling his disciples that his hour
      has not yet come. Now, after riding into Jerusalem on the ass, he
      prophesies his death and Resurrection.

44   **Now is my soul troubled; and what shall I say? Father, save
      me from this hour: but for this cause came I unto this hour.**
      (12:27)
      Jesus prays to God before the crowd in Jerusalem.

45   **Jesus answered and said, This voice came not because of me,
      but for your sakes. Now is the judgment of this world: now
      shall the prince of this world be cast out.**
      (12:30–1)
      Jesus' prayer has been answered by a voice from heaven, and the
      crowd are amazed, saying that angels speak with him.

46   **He riseth from supper, and laid aside his garments; and took
      a towel, and girded himself. After that he poureth water into a
      bason, and began to wash the disciples' feet, and to wipe them
      with the towel wherewith he was girded.**
      (13:4–5)
      At the Last Supper, Jesus takes on the role of a slave and washes the
      disciples' feet – much to Peter's embarrassment.

47   Peter saith unto him, Thou shalt never wash my feet. Jesus
     answered him, If I wash thee not, thou hast no part with me.
     Simon Peter saith unto him, Lord, not my feet only, but also
     my hands and my head.
     (13:8–9)
     Jesus makes Peter understand the symbolic meaning of his washing
     the disciples' feet; Peter's answer, a statement of absolute belief,
     became proverbial.

48   Now there was leaning on Jesus' bosom one of his disciples,
     whom Jesus loved.
     (13:23)
     Some scholars think that this is an autobiographical reference, that
     the man referred to is John himself. As with Mark's mention of his
     own presence in Gethsemane (see Mark 15), the purpose of the
     reference is to authenticate the truth of the events recounted.

49   Then said Jesus unto him, That thou doest, do quickly.
     (13:27)
     Jesus has told the disciples that his betrayer will be the man to
     whom he gives a sop of bread dipped in wine. He then hands Judas
     the sop, with these words, and Judas hurries out.

50   Simon Peter said unto him, Lord, whither goest thou? Jesus
     answered him, Whither I go, thou canst not follow me now,
     but thou shalt follow me afterwards.
     (13:36)
     Peter's question (also well-known in its Latin form, *Quo Vadis*) and
     Jesus' answer have been taken ever since as symbolizing the anxiety
     of the Christian soul facing death, and the reassurance of Jesus'
     Resurrection.

51   Let not your heart be troubled: ye believe in God, believe also
     in me.
     (14:1)
     Jesus comforts Peter, who is heartbroken at the thought that he will
     deny Jesus three times before the cock crows.

52   In my Father's house are many mansions: if it were not so, I
     would have told you. I go to prepare a place for you. And if I
     go and prepare a place for you, I will come again, and receive
     you unto myself; that where I am, there ye may be also.
     (14:2–3)
     Jesus comforts the disciples, who are miserable to think that he is
     going to his death and leaving them. 'Mansions' means 'resting-
     places'.

53   Jesus saith unto him, I am the way, the truth, and the life: no
man cometh unto the Father, but by me.
(14:6)
Thomas, one of the most literal-minded of all Jesus' disciples, has
asked how they can follow Jesus when none of them know the way.
This is Jesus' answer.

54   Peace I leave with you, my peace I give unto you: not as the
world giveth, give I unto you. Let not your heart be troubled,
neither let it be afraid.
(14:27)
Jesus continues to comfort his disciples.

55   This is my commandment, That ye love one another, as I
have loved you. Greater love hath no man than this, that a
man lay down his life for his friends.
(15:12–13)
Jesus is talking to his disciples as they walk from the room of the
Last Supper to the Garden of Gethsemane. He has been reassuring
them of his eternal presence; now he reminds them that they, too,
must tread the path of martyrdom.

56   Ye are my friends, if ye do whatsoever I command you.
Henceforth I call you not servants; for the servant knoweth
not what his lord doeth: but I have called you friends; for all
things that I have heard of my Father I have made known
unto you. Ye have not chosen me, but I have chosen you, and
ordained you, that ye should go and bring forth fruit, and that
your fruit should remain: that whatsoever ye shall ask of the
Father in my name, he may give it you.
(15:14–16)
Jesus is putting heart into his disciples for the ordeals to come.

57   But now I go my way to him that sent me; and none of you
asketh me, Whither goest thou? But because I have said these
things unto you, sorrow hath filled your heart. Nevertheless I
tell you the truth; It is expedient for you that I go away: for if I
go not away, the Comforter will not come unto you; but if I
depart, I will send him unto you.
(16:5–7)
Jesus continues to reassure his disciples. The Comforter is the Holy
Ghost.

58   A little while, and ye shall not see me: and again, a little while
and ye shall see me, because I go to the Father.
(16:16)

These words, referring to Jesus' death and Resurrection, confuse and frighten the disciples.

59   I came forth from the Father, and am come into the world: again, I leave the world, and go to the Father. His disciples said unto him, Lo, now speakest thou plainly, and speakest no proverb.
(16:28–9)
Jesus explains the meaning of his earlier remarks (see John 57), in an image his disciples at last understand.

60   I have glorified thee on the earth: I have finished the work which thou gavest me to do. And now, O Father, glorify thou me with thine own self with the glory which I had with thee before the world was.
(17:4–5)
Before going into the Garden of Gethsemane, where soldiers are waiting to arrest him, Jesus prays to God.

61   Sanctify them through thy truth: thy word is truth. As thou hast sent me into the world, even so have I also sent them into the world.
(17:17–18)
Jesus prays for his disciples.

62   Pilate therefore said unto him, Art thou a king then? Jesus answered, Thou sayest that I am a king. To this end was I born, and for this cause came I into the world, that I should bear witness unto the truth. Every one that is of the truth heareth my voice. Pilate saith unto him, What is truth? And when he had said this, he went out again unto the Jews, and saith unto them, I find in him no fault at all.
(18:37–8)
Pilate interrogates Jesus. 'What is truth?' is usually taken as a joke, the ironic sidestepping of argument by a busy man.

63   Then said the chief priests of the Jews to Pilate, Write not, The King of the Jews; but that he said, I am King of the Jews. Pilate answered, What I have written I have written.
(19:21–2)
The Jewish religious authorities object to Pilate's describing Jesus, in the inscription on his cross, as King of the Jews. They take it as blasphemy. Pilate answers them by crushingly adapting a proverbial phrase enjoining strict obedience to Jewish law, 'What is written, is written'.

64   When Jesus therefore saw his mother, and the disciple
standing by, whom he loved, he saith unto his mother,
Woman, behold thy son! Then saith he to the disciple, Behold
thy mother! And from that hour that disciple took her unto
his own home.
(19:26–7)
From the cross, Jesus sees Mary his mother among the crowd, and
gives her into the care of John himself, the 'disciple whom he loved'.

65   After this, Jesus knowing that all things were now
accomplished, that the scripture might be fulfilled, saith, I
thirst. Now there was set a vessel full of vinegar: and they
filled a spunge with vinegar, and put it upon hyssop, and put
it to his mouth. When Jesus therefore had received the
vinegar, he said, It is finished: and he bowed his head, and
gave up the ghost.
(19:28–30)
The 'scripture' referred to is a psalm verse (see Ps 139) referring to
the ill-treatment by the ungodly of the true servant of God.
Similarly, Jesus' 'It is finished' is taken to refer to an earlier remark
(see John 59), when he talks of having completed the work he was
sent into the world to do. To 'give up the ghost' is a common
Biblical phrase for 'to die', referring to the ancient belief that the
soul was physically separated from the body and floated free from it
at the moment of death. 'Vinegar' simply means cheap wine, the
drink of slaves.

66   But one of the soldiers with a spear pierced his side, and
forthwith came there out blood and water.
(19:34)
This event gave rise to one of the most powerful medieval Christian
legends. The spear used to pierce Jesus' side, and the bowl in which
his blood was collected, were regarded as holy relics – the Holy
Lance and the Holy Grail. They had healing power, and remained
in the hands of mortals so long as goodness predominated over evil
in the world. Gradually, however, evil began to triumph, and the
Lance and Grail faded from human sight, so that only the purest
and noblest mortals of all (such as Sir Galahad) could ever catch
sight of them, and then only after a lengthy and anguished quest.

67   Then came Jesus forth, wearing the crown of thorns, and the
purple robe. And Pilate saith unto them, Behold the man.
(19:5)
The Romans parade Jesus before the people in a parody of royal
attire, and Pilate caps it by quoting Nathan's words to David (see II
Sam 10) accusing him of guilt before God. The phrase 'Behold the
man' never had, for Christians, the ironical overtones of guilt which

Pilate – and, no doubt, the Old Testament scholar who advised him
– intended; instead, it became a declaration of one of the central
'mysteries' of Christianity, Christ's willing acceptance of mortality,
and thence of the guilt of Adam, in order to redeem the human
race.

68   **So they ran both together: and the other disciple did outrun
Peter, and came first to the sepulchre.**
(20:4)
Mary Magdalene has told Peter and John himself (the 'other
disciple' mentioned here) that Jesus' tomb is empty, and they run to
see for themselves.

69   **And they say unto her, Woman, why weepest thou? She saith
unto them, Because they have taken away my Lord, and I
know not where they have laid him.**
(20:13)
Mary Magdalene, left alone in Jesus' empty tomb, sees two angels,
one at the head and one at the feet of where Jesus' body had lain,
and they question her.

70   **Jesus saith unto her, Woman, why weepest thou? whom
seekest thou? She, supposing him to be the gardener, saith
unto him, Sir, if thou have borne him hence, tell me where
thou hast laid him, and I will take him away. Jesus saith unto
her, Mary. She turned herself, and saith unto him, Rabboni;
which is to say, Master. Jesus saith unto her, Touch me not;
for I am not yet ascended to my Father.**
(20:15–17)
Jesus appears to Mary Magdalene outside the empty tomb.

71   **But he said unto them, Except I shall see in his hands the
print of the nails, and put my finger into the print of the nails,
and thrust my hand into his side, I will not believe.**
(20:25)
Jesus has appeared to all the disciples except Thomas, and they tell
Thomas excitedly that Christ is risen. Thomas, always a cautious,
literal-minded man, refuses to take their word for it. The
expression 'a doubting Thomas' owes its origin to this event.

72   **Be not faithless, but believing.**
(20:27)
Jesus rebukes Thomas for doubting his Resurrection.

73   **And Thomas answered and said unto him, My Lord and my
God. Jesus saith unto him, Thomas, because thou hast seen
me, thou hast believed: blessed are they that have not seen,**

and yet have believed. And many other signs truly did Jesus in the presence of his disciples, which are not written in this book: But these are written, that ye might believe that Jesus is the Christ, the Son of God; and that believing ye might have life through his name.
(20:28–31)

Thomas, offered the proofs he demanded of Jesus' resurrection, has been absolutely convinced. John goes on to make the point that stories such as that of Thomas and the others in his Gospel should guide people to Jesus without the need for tangible proof.

74   Simon Peter saith unto them, I go a fishing. They say unto him, We also go with thee.
(21:3)

Some days after the Resurrection, Simon and other disciples briefly return to their old trade of fishing, and Jesus appears to them.

75   So when they had dined, Jesus saith to Simon Peter, Simon, son of Jonas, lovest thou me more than these? He saith unto him, Yea, Lord; thou knowest that I love thee. He saith unto him, Feed my lambs. He saith to him again the second time, Simon, son of Jonas, lovest thou me? He saith unto him, Yea, Lord; thou knowest that I love thee. He saith unto him, Feed my sheep. He saith unto him the third time, Simon, son of Jonas, lovest thou me? Peter was grieved because he said unto him the third time, Lovest thou me? And he said unto him, Lord, thou knowest all things; thou knowest that I love thee. Jesus saith unto him, Feed my sheep.
(21:15–17)

Jesus three times asks Peter if he loves him – a parallel to the three times Peter denied him in the court of the temple earlier – and reminds him, each time, that his duty is to lead the disciples in their mission, to feed the whole world with news of the risen Christ.

76   And there are also many other things which Jesus did, the which, if they should be written every one, I suppose that even the world itself could not contain the books that should be written. Amen.
(21:25)

John has previously said that his Gospel is a selection of stories, designed to bring his readers to a belief in Jesus. Now he ends with a more conventional statement, common in histories of the time, a kind of authorial disclaimer of completeness which has itself become proverbial.

The Acts

1   The former treatise have I made, O Theophilus, of all that Jesus began both to do and teach.
(1:1)
Luke's preface to Acts is addressed to the Greek Theophilus, the dedicatee of his Gospel, either a real individual or a generalized believer (*Theophilus* in Greek means 'beloved of God'). His preface makes clear that Acts takes up where the 'former treatise' (that is, 'earlier book') leaves off. Luke, the only non-Jewish writer in the Bible, is particularly concerned with the spread of Christianity to the Gentiles, and Acts is partly an account of the activities of Luke's friend Paul, for whose Gentile missions Luke's own Gospel may well have been compiled.

2   And he said unto them, It is not for you to know the times or the seasons, which the Father hath put in his own power. But ye shall receive power, after that the Holy Ghost is come upon you: and ye shall be witnesses unto me both in Jerusalem, and in all Judaea, and in Samaria, and unto the uttermost part of the earth.
(1:7–8)
The disciples have asked the risen Jesus if the time of their 'baptism with the Holy Ghost', which he has told them to expect in a few days, will also be the time of the Second Coming. His answer, though vague about the Second Coming, links the coming of the Holy Ghost with the disciples' mission to the Gentiles which is to be the subject of this whole book.

3   And when he had spoken these things, while they beheld, he was taken up; and a cloud received him out of their sight. And while they looked stedfastly toward heaven as he went up, behold, two men stood by them in white apparel; Which also said, Ye men of Galilee, why stand ye gazing up into heaven? this same Jesus, which is taken up from you into heaven, shall so come in like manner as ye have seen him go into heaven.
(1:9–11)
Luke's Gospel ended with the first part of this same scene, Jesus being taken up into heaven. Acts now begins by linking it to his return to earth, and placing that announcement just before the account of the descent of the Holy Ghost at Pentecost. As John did at the beginning of his Gospel (see John 1), Luke is drawing together threads of Old Testament teaching – the cloud, for example, is a symbol of the presence of God himself, first seen by the poeple in the wilderness after Moses built the tabernacle – with their Christian interpretation and extension.

4   **And they gave forth their lots; and the lot fell upon Matthias; and he was numbered with the eleven apostles.**
(1:26)

The disciples choose a twelfth man to take the place of Judas after his suicide. The candidates are Joseph Barsabas and Matthias. Casting lots, a favourite method of choice in the ancient world (because it allowed the gods, not chance, a role in the selection process) is here preceded by prayer to God. 'Guided choice' has been common in many Christian congregations since.

5   **And when the day of Pentecost was fully come, they were all with one accord in one place.**
(2:1)

The day of Pentecost was the last day of harvest, when the first fruits were symbolically offered to God. It took place fifty days after passover. Its non-Christian significance was that it brought together large groups of people – 150, in this case; for Christians, the events of this particular Day of Pentecost gave the idea of 'first fruits' a whole new significance.

6   **And suddenly there came a sound from heaven as of a rushing mighty wind, and it filled all the house where they were sitting. And there appeared unto them cloven tongues like as of fire, and it sat upon each of them.**
(2:2–3)

To many believers, these verses are the fulfilment of the prophecy of John the Baptist (see Matt 10), that Jesus would baptize his followers with the Holy Ghost and with fire.

7   **And they were all filled with the Holy Ghost, and began to speak with other tongues, as the Spirit gave them utterance.**
(2:4)

The plain words of this verse mean that the disciples, instead of speaking in their usual rough country dialect, virtually incomprehensible to strangers, seemed to speak in clear words which everyone present could understand – indeed, in each person's native 'tongue' or language. The idea of 'speaking in tongues', however, is also linked with a well-established phenomenon in many religions of the ancient world. *Glossolalia* (Greek for 'babbling with the tongue'), was the utterance of nonsense-syllables in a kind of ecstatic trance, speaking the language of gods not mortals. (It was the method of prophecy at the Delphic Oracle, for example: a priestess spoke the god Apollo's words in nonsense-syllables, and the priests of the oracle interpreted them.) In later Christian traditions, ranging from medieval monasteries to modern Pentecostalist services, speaking in tongues of this kind is a frequent, well-attested occurrence.

8   And they were all amazed and marvelled, saying one to
    another, Behold, are not all these which speak Galilaeans?
    And how hear we every man in our own tongue, wherein we
    were born? Parthians, and Medes, and Elamites, and the
    dwellers in Mesopotamia, and in Judaea, and Cappadocia, in
    Pontus, and Asia, Phrygia, and Pamphylia, in Egypt, and in
    the parts of Libya about Cyrene, and strangers of Rome, Jews
    and proselytes, Cretes and Arabians, we do hear them speak
    in our tongues the wonderful works of God.
    (2:7–11)
    This is the first reaction of the people who hear the disciples
    'speaking in tongues'. Each of the areas mentioned had a language
    of its own, so that the fact that they all clearly understood the
    disciples is a spectacular reversal of the affliction God sent the
    peoples of the world at the time of the building of the Tower of
    Babel; that is that they should be disunited simply because they
    could not understand each other.

9   Others mocking said, These men are full of new wine.
    (2:13)
    Uncharitable hearers put a less flattering interpretation on the
    disciples' speaking with tongues. Drinking new wine was part of the
    traditional 'first fruits' celebration at Pentecost.

10 These are not drunken, as ye suppose, seeing it is but the
    third hour of the day. But this is that which was spoken by the
    prophet Joel; And it shall come to pass in the last days, saith
    God, I will pour out of my Spirit upon all flesh: and your sons
    and your daughters shall prophesy.
    (2:15–17)
    Peter explains the disciples' speaking in tongues, linking it to Joel's
    prophecy about the coming of the Day of Judgment (see Joel 5).

11 Ye men of Israel, hear these words; Jesus of Nazareth, a man
    approved of God among you by miracles and wonders and
    signs, which God did by him in the midst of you, as ye
    yourselves also know: Him, being delivered by the
    determinate counsel and foreknowledge of God, ye have
    taken, and by wicked hands have crucified and slain: Whom
    God hath raised up, having loosed the pains of death: because
    it was not possible that he should be holden of it.
    (2:22–4)
    For the first time, Peter preaches about the risen Christ, in words
    which have become part of many church prayers and services.

12   Now when they heard this, they were pricked in their heart,
and said unto Peter and to the rest of the apostles, Men and
brethren, what shall we do? Then Peter said unto them,
Repent, and be baptized every one of you in the name of Jesus
Christ for the remission of sins, and ye shall receive the gift of
the Holy Ghost.
(2:37–8)

Peter powerfully sets the events of Pentecost in the context of other
Christian teaching: what has happened to the disciples, and has
been seen by everyone present, can happen to anyone who truly
believes in Christ. Until now, the Holy Ghost has played little part
in Christian teaching, because Jesus himself was there; from these
events onwards, the Holy Ghost or Spirit of God has central
importance.

13   Silver and gold have I none; but such as I have give I thee: In
the name of Jesus Christ of Nazareth rise up and walk.
(3:6)

Peter heals a cripple who asks for alms at the Gate Beautiful of the
temple.

14   And he leaping up stood, and walked, and entered with them
into the temple, walking, and leaping, and praising God.
(3:8)

The once-lame man, now cured, goes into the temple with Peter
and John. The phrase 'walking and leaping and praising God'
deliberately links his reaction when cured to the ecstatic religious
dancing common in the Middle East, not least in Judaism, where
David himself practised it.

15   But ye denied the Holy One and the Just, and desired a
murderer to be granted unto you; And killed the Prince of
life, whom God hath raised from the dead; whereof we are
witnesses.
(3:14–15)

Peter preaches, in vehement, unminced words, to the crowd
amazed at the lame man's dancing. 'Prince of life' entered the
language of the Christian Church.

16   Neither was there any among them that lacked: for as many
as were possessors of lands or houses sold them, and brought
the prices of the things that were sold, And laid them down at
the apostles' feet: and distribution was made unto every man
according as he had need.
(4:34–5)

The miracle of the healing of the lame man is followed by the conversion of many thousands, and by acts of charity.

17 **Why hast thou conceived this thing in thine heart? thou hast not lied unto men, but unto God.**
(5:4)
Peter scolds a man called Ananias who has sold a valued possession to give the money to charity, but has kept part of the price back for himself. Ananias is so affected by Peter's words, and by the realization of what he has done, that he is literally 'mortified', that is, he dies of it.

18 **Then the twelve called the multitude of the disciples unto them, and said, It is not reason that we should leave the word of God, and serve tables. Wherefore, brethren, look ye out among you seven men of honest report, full of the Holy Ghost and wisdom, whom we may appoint over this business.**
(6:2–3)
So many charitable offerings have been made to the new Church that the twelve disciples are spending their time in distributing alms rather than in ministry. Accordingly, they decide to appoint seven secular stewards, from among the Greeks (who have, as it happens, been complaining that the alms are being unfairly distributed). One of the stewards is Stephen, the man later tried and stoned to death by the authorities, the first Christian martyr named in Acts.

19 **The most High dwelleth not in temples made with hands; as saith the prophet, Heaven is my throne, and earth is my footstool: what house will ye build me? saith the Lord.**
(7:48–9)
Stephen is on trial for preaching against the temple, that is repeating Jesus' prophecy that it will be swept away. This is part of his defence – and it is hardly calculated to soften his judges' hearts.

20 **When they heard these things, they were cut to the heart, and they gnashed on him with their teeth.**
(7:54)
Stephen's 'defence', which involves a call to his hearers to repent, finds no favour.

21 **Behold, I see the heavens opened, and the Son of man standing on the right hand of God.**
(7:56)
Stephen sees, and declares, a vision of Jesus in majesty.

22 Then they cried out with a loud voice, and stopped their ears, and ran upon him with one accord, And cast him out of the city, and stoned him: and the witnesses laid down their clothes at a young man's feet, whose name was Saul.
(7:57–8)

Stephen's hearers react to his vision with panic-stricken fury. The introduction of Saul to the narrative which follows is one of the few literary devices Luke permits himself in an otherwise functional, plain narrative. Instead of proclaiming and announcing him in the usual way of the scriptures with major figures, he lets him slip unobtrusively into the story. This allows him to show us Saul's subsequent conversion step by step, as if we were sharing his spiritual awakening.

23 And he kneeled down, and cried with a loud voice, Lord, lay not this sin to their charge. And when he had said this, he fell asleep.
(7:60)

The dying Stephen echoes Jesus' words on the cross (see Luke 66). 'Fell asleep', in this context, is a metaphor carefully chosen to suggest a placid, spiritually easy death.

23 And Saul was consenting unto his death.
(8:1)

At the time of Stephen's death, Saul was probably in his early thirties. He was an educated man, who had trained for ten years to become a rabbi. Some scholars take the word 'consenting' in this verse to imply that he was a member of the Sanhedrin, the Jewish religious court which condemned Stephen to death. Whether or not that is so, Saul's subsequent persecution of Christians, on behalf of the authorities, indicates that he was a man of considerable regard, not only in Jewish religious circles but also with the ruling Romans, and that his zeal matched his reputation.

24 Thy money perish with thee, because thou hast thought that the gift of God may be purchased with money. Thou hast neither part nor lot in this matter: for thy heart is not right in the sight of God.
(8:20–1)

Simon Magus ('Simon the Sorcerer'), who has made a highly successful career out of persuading the people of Samaria that he can work miracles, has heard of the disciples' healing powers through the Holy Ghost, and has offered Peter money if he shares the secret. This is Peter's withering reply.

25 **Understandest thou what thou readest?**
(8:30)
Philip the apostle has been summoned by God into the desert area
now known as the Gaza Strip. He meets an Ethiopian dignitary
there, a eunuch reading Isaiah while riding north to Jerusalem in a
chariot, and asks him this question.

26 **And as they went on their way, they came unto a certain**
water: and the eunuch said, See, here is water; what doth
hinder me to be baptized? And Philip said, If thou believest
with all thine heart, thou mayest. And he answered and said, I
believe that Jesus Christ is the Son of God.
(8:36–7)
Philip has ridden with the Ethiopian and preached Christianity on
the way. The Ethiopian now asks to be baptized. The condition
Philip sets, and the Ethiopian's wholehearted response, have
remained at the heart of the service of Christian baptism ever since.
In medieval legend, one of this Ethiopian's distant relatives was
identified with Prester John, the hero who rose from the grave to
help the Crusaders fight the forces of Islam.

27 **And Saul, yet breathing out threatenings and slaughter**
against the disciples of the Lord, went unto the high priest,
And desired of him letters to Damascus to the synagogues,
that if he found any of this way, whether they were men or
women, he might bring them bound unto Jerusalem.
(9:1–2)
Saul asks permission to extend his persecution of the Christians
beyond the immediate area of Jerusalem. 'Breathing out
threatenings and slaughter', here meant literally, became
proverbial, sometimes blended with the idea of fire and the sword to
produce the phrase 'breathing fire and slaughter'.

29 **And he fell to the earth, and heard a voice saying unto him,**
Saul, Saul, why persecutest thou me?
(9:4)
On the road to Damascus, Saul sees a vision: a blinding light from
heaven.

30 **And he said, Who art thou, Lord? And the Lord said, I am**
Jesus whom thou persecutest: it is hard for thee to kick
against the pricks.
(9:5)
Saul sees and hears a vision of Jesus on the road to Damascus. The
phrase 'road to Damascus' became proverbial for those 'seeing the
light', suddenly realizing that they must radically change their ways.

'To kick against the pricks' means to resist direction. 'Pricks' were the goads used to drive donkeys or oxen.

31 **Go thy way: for he is a chosen vessel unto me, to bear my name before the Gentiles, and kings, and the children of Israel.**
(9:15)
Jesus, in a vision, has told Ananias of Damascus to find Saul, touch him and heal him of blindness. Ananias objects saying that Saul is the man who has been sent to imprison all true believers. This is Jesus' reply. The phrase 'chosen vessel' became proverbial, particularly for those visibly fired with missionary zeal. (The metaphor of the vessel is drawn from pottery, and links with the common Old Testament ideas that human beings are clay and that God is the potter who moulds them into meaningful existence.)

32 **Thy prayers and thine alms are come up for a memorial before God.**
(10:4)
God's angel appears in a vision to the Roman centurion Cornelius, telling him to find Peter and to be converted to Christianity. 'Come up for a memorial before' means 'come to the attention of '.

33 **And saw heaven opened, and a certain vessel descending unto him, as it had been a great sheet knit at the four corners, and let down to the earth: Wherein were all manner of fourfooted beasts of the earth, and wild beasts, and creeping things, and fowls of the air. And there came a voice to him, Rise, Peter; kill, and eat.**
(10:11-13)
Peter is hungry, and while the servants prepare food he dozes on the flat roof and dreams this dream.

34 **What God hath cleansed, that call not thou common.**
(10:15)
Peter's dream continues. He has refused to kill and eat any of the creatures in the sheet, on the grounds that they are not kosher. This is the angel's reply. The dream precedes his converting the Roman centurion Cornelius, and its point is to show him that conversion is not solely available to orthodox Jews: Christianity is for everyone.

35 **But Peter took him up, saying, Stand up; I myself also am a man.**
(10:26)
The centurion Cornelius has knelt at Peter's feet as if to worship him.

36   Then Peter opened his mouth, and said, Of a truth I perceive that God is no respecter of persons: But in every nation he that feareth him, and worketh righteousness, is accepted with him.
(10:34–5)
Peter proclaims his realization that Christianity is open to all, whether Jewish or Gentile.

37   Whosoever believeth in him shall receive remission of sins.
(10:43)
Peter is preaching about Jesus. The context of this verse – a sermon preached to a Gentile group in Joppa – concerns Peter's realization that salvation is open to all true believers, whether Jewish or not. This sermon preceded a second descent of the Holy Ghost, and the first conversions of Gentiles by any of the apostles.

38   God gave them the like gift as he did unto us, who believed on the Lord Jesus Christ; what was I, that I could withstand God?
(11:17)
Jewish Christians have objected to Peter's conversion of Gentiles. This is his reply.

39   And upon a set day Herod, arrayed in royal apparel, sat upon his throne, and made an oration unto them. And the people gave a shout, saying, It is the voice of a god, and not of a man. And immediately the angel of the Lord smote him, because he gave not God the glory: and he was eaten of worms, and gave up the ghost.
(12:21–3)
Herod Agrippa, the Roman-backed king of Judaea, has been savagely persecuting the Christians. He has murdered the disciple James, and imprisoned Peter (who however has been rescued by an angel). Now he sits on the throne and the people receive him with pagan honour: this kind of adulation of royalty was common in ancient Babylon and Egypt, but never in Israel. Herod's sudden death – perhaps from a heart attack or stroke – was explained by both Jewish and Christian writers as God's punishment for blasphemy.

40   He saith also in another psalm, Thou shalt not suffer thine Holy One to see corruption.
(13:35)
Paul is quoting the Old Testament to support his teaching about Jesus' resurrection and its meaning for Christians. Just as God raised Jesus from the dead, so he guarantees eternal life to all believers. 'Thine Holy One' means 'the person who worships and

believes in you'. The psalm quoted is a prayer for spiritual
protection (see Ps 32).

41   **And when the people saw what Paul had done, they lifted up
      their voices, saying in the speech of Lycaonia, The gods are
      come down to us in the likeness of men.**
      (14:11)
      During his first missionary journey with Barnabas to Cyprus and
      Asia Minor, Paul has healed a man lame from birth. The response
      of the local people is to try to sacrifice to the apostles as though they
      are gods: they take Paul for Jupiter and Barnabas for Mercury.

42   **Sirs, why do ye these things? We also are men of like passions
      with you, and preach unto you that ye should turn from these
      vanities unto the living God.**
      (14:15)
      Paul and Barnabas deny that they are gods, the 'vanities' or shadows
      worshipped by the heathen. 'Passions' here means 'human
      weaknesses'.

43   **Sirs, what must I do to be saved?**
      (16:30)
      The keeper of a prison in Philippi finds that Paul, Silas and the
      other Christians have survived an earthquake which has destroyed
      the jail and killed everyone else in it. He responds with this
      awestruck question.

44   **And they said, Believe on the Lord Jesus Christ, and thou
      shalt be saved, and thy house.**
      (16:31)
      Paul's and Silas' words paraphrase Jesus' own, as reported by St
      John (see John 24).

45   **But the Jews which believed not, moved with envy, took unto
      them certain lewd fellows of the baser sort, and gathered a
      company, and set all the city on an uproar.**
      (17:5)
      In Thessalonica, objectors to Paul's and Silas' preaching, and to the
      large crowds it attracts, start a riot. 'Lewd fellows of the baser sort'
      became proverbial. 'Lewd' has none of its limited modern meaning
      here: it implies general wickedness.

46   **These that have turned the world upside down are come
      hither.**
      (17:6)

The people who object to Paul's and Silas' Christian preaching
complain to the authorities. The charge that the Christians were
'turning the world upside down' was not merely a lively form of
speech: it implied political unrest, upsetting the order of society,
and was a serious matter under Roman law.

47 Then certain philosophers of the Epicureans, and of the
Stoicks, encountered him. And some said, What will this
babbler say? other some, He seemeth to be a setter forth of
strange gods: because he preached unto them Jesus, and the
resurrection. And they took him, and brought him unto
Areopagus, saying, May we know what this new doctrine,
whereof thou speakest, is?
(17:18–19)
Paul is in Athens, then a university city and a centre of pagan
philosophical teaching. The philosophers react to him with
withering academic amusement. Areopagus is a hill in the centre of
the city, used from ancient times for public meetings, and as a law
court.

48 Then Paul stood in the midst of Mars' hill, and said, Ye men
of Athens, I perceive that in all things ye are too superstitious.
For as I passed by, and beheld your devotions, I found an
altar with this inscription, TO THE UNKNOWN GOD.
Whom therefore ye ignorantly worship, him declare I unto
you.
(17:24–5)
Paul preaches on Areopagus ('Mars' hill'), neatly using the
philosophers' own logic-chopping style of argument against
themselves. The Greeks and Romans worshipped dozens of gods
and spirits, and put up altars to them all. The altar 'to the unknown
god' was a prudent attempt to make sure no god had been offended
by being left out.

49 God that made the world and all things therein, seeing that he
is Lord of heaven and earth, dwelleth not in temples made
with hands; Neither is worshipped with men's hands, as
though he needed any thing, seeing he giveth to all life, and
breath, and all things.
(17:24–5)
Paul identifies and describes the 'unknown god' to the crowd in
Athens.

50 For in him we live, and move, and have our being.
(17:28)

Paul's sermon in Athens, about the 'unknown god', continues.

51 He said unto them, Have ye received the Holy Ghost since ye believed? And they said unto him, We have not so much as heard whether there be any Holy Ghost.
(19:2)
Paul is visiting Ephesus, one of the major pagan religious centres of the ancient world. He finds a group who believe in the Messiah because of the teaching of John the Baptist, and who know nothing of subsequent events – from Jesus' ministry and resurrection to Pentecost.

52 Many of them also which used curious arts brought their books together, and burned them before all men: and they counted the price of them, and found it fifty thousand pieces of silver.
(19:19)
Even sorcerors and cabalists – flourishing groups in superstition-riddled Ephesus – are converted to Christianity by Paul's teaching. Fifty thousand pieces of silver is a fortune, and indicates that a large number of people must have been so affected by Paul's teaching that they gave up their livelihood. Books in those days were rare and expensive luxuries – and burning them, as this verse suggests, was a very considerable financial sacrifice.

53 And when they heard these sayings, they were full of wrath, and cried out, saying, Great is Diana of the Ephesians.
(19:28)
Demetrius the silversmith has stirred his fellow-workers to riot against Paul for destroying the souvenir trade. They rush through the streets of Ephesus, shouting in honour of Diana. The statue of Diana at Ephesus was one of the seven wonders of the ancient world, and attracted hundreds of thousands of visitors. Silver replicas were favourite souvenirs. The phrase 'Great is Diana of the Ephesians' was once proverbial, used (for example by nineteenth-century British visitors to outposts of the Empire) as an expression of slightly ironical amazement at any wonder of someone else's civilization.

54 Some therefore cried one thing, and some another: for the assembly was confused; and the more part knew not wherefore they were come together.
(19:32)
The riot which was started by Demetrius the silversmith against the Christians has led to a great deal of noise but little sense – a metaphor, to Christian readers of this narrative, for the religious babble of Ephesus itself, and for the confusion in all pagan minds.

55   And now, brethren, I commend you to God, and to the word
of his grace, which is able to build you up, and to give you an
inheritance among all them which are sanctified.
(20:32)
Paul, about to leave Ephesus for Jerusalem, speaks words of
encouragement to the elders of the new Ephesian Christian
community.

56   I have shewed you all things, how that so labouring ye ought
to support the weak, and to remember the words of the Lord
Jesus, how he said, It is more blessed to give than to receive.
(20:35)
Paul, still talking to the Christian elders at Ephesus, is advising
them never to take money for their teaching – pointed advice in a
city where selling religious instruction was a major industry.

57   I am a man which am a Jew of Tarsus, a city in Cilicia, a
citizen of no mean city.
(21:39)
In Jerusalem, the Roman authorities have saved Paul from death at
the hands of the orthodox Jews opposed to Christianity and to his
bringing the Gentiles and Greeks into the temple. The Roman
centurion has taken him for a notorious Egyptian agitator, leader of
a faction of fanatical anti-Roman freedom-fighters. He is therefore
astonished to hear Paul speaking not Egyptian but Greek. Paul here
announces his true identity, in words which have become
proverbial.

58   Then the chief captain came, and said unto him, Tell me, art
thou a Roman? He said, Yea. And the chief captain answered,
With a great sum obtained I this freedom. And Paul said, But
I was free born.
(22:27–8)
The Romans have bound Paul and are about to beat him, when they
discover that he is a Roman citizen, that is, a man above their
summary justice. Their commander has bought his own citizenship,
and is therefore in awe of Paul, who was born a citizen and is
therefore of superior social standing, able to cause trouble if he is
wrongfully arrested.

59   We have found this man a pestilent fellow, and a mover of
sedition among all the Jews throughout the world, and a
ringleader of the sect of the Nazarenes.
(24:5)
The barrister Tertullus prosecutes Paul before the Roman
authorities. He is speaking on behalf of Ananias, the high priest of
Jerusalem, and the charge is one of sedition. To accuse Paul of

leading a sect at that time was tantamount to calling him a terrorist, for the whole province of Judaea was currently full of armed groups trying to break free from Roman rule, and being ruthlessly put down.

60 And herein do I exercise myself, to have always a conscience void of offence toward God, and toward men.
(24:16)
Paul defends himself against the charges brought against him: both the religious charge (blasphemy) which interests the high priest, and the secular charge (sedition) which interests the Romans.

61 And as he reasoned of righteousness, temperance, and judgment to come, Felix trembled, and answered, Go thy way for this time; when I have a convenient season, I will call for thee.
(24:25)
Felix, the Roman governor of Judaea, can find no fault in Paul, and releases him into a kind of probation or house arrest.

62 I appeal unto Caesar.
(25:11)
Festus, the new Roman governor of Judaea, is proposing to send Paul to Jerusalem for trial. Paul exercises his right as a Roman citizen: by appealing to Caesar (that is, in this case, to the Emperor Nero), he puts himself beyond the jurisdiction of local courts, and has to be sent to Rome for trial before the emperor himself. Paul is, however, concerned less with legal niceties than with seizing the chance of going to Rome and preaching Christianity there.

63 Hast thou appealed unto Caesar? unto Caesar shalt thou go.
(25:12)
In a formal phrase, standard legal terminology, Festus accepts Paul's appeal to the emperor. These words would be put in the trial record, and indicate the end of Festus' own responsibility.

64 Why should it be thought a thing incredible with you, that God should raise the dead?
(26:8)
Because the Roman authorities can find no suitable charge to make against Paul in Rome, they invite Agrippa, the Jewish king, to examine him. Agrippa asks Paul to explain himself, and Paul takes the chance to preach Christianity.

65 And as he thus spake for himself, Festus said with a loud voice, Paul, thou art beside thyself; much learning doth make thee mad.
(26:24)

Festus, the Roman governor, is unimpressed by Paul's description of his conversion and of his missionary work: he thinks him a madman. 'Beside oneself ', in Elizabethan English, was roughly equivalent to the modern 'out of one's mind'.

66 **But he said, I am not mad, most noble Festus; but speak forth the words of truth and soberness. For the king knoweth of these things, before whom also I speak freely: for I am persuaded that none of these things are hidden from him; for this thing was not done in a corner.**
(26:25–6)
Paul answers the Roman governor, who has called his beliefs and missionary work the ravings of a madman. His words are also an implicit denial of sedition: he has not plotted in the shadows, but proclaimed his message for all to hear.

67 **Then Agrippa said unto Paul, Almost thou persuadest me to be a Christian. And Paul said, I would to God, that not only thou, but also all that hear me this day, were both almost, and altogether such as I am, except these bonds.**
(26:28–9)
Paul's account of his beliefs almost converts Agrippa – who later says to Festus that he can find no fault in Paul, and would have recommended releasing him in Judaea if he had not appealed to Caesar.

Romans

1 **Paul, a servant of Jesus Christ, called to be an apostle.**
(1:1)
Paul begins this letter, which is a reasoned exposition of Christian doctrine, with a ringing assertion of faith. The phrase 'servant of God' was a standard description, in many ancient languages, for 'priest'; by substituting 'Jesus Christ' for 'God', Paul is not only declaring his own status but also affirming belief in the divinity of Christ. The effect is somewhat muted in translation, especially to readers or hearers who are already Christians; in Paul's own time it would have been both uncompromising and provocative, and was meant to be so.

2 **Jesus Christ our Lord, which was made of the seed of David according to the flesh; And declared to be the Son of God with power, according to the spirit of holiness, by the resurrection from the dead.**
(1:3–4)

Paul continues his blunt assertion of Christ's divinity. At the time, making these statements (which can now seem unexceptionably true) must have been like nailing his colours to the mast: to hold these views openly, as many of his hearers and readers would be uncomfortably aware, was to court arrest and a beating, if not death.

3   **To all that be in Rome, beloved of God, called to be saints: Grace to you and peace.**
    (1:7)
    'Saint' here has none of its later overtones: it is equivalent to 'holy ones' and means simply 'believers', members of the Christian community.

4   **For God is my witness, whom I serve with my spirit in the gospel of his Son, that without ceasing I make mention of you always in my prayers.**
    (1:9)
    This is the first Biblical mention of the use of prayer as a kind of binding force, uniting all believers in intercession before God. In the doubt-ridden, persecution-racked days of early Christianity, Paul established this kind of prayer as a way of building up and strengthening the Christians' feeling of community, the idea that they belonged to a homogeneous group and were not alone.

5   **I am debtor both to the Greeks, and to the Barbarians; both to the wise, and to the unwise.**
    (1:14)
    Paul has been explaining that although he has wanted to make a missionary journey to Rome, he has up to now been delayed. The meaning of this verse, which is much quoted despite its obscurity, is quite simply that he has had many claims on his time. He has owed visits (hence 'debtor') both to Greek and non-Greek ('barbarian') communities, and has been preaching and discussing Christianity both with the learned ('wise') and the uneducated.

6   **For therein is the righteousness of God revealed from faith to faith: as it is written, The just shall live by faith.**
    (1:17)
    Paul quotes the prophet Habbakuk in support of his message that salvation, eternal life, is available to anyone, from whatever race or religious background, who professes faith in Christ.

7   **Professing themselves to be wise, they became fools, And changed the glory of the uncorruptible God into an image made like to corruptible man, and to birds, and four-footed beasts, and creeping things.**
    (1:22–3)

Continuing his assertion that faith in God is all that is needed for
salvation, Paul talks of idolaters, who ignore all the signs of God's
existence and worship images.

8 **Who changed the truth of God into a lie, and worshipped and
served the creature more than the Creator.**
(1:25)
Paul continues to describe idolaters: he is talking of people who
worship statues of animal-gods, bird-gods, gods in the form of
human beings. 'Creature' here means 'created thing'.

9 **For this cause God gave them up unto vile affections: for even
their women did change the natural use into that which is
against nature: And likewise also the men, leaving the natural
use of the woman, burned in their lust one toward another;
men with men working that which is unseemly, and receiving
in themselves that recompence of their error which was meet.**
(1:26–7)
Paul describes God's punishment of idolaters. He is using images
of the perversion and decadence of the aristocratic Roman world –
the world of the 'Roman orgy' beloved of modern epic film-makers.
The 'recompence of their error which was meet' would irresistibly
have suggested to his hearers and readers the Old Testament fate of
Sodom and Gomorrah, where the same practices were also an
outward sign of the inner corruption of idolatry.

10 **Being filled with all unrighteousness, fornication,
wickedness, covetousness, maliciousness; full of envy,
murder, debate, deceit, malignity; whisperers, Backbiters,
haters of God, despiteful, proud, boasters, inventors of evil
things, disobedient to parents, Without understanding,
covenantbreakers, without natural affection, implacable,
unmerciful: Who knowing the judgment of God, that they
which commit such things are worthy of death, not only do
the same, but have pleasure in them that do them.**
(1:29–32)
In a fine rhetorical flourish – the first of many such outbursts in his
letters – Paul itemizes the sins of the idolaters and (in the last verse)
of those who are merely tarnished by association, which is for him
just as great a sin.

11 **Who will render to every man according to his deeds: To
them who by patient continuance in well doing seek for glory
and honour and immortality, eternal life.**
(2:6–7)

Paul describes God on the Day of Judgment, and in a memorable
phrase outlines the conduct which, in marked contrast to the sins of
the ungodly, will be rewarded with everlasting life.

12 **For when the Gentiles, which have not the law, do by nature
    the things contained in the law, these, having not the law, are
    a law unto themselves.**
    (2:14)
    Paul has been saying that adherence to the letter of Jewish law alone
    is no guarantee of salvation: it is deeds, not forms of words, which
    proclaim the true believer. 'To be a law unto oneself ' has come to
    have overtones of arrogance if not criminality; Paul's implication
    here is quite the opposite.

13 **For circumcision verily profiteth, if thou keep the law: but if
    thou be a breaker of the law, thy circumcision is made
    uncircumcision.**
    (2:25)
    Paul reinforces his point that a true believer is declared by his or her
    lifestyle, not by adherence to the letter or practice of Jewish (or any
    other) law.

14 **For what if some did not believe? shall their unbelief make
    the faith of God without effect? God forbid: yea, let God be
    true, but every man a liar.**
    (3:3–4)
    Paul is talking of the Jews' special relationship with God, who chose
    them to bear witness to his presence in the world. He now answers
    those who claim that the wickedness of some of the Jewish people
    (their idolatry, say) invalidates their teaching about God. God is
    God, unaffected by human ideas of morality, such as truth or lies.

15 **Let us do evil, that good may come?**
    (3:8)
    This extraordinary view, Paul says, is attributed by some people to
    the Christians. If God redeems sinners, then the greater the sin the
    greater the redemption. He proceeds briskly to condemn this notion
    – a good life is still the best way to serve God – and to show this
    kind of moral logic-chopping for what it is.

16 **For all have sinned, and come short of the glory of God; Being
    justified freely by his grace through the redemption that is in
    Christ Jesus.**
    (3:23–4)
    Paul's discussion of guilt and innocence moves to a more general
    plane: the guilt of the whole human race, the 'original sin' of Adam
    which God, because he is a just God, is bound to punish. Paul goes

on to state one of the central beliefs of the Christian faith, that it is
this guilt which Christ was sent into the world to redeem, and that
God will forgive anyone who truly repents and believes in Christ.

17 **If Abraham were justified by works, he hath whereof to glory;
but not before God.**
(4:2)
Paul goes back to Abraham (one of the founding fathers of the
Jewish faith, the man with whom God symbolically renewed his
covenant with humanity) to demonstrate his point that there are two
kinds of 'justification', which means 'being righteous'. Justification
by works is living by the moral standards of humankind, and it is
flawed because all human beings, however 'good', are tainted with
original sin and must be punished. Justification by faith, by contrast,
involves both believing that Jesus came into the world to redeem
human sin, and living the 'good life' which such belief necessitates.

18 **Where no law is, there is no transgression.**
(4:15)
Paul has been saying that Abraham was a good man because of his
faith in God, not because of Jewish law (which was not yet
formulated in Abraham's time). This quotation, which has been
widely used since to justify the existence of the rule of law, in fact
implies quite the opposite. The existence of law creates human
scales of good and evil, crime and recompense, but they are
unnecessary or irrelevant once faith enters the argument because
faith transcends human moral reasoning.

19 **Who against hope believed in hope, that he might become the
father of many nations; according to that which was spoken,
So shall thy seed be.**
(4:18)   •
This refers to Abraham's faith in God, when he was told that he and
Sarah would have a child despite his and his wife's extreme old age.
To 'hope against hope' became proverbial.

20 **Therefore being justified by faith, we have peace with God
through our Lord Jesus Christ: By whom also we have access
by faith into this grace wherein we stand, and rejoice in hope
of the glory of God.**
(5:1–2)
Paul brings to a point his comparison of justification by works and
justification by faith.

21 **Where sin abounded, grace did much more abound.**
(5:20)

Paul has been contrasting the way one man (Adam) brought sin into the world, and another (Jesus) brought redemption: the one cancels out the other. The idea of 'grace abounding' (that is, abundant) became proverbial.

22 **Know ye not, that so many of us as were baptized into Jesus Christ were baptized into his death? Therefore we are buried with him by baptism into death: that like as Christ was raised up from the dead by the glory of the Father, even so we also should walk in newness of life.**
(6:3–4)
Acceptance of Christ involves sharing his death as well as his resurrection – and this, Paul goes on to say, is one guarantee of redemption, since death includes the death of sin.

23 **Christ being raised from the dead dieth no more; death hath no more dominion over him.**
(6:9)
Christ's death is, so to speak, a once-for-all payment: redemption needs no repetition.

24 **For the wages of sin is death; but the gift of God is eternal life through Jesus Christ our Lord.**
(6:23)
This is the culmination of a complex theological argument linking sin with death and faith with redemption: each involves and is the other, and in this verse Paul finally offers them to each individual human being as straightforward and mutually exclusive alternatives.

25 **What shall we say then? Is the law sin? God forbid. Nay, I had not known sin, but by the law: for I had not known lust, except the law had said, Thou shalt not covet.**
(7:7)
Having dismissed the ideas that keeping the letter of the law is the way to salvation, and that there is a kind of moral profit-and-loss account for each of us, which has only to balance to win us eternal life, Paul explains the true purpose of human moral codes: not to guarantee, but to teach, to guide, leaving ultimate choice open to each individual.

26 **For the good that I would I do not: but the evil which I would not, that I do.**
(7:19)
Paul memorably states the dilemma of everyone trying to live a truly moral life, being tugged in opposite directions by the flesh and the spirit.

27 O wretched man that I am! who shall deliver me from the
body of this death?
(7:24)
The 'body of this death' is human nature, subject as it is to original
sin and the punishment which that entails.

28 I thank God through Jesus Christ our Lord.
(7:25)
Paul implicitly answers the question he posed in the previous verse:
praise of God and belief in the risen Christ help the true believer to
fight original sin.

29 They that are after the flesh do mind the things of the flesh;
but they that are after the Spirit the things of the Spirit. For to
be carnally minded is death; but to be spiritually minded is
life and peace.
(8:5–6)
The distinction is still between human nature, the 'flesh' which we
have inherited from Adam and which is tainted with original sin,
and the spiritual purity promised us if we have faith that Christ
assumed that same flesh in order to redeem its sin. His choice was
to share our mortality; our choice, faith in him, unshackles us from
mortality.

30 We are the children of God: And if children, then heirs; heirs
of God, and joint-heirs with Christ; if so be that we suffer
with him, that we may be also glorified together.
(8:16–17)
The presence of the Holy Spirit in our lives, and our readiness to
accept it, allies us with Christ in the family of God. In the early days
of Christianity this passage led to the Christians calling themselves
'children of God', a name by which they were known even to their
Roman persecutors. The idea of God's people as a family, common
from earliest times, was given new impetus by the idea of all
Christians being a 'communion of saints', and by the Eucharist by
which that communion was acknowledged and which took its form
from a family meal.

31 All things work together for good to them that love God, to
them who are the called according to his purpose.
(8:28)
Faith in God gives moral direction. Paul has just described the Holy
Spirit as our helper, intercessor and guide.

32 What shall we then say to these things? If God be for us, who
can be against us?
(8:31)

'These things' are the case which Paul has just been stating: that God predestined certain people to be called to righteousness, to be remade in the perfect image of God. The phrase which ends this quotation became a rallying cry to the early Christians, suffering Roman persecution, and has been used as a summons to spiritual courage ever since.

33 I am persuaded, that neither death, nor life, nor angels, nor principalities, nor powers, nor things present, nor things to come, Nor height, nor depth, nor any other creature, shall be able to separate us from the love of God, which is in Christ Jesus our Lord.
(8:38–9)
God's love, shown in his sending his own son to die in redemption of the world's sin, is undeviating and secure, whatever the forces ranged against it. In context, Paul is urging on his hearers and readers an equally unshakeable faith in Christ.

34 Nay but, O man, who art thou that repliest against God? Shall the thing formed say to him that formed it, Why has thou made me thus? Hath not the potter power over the clay, of the same lump to make one vessel unto honour, and another unto dishonour?
(9:20–1)
Paul answers those who ask why, if God loves all human beings equally, he has mercy on some and allows others to suffer: why does he still judge between them? The image of the potter and the clay is a standard Old Testament metaphor for God and his creation (see Isa 44). The potter, not the clay, is in control of the clay's nature and destiny.

35 I beseech you therefore, brethren, by the mercies of God, that ye present your bodies a living sacrifice, holy, acceptable unto God, which is your reasonable service.
(12:1)
From a discussion of God's mercy, freely available to all people, Paul turns to the human side of the relationship, answering the question 'what must we do to be saved?'.

36 For as we have many members in one body, and all members have not the same office: So we, being many, are one body in Christ, and every one members one of another.
(12:4–5)
Earlier, Paul compared the Church to a family; now he compares it to a body, with many limbs ('members') performing different functions ('offices'), but none the less united and indivisible.

37 **Let love be without dissimulation. Abhor that which is evil; cleave to that which is good. Be kindly affectioned one to another with brotherly love.**
(12:9–10)
Paul continues his teaching about true Christian behaviour. 'Brotherly love' was one of his favourite images for the kind of affection people should show one another: it relates to his vision of the Church as a family led by God the loving father.

38 **Bless them which persecute you: bless, and curse not.**
(12:14)
Paul here adapts to contemporary conditions one of Jesus' teachings in the Sermon on the Mount (see Matt 23).

39 **Rejoice with them that do rejoice, and weep with them that weep.**
(12:15)
Paul continues preaching practical Christianity. Here he is recommending 'fellow-feeling', that is identifying with every other member of the human race.

40 **Be of the same mind one toward another. Mind not high things, but condescend to men of low estate. Be not wise in your own conceits. Recompense to no man evil for evil. Provide things honest in the sight of all men. If it be possible, as much as lieth in you, live peaceably with all men. Dearly beloved, avenge not yourselves, but rather give place unto wrath: for it is written, Vengeance is mine; I will repay, saith the Lord.**
(12:16–19)
Paul's teaching about the true Christian life draws on many different sources, ranging from the book of Proverbs to Jesus' Sermon on the Mount. 'Be of the same mind' means 'make no distinctions'; 'condescend to' means 'be on equal terms with'.

41 **Be not overcome of evil, but overcome evil with good.**
(12:21)
Paul is advocating neither passivity nor a kind of arrogant, Pharisaical humility, but patient 'charity' – the Christian love which he later declares was the greatest virtue of them all (see I Cor 22).

42 **Let every soul be subject unto the higher powers. For there is no power but of God: the powers that be are ordained of God.**
(13:1)
Paul is here preaching temporal obedience, acceptance of the hierarchies of human life. 'Power' here is used as we today talk of 'the authorities'. The Romans thought of society as a kind of

pyramid, with each person's place determined by rank and position. By putting God, its creator, not so much at the point of this pyramid but outside it, Paul gives the traditional idea a powerful, if somewhat ironical, new twist.

43 **For rulers are not a terror to good works, but to the evil. Wilt thou then not be afraid of the power? do that which is good, and thou shalt have praise of the same: For he is the minister of God to thee for good. But if thou do that which is evil, be afraid; for he beareth not the sword in vain: for he is the minister of God, a revenger to execute wrath upon him that doeth evil. Wherefore ye must needs be subject, not only for wrath, but also for conscience sake.**
(13:3–5)
Paul extends his teaching about human hierarchies. We should accept the authorities, not resist them, because their position was given them by God and they are the instruments of his justice.

44 **Render therefore to all their dues: tribute to whom tribute is due; custom to whom custom; fear to whom fear; honour to whom honour. Owe no man any thing, but to love one another: for he that loveth another hath fulfilled the law.**
(13:7–8)
Paul's teaching about Christian duty continues by advocating Christian 'charity' in all aspects of society.

45 **Love worketh no ill to his neighbour: therefore love is the fulfilling of the law.**
(13:10)
In the traditional rabbinical manner, followed also by Jesus, Paul rounds off a piece of complex teaching with a pithy, easily remembered summary of the point he has been developing.

46 **The night is far spent, the day is at hand: let us therefore cast off the works of darkness, and let us put on the armour of light. Let us walk honestly, as in the day; not in rioting and drunkenness, not in chambering and wantonness, not in strife and envying. But put ye on the Lord Jesus Christ, and make not provision for the flesh, to fulfil the lusts thereof.**
(13:12–14)
Paul memorably extends the common image of the dawning of the Day of Judgment. By dressing ourselves in the armour of light, by putting on Jesus, we turn Judgment into Salvation. The rioting, drunkenness, chambering (lust: 'chamberer' originally meant chambermaid, then prostitute) and other dark activities are all common Biblical metaphors for ungodliness.

47 **Him that is weak in the faith receive ye, but not to doubtful disputations.**
(14:1)
Paul is concerned that the Christian Church should not fall into the sectarianism of Judaism, a fragmentation of true worship in which each group bases it practice, and its claim to exclusive 'rightness', on obedience to this or that tiny detail of teaching.

48 **For none of us liveth to himself, and no man dieth to himself. For whether we live, we live unto the Lord; and whether we die, we die unto the Lord: whether we live therefore, or die, we are the Lord's. For to this end Christ both died, and rose, and revived, that he might be Lord both of the dead and living.**
(14:7–9)
Paul's preaching against exclusivity, the making of sects, continues. Whatever our beliefs, we are, as he said earlier, 'members' of one another, like the limbs of a body, and Christ died for all of us equally.

49 **Let us not therefore judge one another any more: but judge this rather, that no man put a stumblingblock or an occasion to fall in his brother's way. I know, and am persuaded by the Lord Jesus, that there is nothing unclean of itself: but to him that esteemeth any thing to be unclean, to him it is unclean. But if thy brother be grieved with thy meat, now walkest thou not charitably. Destroy not him with thy meat, for whom Christ died.**
(14:13–15)
In his continued preaching against sectarianism, Paul deliberately chooses as a metaphor one of the most contentious issues between the Jewish and Gentile members of the new Christian Church, the matter of 'clean' and 'unclean' food. What we believe and/or practise, in this as in other matters, is irrelevant to the central issue (that we are all brothers in Christ, equal in redemption); we should not therefore use our beliefs to exclude or mortify others.

50 **Salute one another with an holy kiss.**
(16:16)
The 'holy kiss', or kiss of peace, became a standard form of greeting between Christians. It marked them off from most other peoples of the time, and especially from those educated in Roman ways, for whom there was no such thing as a casual embrace: hugging and kissing were intensely private activities between relatives or lovers, and were never done to strangers. The 'holy kiss' led to the accusation, in Roman times, that Christians were a loose-living, lascivious sect.

I Corinthians

1 **For ye see your calling, brethren, how that not many wise men after the flesh, not many mighty, not many noble, are called: But God hath chosen the foolish things of the world to confound the wise; and God hath chosen the weak things of the world to confound the things which are mighty.**
(1:26–7)

The contrast is between the simplicity (or here, 'foolishness') of the Christian message and the learning (or 'wisdom') of the world. 'Wise men after the flesh' are people regarded as learned in human terms, but (Paul implies) not necessarily in spirit, that is in the faith of God.

2 **And I, brethren, when I came to you, came not with excellency of speech or of wisdom, declaring unto you the testimony of God. For I determined not to know any thing among you, save Jesus Christ, and him crucified.**
(2:1–2)

The Corinthians have been squabbling about different interpretations of the Christian message; Paul reminds them that the word he brought them was simple and unequivocal.

3 **I have planted, Apollos watered; but God gave the increase.**
(3:6)

Some of the Corinthian Christians have been following Paul's teaching, others that of Apollo, a missionary from Alexandria. Paul reminds them that there is only one message, only one seed of truth, whoever sows it or tends it. 'I planted, but God gave the increase' became proverbial as a statement of modest pride in achievement, usually in contexts nothing like Paul's own.

4 **Let a man so account of us, as of the ministers of Christ, and stewards of the mysteries of God.**
(4:1)

Paul has been talking of the achievements of human life. Now he recommends to his hearers the only achievement, the only reputation worth aiming for.

5 **For I think that God hath set forth us the apostles last, as it were appointed to death: for we are made a spectacle unto the world, and to angels, and to men. We are fools for Christ's sake.**
(4:9–10)

Paul is seeking to mortify those Corinthian Christians who have set
themselves up as interpreters of Christianity to other Greeks.
(There was long-standing rivalry between Corinth and Athens as
intellectual centres, seedbeds of philosophical learning.) He
contrasts their 'wisdom', their assumption of knowledge, with the
'foolishness' of himself and the other true apostles. The rhetorical
exaggeration in these verses is quite deliberate: the letter was meant
to be read aloud, and would be more like a modern sermon, with all
the force for persuasion or denunciation which that implies.

6   **For I verily, as absent in body, but present in spirit, have
     judged already, as though I were present, concerning him
     that hath so done this deed.**
     (5:3)
     One of the reasons for Paul's letter is that he has been asked to
     make a ruling about incest among the Corinthian Christians: they
     claim that their faith in Christ has freed them from the constraints
     of earthly morality, and are misbehaving accordingly. Paul here
     apologizes for judging by letter and not in person. 'Absent in body
     but present in spirit' became proverbial.

7   **Your glorying is not good. Know ye not that a little leaven
     leaveneth the whole lump?**
     (5:6)
     The Corinthians are wrong to boast that their faith in Christ puts
     them above ordinary moral law. 'Leaven' here, yeast, is a metaphor
     for sin: just as a little sour yeast spoils the whole lump of dough, so a
     little sin spoils a congregation.

8   **Purge out therefore the old leaven, that ye may be a new
     lump, as ye are unleavened. For even Christ our passover is
     sacrificed for us: Therefore let us keep the feast, not with old
     leaven, neither with the leaven of malice and wickedness; but
     with the unleavened bread of sincerity and truth.**
     (5:7–8)
     The phrase 'Christ our passover' recalls the passover lamb killed in
     token of God's forgiveness. Christ, crucified at the time of passover,
     is such a lamb, and the Christian remembering that should give up
     the 'leaven' of sin and become pure bread again, like the
     unleavened bread of passover.

9   **What? know ye not that your body is the temple of the Holy
     Ghost which is in you, which ye have of God, and ye are not
     your own? For ye are bought with a price: therefore glorify
     God in your body, and in your spirit, which are God's.**
     (6:19–20)

The context is a passage of teaching about purity, fleshly abstinence. Two ideas are blended: that our bodies are shrines for the Holy Ghost, and that we are God's slaves, bought by Jesus' blood, and are not our own property to dispose of as we choose.

10   **It is better to marry than to burn.**
     (7:9)
     The context of this much-quoted remark is a sermon against fornication. In general, Paul advocates sexual abstinence, but he recommends that those who find celibacy difficult should marry rather than risk the flames of hell by promiscuous behaviour.

11   **He that is unmarried careth for the things that belong to the**
     Lord, how he may please the Lord: But he that is married
     careth for the things that are of the world, how he may please
     his wife.
     (7:32–3)
     These verses have been taken as Paul's justification of a celibate life, and are in part the origin of the monastic tradition of celibacy. Their context is more urgent. Paul has been predicting dangerous times immediately ahead for his Corinthian Christian hearers, and says that they should think twice about marrying in such circumstances. The contrast is between the needs of the flesh (since it is better to marry than to burn: see I Cor 10) and the need to keep one's mind entirely on God in times of persecution.

12   **I am made all things to all men, that I might by all means save**
     some.
     (9:22)
     Paul is talking of his own self-discipline, his willingness, for the sake of conversion, to talk to each group of people in their own terms. The phrase 'all things to all men' has since become proverbial of a less estimable kind of pliability.

13   **Know ye not that they which run in a race run all, but one**
     receiveth the prize? So run, that ye may obtain. And every
     man that striveth for the mastery is temperate in all things.
     Now they do it to obtain a corruptible crown; but we an
     incorruptible.
     (9:24–5)
     The context of this verse is Paul's teaching about self-discipline: it is the person who trains for the race who wins, whether the prize is the laurel wreath of a mortal athletics contest, which will wither and die, or the incorruptible crown of glory awarded to all true believers.

14 **All things are lawful for me, but all things are not expedient: all things are lawful for me, but all things edify not.**
(10:23)
The Corinthians have been claiming that their faith makes them immune to ordinary moral or human law, and in particular that they can meet and eat with pagans without taint. This is Paul's answer. 'For me' here means 'in my opinion'.

15 **But if a woman have long hair, it is a glory to her; for her hair is given her for a covering.**
(11:15)
From this verse, which is part of a long piece of teaching on whether or not a woman should cover her hair to pray, comes the common description of hair as a person's 'crowning glory'.

16 **Wherefore whosoever shall eat this bread, and drink this cup of the Lord, unworthily, shall be guilty of the body and blood of the Lord.**
(11:27)
Continuing his sermon on moral purity, Paul says that anyone who takes communion, symbolically eating bread and drinking wine in remembrance of Christ's self-sacrifice for the remission of sins, knowing that he or she is unworthy because of sin, is in the same moral and theological position as those who rejected and murdered Christ.

17 **Now there are diversities of gifts, but the same Spirit.**
(12:4)
Corinth prided itself as a kind of spiritual marketplace, welcoming people from all traditions and tolerantly accepting religious practices – entranced dancing, ritual prostitution, self-mutilation – which were frowned on elsewhere. Though the Corinthian Christians eschewed the more bizarre of these activities, they did boast a variety of 'gifts', as Paul calls them here, ranging from flagellation to speaking in tongues, for which some of them were renowned. Paul reminds them of the indivisible truth at the heart of Christianity, and of the Holy Spirit which transmits that truth.

18 **For by one Spirit are we all baptized into one body, whether we be Jews or Gentiles, whether we be bond or free; and have been all made to drink into one Spirit. For the body is not one member, but many.**
(12:13–14)
Paul repeats one of his favourite metaphors, that the Church is a body. The diversity of religious 'gifts' or practices to which he has been alluding, like the different 'members' of the body, have point

and meaning only because they are all aspects or parts of the same thing.

19 **Though I speak with the tongues of men and of angels, and have not charity, I am become as sounding brass, or a tinkling cymbal. And though I have the gift of prophecy, and understand all mysteries, and all knowledge; and though I have all faith, so that I could remove mountains, and have not charity, I am nothing. And though I bestow all my goods to feed the poor, and though I give my body to be burned, and have not charity, it profiteth me nothing.**
(13:1–3)
Pursuing his teaching about the outward manifestations of inward faith, Paul singles out Faith, Hope and Charity as the three most desirable 'gifts', and places Charity, that is *caritas* or Christian love, above them all. Here he lists some of the 'gifts' it surpasses: speaking in tongues, prophetic knowledge, absolute faith, self-dedication even to the point of bankruptcy and death. In many versions, 'charity' is translated as 'love' throughout.

20 **Charity suffereth long, and is kind; charity envieth not; charity vaunteth not itself, is not puffed up, Doth not behave itself unseemly, seeketh not her own, is not easily provoked, thinketh no evil; Rejoiceth not in iniquity, but rejoiceth in the truth; Beareth all things, believeth all things, hopeth all things, endureth all things.**
(13:4–7)
Paul describes the characteristics of Christian love ('charity').

21 **Charity never faileth: but whether there be prophecies, they shall fail; whether there be tongues, they shall cease; whether there be knowledge, it shall vanish away. For we know in part, and we prophesy in part. But when that which is perfect is come, then that which is in part shall be done away. When I was a child, I spake as a child, I understood as a child, I thought as a child: but when I became a man, I put away childish things. For now we see through a glass, darkly; but then face to face: now I know in part; but then shall I know even as also I am known.**
(13:8–12)
Christian love is here linked with full knowledge, the perfect union with God which from Old Testament times had been proclaimed as the reward of all true believers at the Day of Judgment. While we are in the world, we understand only dimly (as if through a distorting glass) what true Christian love is; on the Day of Judgment we will understand it perfectly, and be at one with God.

22   And now abideth faith, hope, charity, these three; but the greatest of these is charity.
(13:13)
Paul rounds off his poem in praise of Christian love. 'Now abideth' implies 'are eternal and unchanged' – qualities which mark Faith, Hope and Charity from all the other spiritual 'gifts' he has been considering.

23   For if the trumpet give an uncertain sound, who shall prepare himself to the battle?
(14:8)
Discussing the value of speaking in tongues – one of the 'gifts' on which the Corinthian Christians most prided themselves – Paul asks what the point of it is if no one understands. Speech without sense, like the 'uncertain sound' of a trumpet (a fanfare no one understands) is mere entertainment – something for which Paul, with his sense of the urgency of the spiritual battle to be fought, has little time.

24   Brethren, be not children in understanding: howbeit in malice be ye children, but in understanding be men.
(14:20)
'Malice' here means 'guile'. Paul is recommending a kind of childlike spiritual innocence, and makes clear that he means not ignorance (innocence of all understanding) but honesty (innocent, that is unsinful, use of one's knowledge of God).

25   God is not the author of confusion, but of peace.
(14:33)
Paul is preaching against the indiscriminate speaking in tongues which, he says, is a feature of Corinthian Christian services. The idea in his mind is of Babel, of meaningless babble inspired by Satan, lord of confusion and father of lies. By contrast, God sends unequivocal, clear messages, and Paul would, he says, prefer people to speak one at a time, and if necessary have someone at hand to explain their ecstatic utterances.

26   Let all things be done decently and in order.
(14:40)
This verse ends, and summarizes, Paul's attempts to bring some discipline into the chaotic, rowdy services of the Corinthian Christians. It became a favourite instruction in the Middle Ages, both in the more spartan monastic traditions and at the time of the Reformation.

27 Christ died for our sins according to the scriptures; And that he was buried, and that he rose again the third day according to the scriptures.

(15:3–4)

In simple language, Paul states the core of Christian belief. His words were later incorporated into the Creed, the recital of belief which is at the centre of much Christian worship.

28 And last of all he was seen of me also, as of one born out of due time. For I am the least of the apostles, that am not meet to be called an apostle, because I persecuted the church of God. But by the grace of God I am what I am: and his grace which was bestowed upon me was not in vain; but I laboured more abundantly than they all: yet not I, but the grace of God which was with me. Therefore whether it were I or they, so we preach, and so ye believed.

(15:8–11)

Paul has been saying that the risen Christ appeared to many people, several of whom were still alive at the time of writing. He now adds himself to the list, referring to his vision of Christ on the road to Damascus. He is, perhaps, one of the most unlikely people in the world to be chosen, but his point is that it is the message, not the messenger, which counts: the transmission of God's grace is all that matters. 'Born out of due time' simply refers to his being a generation or so younger than the other 'witnesses'.

29 But now is Christ risen from the dead, and become the firstfruits of them that slept. For since by man came death, by man came also the resurrection of the dead. For as in Adam all die, even so in Christ shall all be made alive.

(15:20–2)

This is a simple statement of one of the most constant themes of Paul's teaching. Just as all human beings are one in sin, because of Adam's fall, so they are one in hope because of Christ's resurrection. Belief in that is the core of faith, and faith is the path to eternal life, to escaping the bonds of death as Christ himself escaped. To describe Christ as the firstfruits of the dead (that is, 'them that slept') is to imply that the harvest of souls has started, that all is now being safely gathered in.

30 The last enemy that shall be destroyed is death.

(15:26)

Paul continues to preach the eternal life of all believers, guaranteed by the resurrection of Christ himself. 'The last enemy' became a proverbial phrase for death.

31   There is one glory of the sun, and another glory of the moon,
and another glory of the stars: for one star differeth from
another star in glory. So also is the resurrection of the dead. It
is sown in corruption; it is raised in incorruption.
(15:41–2)
The contrast is between the glory of the risen body and the
corruption from which it arose. Paul has been reflecting on the
many forms of earthly existence, and talks of the resurrection of the
dead as if it were a plant, transcending the world as a seed
transcends the soil (an essential medium, and one made by
corruption and decay) in which it grows. The glory of the
resurrection will be as different from this seed as the sun is from the
moon in the sky.

32   The first man is of the earth, earthy: the second man is the
Lord from heaven.
(15:47)
The two sides of human nature, worldly and spiritual, are described
as if they were two distinct individuals.

33   Now this I say, brethren, that flesh and blood cannot inherit
the kingdom of God; neither doth corruption inherit
incorruption.
(15:50)
Before we can enter God's kingdom, we must shed our worldliness
as a plant sheds the 'corruption' in which it grows (see I Cor 31).

34   Behold, I shew you a mystery; We shall not all sleep, but we
shall all be changed, In a moment, in the twinkling of an eye,
at the last trump: for the trumpet shall sound, and the dead
shall be raised incorruptible, and we shall be changed. For
this corruptible must put on incorruption, and this mortal
must put on immortality. So when this corruptible shall have
put on incorruption, and this mortal shall have put on
immortality, then shall be brought to pass the saying that is
written, Death is swallowed up in victory.
(15:51–4)
Paul continues to describe the resurrection of all believers in terms
of the transformation of a seed into a plant. 'Twinkling of an eye',
here simply meaning 'blink', became proverbial.

35   O death, where is thy sting? O grave, where is thy victory? The
sting of death is sin; and the strength of sin is the law. But
thanks be to God, which giveth us the victory through our
Lord Jesus Christ.
(15:55–7)

Paul rounds off his teaching on the resurrection, quoting from and expounding Old Testament texts.

36 **Watch ye, stand fast in the faith, quit you like men, be strong. Let all your things be done with charity.**
(16:13–14)
As always, Paul's instructions to his congregation are a blend of the military – he saw conversion as a kind of tactical exercise, a battle against unbelief; there were also the (literal) armies of the ungodly, the Roman authorities, to be faced – and the pastoral. Here he simultaneously recommends soldierly fortitude and the charity, or Christian love, which has been a major theme throughout this letter. The instruction is uncompromising – Paul never conceals the problems his congregation will have to face – but it is clear and unequivocal, as his Corinthian followers had requested.

37 **If any man love not the Lord Jesus Christ, let him be Anathema Maranatha.**
(16:22)
The Greek word *anathema* means something or someone set apart, taboo. *Maranatha* is Aramaic for 'May God come!' Although the two expressions are quite separate in this verse, they have often been proverbially run together since, to mean something like 'beyond the pale'.

II Corinthians

1 **Moreover I call God for a record upon my soul, that to spare you I came not as yet unto Corinth. Not for that we have dominion over your faith, but are helpers of your joy: for by faith ye stand.**
(1:23–4)
Matters have gone from bad to worse at Corinth, and Paul has been asked to make a pastoral visit to sort things out. He has delayed his visit, he says, hoping that the Corinthian Christians will settle their own differences, and now reminds them that they are united in a single faith, a faith which should lead to joy, not argument.

2 **Our sufficiency is of God; Who also hath made us able ministers of the new testament; not of the letter, but of the spirit: for the letter killeth, but the spirit giveth life.**
(3:5–6)
Anti-Paul factions have arisen in the Corinthian church. He has just asked, with mild sarcasm, if he needs letters of introduction to the congregation there, and then answers his own question by

saying that the Corinthian Christians *are* his 'letters', because he founded the Church there. He now links this thought to another, common in his preaching, that spiritual truth transcends any 'letter of the law'.

3   **For God, who commanded the light to shine out of darkness, hath shined in our hearts, to give the light of true knowledge of the glory of God in the face of Jesus Christ.**
(4:6)
The contrast is between the transitory law of Moses, which Paul likens to a light only partially revealed, and the light of true knowledge revealed in Christ. As often, Paul takes up an image from earlier teaching (also present in the opening of St John's Gospel), and develops it: the light of the world is not external, but inside every one of us.

4   **For we know that if our earthly house of this tabernacle were dissolved, we have a building of God, an house not made with hands, eternal in the heavens.**
(5:1)
Continuing his theme that the light of faith irradiates the inner soul, Paul uses a traditional Greek idea, that the body is a tent (or 'tabernacle') of flesh, housing the spirit which is the true personality. By identifying that spirit with the Holy Ghost, Paul adds Christian urgency to what his hearers would have considered a well-worn philosophical cliché.

5   **If any man be in Christ, he is a new creature: old things are passed away; behold, all things are become new.**
(5:17)
This links up with Paul's earlier teaching, that faith in Christ makes the true believer grow like a seed, new spiritual life being born from the corruption of the flesh.

6   **Behold, now is the accepted time; behold, now is the day of salvation.**
(6:2)
The Corinthian Christians had been frittering away their time and spiritual energy in futile disagreements. Paul urges them to change their ways at once: the need for spiritual regeneration is pressing.

7   **As unknown, and yet well known; as dying, and, behold, we live; as chastened, and not killed; As sorrowful, yet alway rejoicing; as poor, yet making many rich; as having nothing, and yet possessing all things.**
(6:9–10)

Paul describes the ideal Christian, at once the vessel and the minister of faith.

8   **Be ye not unequally yoked together with unbelievers: for what fellowship hath righteousness with unrighteousness? and what communion hath light with darkness? And what concord hath Christ with Belial? or what part hath he that believeth with an infidel?**
(6:14–15)
Just as Paul regularly preached the equal fellowship of all who believed in Christ, whatever their backgrounds, so he often reminded his congregations to keep themselves apart from idolaters. In Corinth, where seductive religions of all kinds were practised, this instruction was particularly necessary – and it is delivered here with suitable vehemence.

9   **For ye know the grace of our Lord Jesus Christ, that, though he was rich, yet for your sakes he became poor, that ye through his poverty might be rich.**
(8:9)
Paul develops his contrast between worldly poverty and the spiritual riches guaranteed by Jesus.

10 **Every man according as he purposeth in his heart, so let him give; not grudgingly, or of necessity: for God loveth a cheerful giver.**
(9:7)
Although this verse has come to have a general application, its original circumstances were highly specific: Paul was urging the Corinthians to send money to help needy Christians in Jerusalem.

11 **He that glorieth, let him glory in the Lord. For not he that commendeth himself is approved, but whom the Lord commendeth.**
(10:17–18)
Some of Paul's critics in the Corinthian congregation have been boasting ('glorying'), saying that they are more successful in the world's terms, not to mention more devout, than he is. This is the beginning of his reply.

12 **Though I be rude in speech, yet not in knowledge.**
(11:6)
Paul is comparing himself to other Christian apostles, who are (he says) smoother tongued but not necessarily more authoritative for that. 'Rude' means 'plain', 'uneducated'; it is a highly sarcastic claim, as Paul was one of the best-educated of all Christ's early followers.

13   **For ye suffer fools gladly, seeing ye yourselves are wise.**
      (11:19)
      The 'fools' Paul is complaining that the Corinthian Christians
      respect ('suffer gladly') are clever windbags: they preach the Gospel
      in a showy, shallow way, in complete contrast to his own urgent
      simplicity.

14   **Are they Hebrews? so am I. Are they Israelites? so am I. Are**
      they the seed of Abraham? so am I. Are they ministers of
      Christ? (I speak as a fool) I am more; in labours more
      abundant, in stripes above measure, in prisons more
      frequent, in deaths oft.
      (11:22–3)
      Paul continues to compare himself with the other, more plausible-
      seeming, missionaries who have been welcomed in Corinth.

15   **Of the Jews five times received I forty stripes save one. Thrice**
      was I beaten with rods, once was I stoned, thrice I suffered
      shipwreck, a night and a day I have been in the deep; In
      journeyings often, in perils of waters, in perils of robbers, in
      perils by mine own countrymen, in perils by the heathen, in
      perils in the city, in perils in the wilderness, in perils in the
      sea, in perils among false brethren; In weariness and
      painfulness, in watchings often, in hunger and thirst, in
      fastings often, in cold and nakedness.
      (11:24–7)
      This description of Paul's suffering for Christ has become a symbol
      for the worldly torments which assail all Christian souls, and has
      been the inspiration of prayers, hymns and meditations in many
      denominations.

16   **I knew a man in Christ above fourteen years ago, (whether in**
      the body, I cannot tell; or whether out of the body, I cannot
      tell: God knoweth;) such an one caught up to the third
      heaven.
      (12:2)
      From physical hardships suffered for Christ, Paul goes on to tell of
      revelations and mystical experiences. The man he mentions here
      was carried, in a vision, to the highest heaven of all, into the
      presence of God himself. Unlike some other traditions, which
      believed in seven tiers of heaven (hence the expression 'seventh
      heaven'), the Jewish scriptures taught that there were three, one
      above the other, and that the third or highest heaven was the home
      of God. In some versions of this verse, 'third heaven' is translated
      'highest heaven', so giving the language a phrase – akin to 'seventh
      heaven' – for ecstasy.

17 Lest I should be exalted above measure through the abundance of the revelations, there was given to me a thorn in the flesh, the messenger of Satan to buffet me, lest I should be exalted above measure.
(12:7)

Not all Paul's visions are comfortable ones. Here he describes the coming of a tempter, an emissary of the Devil. Some take the phrase to refer to a recurring illness, a constant reminder to him of the weakness of the flesh.

18 For this thing I besought the Lord thrice, that it might depart from me. And he said unto me, My grace is sufficient for thee: for my strength is made perfect in weakness.
(12:8–9)

In his vision, Paul begs Christ to free him from the 'thorn in the flesh', and Christ answers that out of temptations, out of weakness, comes spiritual strength.

19 The grace of the Lord Jesus Christ, and the love of God, and the communion of the Holy Ghost, be with you all. Amen.
(13:14)

This the fullest form of a formula of blessing Paul uses to end all his letters. It has been adapted as a Christian benediction, usually to round off meetings or services.

Galatians

1 It pleased God, who separated me from my mother's womb, and called me by his grace, To reveal his Son in me, that I might preach him among the heathen.
(1:15–16)

Paul was the first Christian missionary to Galatia (most of modern Turkey), founding churches at such important cities as Antioch, which became centres of the new faith. But now he has been told that other Christian missionaries have visited the Galatians, and have persuaded the people that faith in Christ is not enough for salvation: circumcision and observation of kosher and other orthodox Jewish laws are also essential. Paul writes in horror to the Galatians to correct this teaching, and begins by reminding his hearers that his authority comes from God himself.

2 And when James, Cephas, and John, who seemed to be pillars, perceived the grace that was given unto me, they gave to me and Barnabas the right hands of fellowship; that we should go unto the heathen, and they unto the circumcision.
(2:9)

Paul is referring to his acceptance as an apostle by the chief 'pillars' of Christianity, when it was first decided to evangelize among Gentiles ('the heathen') as well as Jews ('the circumcision'). His authority is thus not only from God but from the founders of the early Church themselves. 'The right hand of fellowship' was originally a Roman custom: you grasped someone's right arm in your right hand as a sign that you were unarmed, were a friend. The phrase has become proverbial.

3   **Wherefore the law was our schoolmaster to bring us unto Christ, that we might be justified by faith. But after that faith is come, we are no longer under a schoolmaster.**
(3:24–5)
The point – reiterated throughout Paul's teaching, but particularly relevant in the circumstances of this letter – is that faith in Christ is all we need for salvation, that it transcends or underlies all other religious teaching and practice.

4   **For ye are all the children of God by faith in Christ Jesus. For as many of you as have been baptized into Christ have put on Christ. There is neither Jew nor Greek, there is neither bond nor free, there is neither male nor female: for ye are all one in Christ Jesus.**
(3:26–8)
Paul reiterates that there are no earthly distinctions between Christians: all who have faith in Christ are like members, or limbs, of a single body. 'Bond' means 'slave'.

5   **Christ is become of no effect unto you, whosoever of you are justified by the law; ye are fallen from grace.**
(5:4)
This bluntly worded denunciation of the Galatians must have been terrifying, coming from someone of Paul's authority. 'Grace' is God's favour towards mortals, the source of their salvation; to be 'fallen' from it is to be in the position of Satan who was cast from heaven into hell.

6   **If ye be led of the Spirit, ye are not under the law.**
(5:18)
Once again Paul spells out his message that faith transcends all religious laws.

7   **Now the works of the flesh are manifest, which are these; Adultery, fornication, uncleanness, lasciviousness, Idolatry, witchcraft, hatred, variance, emulations, wrath, strife, seditions, heresies, Envyings, murders, drunkenness,**

revellings, and such like: of the which I tell you before, as I
have also told you in time past, that they which do such things
shall not inherit the kingdom of God.
(5:19–21)

Paul is contrasting the behaviour of those who follow earthly laws,
the imperatives of the flesh, with those who are guided by faith.
This catalogue of vice, perhaps a little over-emphatic in order to
make Paul's point, was a favourite sermon-text in Puritan England
at the time of Cromwell.

8   But the fruit of the Spirit is love, joy, peace, longsuffering,
      gentleness, goodness, faith, Meekness, temperance: against
      such there is no law.
      (5:22–3)

In contrast to the 'works of the flesh' in previous verses, Paul
catalogues the qualities of those who lead a true Christian life. They
have been guided by the Spirit and set free by the grace of God
from the 'bondage', or slavery, of strict religious laws.

9   If we live in the Spirit, let us also walk in the Spirit.
      (5:25)

Faith is its own imperative: it is not an invitation to licence, but a
commitment even more demanding than the religious laws it
transcends.

10   Be not deceived; God is not mocked: for whatsoever a man
      soweth, that shall he also reap. For he that soweth to his flesh
      shall of the flesh reap corruption; but he that soweth to the
      Spirit shall of the Spirit reap life everlasting.
      (6:7–8)

In context, this is a blunt summons to repentance: Paul has earlier
made clear that by the 'flesh' he means the extra laws, irrelevant to
Christian faith, with which his hearers are burdening themselves to
the exclusion of faith itself.

11   Let us not be weary in well doing: for in due season we shall
      reap, if we faint not.
      (6:9)

Paul regularly uses this phrase in his letters, as an injunction to lead
the truly spiritual, truly Christian life.

Ephesians

1   I also, after I heard of your faith in the Lord Jesus, and love
unto all the saints, Cease not to give thanks for you, making
mention of you in my prayers; That the God of our Lord Jesus
Christ, the Father of glory, may give unto you the spirit of
wisdom and revelation in the knowledge of him: The eyes of
your understanding being enlightened; that ye may know
what is the hope of his calling, and what the riches of the
glory of his inheritance in the saints.
(1:15–18)
The immediate cause of this letter is uncertain, but it is thought to
have been a disagreement among the Christians at Ephesus, the
Gentile Ephesians regarding themselves as better Christians than
the Jewish Ephesians. Paul begins by praising the general Christian
devotion at Ephesus, and praying for its increase.

2   Wherein in time past ye walked according to the course of
this world, according to the prince of the power of the air, the
spirit that now worketh in the children of disobedience.
(2:2)
This is a direct reference to the Gentile Christians at Ephesus, who
before their conversion followed the pagan Greek religion, whose
chief deity was Zeus, lord of the sky, and whom Paul here identifies
with Satan. 'Children of disobedience' are pagans, Zeus-
worshippers: their disobedience is to the First Commandment.

3   And came and preached peace to you which were afar off, and
to them that were nigh.
(2:17)
As always to divided congregations, Paul preaches the unity of all
Christians, that the Church is one body. Those 'afar off ' were
Gentiles, strangers to what Paul calls the 'commonwealth of Israel'
(that is, the Jewish faith); 'them that were nigh' were Jews.

4   Unto me, who am less than the least of all saints, is this grace
given, that I should preach among the Gentiles the
unsearchable riches of Christ.
(3:8)
This description of himself recurs in Paul's letters: he is contrasting
his unworthiness with the glorious summons he has had to preach
the Gospel. 'Saints' here simply means 'believers'.

5   For this cause I bow my knees unto the Father of our Lord
Jesus Christ, Of whom the whole family in heaven and earth
is named, That he would grant you, according to the riches of

his glory, to be strengthened with might by his Spirit in the inner man; That Christ may dwell in your hearts by faith; that ye, being rooted and grounded in love, May be able to comprehend with all saints what is the breadth, and length, and depth, and height; And to know the love of Christ, which passeth knowledge, that ye might be filled with all the fulness of God.
(3:14–19)
Paul prays for the congregation of Ephesus, in words which have passed into common church use.

6   Now unto him that is able to do exceeding abundantly above all that we ask or think, according to the power that worketh in us, Unto him be glory in the church by Christ Jesus throughout all ages, world without end. Amen.
(3:20–1)
This form of words, which Paul uses to end his prayer for the Christians at Ephesus, is often still used today in place of the Doxology ('Glory be to the Father...').

7   There is one body, and one Spirit, even as ye are called in one hope of your calling; One Lord, one faith, one baptism, One God and Father of all, who is above all, and through all, and in you all.
(4:4–6)
Paul continues to preach the unity of all who have faith in Christ.

8   When he ascended up on high, he led captivity captive, and gave gifts unto men.
(4:8)
By his resurrection Jesus conquered death, the force which had previously enslaved the human race.

9   And he gave some, apostles; and some, prophets; and some, evangelists; and some, pastors and teachers; For the perfecting of the saints, for the work of the ministry, for the edifying of the body of Christ: Till we all come in the unity of the faith, and of the knowledge of the Son of God, unto a perfect man, unto the measure of the stature of the fulness of Christ.
(4:11–13)
Paul has just been discussing Christ's 'gifts' to the human race. The greatest gift of all is grace, and the apostles, prophets and evangelists are its ministers, God's go-betweens. The 'body of Christ' is the community of all Christians.

10 That we henceforth be no more children, tossed to and fro,
and carried about with every wind of doctrine, by the sleight
of men, and cunning craftiness, whereby they lie in wait to
deceive; But speaking the truth in love, may grow up into him
in all things, which is the head, even Christ: From whom the
whole body fitly joined together and compacted by that which
every joint supplieth, according to the effectual working in
the measure of every part, maketh increase of the body unto
the edifying of itself in love.
(4:14–16)
Paul spells out Christ's purpose in sending apostles and ministers of
grace. In the process he develops two of his favourite metaphors for
the Christian Church: a body made up of many limbs, and a family
in which we mature in grace.

11 For we are members one of another.
(4:25)
Paul brings to a point his teaching about the Church as a single
body. 'Members' means limbs.

12 Be ye angry, and sin not: let not the sun go down upon your
wrath.
(4:26)
Having declared that faith in God requires a commitment to a new
life, Paul begins a series of moral instructions on how to live in
Christian grace.

13 Walk in love, as Christ also hath loved us, and hath given
himself for us an offering and a sacrifice to God for a
sweetsmelling savour. But fornication, and all uncleanness,
or covetousness, let it not be once named among you, as
becometh saints; Neither filthiness, nor foolish talking, nor
jesting, which are not convenient: but rather giving of thanks.
(5:2–4)
Paul continues to prescribe the ideal Christian life. 'Convenient'
means appropriate. 'Named' means spoken about, much less
performed.

14 See then that ye walk circumspectly, not as fools, but as wise,
Redeeming the time, because the days are evil.
(5:15–16)
The exemplary behaviour of Christians will make their 'wisdom'
shine like a light in the world, compensating for ('redeeming') the
darkness of evil times.

15 Be not drunk with wine, wherein is excess; but be filled with
the Spirit; Speaking to yourselves in psalms and hymns and
spiritual songs, singing and making melody in your heart to
the Lord.
(5:18–19)
Paul's instructions on the Christian life continue.

16 For this cause shall a man leave his father and mother, and
shall be joined unto his wife, and they two shall be one flesh.
This is a great mystery: but I speak concerning Christ and the
church.
(5:31–2)
Paul, quoting Genesis, likens Christ's relationship with his Church
to the bond between husband and wife. The idea is an extension of
earlier teaching, in which Christ is the bridegroom and his Church
is the bride.

17 Servants, be obedient to them that are your masters
according to the flesh, with fear and trembling, in singleness
of your heart, as unto Christ; Not with eyeservice, as men-
pleasers; but as the servants of Christ, doing the will of God
from the heart; With good will doing service, as to the Lord,
and not to men.
(6:5–7)
These verses take up some earlier teaching of Paul, that the
hierarchies of human life should not be overthrown, but should be
observed because they are created or sanctioned by God. We work
ostensibly for our masters, but actually for God who is the father
and overseer of masters and servants alike.

18 Finally, my brethren, be strong in the Lord, and in the power
of his might. Put on the whole armour of God, that ye may be
able to stand against the wiles of the devil.
(6:10–11)
Paul ends his summons to the Christian life by developing the
common ideas that there is a battle to be fought between the powers
of light and of darkness, and that God is the armour of those who
have faith in him.

19 Wherefore take unto you the whole armour of God, that ye
may be able to withstand in the evil day, and having done all,
to stand. Stand therefore, having your loins girt about with
truth, and having on the breastplate of righteousness; And
your feet shod with the preparation of the gospel of peace;
Above all, taking the shield of faith, wherewith ye shall be
able to quench all the fiery darts of the wicked. And take the
helmet of salvation, and the sword of the Spirit, which is the

word of God: **Praying always with all prayer and supplication
in the Spirit, and watching thereunto with all perseverance
and supplication for all saints.**
(6:13–18)
The 'armour of righteousness' is an idea as old as Moses, and Paul
here draws on phrases from earlier writings as diverse as the
Psalms, the prophets and the Gospels to produce a passage of
stirring poetic rhetoric, a call to spiritual arms as memorable as his
earlier poem on the nature of Christian love (see I Cor 19).

Philippians

1   **God is my record, how greatly I long after you all in the
bowels of Jesus Christ.**
(1:8)
The ancients believed that the 'affections', feelings of, for example,
mercy, sympathy, jealousy and scorn, were governed by the
'bowels', that is, the bile, liver, kidneys and other internal organs.
(We still use words like 'bilious' and 'liverish' for people displaying
grumpiness.) Paul uses 'bowels of Jesus Christ' here to link two
ideas, that he longs to see his friends in Philippi for whom he has
warm fellow-feeling, and that that fellow-feeling results from them
all being 'members' or limbs of the body of Christ (that is, the
Christian Church). 'Bowels of Jesus Christ!' or 'Jesus' bowels!'
became proverbial, as a slang expression of irritated amazement and
as a particularly vehement oath.

2   **For to me to live is Christ, and to die is gain.**
(1:21)
Paul has been talking of his imprisonment – he probably sent this
letter from gaol in Rome – and of the possibility of his martyrdom.
In this verse he says that his whole life is dedicated to Christ, as (in
Thomas à Kempis' later words) an 'imitation of Christ', and that his
death will perfect the process, bringing him into unity with Christ.

3   **Let this mind be in you, which was also in Christ Jesus: Who,
being in the form of God, thought it not robbery to be equal
with God: But made himself of no reputation, and took upon
him the form of a servant, and was made in the likeness of
men: And being found in fashion as a man, he humbled
himself, and became obedient unto death, even the death of
the cross.**
(2:5–8)

Although Jesus shared God's nature by right (that is, it was 'not robbery'), he chose to take on the nature of mortals, humbling himself even to accept death. His humility should inspire our own: we should let his mind be in us.

4 **Wherefore God also hath highly exalted him, and given him a name which is above every name: That at the name of Jesus every knee should bow, of things in heaven, and things in earth, and things under the earth; And that every tongue should confess that Jesus Christ is Lord, to the glory of God the Father.**
(2:9–11)

Jesus' humility, his acceptance of mortality, has resulted in his exaltation above all creation. Paul is preaching Christian humility and acceptance to his hearers; their reward will be eternal life.

5 **Wherefore, my beloved, as ye have always obeyed, not as in my presence only, but now much more in my absence, work out your own salvation with fear and trembling. For it is God which worketh in you both to will and to do of his good pleasure.**
(2:12–13)

Although the surface meaning of this passage is literal – without Paul physically there to guide them, the Philippian Christians are to manage their own spiritual lives – it also refers to a consistent theme in Paul's teaching, that we have free will, that the way of faith is open, with God as guide, but it is for us to choose to walk it. To 'work out one's own salvation' became proverbial in a somewhat bleaker sense, meaning to be left with no resources other than one's own.

6 **Circumcised the eighth day, of the stock of Israel, of the tribe of Benjamin, an Hebrew of the Hebrews; as touching the law, a Pharisee; Concerning zeal, persecuting the church; touching the righteousness which is in the law, blameless.**
(3:5–6)

As elsewhere in his ministry, Paul has found that the congregation at Philippi has been beset by Judaizers, missionaries who refuse to allow anyone to convert to Christianity unless they first accept orthodox Judaism's circumcision, kosher laws and the like. As elsewhere, he angrily refutes this teaching, saying that faith in Christ is all that is essential, and backs up his teaching by pointing out that he was himself the most orthodox of Jews, and that this former orthodoxy is irrelevant (see Phil 7). 'Hebrew of the Hebrews' became proverbial.

7   But what things were gain to me, those I counted loss for
     Christ. Yea doubtless, and I count all things but loss for the
     excellency of the knowledge of Christ Jesus my Lord: for
     whom I have suffered the loss of all things, and do count them
     but dung, that I may win Christ.
     (3:7–8)
     Developing his theme that following human laws is not an essential
     prerequisite for Christianity, Paul describes how he himself has
     shed for Christ all the trappings of his Jewish orthodoxy, and
     regards the symbols of worldly rank or position as a hindrance,
     ('loss'), compared to the 'excellency' of Christian belief.

8   Brethren, I count not myself to have apprehended: but this
     one thing I do, forgetting those things which are behind, and
     reaching forth unto those things which are before, I press
     toward the mark for the prize of the high calling of God in
     Christ Jesus.
     (3:13–14)
     True 'apprehension', that is 'understanding', comes at the moment
     of death, when we are united with Christ in everlasting life. The
     way to achieve it is not to struggle for understanding in our worldly
     lives, but to press forward 'towards the mark' (that is, to the
     finishing post) as runners press forward in a race.

9   For many walk, of whom I have told you often, and now tell
     you even weeping, that they are the enemies of the cross of
     Christ: Whose end is destruction, whose God is their belly,
     and whose glory is in their shame, who mind earthly things.
     (3:18–19)
     Paul warns the Philippians against false ministers, those whose
     concern is earthly things (in this case, insistence on orthodox Jewish
     practices). Their God is appetite ('belly'), their pleasure is
     perversion, and their end will not be eternal life, spiritual fulfilment,
     but the fleshly 'fulfilment' of rotting in the grave.

10   Rejoice in the Lord alway: and again I say, Rejoice. Let your
     moderation be known unto all men. The Lord is at hand. Be
     careful for nothing; but in every thing by prayer and
     supplication with thanksgiving let your requests be made
     known unto God.
     (4:4–6)
     Paul lays down guidelines for the Christian life: praise of God;
     spiritual moderation and watchfulness; prayer to and trust in God.

11   And the peace of God, which passeth all understanding, shall
     keep your hearts and minds through Christ Jesus.
     (4:7)

In context, this is the reward Paul promises the true Christian believer. The words have been adapted into one of the best-loved of all prayers of blessing.

12 **Finally, brethren, whatsoever things are true, whatsoever things are honest, whatsoever things are just, whatsoever things are pure, whatsoever things are lovely, whatsoever things are of good report; if there be any virtue, and if there be any praise, think on these things.**
(4:8)
Other preachers have been directing the Philippians' thoughts to such matters as keeping the letter of the Jewish law, attention to ritual detail. Paul, literally, gives his hearers something else to think about, if they want to be virtuous (that is, if they want to live the 'good life' which adherence to the law once seemed to promise) and to be praised (that is, to seem 'virtuous' in other people's eyes, as was once also promised to those who observed the law).

13 **I can do all things through Christ which strengtheneth me.**
(4:13)
The Philippians have written to Paul in prison, asking if he needs anything. He thanks them for their concern, but also takes the opportunity to make this theological point.

Colossians

1 **That ye might walk worthy of the Lord unto all pleasing, being fruitful in every good work, and increasing in the knowledge of God; Strengthened with all might, according to his glorious power, unto all patience and longsuffering with joyfulness.**
(1:10–11)
Paul begins his letter by praying for the spiritual growth of his hearers. The placing of these ideas here was deliberate. They are not merely the pious platitudes to be expected of any holy man, but a reminder of Christian duty. Colossae in Turkey had a thriving Christian community, but one of the reasons for its thriving was that it admitted into Christian worship ideas and practices from other traditions: circumcision and kosher laws from Judaism, the Phrygian notion of minor, second-rank deities (identified by the Colossians with angels), and moral teaching from Greek philosophy.

2   **Beware lest any man spoil you through philosophy and vain deceit, after the tradition of men, after the rudiments of the world, and not after Christ.**
(2:8)
Paul warns his hearers to keep away from non-Christian moral teaching; it is worldly (and therefore doomed to die) and not of the Spirit (which would imbue it with the promise of eternal life).

3   **Touch not; taste not; handle not.**
(2:21)
The laws and practices of the non-Christian world, Paul says, are being offered invitingly to his Colossian hearers – and they should have nothing to do with them.

4   **Ye have put off the old man with his deeds; And have put on the new man, which is renewed in knowledge after the image of him that created him: Where there is neither Greek nor Jew, circumcision nor uncircumcision, Barbarian, Scythian, bond nor free: but Christ is all, and in all.**
(3:9–11)
The 'old man' is the former self, the 'old Adam' whose concerns are worldly; the 'new man' is the human being reborn in the faith of Christ, and guided by the Holy Spirit. Faith in Christ, Paul says, contains neither hierarchies nor boundaries.

5   **And whatsoever ye do, do it heartily, as to the Lord, and not unto men.**
(3:23)
This is a frequent theme in Paul's teaching, we should live our lives in conformity to the demands of our Christian faith, and not by laws made by mortals. Some of his hearers wrongly took this as an encouragement to ignore the constraints of the society they lived in. Paul, however, taught – and implies here – that our own obedience to God should give zest to, rather than replace, the tasks, duties and responsibilities of everyday life. 'Heartily' means 'with all your heart', that is (since the heart was considered the seat of intelligence) as we would say 'with your full mind'.

6   **Luke, the beloved physician, and Demas, greet you.**
(4:14)
Most of Paul's letters close with personal messages of this kind: apart from anything else, they helped to bind the Christian community together in a world where communication was slow and difficult. The Luke referred to here is the gospel-writer and author of Acts, Paul's close friend and fellow-missionary at the time when the Church was established at Colossae.

I Thessalonians

1   **Furthermore then we beseech you, brethren, and exhort you by the Lord Jesus, that as ye have received of us how ye ought to walk and to please God, so ye would abound more and more. (4:1)**

The Christian community at Thessalonica was small, and had suffered persecution. But by the time of this letter it was beginning to thrive, and Paul – its founder, as he implies here – sends appropriately encouraging words. 'Abound' means 'flourish'.

2   **And that ye study to be quiet, and to do your own business, and to work with your own hands, as we commanded you. (4:11)**

As always, Paul's teaching is that the Christian life involves diligence and humility. There were those in the Church – and in the congregation of Thessalonica – who thought that Jesus' Second Coming was imminent and that hard work of any kind was therefore pointless: better to spend the time praying and meditating spiritual readiness, while living off charity. This is not what Paul recommends.

3   **I would not have you to be ignorant, brethren, concerning them which are asleep, that ye sorrow not, even as others which have no hope. For if we believe that Jesus died and rose again, even so them also which sleep in Jesus will God bring with him. (4:13–14)**

Some of the Thessalonians have anxiously asked Paul what will happen to those who die (that is, 'fall asleep') before Christ's Second Coming. Will they be denied eternal life? Paul's answer became one of the fundamental teachings of the Christian Church.

4   **For the Lord himself shall descend from heaven with a shout, with the voice of the archangel, and with the trump of God: and the dead in Christ shall rise first: Then we which are alive and remain shall be caught up together with them in the clouds, to meet the lord in the air: and so shall we ever be with the Lord. (4:16–17)**

Paul's teaching on the Second Coming continues.

5   **The day of the Lord so cometh as a thief in the night. (5:2)**

Some Thessalonians have asked Paul when the Second Coming can be expected. (This was a common anxiety among the very early Christians, who believed that it was imminent and found it hard to organize their lives to suit their belief.) Here he answers in a phrase adapted from Jesus' own words (see Matt 140).

6 **Prove all things; hold fast that which is good.**
(5:21)
This is the climax of a series of instructions on how to live one's life in expectation of the Second Coming. 'Prove' means 'test': taking nothing for granted, spiritual vigilance, is one of Paul's most constant pieces of advice.

II Thessalonians

1 **Now we beseech you, brethren, by the coming of our Lord Jesus Christ, and by our gathering together unto him, That ye be not soon shaken in mind, or be troubled, neither by spirit, nor by word, nor by letter as from us, as that the day of Christ is at hand.**
(2:1–2)
The Thessalonians, already worried about the imminence of the Second Coming, have been thrown into confusion by Paul's earlier letter. He reassures them. His words meant that the Day of Judgment was spiritually imminent, that we should live each moment spiritually as if it were our last. This is not to say, that the end of the world is literally only moments away.

2 **Even when we were with you, this we commanded you, that if any would not work, neither should he eat.**
(3:10)
Paul reinforces his earlier teaching, that expectation of the Second Coming is no justification for refusing to do an honest day's work. Particularly in a small church like that at Thessalonica, there is no excuse, spiritual or otherwise, for living on others' charity.

I Timothy

1 **As I besought thee to abide still at Ephesus, when I went into Macedonia, that thou mightest charge some that they teach no other doctrine, Neither give heed to fables and endless genealogies, which minister questions, rather than godly edifying which is in faith: so do.**
(1:3–4)

Timothy was Paul's assistant and close friend, who went with him on all his missionary journeys except the first. Here Paul leaves him for a while in Ephesus, to oversee Christian doctrine there, and warns him against the ideas from other faiths which are being imported into Christianity. In a multi-religious centre such as Ephesus (home of the statue of Diana, one of the seven wonders of the world), 'fables and endless genealogies' would be the stock-in-trade of every religious huckster who set out to 'minister' (that is answer questions). In this situation, Paul advocates Christian behaviour as well as teaching. The contrast with other people's commerciality must have been remarkable.

2 **Some having swerved have turned aside unto vain jangling. (1:6)**
Paul complains that even Christian preachers have been seduced by the commercial atmosphere of Ephesus into adulterating their message.

3 **I thank Christ Jesus our Lord, who hath enabled me, for that he counted me faithful, putting me into the ministry; Who was before a blasphemer, and a persecutor, and injurious: but I obtained mercy, because I did it ignorantly in unbelief. (1:12–13)**
Paul uses his own conversion as an example: the worst sinner can be converted, by the grace of God. What he did before was done in ignorance of God; his belief, now, brings certainty.

4 **For this cause I obtained mercy, that in me first Jesus Christ might shew forth all longsuffering, for a pattern to them which should hereafter believe on him to life everlasting. Now unto the King eternal, immortal, invisible, the only wise God, be honour and glory for ever and ever. Amen. (1:16–17)**
Throughout his life, Paul has preached that Jesus did not come into the world to save the faithful, but sinners. Once again, he uses himself as an example. This use of oneself as proof that redemption was possible was a common method of teaching in the early Church, where many of the apostles had seen Christ, or knew people who had seen Christ, in person.

5 **I exhort therefore, that, first of all, supplications, prayers, intercessions, and giving of thanks, be made for all men; For kings, and for all that are in authority; that we may lead a quiet and peaceable life in all godliness and honesty. (2:1–2)**

The first duty of the Church is prayer; the second is Christian humility.

6   **There is one God, and one mediator between God and men, the man Christ Jesus; Who gave himself a ransom for all, to be testified in due time.**
(2:5–6)
This assertion of the uniqueness of Christ would have particular force in the babble of conflicting religious claims in Ephesus. One of the purposes of Paul's letters was to put essential truths into simple, unequivocal language, so that they could then be quoted and relied on, in the way of modern legal precedents. These verses are a memorable example. 'To be testified' means 'to be witnessed to': Paul is referring both to the Christian witness of apostles such as himself, and to the witness that Christ is Lord by the countless redeemed souls on the Day of Judgment.

7   **A bishop then must be blameless, the husband of one wife, vigilant, sober, of good behaviour, given to hospitality, apt to teach; Not given to wine, no striker, not greedy of filthy lucre; but patient, not a brawler, not covetous.**
(3:2–3)
Bishops (*episkopoi* or 'overseers' in Greek) were church elders, a kind of committee who administered both the secular and spiritual life of their community.

8   **Refuse profane and old wives' fables, and exercise thyself rather unto godliness.**
(4:7)
Paul warns once again that the myths favoured by other religions have no place in Christianity. This verse is the origin of the phrase 'old wives' tales'. 'Profane' means 'common', that is (here) uneducated, without authority.

9   **Drink no longer water, but use a little wine for thy stomach's sake and thine often infirmities.**
(5:23)
This was meant as specific advice to Timothy. He was a sickly man, and Paul is recommending him to drink undiluted wine to counteract the effects of the impure water in Ephesus (a marshy, notoriously unhealthy place). This verse has since been used humorously, as a jokey excuse for tippling.

10   **He is proud, knowing nothing, but doting about questions and strifes of words, whereof cometh envy, strife, railings, evil surmisings, Perverse disputings of men of corrupt minds,**

and destitute of the truth, supposing that gain is godliness:
from such withdraw thyself.
(6:4–5)
Paul thunderously denounces the kind of false prophet who
abounds in Ephesus. The idea that idolators make gain their god is
common throughout the Bible, probably because of the
extraordinary lavishness of many pagan temples; here, in Ephesus,
Paul gives it sharp commercial point.

11   For we brought nothing into this world, and it is certain we
can carry nothing out.
(6:7)
As often in Paul, a familiar idea is both given memorably simple
utterance and linked to a deeper theological point – in this case that
love of gain seduces people from true religion.

12   For the love of money is the root of all evil: which while some
coveted after, they have erred from the faith, and pierced
themselves through with many sorrows.
(6:10)
Paul develops his denunciation of those who make gain their god.
The riches of the world are to be shunned in favour of the riches of
the spirit.

13   Fight the good fight of faith, lay hold on eternal life.
(6:12)
The idea that apostleship was a battle was one of Paul's favourites,
and has become so well-known that it hardly nowadays seems
metaphorical. 'Lay hold on' means 'hold tight to': the idea is not so
much that eternal life is the goal to be fought for as that it is the
security which gives us confidence to fight at all.

14   Charge them that are rich in this world, that they be not
highminded, nor trust in uncertain riches, but in the living
God, who giveth us richly all things to enjoy.
(6:17)
Paul summarizes his teaching about the relative values of earthly
and spiritual riches. To be 'highminded' was to be proud, to think
oneself above ordinary people.

II Timothy

1   To Timothy, my dearly beloved son: Grace, mercy, and
peace, from God the Father and Christ Jesus our Lord. I
thank God, whom I serve from my forefathers with pure

conscience, that without ceasing I have remembrance of thee
in my prayers night and day; Greatly desiring to see thee,
being mindful of thy tears, that I may be filled with joy.
(1:2–4)

Writing this letter from prison, knowing that execution is imminent,
Paul allows himself an uncharacteristic display of personal affection
to his friend and beloved colleague Timothy. 'My beloved son' was
a common expression of affection in Greek, often used by Paul of
younger colleagues (see, for example, Titus 1).

2   **God hath not given us the spirit of fear; but of power, and of
love, and of a sound mind.**
(1:7)

The idea that our strength is in the Lord, that we have nothing to
fear, was particularly apposite to the circumstances of this letter.
Paul is, so to speak, handing the mantle of his apostleship over to
Timothy, and in the process reminding him that there is no cause to
grieve for Paul's coming death. 'Sound' here means not so much
'sane' as 'untroubled'.

3   **Thou therefore, my son, be strong in the grace that is in
Christ Jesus. And the things that thou hast heard of me
among many witnesses, the same commit thou to faithful
men, who shall be able to teach others also. Thou therefore
endure hardness, as a good soldier of Jesus Christ.**
(2:1–3)

Paul continues to encourage Timothy in his forthcoming role as
heir to Paul's apostleship.

4   **All scripture is given by inspiration of God, and is profitable
for doctrine, for reproof, for correction, for instruction in
righteousness: That the man of God may be perfect,
throughly furnished unto all good works.**
(3:16–17)

The specific point of these verses is that when Timothy no longer
has Paul to consult about spiritual matters, he will have the
scriptures, in particular the Gospels and Paul's letters, as guides:
they will 'throughly furnish' him (that is, thoroughly equip him).
The verses have often been taken since as a statement that the
scriptures are not only inspired by God, but that they are his own
actual, infallible words.

5   **I am now ready to be offered, and the time of my departure is
at hand. I have fought a good fight, I have finished my course,
I have kept the faith: Henceforth there is laid up for me a
crown of righteousness, which the Lord, the righteous judge,**

shall give me at that day: and not to me only, but unto all
them also that love his appearing.
(4:6–8)
Paul reflects on his coming death and on his and every other true
Christian's certainty of eternal life. (As a Roman citizen, Paul had
the right to be beheaded, not crucified as many less fortunate
Christians were in this outbreak of savage persecution.)

Titus

1   To Titus, mine own son after the common faith: Grace,
mercy, and peace, from God the Father and the Lord Jesus
Christ our Saviour.
(1:4)
This letter is addressed to one of Paul's first converts and most
trusted assistants: Paul calls him 'son after the common faith'
because of his teaching that all Christians were like members of one
family. Scholars think that Paul wrote this letter from prison, at the
end of his life. Titus was leader of the Christian community in
Crete, and was having to deal with the same kind of problems as
Timothy faced in Ephesus: the maintenance of pure belief and
worship in the face of the colourful and seductive practices of other
religions.

2   One of themselves, even a prophet of their own, said, The
Cretians are alway liars, evil beasts, slow bellies. This witness
is true. Wherefore rebuke them sharply, that they may be
sound in the faith.
(1:12–13)
Advising Titus against believing the claims of false prophets, Paul
refers to a famous ancient Greek proverb. Taken from the works of
the Cretan poet Epimenides, it was worked into a famous
philosophical paradox. 'All Cretans are liars. A Cretan told me so
himself, so it must be true. Or must it?'

3   Unto the pure all things are pure: but unto them that are
defiled and unbelieving is nothing pure; but even their mind
and conscience is defiled.
(1:15)
All that matters is faith in Christ: the light of Christian belief
irradiates everything a person says or does. If that faith is missing,
however, nothing about the person, however good it may seem or
worthily it may be meant, has any value.

Philemon

1   I beseech thee for my son Onesimus, whom I have begotten in
my bonds: Which in time past was to thee unprofitable, but
now profitable to thee and to me: Whom I have sent again:
thou therefore receive him.
(1:10–12)
Onesimus, a slave of Paul's Christian friend Philemon, has run
away to Paul and been converted to Christianity. Paul has 'begotten
him in his bonds', that is, converted him, given him rebirth as a
Christian, while in prison. Now he sends Onesimus back to
Philemon, begging his friend to treat the young man with leniency
and not the harshness Roman law laid down for escaped slaves. The
idea that the boy was once unprofitable and is now profitable is a
pun on his name: *Onesimus* literally means 'profitable'.

Hebrews

1   God, who at sundry times and in divers manners spake in
time past unto the fathers by the prophets, Hath in these last
days spoken unto us by his Son, whom he hath appointed heir
of all things, by whom also he made the worlds; Who being
the brightness of his glory, and the express image of his
person, and upholding all things by the word of his power,
when he had by himself purged our sins, sat down on the
right hand of the Majesty on high; Being made so much better
than the angels, as he hath by inheritance obtained a more
excellent name than they. For unto which of the angels said
he at any time, Thou art my Son, this day have I begotten
thee? And again, I will be to him a Father, and he shall be to
me a Son?
(1:1–5)
Scholars believe that although this letter is attributed to Paul, its
style is so unlike his that is is almost certainly by someone else. It is
less a letter than an essay, and its purpose is to link the teachings of
the Old and New Testaments, to place Christianity in the context of
Judaism and vice versa.

2   But to which of the angels said he at any time, Sit on my right
hand, until I make thine enemies thy footstool? Are they not
all ministering spirits, sent forth to minister for them who
shall be heirs of salvation?
(1:13–14)

The writer contrasts Jesus, the Son of God, with the angels who are no more than servants. The idea of a 'ministering angel' became proverbial.

3 **For finding fault with them, he saith, Behold, the days come, saith the Lord, when I will make a new covenant with the house of Israel and with the house of Judah.**
(8:8)
Paul quotes Jeremiah (see Jer 33), and goes on to say that the coming of Jesus is a sign of the 'new covenant' which is to replace the old, and that belief in Christ is the only requirement made of mortals, unlike the long list of ritual observances which the old covenant contained.

4 **And almost all things are by the law purged with blood; and without shedding of blood is no remission.**
(9:22)
The writer has been describing blood-sacrifice in ancient Judaic practice and Moses' sprinkling of the tabernacle with blood as a token of the covenant between God and mortals. Now he makes his point: blood has always been a sign that God and his people are reconciled, and Christ's shedding of his own blood for the remission, or forgiveness, of sins is the renewal of that same covenant.

5 **Now faith is the substance of things hoped for, the evidence of things not seen.**
(11:1)
Up till now, the writer of this letter has been proving that Jesus' acceptance of mortality and death is the renewal of the ancient covenant between God and mortals. Now, assuming that we accept this argument, that we have faith, he passes on to show us the implications of that faith for our daily lives. 'Substance' here means 'grounds for believing in'.

6 **These all died in faith, not having received the promises, but having seen them afar off, and were persuaded of them, and embraced them, and confessed that they were strangers and pilgrims on the earth.**
(11:13)
The patriarchs of the Old Testament, Noah, Abraham and the others, all showed exemplary faith, and treated their earthly existence as a temporary thing, a prologue to eternal life. Their faith in the unprovable truths of the spirit should guide our own.

7   They were stoned, they were sawn asunder, were tempted, were slain with the sword: they wandered about in sheepskins and goatskins; being destitute, afflicted, tormented; (Of whom the world was not worthy:) they wandered in deserts, and in mountains, and in dens and caves of the earth.
(11:37–8)

After enumerating the patriarchs, the writer moves on to the (Old Testament) prophets and others who suffered for their faith.

8   Wherefore seeing we also are compassed about with so great a cloud of witnesses, let us lay aside every weight, and the sin which doth so easily beset us, and let us run with patience the race that is set before us, Looking unto Jesus the author and finisher of our faith; who for the joy that was set before him endured the cross, despising the shame, and is set down at the right hand of the throne of God.
(12:1–2)

Encouraged by the example of all the Old Testament patriarchs and prophets, and by Jesus' suffering and death, we should put aside worldly fears and ambitions and live by the light of faith.

9   And ye have forgotten the exhortation which speaketh unto you as unto children, My son, despise not thou the chastening of the Lord, nor faint when thou art rebuked of him: For whom the Lord loveth he chasteneth, and scourgeth every son whom he receiveth. If ye endure chastening, God dealeth with you as with sons; for what son is he whom the father chasteneth not?
(12:5–7)

Quoting Proverbs, the writer says that the very fact that we suffer in the world is proof that we are God's own children: punishment is meant to improve, as a child is beaten to help it learn. The writer's zeal to make his point leads him to a markedly Old Testament view of child-rearing.

10   But ye are come unto mount Sion, and unto the city of the living God, the heavenly Jerusalem, and to an innumerable company of angels, To the general assembly and church of the firstborn, which are written in heaven, and to God the Judge of all, and to the spirits of just men made perfect.
(12:22–3)

Our faith leads us to the New Jerusalem, to the company of God, his angels, and all who have ever preceded us in faith and have been 'made perfect' (that is, freed of the imperfection of mortality) by it.

11 **Let brotherly love continue. Be not forgetful to entertain strangers: for thereby some have entertained angels unawares.**
(13:1–2)
The letter-writer moves from general exhortations about faith to specific instructions on leading the Christian life.

12 **Remember them which have the rule over you, who have spoken unto you the word of God: whose faith follow, considering the end of their conversation. Jesus Christ the same yesterday, and today, and for ever.**
(13:7–8)
For the first time in the letters, a church hierarchy is recommended, with some members not merely set to guide others, but placed in authority over them. The authority is nevertheless not temporal but spiritual, vested in teaching of the eternity of Jesus. These verses were one of the main sources of the idea of the authority of the Church, the apostolic line which passes unbroken from the disciples right down to the priests and ministers of today.

13 **Here have we no continuing city, but we seek one to come.**
(13:14)
This familiar verse picks up the idea of the New Jerusalem, the city of God, built not with stones but with faith, and longer-lasting than even the most 'continuing' ancient cities of the world.

14 **Now the God of peace, that brought again from the dead our Lord Jesus, that great shepherd of the sheep, through the blood of the everlastng covenant, Make you perfect in every good work to do his will, working in you that which is well-pleasing in his sight, through Jesus Christ; to whom be glory for ever and ever. Amen.**
(13:20–1)
The writer ends his letter by drawing together quotations from many New Testament sources (the Gospels, Acts, the Letters) into a single prayer. It is still often used today.

James

1 **My brethren, count it all joy when ye fall into divers temptations; Knowing this, that the trying of your faith worketh patience. But let patience have her perfect work, that ye may be perfect and entire, wanting nothing.**
(1:2–4)

The author of this letter is otherwise unknown, unless he is (as some say) Jesus' brother James. His subject is the Christian life, and he begins by imagining the Christian beset by temptations as a fortress is beseiged by enemies. The way to survive is by endurance ('patience'), and since that endurance is founded on faith, we should welcome it ('count it all joy') rather than fear each test. 'Perfection' is the state of absolute oneness with God and Christ to which our faith is leading us.

2   **If any of you lack wisdom, let him ask of God, that giveth to all men liberally, and upbraideth not; and it shall be given him. But let him ask in faith, nothing wavering. For he that wavereth is like a wave of the sea driven with the wind and tossed.**
(1:5–6)
James pursues his themes that the Christian life is founded on unshakeable faith, and that faith is abundantly available, the gift of God.

3   **Blessed is the man that endureth temptation: for when he is tried, he shall receive the crown of life, which the Lord hath promised to them that love him.**
(1:12)
Eternal life is the reward for steadfast Christian endurance. 'Temptation', testing, refers both to the physical risks of being a Christian in the Roman world of the time and to spiritual seductions to stray from the path of true faith.

4   **Every good gift and every perfect gift is from above, and cometh down from the Father of lights, with whom is no variableness, neither shadow of turning.**
(1:17)
'Lights' are what we might call 'insights', revelations of truth. 'Father of lights', apart from its obvious connection with God the father of all, therefore means something like 'truth of truths', the unwavering beam which, as John's Gospel said, lights every human being who comes into the world.

5   **Wherefore, my beloved brethren, let every man be swift to hear, slow to speak, slow to wrath: For the wrath of man worketh not the righteousness of God.**
(1:19–20)
James expands his idea of 'patience', which he has earlier declared to be a main pillar of Christian life.

6   Wherefore lay apart all filthiness and superfluity of
     naughtiness, and receive with meekness the engrafted word,
     which is able to save your souls. But be ye doers of the word,
     and not hearers only, deceiving your own selves. For if any be
     a hearer of the word, and not a doer, he is like unto a man
     beholding his natural face in a glass: For he beholdeth
     himself, and goeth his way, and straightway forgetteth what
     manner of man he was. But whoso looketh into the perfect
     law of liberty, and continueth therein, he being not a forgetful
     hearer, but a doer of the work, this man shall be blessed in his
     deed.
     (1:21–5)
     In homely metaphors, James describes the place of God's word in
     human lives. It is grafted on to us as new stock is grafted on to a
     tree: it gives new life to the old wood and gradually becomes the
     main stem of the whole tree. It is a mirror showing us ourselves, and
     we must continually act on what it shows us, rather than merely
     glance in its direction now and then.

7   If any man among you seem to be religious, and bridleth not
     his tongue, but deceiveth his own heart, this man's religion is
     vain. Pure religion and undefiled before God and the Father
     is this, To visit the fatherless and widows in their affliction,
     and to keep himself unspotted from the world.
     (1:26–7)
     James gives three further examples of truly Christian behaviour. He
     is talking not of faith (which he takes for granted here, as an
     essential prerequisite), but of the 'works' which flow from and
     reveal that faith.

8   For as the body without the spirit is dead, so faith without
     works is dead also.
     (2:26)
     There were those at the time who said that faith in Christ was all
     that was needed to be a Christian: Christian duty lay solely in
     cultivating and concentrating on that faith, withdrawing from the
     world. Others said that 'works' were all that mattered: if you were
     honest, charitable, friendly and peaceable, what need was there of
     any specific faith? James takes a third position: that faith and works
     are like soul (or 'spirit') and body, and that neither can exist without
     the other.

9   Behold, we put bits in the horses' mouths, that they may obey
     us; and we turn about their whole body. Behold also the ships,
     which though they be so great, and are driven of fierce winds,
     yet are they turned about with a very small helm,
     whithersoever the governor listeth. Even so the tongue is a

little member, and boasteth great things. Behold, how great a matter a little fire kindleth!
(3:3-5)

Descriptions of the power of speech, of uncontrollable growth from tiny beginnings, were common in the literature of the time. James is here advocating self-discipline, especially in those who preach God's word. 'Governor' means helmsman; 'listeth' means chooses; 'member' means 'part of the body'.

10 Out of the same mouth proceedeth blessing and cursing. My brethren, these things ought not so to be. Doth a fountain send forth at the same place sweet water and bitter? Can the fig tree, my brethren, bear olive berries? either a vine, figs? so can no fountain both yield salt water and fresh. Who is a wise man and endued with knowledge among you? let him shew out of a good conversation his works with meekness of wisdom.
(3:10-13)

James' point is *not* that the tongue is an uncontrollable monster, but that it should be governed to express truly the Christian approach to life.

11 Go to now, ye that say, To day or to morrow we will go into such a city, and continue there a year, and buy and sell, and get gain: Whereas ye know not what shall be on the morrow. For what is your life? It is even a vapour, that appeareth for a little time, and then vanisheth away.
(4:13-14)

We should not prefer worldly claims – in this case, commercial ambition – above those of the spirit. However urgent our lives on earth seem as we live them, the world of the flesh is like a wisp of mist when it is measured against eternal life. 'Go to now' means 'Be quiet'.

12 Be patient therefore, brethren, unto the coming of the Lord. Behold, the husbandman waiteth for the precious fruit of the earth, and hath long patience for it, until he receive the early and latter rain.
(5:7)

This is the reason for the Christian 'patience', that is endurance and spiritual expectation, which James has been advocating throughout this letter. The Second Coming is the reward of the patient believer, a harvest of souls to equal the earthly harvest for which the farmer must wait in patience.

13 But above all things, my brethren, swear not, neither by
    heaven, neither by the earth, neither by any other oath: but let
    your yea be yea and your nay, nay; lest ye fall into
    condemnation.
    (5:12)
    James summarizes his teaching about true speaking being an
    essential sign of the genuine Christian: it is one of the 'works' which
    reveal the 'spirit'.

14 Pray one for another, that ye may be healed. The effectual
    fervent prayer of a righteous man availeth much.
    (5:16)
    The letter ends with a series of teachings about the Christian
    community, about how each church group is one entity whose
    people are 'members' of each other. One of the ways to cement and
    celebrate this unity is prayer for one another, linking the community
    directly with its father, God.

I Peter

1   Ye greatly rejoice, though now for a season, if need be, ye are
    in heaviness through manifold temptations: That the trial of
    your faith, being much more precious than of gold that
    perisheth, though it be tried with fire, might be found unto
    praise and honour and glory at the appearing of Jesus Christ:
    Whom having not seen, ye love; in whom, though now ye see
    him not, yet believing, ye rejoice with joy unspeakable and
    full of glory: Receiving the end of your faith, even the
    salvation of your souls. Of which salvation the prophets have
    inquired and searched diligently, who prophesied of the grace
    that should come unto you.
    (1:6–10)
    This letter, from Peter to the Christians in Turkey, was written at
    the time of the merciless persecution under Nero who made the
    Christians scapegoats for the Great Fire of Rome. Peter reminds
    them that despite the dangers that face them on all sides, the
    'manifold temptations', they should be comforted by their faith,
    which is the guarantee of eternal life.

2   Gird up the loins of your mind, be sober, and hope to the end
    for the grace that is to be brought unto you at the revelation of
    Jesus Christ.
    (1:13)

Peter preaches spiritual vigilance, a state of constant preparedness for the Second Coming.

3 **See that ye love one another with a pure heart fervently: Being born again, not of corruptible seed, but of incorruptible, by the word of God, which liveth and abideth for ever. For all flesh is as grass, and all the glory of man as the flower of grass. The grass withereth, and the flower thereof falleth away: But the word of the Lord endureth for ever. And this is the word which by the gospel is preached unto you.**
(1:22–5)
Peter urges his people to live by the standards not of their former lives, but of their new Christian selves. The old life, based on worldly standards and ambitions ('the flesh') was ephemeral; the new life, by contrast, like God's word which enlightens and guarantees it, is everlasting. The Old Testament quotation given new direction here is from Isaiah. (See Isa 62.)

4 **As newborn babes, desire the sincere milk of the word, that ye may grow thereby: If so be ye have tasted that the Lord is gracious.**
(2:2–3)
The idea of 'being reborn in Christ' inspires Peter to a simple but remarkable metaphor. 'Sincere' here means pure, unadulterated.

5 **Honour all men. Love the brotherhood. Fear God. Honour the king.**
(2:17)
The Christian's duty, even in a hostile world ruled by an insane emperor (Nero, here called 'the king') is not to concentrate on spiritual or temporal loyalty exclusively, but to balance the two.

6 **For what glory is it, if, when ye be buffeted for your faults, ye shall take it patiently? but if, when ye do well, and suffer for it, ye take it patiently, this is acceptable with God.**
(2:20)
Peter here preaches true Christian humility: long-suffering even when wronged. In the context of irrational, cruel persecution, this advice had especial force.

7 **Ye were as sheep going astray; but are now returned unto the Shepherd and Bishop to your souls.**
(2:25)
Peter has quoted Christ as the example of true long-suffering which all Christians should follow. Jesus' suffering was for the redemption

of the human race, and our suffering is part of our redemption. 'Bishop' means 'overseer' or 'examiner'.

8 **Let it be the hidden man of the heart, in that which is not corruptible, even the ornament of a meek and quiet spirit, which is in the sight of God of great price.**
(3:4)

Peter has been warning women against what he calls 'outward adorning'; here he describes what true adornment is. From earliest times, Jewish scriptures had preached that make-up, braided hair and colourful clothes were sure signs of licentious, not to say idolatrous behaviour, and this view persisted well into Christian times. Fashionable Roman women, by contrast, spent fortunes on their appearance. The moral implications, for those in the beleaguered Christian community, hardly needed spelling out.

9 **Finally, be ye all of one mind, having compassion one of another, love as brethren, be pitiful, be courteous: Not rendering evil for evil, or railing for railing: but contrariwise blessing; knowing that ye are thereunto called, that ye should inherit a blessing.**
(3:8–9)

This is Peter's advice to the two partners in marriage: their relationship is a microcosm of all true Christian relationships. 'Pitiful' means 'forgiving'.

10 **But the end of all things is at hand: be ye therefore sober, and watch unto prayer.**
(4:7)

Although statements like this must have seemed to their hearers at the time to be intimations of an imminent apocalypse, they were actually advocating spiritual rather than earthly vigilance. It is more dangerous for the soul to be taken unawares by the Second Coming than for the body.

11 **Above all things have fervent charity among yourselves: for charity shall cover the multitude of sins.**
(4:8)

Charity is the quality of Christian love so highly praised by Paul (see I Cor 19). The phrase 'cover a multitude of sins' became proverbial.

12 **Be sober, be vigilant; because your adversary the devil, as a roaring lion, walketh about, seeking whom he may devour.**
(5:8)

Peter reiterates his teaching on spiritual vigilance, in words which have since been adapted for liturgical use, in the service of compline. When Satan, the 'adversary', described his own walking

about the world (see Job 2), he made it sound innocent and carefree;
Peter puts it in a far more sinister light, especially to those who
would be daily hearing tales of Christians being thrown to lions in
the arena.

II Peter

1   We have not followed cunningly devised fables, when we
made known unto you the power and coming of our Lord
Jesus Christ, but were eyewitnesses of his majesty. For he
received from God the Father honour and glory, when there
came such a voice to him from the excellent glory, This is my
beloved Son, in whom I am well pleased. And this voice which
came from heaven we heard, when we were with him in the
holy mount. We have also a more sure word of prophecy;
whereunto ye do well that ye take heed, as unto a light that
shineth in a dark place, until the day dawn, and the day star
arise in your hearts.
(1:16–19)
Unlike some other religions, which use myths and imaginative
fiction, Peter says that Christianity can draw on actual eye-witness
accounts. He here reminds his hearers that he personally witnessed
Christ's ascension into heaven, and says that his evidence should
guide them until they see a similar radiance, the dawn of the
Second Coming, for themselves.

2   For if after they have escaped the pollutions of the world
through the knowledge of the Lord and Saviour Jesus Christ,
they are again entangled therein, and overcome, the latter
end is worse with them than the beginning. For it had been
better for them not to have known the way of righteousness,
than, after they have known it, to turn from the holy
commandment delivered unto them. But it is happened unto
them according to the true proverb, The dog is turned to his
own vomit again; and the sow that was washed to her
wallowing in the mire.
(2:20–2)
Peter is here denouncing those who have been converted to
Christianity, only to reject it because of the world's pressures.

3   Beloved, be not ignorant of this one thing, that one day is with
the Lord as a thousand years, and a thousand years as one
day. The Lord is not slack concerning his promise, as some
men count slackness; but is longsuffering to us-ward, not

willing that any should perish, but that all should come to repentance.
(3:8–9)

Peter answers people who have demanded the exact date of the Second Coming. God is not bound by human ideas of time; the apparent delay is not because he has forgotten his promise, but is to give the whole human race time to repent.

4   We, according to his promise, look for new heavens and a new earth, wherein dwelleth righteousness. Wherefore, beloved, seeing that ye look for such things, be diligent that ye may be found of him in peace, without spot, and blameless.
(3:13–14)

However long it appears to be delayed, the Second Coming is certain. That being so, Peter says, we should shape our lives accordingly.

I John

1   If we say that we have no sin, we deceive ourselves, and the truth is not in us. If we confess our sins, he is faithful and just to forgive us our sins, and to cleanse us from all unrighteousness.
(1:8–9)

John, the evangelist, wrote this letter at the end of his life. Its purpose was to refute the teaching of the Gnostics, people who rigorously separated the two natures of human beings, spiritual and temporal. If we are spiritually pure, they said, we are above earthly sin – a teaching some of their followers took as licence to do as they pleased, and a view which John absolutely rejects. If human beings were sinless, what would be the point of Christ's redemption?

2   My little children, these things write I unto you, that ye sin not. And if any man sin, we have an advocate with the Father, Jesus Christ the righteous: And he is the propitiation for our sins: and not for ours only, but also for the sins of the whole world.
(2:1–2)

We are not sinless, but to be sinless should be our ambition. Our guide and help is Jesus: he was the 'propitiation', the scapegoat offered up on our behalf.

3   Whoso hath this world's good, and seeth his brother have need, and shutteth up his bowels of compassion from him, how dwelleth the love of God in him?
(3:17)

John is here preaching against the Gnostic view that concentration on matters of the spirit absolves us from worldly concern (in this case, helping our fellow human beings). 'Bowels of compassion' became proverbial. The ancients believed that pity, forgiveness, love and other 'affections' were situated not in the brain but in other organs, the liver, spleen, pancreas and so on, which they collectively called 'bowels'.

4   Beloved, let us love one another: for love is of God; and every one that loveth is born of God, and knoweth God. He that loveth not knoweth not God; for God is love. In this was manifested the love of God toward us, because that God sent his only begotten Son into the world, that we might live through him.
(4:7–9)
God's love for us should inspire our love for each other: it is one of the 'works' which are a sign of faith, not separate as the Gnostics taught but irrevocably intertwined.

5   Herein is our love made perfect, that we may have boldness in the day of judgment: because as he is, so are we in this world. There is no fear in love; but perfect love casteth out fear: because fear hath torment. He that feareth is not made perfect in love.
(4:17–18)
Just as Jesus' love led him to conquer the fear of death, so his followers' love of him should cancel out their fear, not only of earthly suffering but of the Day of Judgment.

6   If a man say, I love God, and hateth his brother, he is a liar: for he that loveth not his brother whom he hath seen, how can he love God whom he hath not seen?
(4:20)
Love of God is not only an inward-looking, comforting emotion: it contains a powerful moral imperative as well. This is another example of the teaching that 'works' and 'spirit' cannot be separated, that they are intertwined and mutually essential.

II John

1   The elder unto the elect lady and her children, whom I love in the truth; and not I only, but also all they that have known the truth.
(1:1)

The second letter of John the Evangelist is written to a sister church and its congregation: the 'elect lady and her children' of this quotation. As in his first letter, John's subject in this one is Christian love.

2 **And this is love, that we walk after his commandments.**
(1:6)
John pithily defines Christian love in terms of obedience to Christ.

III John

1 **Beloved, follow not that which is evil, but that which is good.**
He that doeth good is of God: but he that doeth evil hath not
seen God.
(1:11)
The third letter of John the Evangelist was sent to Gaius, an elder of the Christian community at Pergamum. Its purpose was to warn of a false apostle, Diotrephes, whose teaching was contrary to John's. John here quotes from his own Gospel, before going on to say that he will write no more, but will soon visit Pergamum in person.

Jude

1 **Jude, the servant of Jesus Christ, and brother of James, to**
them that are sanctified by God the Father, and preserved in
Jesus Christ, and called: Mercy unto you, and peace, and love,
be multiplied.
(1:1–2)
Jude, identified by some as the brother of Jesus and of James, writes to warn against false apostles, those who preach the separation of worldly and spiritual matters.

2 **There are certain men crept in unawares, who were before of**
old ordained to this condemnation, ungodly men, turning the
grace of our God into lasciviousness, and denying the only
Lord God, and our Lord Jesus Christ.
(1:4)
Jude's condemnation of the false apostles was widely quoted at the time of the Reformation, both by Roman Catholic priests fulminating against reformers, and vice versa.

3 These are spots in your feasts of charity, when they feast with you, feeding themselves without fear: clouds they are without water, carried about of winds; trees whose fruit withereth, without fruit, twice dead, plucked up by the roots; Raging waves of the sea, foaming out their own shame; wandering stars, to whom is reserved the blackness of darkness for ever. (1:12–13)

Jude's thunderous denunciation of false apostles continues. The vividness of his language comes from his use of two apocalyptic books in Old Testament style which would be well-known to his hearers, *The Assumption of Moses* and the *Book of Enoch*.

4 Now unto him that is able to keep you from falling, and to present you faultless before the presence of his glory with exceeding joy, To the only wise God our Saviour, be glory and majesty, dominion and power, both now and ever. Amen. (1:24–5)

Jude's closing prayer for his hearers has been taken over, both completely and in parts, into the liturgy of the Church.

Revelation

1 John to the seven churches which are in Asia: Grace be unto you, and peace, from him which is, and which was, and which is to come; and from the seven Spirits which are before his throne; And from Jesus Christ, who is the faithful witness and the first begotten of the dead, and the prince of the kings of the earth. (1:4–5)

Revelation, a vision of the Day of Judgment – *Apocalypse* is Greek for 'revelation' – may be the work of John the Evangelist, written in exile on Patmos at the end of his life. The greeting in this passage is similar to the words which begin his pastoral letters. John uses the number seven frequently throughout his vision, as a perfect number and a symbol of the 'perfection' or completeness of God which faithful mortals are at last allowed to see. (The fact that there are seven churches receiving this account in Asia is, however, no more than happy coincidence.) Jesus is the 'faithful witness' because he spoke truly of God to mortals; he is the 'first begotten of the dead' because he was the first person to be born again from death, to rise, in John's words, from corruption to incorruption.

2 Behold, he cometh with clouds; and every eye shall see him, and they also which pierced him. (1:7)

The vision of Jesus riding 'with clouds' is derived from Old Testament ideas of God riding among his *cherubim* or storm-winds. The idea that on the Day of Judgment every eye shall be opened, to see Christ plainly, picks up earlier teaching by Paul (see I Cor 22). 'They which pierced him' refers to the Romans, who crucified Jesus: even they will bear him witness.

3   **I am Alpha and Omega, the beginning and the ending, saith the Lord, which is, and which was, and which is to come, the Almighty.**
(1:8)
In Greek (in which Revelation was written) *alpha* is the first letter of the alphabet and *omega* the last.

4   **I John, who also am your brother, and companion in tribulation, and in the kingdom and patience of Jesus Christ, was in the isle that is called Patmos, for the word of God, and for the testimony of Jesus Christ. I was in the Spirit on the Lord's day, and heard behind me a great voice, as of a trumpet, Saying, I am Alpha and Omega, the first and the last: and, What thou seest, write in a book, and send it into the seven churches which are in Asia; unto Ephesus, and unto Smyrna, and unto Pergamos, and unto Thyatira, and unto Sardis, and unto Philadelphia, and unto Laodicea. And I turned to see the voice that spake with me. And being turned, I saw seven golden candlesticks; And in the midst of the seven candlesticks one like unto the Son of man, clothed with a garment down to the foot, and girt about the paps with a golden girdle. His head and his hairs were white like wool, as white as snow; and his eyes were as a flame of fire; And his feet like unto fine brass, as if they burned in a furnace; and his voice as the sound of many waters. And he had in his right hand seven stars: and out of his mouth went a sharp two-edged sword: and his countenance was as the sun shineth in his strength.**
(1:9–16)
John describes the circumstances of his vision, beginning like a witness in court by giving a precise place and location. 'I was in the Spirit' means 'I was meditating'. 'Paps' are the chest.

5   **Fear not: I am the first and the last: I am he that liveth, and was dead; and, behold, I am alive for evermore, Amen; and have the keys of hell and of death.**
(1:17–18)
Jesus speaks to John in his vision. The fact of the Resurrection, of Jesus opening the gates of death, is the first and most basic element in John's whole account.

6   The mystery of the seven stars which thou sawest in my right hand, and the seven golden candlesticks. The seven stars are the angels of the seven churches: and the seven candlesticks which thou sawest are the seven churches.
(1:20)
Jesus explains part of John's vision. The 'angels' are either the elders of each of the seven churches, or their guardian angels. The next two chapters of Revelation contain specific messages for each of the seven churches.

7   I have somewhat against thee, because thou hast left thy first love. Remember therefore from whence thou art fallen, and repent, and do the first works; or else I will come unto thee quickly, and will remove thy candlestick out of his place, except thou repent.
(2:4–5)
This message is to the Christians at Ephesus. Diligent in all outward matters, they have nevertheless lost the spirit of true Christian love, or 'charity', which the apostles all said was the essential obligation of Christian life.

8   He that hath an ear, let him hear what the Spirit saith unto the churches; To him that overcometh will I give to eat of the tree of life, which is in the midst of the paradise of God.
(2:7)
Jesus offers each of the seven churches a symbolic gift in the verses which follow; either a renewal of some Old Testament sign of God's favour to the human race, or a place in his spiritual temple (for example a pillar to stand beside, as he offers the Philadelphians; see Rev 14).

9   Be thou faithful unto death, and I will give thee a crown of life.
(2:10)
The Christian community at Smyrna was small and suffering persecution. Jesus, in John's vision, urges them to emulate his own faithfulness, and promises them everlasting life.

10 Repent; or else I will come unto thee quickly, and will fight against them with the sword of my mouth.
(2:16)
The Christians at Pergamos have been generally faithful, but have taken part in the Zeus-worship of which the city was a centre. Jesus warns them to change their ways, threatening them with the sword that John saw in his vision issuing from Jesus' mouth: that is, the sword of words, denouncing them to God on the Day of Judgment.

11 And he that overcometh, and keepeth my works unto the end, to him will I give power over the nations: And he shall rule them with a rod of iron; as the vessels of a potter shall they be broken to shivers: even as I received of my Father. And I will give him the morning star.
(2:26–8)
This is the reward promised to the church of Thyatira, if they keep the true faith untainted by idolatry. 'Rod of iron' became proverbial, though more in the sense of harshness than of sternness, as here.

12 He that overcometh, the same shall be clothed in white raiment; and I will not blot out his name out of the book of life, but I will confess his name before my Father, and before his angels.
(3:5)
Jesus promises this reward to the church at Sardis. It was a small community of Christians, so smug with the certainty of their own salvation that they made no effort to find new converts, with the result that their church was dwindling away. The idea of the 'book of life', in which was written the names of everyone to be saved at the Day of Judgment, becomes vitally important later in John's vision (see Rev 75). White is the colour of purity.

13 I know thy works: behold, I have set before thee an open door, and no man can shut it: for thou hast a little strength, and hast kept my word, and hast not denied my name.
(3:8)
These words are addressed to the Christians at Philadelphia, who are few in number but blamelessly faithful. The door leads to eternal life.

14 Him that overcometh will I make a pillar in the temple of my God, and he shall go no more out: and I will write upon him the name of my God, and the name of the city of my God, which is new Jerusalem, which cometh down out of heaven from my God: and I will write upon him my new name.
(3:12)
These are the rewards Jesus promises to the faithful Christians at Philadelphia. This is one of John's first mentions of the 'New Jerusalem', the home of the blessed after the Day of Judgment.

15 I know thy works, that thou art neither cold nor hot: I would thou wert cold or hot. So then because thou art lukewarm, and neither cold nor hot, I will spue thee out of my mouth.
(3:15–16)

Jesus warns the Christians of Laodicea, who are so sure of salvation
that they neglect their church and the practice of their faith. The
word 'Laodicean' came to be used proverbially for someone too
lackadaisical to make up his or her mind on any matter, and most of
all on the choice of religious or political loyalty.

16 **Behold, I stand at the door, and knock: if any man hear my
voice, and open the door, I will come in to him, and will sup
with him, and he with me.**
(3:20)
The door, as always in Revelation, is the gateway between this
world and the next, between earthly and spiritual life. The promise
to the faithful is that just as Jesus can pass through the door, and
has shown it by taking on mortality, so, by belief, can they, and take
on eternal life.

17 **After this I looked, and, behold, a door was opened in heaven:
and the first voice which I heard was as it were of a trumpet
talking with me; which said, Come up hither, and I will shew
thee things which must be hereafter. And immediately I was
in the spirit: and, behold, a throne was set in heaven, and one
sat on the throne. And he that sat was to look upon like a
jasper and a sardine stone: and there was a rainbow round
about the throne, in sight like unto an emerald. And round
about the throne were four and twenty seats: and upon the
seats I saw four and twenty elders sitting, clothed in white
raiment; and they had on their heads crowns of gold.**
(4:1–4)
From advice to each of the seven churches to which Revelation is
addressed, John moves on to tell of a vision of heaven itself.
'Sardine stone' means 'sardonyx' a semi-precious stone.

18 **And out of the throne proceeded lightnings and thunderings
and voices: and there were seven lamps of fire burning before
the throne, which are the seven Spirits of God.**
(4:5)
The 'seven Spirits' means the Holy Ghost. It hovered over the
seven lamps as the flame of God's presence hovered over the
tabernacle built by Moses in the desert.

19 **And before the throne there was a sea of glass like unto
crystal: and in the midst of the throne, and round about the
throne, were four beasts full of eyes before and behind. And
the first beast was like a lion, and the second beast like a calf,
and the third beast had a face as a man, and the fourth beast
was like a flying eagle.**
(4:6–7)

The four beasts symbolize the four Evangelists: the lion is Mark, the calf Luke, the man Matthew and the eagle John himself, author of this account. 'Full of eyes' means covered all over with eyes, like a peacock's tail.

20   The four and twenty elders fall down before him that sat on the throne, and worship him that liveth for ever and ever, and cast their crowns before the throne, saying, Thou art worthy, O Lord, to receive glory and honour and power: for thou hast created all things, and for thy pleasure they are and were created.
(4:10–11)
The elders of John's vision represent the leaders of all people who have faith in God. They worship God in a parallel of the ceremony in which subject kings vowed loyalty to the Roman emperor: a familiar scene to John's hearers, given sublime transformation by its setting here and by the language he uses to describe it.

21   And I saw in the right hand of him that sat on the throne a book written within and on the backside, sealed with seven seals. And I saw a strong angel proclaiming with a loud voice, Who is worthy to open the book, and to loose the seals thereof?
(5:1–2)
The book, or scroll, with seven seals, contains the future of creation. Until now it has remained sealed, and its opening will herald the apocalypse.

22   And I beheld, and, lo, in the midst of the throne and of the four beasts, and in the midst of the elders, stood a Lamb as it had been slain, having seven horns and seven eyes, which are the seven Spirits of God sent forth into all the earth.
(5:6)
Christ, the Lamb of God, comes forward to open the book with seven seals.

23   And when he had taken the book, the four beasts and four and twenty elders fell down before the Lamb, having every one of them harps, and golden vials full of odours, which are the prayers of saints.
(5:8)
The elders who are the leaders of God's faithful, and the beasts which symbolize the four evangelists, worship the Lamb of God. It was from this verse that the traditional idea arose of every being in heaven playing a harp and singing eternal hymns of praise.

24   And I beheld, and I heard the voice of many angels round
about the throne and the beasts and the elders: and the
number of them was ten thousand times ten thousand, and
thousands of thousands; Saying with a loud voice, Worthy is
the Lamb that was slain to receive power, and riches, and
wisdom, and strength, and honour, and glory, and blessing.
(5:11–12)
Every being in heaven joins in praise of the Lamb of God.

25   And I saw when the Lamb opened one of the seals, and I
heard, as it were the noise of thunder, one of the four beasts
saying, Come and see. And I saw, and behold a white horse:
and he that sat on him had a bow; and a crown was given unto
him: and he went forth conquering, and to conquer.
(6:1–2)
Opening the first four seals of the book with seven seals unleashes
disaster, in the form of the four horsemen of the apocalypse. The
first rider (on a white horse) is Conquest, the second (on a 'red'
horse) is Slaughter, the third (on a black horse) is Famine and the
fourth (on a 'pale' horse) is Disease or Death.

26   And I looked, and behold a pale horse: and his name that sat
on him was Death, and Hell followed with him.
(6:8)
This is John's vision of the fourth horseman of the apocalypse:
Death which comes from plague.

27   And when he had opened the fifth seal, I saw under the altar
the souls of them that were slain for the word of God, and for
the testimony which they held: And they cried with a loud
voice, saying, How long, O Lord, holy and true, dost thou not
judge and avenge our blood on them that dwell on the earth?
(6:9–10)
Opening the fifth seal of the book with seven seals reveals everyone
who has been martyred for the faith, crying for revenge. 'Under the
altar' means 'at the foot of the altar'.

28   And I beheld when he had opened the sixth seal, and, lo, there
was a great earthquake; and the sun became black as
sackcloth of hair, and the moon became as blood; And the
stars of heaven fell unto the earth, even as a fig tree casteth
her untimely figs, when she is shaken of a mighty wind. And
the heaven departed as a scroll when it is rolled together; and
every mountain and island were moved out of their places.
(6:12–14)

Opening the sixth seal of the book with seven seals reveals the earthquake which is the beginning of the Day of Judgment.

29 And the kings of the earth, and the great men, and the rich men, and the chief captains, and the mighty men, and every bondman, and every free man, hid themselves in the dens and in the rocks of the mountains; And said to the mountains and rocks, Fall on us, and hide us from the face of him that sitteth on the throne, and from the wrath of the Lamb: For the great day of his wrath is come; and who shall be able to stand?
(6:15-17)
The whole human race, from the highest to the lowest, is thrown into consternation by the coming of the Day of Judgment. These verses, and particularly the last one quoted, were one inspiration of the powerful medieval poem *Dies Irae* ('Day of Wrath'), now central to the Catholic requiem mass.

30 And after these things I saw four angels standing on the four corners of the earth, holding the four winds of the earth, that the wind should not blow on the earth, nor on the sea, nor on any tree. And I saw another angel ascending from the east, having the seal of the living God: and he cried with a loud voice to the four angels, to whom it was given to hurt the earth and the sea, Saying, Hurt not the earth, neither the sea, nor the trees, till we have sealed the servants of our God in their foreheads.
(7:1-3)
While four angels hold back the winds of destruction, that is the four horsemen of the apocalypse, a fifth angel marks God's faithful for salvation. The idea is a development of the marking of the Israelites' doors before the last of the ten plagues of Egypt, the slaughter of the firstborn.

31 After this I beheld and, lo, a great multitude, which no man could number, of all nations, and kindreds, and people, and tongues, stood before the throne, and before the Lamb, clothed with white robes, and palms in their hands; And cried with a loud voice, saying, Salvation to our God which sitteth upon the throne, and unto the Lamb.
(7:9-10)
In the preceding verses, John has enumerated the 'saved' from each of the tribes of Israel: 144,000 in all. Now he describes the countless host of Gentiles who have also been saved.

32 What are these which are arrayed in white robes? and whence came they?
(7:13)

One of the elders of heaven asks John, in his vision, who the host of people are who are worshipping God.

33   **These are they which came out of great tribulation, and have washed their robes, and made them white in the blood of the Lamb.**
(7:14)
The elder answers his own question. From this verse comes a proverbial image for Christian salvation, 'washed in the blood of the Lamb'.

34   **They shall hunger no more, neither thirst any more; neither shall the sun light on them, nor any heat. For the Lamb which is in the midst of the throne shall feed them, and shall lead them unto living fountains of waters: and God shall wipe away all tears from their eyes.**
(7:16–17)
In John's vision, the heavenly elder tells him of the happiness the souls of the saved will have in paradise.

35   **And when he had opened the seventh seal, there was silence in heaven about the space of half an hour. And I saw the seven angels which stood before God; and to them were given seven trumpets.**
(8:1–2)
The opening of the seventh seal of the book with seven seals is the signal for the actual beginning of the Day of Judgment. During the silence which immediately follows, God's angels prepare to send out the trumpet-calls which will begin each apocalyptic stage.

36   **The first angel sounded, and there followed hail and fire mingled with blood, and they were cast upon the earth: and the third part of trees was burnt up, and all green grass was burnt up.**
(8:7)
The sequence of destruction of the mortal world begins.

37   **And I beheld, and heard an angel flying through the midst of heaven, saying with a loud voice, Woe, woe, woe, to the inhabiters of the earth by reason of the other voices of the trumpet of the three angels, which are yet to sound!**
(8:13)
The sounding of the first four angels' trumpets has brought earthquake, fire, poisoned water and supernatural darkness to the world. There is now a pause before the apocalyptic sequence resumes.

38 And the fifth angel sounded, and I saw a star fall from heaven
    unto the earth: and to him was given the key of the bottomless
    pit. And he opened the bottomless pit; and there arose a
    smoke out of the pit, as the smoke of a great furnace; and the
    sun and the air were darkened by reason of the smoke of the
    pit. And there came out of the smoke locusts upon the earth:
    and unto them was given power, as the scorpions of the earth
    have power.
    (9:1–3)
    The fifth trumpet sounds, and unleashes tormentors from the pit of
    hell. 'Bottomless pit' became proverbial.

39 And in those days shall men seek death, and shall not find it;
    and shall desire to die, and death shall flee from them.
    (9:6)
    John predicts that there will be a time of torment, brought by the
    creatures from the pit of hell. Because the people are godless, none
    of their prayers – not even prayers for death – are granted.

40 And they had tails like unto scorpions, and there were stings
    in their tails.
    (9:10)
    John imagines that the hellish locusts which torment the world are
    venomous. The idea of a 'sting in the tail', something vicious but
    unexpected, derives from this verse.

41 And the number of the army of the horsemen were two
    hundred thousand thousand and I heard the number of them.
    And thus I saw the horses in the vision, and them that sat on
    them, having breastplates of fire, and of jacinth, and
    brimstone: and the heads of the horses were as the heads of
    lions; and out of their mouths issued fire and smoke and
    brimstone.
    (9:16–17)
    The sixth trumpet is blown and the cavalry of heaven ride out across
    the world to slaughter everyone not marked for salvation.

42 And I took the little book out of the angel's hand, and ate it
    up; and it was in my mouth sweet as honey: and as soon as I
    had eaten it, my belly was bitter.
    (10:10)
    After locusts and the angel army have tormented the world and have
    failed to make the human race repent, John is given a scroll with the
    Christian message on it. He himself finds the message pleasant; his
    bitterness is because he must tell the human race of the fate
    awaiting those who ignore God's word.

43   And there appeared a great wonder in heaven; a woman
clothed with the sun, and the moon under her feet, and upon
her head a crown of twelve stars: And she being with child
cried, travailing in birth, and pained to be delivered.
(12:1–2)
John is shown a vision of the war in heaven between the forces of
good and evil which led to Satan being cast into hell. The woman
mentioned here stands for God's chosen people, pregnant with the
Messiah.

44   And there appeared another wonder in heaven; and behold a
great red dragon, having seven heads and ten horns, and
seven crowns upon his heads. And his tail drew the third part
of the stars of heaven, and did cast them to the earth: and the
dragon stood before the woman which was ready to be
delivered, for to devour her child as soon as it was born. ·
(12:3–4)
This dragon stands for Satan, leader of the powers of evil in the
heavenly battle.

45   And there was war in heaven: Michael and his angels fought
against the dragon; and the dragon fought and his angels.
(12:7)
The archangel Michael leads the forces of light against the powers
of darkness.

46   And the great dragon was cast out, that old serpent, called the
Devil, and Satan, which deceiveth the whole world: he was
cast out into the earth, and his angels were cast out with him.
(12:9)
The forces of light triumph, and Satan is hurled out of heaven.

47   Therefore rejoice, ye heavens, and ye that dwell in them. Woe
to the inhabiters of the earth and of the sea! for the devil is
come down unto you, having great wrath, because he knoweth
that he hath but a short time.
(12:12)
Satan will only be able to work his evil on earth until people realize
that the Messiah has given them power over evil, and use that
power. The shortness of time before that happens makes him even
more determined.

48   And I stood upon the sand of the sea, and saw a beast rise up
out of the sea, having seven heads and ten horns, and upon
his horns ten crowns, and upon his heads the name of
blasphemy. And the beast which I saw was like unto a
leopard, and his feet were as the feet of a bear, and his mouth

as the mouth of a lion: and the dragon gave him his power, and his seat, and great authority.
(13:1–2)

A beast is born from the evil of the world, with the crowns of authority and the horns of power. It symbolizes idolatry, and its aim is to tyrannize the world.

49 And they worshipped the beast, saying, Who is like unto the beast? who is able to make war with him?
(13:4)

The peoples of the world fall into idolatry. The picture in John's mind is of people falling down and worshipping one of the huge statues of hybrid monsters which adorned pagan temples, particularly in the Babylonian religion – which he later uses as a symbol for Rome and for everything evil in the world.

50 And all that dwell upon the earth shall worship him, whose names are not written in the book of life of the Lamb slain from the foundation of the world. If any man have an ear, let him hear.
(13:8–9)

Only the chosen people – not here Jews, but Christians – are exempt from idolatry, worship of the beast, because they believe in the Messiah. The second verse quoted is a clear hint to John's hearers that they too, if they choose, can be of that number. It was a phrase traditionally used – not least in Jesus' teaching – to indicate that a parable was over and that it was time to draw the moral.

51 And that no man might buy or sell, save he that had the mark, or the name of the beast, or the number of his name.
(13:17)

The 'mark of the beast' was like the owners' marks tattooed or branded on slaves. In John's vision, it declared its wearers for death as surely as the seal of God marked out believers for eternal life. 'The number of his name' is simply the owner's number, that is the beast's number, branded on his possessions.

52 Here is wisdom. Let him that hath understanding count the number of the beast: for it is the number of a man; and his number is Six hundred threescore and six.
(13:18)

Scholars variously explain the number 666. Some say that it may have been the number of the Roman emperor, the head of the 'beast' which was the power of idolatry. In Hebrew, letters of the alphabet were also used as figures, and the letters of the name Neron Caesar ('Emperor Nero') added up to 666. The letters of *Lateinos*, the Hebrew for 'the Roman empire' reach the same total.

Others say that recurring sixes are a symbol of irredeemable evil, since however often they are repeated they can never equal the 'perfect' number seven. Number-symbolists ever since have twisted 666 to fit the names of anyone currently identified as anti-Christ, including Luther, Napoleon and the Pope (any pope).

53 **And I looked, and, lo, a Lamb stood on the mount Sion, and with him an hundred forty and four thousand, having his Father's name written in their foreheads. And I heard a voice from heaven, as the voice of many waters, and as the voice of a great thunder: and I heard the voice of harpers harping with their harps: And they sung as it were a new song before the throne, and before the four beasts, and the elders: and no man could learn that song but the hundred and forty and four thousand, which were redeemed from the earth.**
(14:1–3)
John's vision moves from the beast of idolatry to the holy city of Jerusalem, where the chosen people, those bearing the seal of salvation and not the mark of the beast, are singing God's praise. The number 144,000, he has already said, refers specifically to the tribes of Israel. There are in addition, though not gathered here, countless millions of Gentiles.

54 **These are they which were not defiled with women; for they are virgins. These are they which follow the Lamb whithersoever he goeth. These were redeemed from among men, being the firstfruits unto God and to the Lamb. And in their mouth was found no guile: for they are without fault before the throne of God.**
(14:4–5)
The chosen people are the 'firstfruits' of the harvest of all saved souls.

55 **And I saw another angel fly in the midst of heaven, having the everlasting gospel to preach unto them that dwell on the earth, and to every nation, and kindred, and tongue, and people, Saying with a loud voice, Fear God, and give glory to him; for the hour of his judgment is come: and worship him that made heaven, and earth, and the sea, and the fountains of waters.**
(14:6–7)
An angel carries the message and chance of redemption beyond the hill of Zion to the whole world.

56 **If any man worship the beast and his image, and receive his mark in his forehead, or in his hand, The same shall drink of the wine of the wrath of God, which is poured out without**

mixture into the cup of his indignation; and he shall be
tormented with fire and brimstone in the presence of the holy
angels, and in the presence of the Lamb.
(14:9–10)
A third angel, in John's vision, predicts eternal suffering for those
who persist in idolatry despite all warnings and calls to repentance.

57 And I heard a voice from heaven saying unto me, Write,
Blessed are the dead which die in the Lord from henceforth:
Yea, saith the Spirit, that they may rest from their labours;
and their works do follow them.
(14:13)
John is here referring to martyrs. 'Martyr' is Greek for 'witness',
and gives those Christians murdered for their faith a very different
status from the Roman view that they were worthless criminals.
'Their works do follow them' refers to those they bring to the faith
by their example, who will in turn witness for them on the Day of
Judgment, as a farmer's harvested crops (say) witness to his
diligence.

58 And I looked, and behold a white cloud, and upon the cloud
one sat like unto the Son of man, having on his head a golden
crown, and in his hand a sharp sickle. And another angel
came out of the temple, crying with a loud voice to him that
sat on the cloud, Thrust in thy sickle, and reap: for the time is
come for thee to reap; for the harvest of the earth is ripe.
(14:14–15)
This figure is not Jesus but an angel in the form of a man. The idea
of the 'grim reaper', scything the human race to death, derives from
these lines, though it was later applied not to avenging angels but to
Time.

59 And the angel thrust in his sickle into the earth, and gathered
the vine of the earth, and cast it into the great winepress of
the wrath of God. And the winepress was trodden without the
city, and blood came out of the winepress, even unto the
horse bridles, by the space of a thousand and six hundred
furlongs.
(14:19–20)
The harvest of the human race begins. Ancient winepresses were
worked by horses, trundling a heavy stone round and round to
crush the juice from the grapes: hence the idea of the blood rising
as far as the 'bridles' or harness. The 1600 furlongs is a symbolic
number: 4 traditionally symbolized the whole world, and therefore
4 x 4 x 10 x 10 means something like 'the world multiplied by itself
ten times ten times', that is, 'to infinity'.

60   **And I saw as it were a sea of glass mingled with fire: and them
that had gotten the victory over the beast, and over his image,
and over his mark, and over the number of his name, stand on
the sea of glass, having the harps of God. And they sing the
song of Moses the servant of God, and the song of the Lamb,
saying, Great and marvellous are thy works, Lord God
Almighty; just and true are thy ways, thou King of saints.
Who shall not fear thee, O Lord, and glorify thy name? for
thou only art holy: for all nations shall come and worship
before thee; for thy judgments are made manifest.**
(15:2–4)
As disasters are poured out, in John's vision, over the idolaters and
evildoers of the world, the redeemed stand apart, singing God's
praise. Some scholars think that 'sea of glass mingled with fire'
came into John's mind from a memory (or someone else's account)
of the lava-flow from a volcano such as Etna in Sicily, which was
active at this time.

61   **And I heard a great voice out of the temple saying to the seven
angels, Go your ways, and pour out the vials of the wrath of
God upon the earth.**
(16:1)
The seven vials of the wrath of God are golden containers, each of
which holds a different plague to torment idolaters.

62   **And he gathered them together into a place called in the
Hebrew tongue Armageddon.**
(16:16)
God gathers the forces of good for the final battle. *Armageddon* is
Hebrew for 'mound of Megiddo'; John sites his imaginary battle in
a real place, a town which guarded a pass through the Carmel Hills
and was often the site of bitter battles. Armageddon, used
symbolically here, became proverbial for the site of any particularly
bloody and devastating battle.

63   **Come hither; I will shew unto thee the judgment of the great
whore that sitteth upon many waters: With whom the kings of
the earth have committed fornication, and the inhabitants of
the earth have been made drunk with the wine of her
fornication.**
(17:1–2)
An angel summons John to see the fall of 'Babylon', that is of the
empire of idolatry that tyrannizes the whole world.

64   **So he carried me away in the spirit into the wilderness: and I
saw a woman sit upon a scarlet coloured beast, full of names
of blasphemy, having seven heads and ten horns. And the**

woman was arrayed in purple and scarlet colour, and decked with gold and precious stones and pearls, having a golden cup in her hand full of abominations and filthiness of her fornication: And upon her forehead was a name written, MYSTERY, BABYLON THE GREAT, THE MOTHER OF HARLOTS AND ABOMINATIONS OF THE EARTH. And I saw the woman drunken with the blood of the saints, and with the blood of the martyrs of Jesus: and when I saw her, I wondered with great admiration.
(17:3–6)

The reference to Christian martyrs in the last verse quoted makes it clear that John identifies 'Babylon' as Rome. This sonorous passage also gave rise to the expression 'scarlet woman', used proverbially of any woman of whose morals – the implication is usually sexual – the speaker disapproves. 'Admiration' in the last quoted verse means 'amazement'.

65 Babylon the great is fallen, is fallen, and is become the habitation of devils, and the hold of every foul spirit, and a cage of every unclean and hateful bird.
(18:2)

An angel announces the coming destruction of 'Babylon', before calling every evil-doer who lives there to repent and be saved. The Elizabethan past tense 'is fallen' (that is, 'has fallen') refers not to the actual physical state of the city, but to the fact that its fate is irrevocably settled – as we might say, 'is as good as fallen'.

66 How much she hath glorified herself, and lived deliciously, so much torment and sorrow give her: for she saith in her heart, I sit a queen, and am no widow, and shall see no sorrow.
(18:7)

Not the least of 'Babylon's' crimes is thinking herself above God's law, immune to the torments which will plague other evil-doers.

67 Alas, alas, that great city, that was clothed in fine linen, and purple, and scarlet, and decked with gold, and precious stones, and pearls! For in one hour so great riches is come to nought. And every shipmaster, and all the company in ships, and sailors, and as many as trade by sea, stood afar off.
(18:16–17)

The merchants of the world, who have traded with 'Babylon', bewail the city's fall.

68 And a mighty angel took up a stone like a great millstone, and cast it into the sea, saying, Thus with violence shall that great city Babylon be thrown down, and shall be found no more at all.
(18:21)

Once again an angel prophesies the end of 'Babylon'. There are warnings after warnings, each one offering the city's people another chance to repent.

69 And a voice came out of the throne, saying, Praise our God, all ye his servants, and ye that fear him, both small and great. And I heard as it were the voice of a great multitude, and as the voice of many waters, and as the voice of mighty thunderings, saying, Alleluia: for the Lord God omnipotent reigneth.
(19:5-6)
The whole congregation of the saved sing praise to God for the fall of 'Babylon'.

70 Let us be glad and rejoice, and give honour to him: for the marriage of the Lamb is come, and his wife hath made herself ready.
(19:7)
After the rout of evil, John's vision moves to foretell a wedding feast, a celebration of the marriage of Christ and his bride the Church.

71 And he saith unto me, Write, Blessed are they which are called unto the marriage supper of the Lamb. And he saith unto me, These are the true sayings of God.
(19:9)
The guests at the wedding of Christ and the Church are all true believers, redeemed by faith.

72 And I saw heaven opened, and behold a white horse; and he that sat upon him was called Faithful and True, and in righteousness he doth judge and make war.
(19:11)
The fifth horseman of the apocalypse rides out to destroy Satan.

73 And he hath on his vesture and on his thigh a name written, KING OF KINGS, AND LORD OF LORDS.
(19:16)
John sees the fifth horseman's name. The horseman is not Christ himself, but carries his insignia.

74 And I saw an angel come down from heaven, having the key of the bottomless pit and a great chain in his hand. And he laid hold on the dragon, that old serpent, which is the Devil, and Satan, and bound him a thousand years, And cast him into the bottomless pit, and shut him up, and set a seal upon him,

that he should deceive the nations no more, till the thousand years should be fulfilled. (20:1-3)

Satan is cast for a second time into hell. The figure of 1,000 years, probably meant as symbolically as every other number in Revelation, has been taken literally by generation after generation, to their great distress. In particular, it has given rise to 'millenarianism', the certainty, towards the close of each millenium, that the end of the world is imminently at hand. To the people of John's time, 'a thousand years', the 'millenium' of Christ's earthly rule, probably meant no more than 'for the foreseeable future': it concerns spiritual, not worldly, calendars.

75 And I saw a great white throne, and him that sat on it, from whose face the earth and the heaven fled away; and there was found no place for them. And I saw the dead, small and great, stand before God; and the books were opened: and another book was opened, which is the book of life: and the dead were judged out of those things which were written in the books, according to their works. And the sea gave up the dead which were in it; and death and hell delivered up the dead which were in them: and they were judged every man according to their works. (20:11-13)

The Last Judgment itself begins, as the souls of the dead appear one after another before God's judgment seat.

76 And I saw a new heaven and a new earth: for the first heaven and the first earth were passed away; and there was no more sea. And I John saw the holy city, new Jerusalem, coming down from God out of heaven, prepared as a bride adorned for her husband. (21:1-2)

With evil routed and judgment complete, John's final vision is of the new age of Christ, the unity of all God's faithful people with their creator and redeemer. The sea is 'no more' because the Hebrew scriptures believed that it was the home of all evils, all impurities.

77 God is with men, and he will dwell with them, and they shall be his people, and God himself shall be with them, and be their God. And God shall wipe away all tears from their eyes; and there shall be no more death, neither sorrow, nor crying, neither shall there be any more pain: for the former things are passed away. And he that sat upon the throne said, Behold, I make all things new. And he said unto me, Write: for these words are true and faithful. (21:3-5)

In the New Jerusalem, the paradisal state of human beings reconciled with God, the 'former things', that is the constraints of previous existence on earth, have no more power.

78   **I will give unto him that is athirst of the fountain of the water of life freely.**
(21:6)
In John's vision, the Old Testament idea of God filling the cups of his faithful is repeated and transfigured. What was once a workaday metaphor, appropriate to a country of deserts and baking heat, is now given spiritual overtones which transcend its origins.

79   **And the foundations of the wall of the city were garnished with all manner of precious stones. The first foundation was jasper; the second, sapphire; the third, a chalcedony; the fourth, an emerald; The fifth, sardonyx; the sixth, sardius; the seventh, chrysolite; the eighth, beryl; the ninth, a topaz; the tenth, a chrysoprasus; the eleventh, a jacinth; the twelfth, an amethyst. And the twelve gates were twelve pearls; every several gate was of one pearl: and the street of the city was pure gold, as it were transparent glass. And I saw no temple therein: for the Lord God Almighty and the Lamb are the temple of it.**
(21:19–22)
John sees a vision of the New Jerusalem, the home of those at one with God. It is a transfigured version of the old Jerusalem, with the powerful exception mentioned in the last quoted verse. The phrase 'pearly gates' and the idea of streets of gold are derived from this passage.

80   **And the nations of them which are saved shall walk in the light of it: and the kings of the earth do bring their glory and honour into it. And the gates of it shall not be shut at all by day: for there shall be no night there.**
(21:24–5)
Unlike earthly cities, which are constantly on guard against attack, the New Jerusalem has nothing to fear, and does not shut its gates either by day or by night.

81   **And he shewed me a pure river of water of life, clear as crystal, proceeding out of the throne of God and of the Lamb. In the midst of the street of it, and on either side of the river, was there the tree of life, which bare twelve manner of fruits, and yielded her fruit every month: and the leaves of the tree were for the healing of the nations.**
(22:1–2)

John's vision of the New Jerusalem incorporates two standard Old
Testament ideas, the river of life, the faith from which all may drink
salvation, and the tree of life which feeds the human race with true
knowledge of God. Both were features of Eden, from which Adam's
fall barred humanity; now, thanks to Christ's redemption, they are
once more available to all.

82   **Behold, I come quickly: blessed is he that keepeth the sayings
     of the prophecy of this book.**
     (22:7)
     The angel tells John that the imminence of Christ's Second
     Coming makes it imperative that people heed the message of the
     vision and repent.

83   **Blessed are they that do his commandments, that they may
     have right to the tree of life, and may enter in through the
     gates into the city. For without are dogs, and sorcerers, and
     whoremongers, and murderers, and idolaters, and whosoever
     loveth and maketh a lie.**
     (22:14–15)
     John spells out the meaning of his vision, the moral of his parable.

84   **He which testifieth these things saith, Surely I come quickly.
     Amen. Even so, come, Lord Jesus. The grace of our Lord
     Jesus Christ be with you all. Amen.**
     (22:20–1)
     'He which testifieth' is Jesus, speaking through his angel and from
     the angel through John himself. John's prayers close the book, and
     bring the account of his revelation to an end.

Index

Each headword in this index represents a key word in the quotation which
follows. The key word in the quotation is replaced by a swung dash. The
numbers refer to the number of the page on which the quotation appears
or begins, followed by the quotation number. Some quotations have more
than one key word. In these cases, they are indexed again under each key
word.

Bears:
  There came forth two she ~ 55.4
Beast:
  count the number of the
    ~ 361.52
  God formed every ~ of the field
    3.11
  like unto the ~ 361.49
  mark, or the name of the ~
    361.51
  saw a ~ rise up 360.48
Beasts:
  Four great ~ came up 175.17
Beauty:
  ~ of holiness 80.45
  ~ of Israel is slain 47.1
  perfection of ~ 162.4
Bed:
  take up thy ~ and walk 268.19
Bedstead:
  his ~ was a bedstead of iron 32.1
Beg:
  to ~ I am ashamed 261.51
Begat:
  Abraham ~ Isaac 217.1
Beginning:
  In the ~ God created the heaven
    1.1
  In the ~ was the Word 265.1
Begotten:
  thy only ~ 195.12
Behemoth:
  Behold now ~ 71.60
Behold:
  ~ the man 277.67
Being:
  we live, and move, and have our
    ~ 290.50
Belial:
  concord hath Christ with ~ 315.8
  sons of ~ 43.1
  thou man of ~ 49.12
Believe:
  ~ on the Lord Jesus 289.44
Belly:
  ~ of hell 181.3
  formed thee in the ~ 155.1
  God is their ~ 326.9
  Jonah was in the ~ 181.2
Beloved:
  My ~ is mine 134.7

Bethlehem:
  ~ Ephratah, though thou be little
    182.4
Betrayed:
  Son of man is ~ 247.159
Bind:
  To ~ his princes 105.181
Birthright:
  he sold his ~ 11.50
Bishop:
  A ~ then must be blameless 332.7
  Shepherd and ~ to your souls
    344.7
Bitter:
  ~ in soul? 64.14
  ~ with hard bondage 14.3
Bitterness:
  ~ of my soul 65.24
Black:
  ~ but comely 134.2
Blasphemy:
  name of ~ 360.48
Bless:
  Lord ~ thee, and keep thee 29.3
Blessed:
  ~ art thou among women 252.2;
    253.5
  ~ be he that cometh 109.204
  ~ is he that cometh 239.121
  ~ is the fruit of thy womb 253.5
  Jesus took bread, and ~ it
    246.154
  thou hast ~ them altogether
    32.18
Blind:
  ~ leaders of the blind 235.100
  I was ~ now I see 272.36
Blood:
  ~ into her streets 169.28
  ~ of the men that went in
    jeopardy 49.18
  His ~ be on us 248.166
  pour out the ~ 27.8
  Their ~ shall be poured 184.2
  there was ~ throughout all the
    land 18.21
  this is my ~ of the new testament
    246.154
  thy brother's ~ crieth 5.22
  white in the ~ of the Lamb
    358.33

sewed ~ leaves together 4.*16*
Fight:
~ the good fight 333.*13*
Fill:
let us take our ~ of love 120.*18*
Filthiness:
lay apart all ~ 341.*6*
Findeth:
He that ~ his life 230.*73*
whoso ~ me findeth life 120.*20*
Finger:
~ of God 18.*24*
My little ~ 52.*13*
Fingers:
~ of a man's hand 174.*12*
Finished:
I have ~ the work 276.*60*
It is ~ 277.*65*
Fir:
~ trees shall be terribly shaken 182.*1*
Howl, ~ tree 186.*7*
Fire:
amber, as the appearance of ~ round about within it 164.*1*
by ~ and by his sword 155.*108*
by night in a pillar of ~ 21.*39*
cloven tongues like as of ~ 281.*6*
devouring ~ 24.*50*
fill thine hand with coals of ~ 166.*11*
~ and brimstone 76.*25*
~ by night 29.*4*
~ in his bosom 120.*17*
God is a consuming ~ 33.*2*
great a matter a little ~ kindleth! 341.*9*
in the midst of the ~ 173.*7*
Firebrand:
~ plucked out of the burning 179.*3*
First:
the ~ and the last 351.*4*
Firstborn:
all the ~ are mine 28.*2*
~ in the land of Egypt shall die 20.*33*
Firstfruits:
~ of them that slept 311.*29*
~ unto God 362.*54*

Fish:
piece of a broiled ~ 265.*73*
Fishers:
I will make you ~ of men 219.*14*
Flagons:
Stay me with ~ 134.*4*
Flame:
behind them a ~ burneth 177.*3*
Fled:
the earth and the heaven ~ away 367.*75*
Flee:
~ from the wrath to come? 218.*9*
Flesh:
~ and blood cannot inherit 312.*33*
~ and blood hath not revealed it 236.*103*
~ is weak 247.*158*
~ of a little child 56.*8*
~ of my flesh 3.*13*
I will give them ~ 29.*7*
in my ~ shall I see 68.*38*
life of all ~ 27.*8*
out of my Spirit upon all ~ 282.*10*
pour out my spirit upon all ~ 178.*5*
They that are after the ~ 300.*29*
thorn in the ~ 317.*17*
two shall be one ~ 323.*16*
we sat by the ~ pots 22.*45*
Who shall give us ~ to eat? 29.*6*
Word was made ~ 266.*4*
works of the ~ are manifest 318.*7*
Flies:
~ in the ointment 131.*26*
Flock:
but ye feed not the ~ 170.*31*
Fear not, little ~ 258.*34*
He shall feed his ~ 146.*63*
Floods:
~ clap their hands 104.*173*
in the ~ of great waters 82.*55*
Flourish:
~ as the green bay tree 84.*68*
Flower:
in the ~ of their age 43.*2*
Foes:
~ shalt be they of his own household 230.*73*

Graves:
  I will open your ~ 170.*36*
  there were no ~ in Egypt 21.*40*
Great:
  be ~ in the sight of the Lord
    252.*1*
  ~ men are not always wise
    70.*48*
Greatest:
  he that is ~ among you 241.*128*
Greatness:
  according to his excellent ~
    116.*242*
Greek:
  neither ~ nor Jew 328.*4*
Greeks:
  debtor both to the ~ 295.*5*
Grief:
  acquainted with ~ 149.*81*
  ~ in a strange land 214.*3*
Griefs:
  he hath borne our ~ 150.*82*
Grind:
  ~ the face of the poor? 137.*7*
Ground:
  Israelites passed over on dry ~
    38.*6*
  place whereon thou standest is
    holy ~ 16.*10*
Guilty:
  ~ of the body and blood 308.*16*
Gulf:
  great ~ fixed 262.*57*

Hail:
  ~ and fire mingled with blood
    358.*36*
  ~ thou that art highly favoured
    252.*2*
  ~ upon the land of Egypt 19.*28*
Hair:
  not one ~ of his head fall 44.*9*
Hairs:
  gray ~ with sorrow to the grave
    14.*64*
  ~ of your head are all numbered
    230.*71*
Hairy:
  my brother is a ~ man 11.*51*
Half:
  ~ was not told me 51.*10*

Hammer:
  like a ~ that breaketh the rock
    160.*30*
Hand:
  delivered him into mine ~ 46.*22*
  every man's ~ against him 8.*40*
  fingers of a man's ~ 174.*12*
  ~ of our God was upon us 59.*1*
  have the upper ~ 76.*23*
  Into thine ~ I commit my spirit
    81.*52*
  know the ~ of the Lord 38.*7*
  let not thy left ~ know 222.*25*
  like a man's ~ 53.*22*
  part of the ~ that wrote 174.*12*
  put his ~ to the plough 256.*24*
  put not forth thine ~ 63.*5*
  the day of the Lord is at ~ 140.*23*
Handmaid:
  Behold the ~ of the Lord 253.*4*
Hands:
  Behold my ~ 265.*72*
  ~ are the hands of Esau 11.*52*
  house not made with ~ 314.*4*
  into thy ~ I commend my spirit
    264.*68*
  little folding of the ~ 119.*16*
  temples made with ~ 284.*19*
  washed his ~ before the
    multitude 248.*165*
  with one of his ~ wrought 60.*2*
  wounds in thine ~ 187.*9*
Harlot:
  faithful city become an ~ 136.*4*
  O ~ hear the word 167.*18*
  played the ~ 168.*23*
Harlots:
  devoured thy living with ~ 260.*49*
  he that cleaveth to ~ 207.*19*
  mother of ~ and abominations
    364.*64*
Harpers:
  voice of ~ harping 362.*53*
Harps:
  ~ and golden vials 355.*23*
Hart:
  As the ~ panteth 86.*77*
  lame man leap as an ~ 145.*55*
Harvest:
  While the earth remaineth,
    seedtime and ~ 8.*36*

hills, from whence cometh my ~
110.*207*
in me is thine ~ 176.*5*
O Israel, thou hast destroyed
thyself; but in me is thine ~
176.*5*

Hem:
touched the ~ of his garment
228.*58*

Hen:
as a ~ gathereth her chickens
242.*131*

Herbs:
Better is a dinner of ~ 123.*36*

Hereafter:
things which must be ~ 354.*17*

Hewers:
Let them be ~ of wood 38.*10*

Hidden:
~ man of the heart 345.*8*

High:
prize of the ~ calling of God
326.*8*

Higher:
Friend, go up ~ 258.*37*

High-minded:
I am not ~ 112.*216*

Highways:
Go out into the ~ 259.*42*
Go ye therefore into the ~
240.*124*

Hills:
~ from whence cometh my help
110.*207*
little ~ rejoice 95.*130*
Why leap ye, ye high ~ 97.*135*

Hip:
He smote them ~ and thigh
40.*12*

Hire:
labourer is worthy of his ~256.*26*

Hissing:
this city desolate, and an ~
160.*28*

Hoarfrost:
he scattereth the ~ 115.*237*

Hold:
~ fast that which is good 330.*6*
lay ~ on eternal life 333.*13*

Holier:
~ than thou 155.*106*

Holiness:
worship the Lord in the beauty of
~ 103.*172*

Hollow:
~ of his thigh 12.*58*

Holy:
~, holy, holy, is the Lord 138.*11*

Honey:
in my mouth sweet as ~ 359.*42*
land flowing with milk and ~
16.*11*
sweeter also than ~ 78.*36*

Honour:
A prophet is not without ~
234.*95*
~ thy father and thy mother
22.*47*
whom the king delighteth to ~
61.*4*

Hoof:
parteth the ~ and is clovenfooted
26.*4*

Hope:
against ~ believed in hope
298.*19*
~ and quietly wait 163.*7*
~ deferred 122.*30*
~ of the ungodly 202.*10*
now abideth faith, ~, charity
310.*22*
prisoners of ~ 186.*6*
secure, because there is ~ 66.*28*

Horse:
Be ye not as the ~ 82.*56*
behold a pale ~ 356.*26*
behold a white ~ 356.*25; 366.72*

Horsemen:
~ running in the air 215.*2*

Horses:
They were as fed ~ 157.*11*

Hosanna:
~ in the highest 239.*121*
~ to the Son of David 239.*121*

Host:
~ of Midian 40.*8*

Hour:
~ is at hand 247.*159*
~ is come 273.*43*
mine ~ is not yet come 266.*8*

House:
an ~ to dwell in 51.*7*

~ shall be great among the
　　heathen 187.*1*
sing praise to the ~ 75.*18*
their ~ liveth for evermore
　　209.*33*
Narrow:
　~, full of sorrow 195.*13*
　Strait is the gate, and ~ 225.*41*
Nation:
　~ shall not lift up sword 137.*6*
　~ shall rise against nation
　　242.*134*
　Righteousness exalteth a ~ 122.*33*
　to a rebellious ~ 164.*2*
Naughtiness:
　bewitching of ~ 201.*6*
　~ of thine heart 45.*14*
Nazareth:
　any good thing come out of ~
　　266.*7*
Need:
　according as he had ~ 283.*16*
　The Lord hath ~ of them
　　239.*119*
Needle:
　camel to go through the eye of a
　　~ 239.*116*
Neighbour:
　love thy ~ as thyself 28.*11*;
　　241.*127*
Net:
　~ is spread 117.*3*
New:
　all things are become ~ 314.*5*
　~ every morning 163.*6*
Newness:
　~ of life 299.*22*
News:
　good ~ from a far country 126.*53*
Night:
　fire by ~ 29.*4*
　there shall be no ~ there 368.*80*
Nimrod:
　~ the mighty hunter 8.*38*
Noise:
　joyful ~ to the rock of our
　　salvation 103.*169*
　joyful ~ unto the Lord 104.*174*
　Make a joyful ~ 96.*131*
　There is a ~ of war in the camp
　　24.*52*

None:
　there is ~ else 147.*70*
Nostrils:
　glory of his ~ 71.*59*
Nothing:
　having ~ and yet possessing all
　　314.*7*
　we brought ~ into this world
　　333.*11*
Nought:
　great riches is come to ~ 365.*67*
Number:
　count the ~ of the beast 361.*52*
　~ of the army of the horsemen
　　359.*41*
　teach us to ~ our days 101.*159*

Obedient:
　~ unto death 324.*3*
Obey:
　to ~ is better than sacrifice
　　44.*10*
Occasion:
　any ~ against this Daniel 174.*15*
Offence:
　conscience void of ~ 293.*60*
Offering:
　delightest not in burnt ~ 90.*100*
Og:
　~ the king of Bashan 31.*15*
Oil:
　anointest my head with ~ 79.*39*
　cruse of ~ 52.*18*
　~ of gladness 87.*84*
Ointment:
　alabaster box of very precious ~
　　246.*150*
　flies in the ~ 131.*26*
Old:
　waxen ~ in wickedness 212.*1*
Olive:
　in her mouth was an ~ leaf 7.*34*
Onan:
　~ knew that the seed should not
　　be his 13.*61*
One:
　ye are all ~ in Christ 318.*4*
Opinions:
　between two ~ 52.*19*
Oppressed:
　let the ~ go free 153.*97*

Oppression:
  looked for judgment, but behold
    ~ 137.*10*
Orion:
  loose the bands of ~ 71.*58*
Ornaments:
  Can a maid forget her ~ 156.*7*
Outgoings:
  ~ of the morning and evening
    95.*129*
Ox:
  as an ~ goeth to the slaughter
    120.*19*
  ~ knoweth his owner 136.*1*
  Thou shalt not muzzle the ~ 35.*13*

Pain:
  neither shall there be any more ~
    367.*77*
Painted:
  she ~ her face 56.*13*
Palmerworm:
  That which the ~ hath left 177.*1*
Palms:
  ~ of her hands 57.*14*
Palsy:
  bringing one sick of the ~ 249.*2*
Parables:
  wise sayings, dark sentences, and
    ~ 204.*1*
Paradise:
  with me in ~ 264.*67*
Part:
  chosen that good ~ 257.*30*
  neither ~ nor lot 285.*24*
Parting:
  at the ~ of the way 168.*22*
Partridge:
  As the ~ sitteth on eggs 159.*26*
Pass:
  all ye that ~ 162.*2*
Passage:
  a large and safe ~ 192.*1*
Passed:
  ~ by on the other side 257.*27*
Passions:
  men of like ~ 289.*42*
Passover:
  it is the Lord's ~ 20.*36*
Pastures:
  lie down in green ~ 79.*39*

Paths:
  all her ~ are peace 118.*7*
  in the ~ of righteousness 79.*39*
Patience:
  In your ~ possess ye your souls
    264.*64*
  let ~ have her perfect work 339.*1*
Patient:
  Be ~ therefore 342.*12*
Pay:
  ~ me that thou owest 238.*111*
Peace:
  all her paths are ~ 118.*7*
  feet into the way of ~ 253.*7*
  I came not to send ~ 230.*72*
  lay me down in ~ 74.*9*
  Mercy unto you, and ~ 349.*1*
  no ~, ..., the wicked 148.*75*
  on earth ~ good will toward men
    254.*12*
  ~ be to this house 256.*25*
  ~ I leave with you 275.*54*
  ~ of God, which passeth all
    understanding 326.*11*
  ~ to you which were afar off 320.*3*
  Pray for the ~ of Jerusalem
    110.*209*
  Prince of ~ 139.*19*
Peacemakers:
  Blessed are the ~ 219.*15*
Peacocks:
  ivory, and apes, and ~ 51.*11*
Pearl:
  one ~ of great price 234.*94*
Pearls:
  neither cast ye your ~ before
    swine 224.*37*
Pelican:
  like a ~ of the wilderness 104.*176*
Pentecost:
  day of ~ was fully come 281.*5*
People:
  let my ~ go 18.*25;* 19.*29*
  my ~ love to have it so 157.*14*
  thy ~ shall be my people 42.*2*
Perfect:
  Be ye therefore ~ 222.*24*
  made ~ in a short time 201.*7*
  unto the ~ day 118.*12*
Perfecting:
  ~ of the saints 321.*9*

~ the Lord, O my soul 115.*233*
Pray:
~ one for another 343.*14*
Prayer:
Give ear to my ~ 90.*101*
Hear my ~ 85.*71*
Let my ~ be set forth 113.*224*
Praying always with all ~ 323.*19*
the Lord will receive my ~ 75.*16*
Prayers:
mention of you always in my ~ 295.*4*
Prepare:
~ to meet thy God 179.*4*
Press:
~ toward the mark 326.*8*
Prevail:
let not man ~ 76.*23*
Pride:
hath ~ profited us? 201.*9*
~ goeth before destruction 123.*38*
Prince:
~ of life 283.*15*
~ of this world be cast out 273.*45*
Who made thee a ~ and a judge 15.*7*
Princes:
~ in all the earth 87.*86*
Put not your trust in ~ 115.*234*
Principalities:
nor ~, nor powers 301.*33*
Printed:
they were ~ in a book! 67.*37*
Prisoners:
~ of hope 186.*6*
Profit:
In all labour there is ~ 122.*32*
Profited:
what is a man ~ 236.*105*
Prologue:
a foolish thing to make a long ~ 215.*1*
Prophet:
A ~ is not without honour 234.*95*
He is a ~ 271.*34*
~ of the Highest 253.*7*
Prophets:
~ do they live for ever? 185.*1*
Saul also among the ~ 46.*21*
Propitiation:
~ for our sins 347.*2*

Provoke:
How long will this people ~ me? 30.*10*
Psalmist:
sweet ~ of Israel 49.*17*
Publicans:
~ and sinners? 227.*55*
Pure:
Blessed are the ~ 219.*15*
Unto the ~ all things are pure 335.*3*
Pursuing:
faint, yet ~ 40.*9*

Quails:
~ from the sea 30.*8*
Quaking:
eat thy bread with ~ 166.*14*
Quickeneth:
It is the spirit that ~ 270.*26*
Quiet:
~ and peaceable life 331.*5*
Quit:
~ yourselves like men 44.*6*
Quiver:
man that hath his ~ full 111.*212*

Race:
~ is not to the swift 131.*25*
they which run in a ~ 307.*13*
Raged:
The heathen ~ 88.*89*
Rain:
Hath the ~ a father? 71.*57*
I will cause it to ~ upon the earth 6.*28*
My doctrine shall drop as the ~ 35.*16*
~ on the just and on the unjust 221.*23*
Raised:
dead shall be ~ incorruptible 312.*34*
Ram:
~ caught in a thicket 10.*46*
Rams:
mountains skipped like ~ 107.*191*
Ran:
they ~ both together 278.*68*
Ransomed:
~ of the Lord shall return 145.*57*

Safe:
  Is the young man Absalom ~?
    49.*13*
Said:
  Thou hast ~ 248.*162*
Saints:
  called to be ~ 295.*3*
Sakes:
  for your ~ he became poor 315.*9*
Salt:
  a pillar of ~ 9.*43*
  Ye are the ~ of the earth 220.*16*
Salvation:
  helmet of ~ 323.*19*
  ~ is of the Lord 181.*4*
  ~ prospered in his hand 213.*2*
  work out your own ~ 325.*5*
Sanctify:
  ~ them through thy truth 276.*61*
Sanctuary:
  as a little ~ 166.*12*
  Praise God in his ~ 116.*242*
Sapphire:
  paved work of a ~ 23.*49*
Satan:
  Get thee behind me, ~ 236.*104*
Saul:
  ~ why persecutest thou me?
    286.*29*
  whose name was ~ 285.*22*
Save:
  himself he cannot ~ 249.*168*
Saved:
  what must I do to be ~? 289.*43*
  world through him might be ~
    268.*14*
Saviour:
  ~ which is Christ 254.*11*
Savour:
  Lord smelled a sweet ~ 8.*36*
  Of a sweet ~ unto the Lord 26.*2*
  ointment of sweet ~ 192.*3*
Sayings:
  dark ~ of old 98.*144*
Scapegoat:
  lot fell to be the ~ 26.*6*
Scarlet:
  arrayed in purple and ~ 364.*64*
  they that were brought up in ~
    163.*9*
  This line of ~ thread 37.*4*

though your sins be as ~ 136.*3*
  thread of ~ 135.*8*
Scatter:
  Lord shall ~ you 33.*3*
Schoolmaster:
  law was our ~ 318.*3*
Scorn:
  Laugh no man to ~ 205.*10*
Scornful:
  sitteth in the seat of the ~ 72.*1*
Scorning:
  drinketh up ~ like water? 70.*51*
Scorpions:
  chastise you with ~ 52.*14*
Scourge:
  overflowing ~ 143.*41*
Scripture:
  ~ is given by inspiration 334.*4*
Sea:
  go down to the ~ in ships
    106.*184*
  He gathereth the waters of the ~
    83.*58*
  Let the ~ roar 58.*3*
  The ~ is his 103.*170*
Seal:
  opened the seventh ~ 358.*35*
  ~ of the living God 357.*30*
  Set me as a ~ 136.*12*
Seals:
  sealed with seven ~ 355.*21*
Search:
  ~ me, O God 113.*223*
Searched:
  thou hast ~ me 112.*219*
Searching:
  by ~ find out God? 66.*27*
Season:
  now for a ~ 343.*1*
  their meat in due ~ 114.*231*
  there is a ~ and a time 129.*11*
  word spoken in due ~ 123.*37*
Secret:
  Father which seeth in ~ 222.*27*
  ~ things belong unto the Lord
    35.*15*
Secrets:
  knoweth the ~ of the heart 87.*82*
See:
  they which ~ not might see
    272.*37*